ECONOMICS

MEASUREMENT

THEORIES

CASE STUDIES

ECONOMICS

MEASUREMENT
THEORIES
CASE STUDIES

by George Soule

With the editorial assistance of

Leland E. Traywick
Michigan State University

and

Francis C. Boddy
University of Minnesota

HOLT, RINEHART AND WINSTON, INC.
NEW YORK

Copyright © 1961 by
Holt, Rinehart and Winston, Inc.

Library of Congress
Catalog Card Number: 61-11282

28048-0411

Printed in the United States of America

PREFACE / This book is designed for use by that

large body of students who need a knowledge of economics as an essential part of a liberal education and a preparation for responsible citizenship, but who do not expect to specialize in the subject. It is based on years of experience in the teaching of a course so conceived. In spite of the apparent limitation of aim, the course always turned out some students who became so intrigued with the subject that they went on to more advanced material and, as a rule, were able to master it with little difficulty.

The book embodies the following distinguishing features:

1. Part I explains important "tools of the trade"—methods of economic measurement, such as business, governmental, personal, and social accounts; and common statistical measures, such as index numbers, sampling, and simple graphs. Part II continues with a description of how the economy works, recurrent themes being allocation of resources, business cycles, and economic growth. Without undue complexity, it examines markets, price theory, and the theory of a firm. It then indicates the influences on markets exerted by such institutions as types of business organization and departures from competition, and by money and its management, governmental activities, labor policy, agricultural policy, behavior of consumers, and foreign transactions. Part II concludes with an examination of the broad outcome of our economic practices, such as advances in technology, growth of income and changes in its distribution, and "big government"; and with a comparative assessment of our society as an "economic system."

2. Part III, comprising almost one third of the volume, consists of case studies involving principles and other material presented in Parts I and II. These cases are not imagined; they are based on documents issued to influence opinion or to throw light on important contemporary problems. Like all policy problems, each involves more than one of the formal principles as they are usually separated for the purpose of teaching; each may be referred back to the several pertinent chapters in

Parts I and II. Whatever confusion this may introduce into an orderly presentation of the discipline is far outweighed by the sense of reality derived by the student and by the opportunity for vivid discussion.

The cases are intended not merely as exercises but also as illustrations of the method, which may be employed and extended by the instructor on the basis of contemporary material which comes in the mail to every economist.

Some instructors may prefer the procedure of completing Parts I and II before tackling the case studies in Part III, and then using these studies as a review and application of the principles discussed. Others may wish immediately to apply the principles described in an early chapter to an appropriate case study; then turn back to a chapter relevant to the case but not yet assigned to the class. There are good arguments to support either procedure; the choice will depend on the preference of the instructor and on the bent of a particular group of students.

I am deeply indebted to Dean Leland E. Traywick, of Michigan State University, and to Professor Francis E. Boddy, of the University of Minnesota, for their help in the preparation of this book. Both read early and final drafts of the manuscript and made many invaluable suggestions. Though I assume full responsibility for the final product, including defects that may be discovered by its users, the book derives much of any merit it may possess from the conscientious and friendly efforts of these two editorial advisers.

March, 1961   GEORGE SOULE

CONTENTS

PART II / HOW OUR INSTITUTIONS OPERATE

of Consumption and Saving / Reasons for Business Investment / Investment Multiplier / Keynesian Equilibrium / Keynesian Prescription for Full Employment / Keynesian Remedy for Inflation / Deflationary and Inflationary Gaps

PART III / CASE STUDIES

PART I / ECONOMIC MEASUREMENT

The study of economics often begins with an outline of the basic economic problems. "Crusoe economics"—named after Daniel Defoe's classic novel—shows how a single castaway on a solitary island must go about satisfying his wants. He needs the material resources from which he can produce food, clothing, and shelter; skill in shaping these resources to fit his needs; judgment in deciding how best to use his time, energies, and the materials at his disposal. Such activities involve the economic problems of *production* and of *allocation* of the available resources.

Any group or society of human beings, all the way from a self-sustaining farm family or pioneer community to a great nation or community of nations, has to solve the same problems. Modern societies are concerned with many more problems and must deal with more complex situations than the pioneer. Work is divided; jobs become specialized. Needs and desires differ. Goods are exchanged not only directly by barter but also through the use of a medium of exchange—money. The making of decisions does not rest with *one* man alone but is spread among millions of people, acting now as consumers, now as workers, now as managers of production or distribution.

How can we proceed to make sense out of such a complex state of affairs? How can we identify its parts, learn the behavior and the results of each part, trace interrelationships? Once we have gained this knowledge, how shall we arrange it to make possible intelligent decisions, management, and planning?

1

The modern economy is like a city with many avenues. A stranger entering at any one of these avenues may gain some knowledge of the city. For example, one may study the history and development of modern economy; may examine the various bodies of theory developed by economists to describe and explain it; or may plunge into the middle of things as they are and observe what goes on.

Books intended to help the beginning student of economics have used various approaches—most of them good—to the introduction of the subject. But no matter what the approach, one tool of discovery is essential if the student is to gain anything like scientific or accurate understanding. This tool is "measurement." Impressionistic observations are indeed often interesting; speculative or imaginative thinking may furnish indispensable illuminations; qualitative analysis may yield valuable results. No matter what the situation we wish to understand, however, we shall be unable to make intelligent judgments unless we are able to answer such questions about the whole or its interrelated parts as how many? how big? how much? For both understanding and decision making, quantitative comparisons are essential in any practical device or problem. Knowledge of how to measure and how to calculate is an elementary requirement. Part I of this book, therefore, deals with elementary economic measurement.

As important examples of such measurement, we shall examine somewhat simplified accounts of (1) a business, (2) government, (3) an individual, (4) the national economy as a whole. We shall then briefly explain some of the commonly used statistical devices used in measuring economic change or relationships, such as index numbers of prices or production and simple graphs or charts.

In the course of examining such accounts and statistics, we shall learn important facts about how our economy operates, as well as the meaning of terms often used in the discussion of economics.

1 / BUSINESS FINANCIAL STATEMENTS /

No science can make much headway without measurement, and this is particularly true of economics. The unit of measurement useful in economics depends, as in other sciences, largely on what is being measured. If you wanted to judge the amount of unemployment, you would have to know how many people were without jobs; the unit of measure might be one worker. If you were interested in the output of steel, the unit of measure would probably be a ton. But if you wanted to measure different commodities and services together, you would have to use a measure common to them all. You could not add tons of steel, hours of work, and all the other separate units that go into the production and consumption of a nation or a business; the sum would mean nothing. In a civilization like ours, a measure common to commodities and services is the unit of money used to buy them. Measurement of economic activity in terms of money is commonly used.

Monetary measuring or counting has come to be called "accounting," which developed in the first place, in the form of accounts used for a business enterprise. It is well to begin, therefore, with a look at the major kinds of accounts used in business. The material presented will not teach anyone how to keep books, how to run a business, or how to pick good investments in the stock market. However, understanding something about business accounting will help one understand how business affects all of us, and is basic to the other measurements discussed in later chapters.

INFORMATION DESIRED BY THE BUSINESSMAN

Among the many things a good businessman wishes to know about his firm is, first of all, how much income it has earned by its operations.

He also wants to know how much it has cost, in current expense, to realize this income, so that he can see the relationship between his costs and his total revenue. He may ask himself whether he can increase his earnings by selling the same amount and at the same time cutting any of his costs. Or, alternatively, can he increase his earnings by selling more without increasing his operating costs proportionately? In other words, is he making the most efficient use of materials, labor, plant, and machinery?

The businessman also wants to know what income his firm might be deriving from any source other than its ordinary operations, and what expenses it might have which are not directly related to its operations. Finally, he requires a record of how much of the firm's net income has been distributed in dividends and how much has remained for reinvestment in the business.

The financial statement or account that reveals the above facts is called the "income (or profit and loss) statement."

THE INCOME (OR PROFIT AND LOSS) STATEMENT

How does the head of a business figure the amount of money it has made in a year? Obviously he adds up all the money the business has taken in during the year and subtracts from it what the business has spent. The difference represents the amount the business has earned. Such a statement could then go on to show what was done with the earnings—for example income taxes or dividends were paid. The amount remaining is commonly called "retained income." Here is an income statement for an imaginary company.

Each of the terms used in the income statement has a meaning set by accounting tradition. Let us comment on the terms in order.

Gross Sales is the amount billed for the goods sold during the year.

Net Sales is the amount actually received, and it must cover all the money distributed by the business. "Net" means that from Gross Sales such items as cash discounts, credits to customers for returned items, and sales allowances have been deducted.

Operating Costs and Expenses covers all the costs incurred in the operations of the business. Cost of Goods Sold includes the materials, productive labor, power, rent, and other costs needed to make the goods. Selling and Administrative Expenses includes money spent for salesmen's salaries and commissions, advertising, executive salaries, general office staff, and insurance, for example. Depreciation is the expense for estimated loss in value of the plant and tools, resulting from wear and tear or from obsolescence during the year: these will be discussed later. Maintenance and Repairs covers what was spent to keep the plant and machinery in good working condition. Taxes include taxes paid to the town or city where the plant is located, any state taxes, and federal

TABLE 1/1

NATIONAL BUSINESS COMPANY, INC.
INCOME FOR YEAR ENDED DECEMBER 31, 19___

Gross Sales		$1,040,000
Net Sales		$1,000,000
Operating Costs and Expenses		
Cost of Goods Sold	$600,000	
Selling and Administrative Expenses	50,000	
Depreciation	30,000	
Maintenance and Repairs	30,000	
Taxes (Other Than Federal Income Taxes)	65,000	775,000
Net Income from Operations		$ 225,000
Other Income		
Interest from Government Bonds and Other Investments		5,000
Total Income		$ 230,000
Other Expenses		
Interest on Mortgage	$ 5,000	
Other Interest	10,000	
Total Other Expenses		$ 15,000
Net Income before Federal Income Taxes		$ 215,000
Provision for Federal Corporate Income Taxes		102,500
Net Income		$ 112,500
Dividends, Common Stock		50,000
Balance Carried to Retained Income		$ 62,500

taxes—such as social security taxes or taxes on the product at so much per unit.

Net Income from Operations is obtained by subtracting Operating Costs and Expenses from Net Sales. This figure represents the money the company made from selling its product. Any receipts from outside investments are not regarded as profit from operations but are added as separate items; these are listed under *Other Income*—Interest on Government Bonds and Other Investments. Moreover, before net profit can be disposed of by the owners, certain charges—not regarded as operating expenses—have to be deducted from it; these are listed as *Other Expenses*.

Interest paid is one of the deducted charges. To set up its business, the company borrowed money from the bank, and it has to pay interest on the loan. As security for the loan, the bank holds a mortgage on the company's main building. If the company did not pay the interest on this loan, the bank could demand that the amount borrowed be repaid; if the company defaulted, the bank could take possession of the building. (This interest is listed as Interest on Mortgage.)

This company, like many others, also borrows money from the bank for short periods. It borrows when it must meet heavy expenses for materials or labor, and repays the loan when the customers pay for the goods. Interest must be paid on these loans. (This interest is shown as Other Interest.)

Interest paid out is not regarded as an *operating* expense because the company could make and sell the same goods without incurring any debts on which interest must be paid. But interest *is* an expense, which must be deducted before income taxes or dividends are paid.

Provision for Federal Corporate Income Taxes, under *Net Income Before Federal Income Taxes,* is what the company knows it will have to pay to the federal government on the money it has made in the year covered by the statement. Income taxes are a certain percentage of the income, and therefore cannot be figured accurately until the income is known. They are not an expense of doing business, either logically or legally. Nevertheless, they have to be deducted before the company knows how much it can pay out to its owners or use for their benefit.

Net Income is the profit that belongs to the owners of the business, after all obligations of the year have been met.

Dividends are the payments made to the owners, or stockholders. In a corporation, each owner's share of the dividends is determined by the number of shares of stock he owns. In this case, a dividend of $2 a share is paid on the 25,000 shares of common stock.

Balance Carried to Retained Earnings is what is left. Growing companies usually use this balance to expand their business, by enlarging the plant or by making other investments. Retained earnings are "savings," but this does not mean that the money is usually held in the form of cash or can be drawn out of the bank.

This business is apparently doing pretty well. From net sales of $1,000,000 during the year, it has derived a net income from operations of $225,000, or 22.5 percent. Or, to put it another way, by spending $775,000 in its operations, it has earned, clear, one third more than it has spent. Although a large part of this sum had to be paid to the government in income taxes, there was enough left to pay $50,000 in dividends and to reinvest $62,500 in the business or to put it into some other investment.

The income statement is regarded as a fairly good measurement of the performance of a business during the period which it covers. Unless the figures are inaccurate or dishonest, the statement should offer some idea of whether the business is doing well or badly. Nevertheless, it is by no means complete. For example, it reveals nothing about the relationship of the profit to the sum invested in the business.

Suppose you owned a share in this business and received a $2 dividend on your share. If your share had cost you $10, you would think you were doing very well indeed, since the dividend represents a 20 percent cash return on your investment. In addition, the company would have made more than half as much again, which it did not pay out but was using for expansion. On the other hand, if you had paid $200 for your share, you would be receiving only a 1 percent cash return—less than you could have obtained by putting your money in a savings bank, with almost no risk of loss.

THE BALANCE SHEET

To find out how much a business is worth on any date, it is necessary first to estimate the value of what it *owns* and then to subtract from that sum the amount that it *owes*. What it owns is called "assets"; what it owes is called "liabilities."

Here is the balance sheet of the National Business Company, Inc., whose income statement we have just inspected. Note that this balance sheet, like those usually used in actual accounting, includes under Lia-

TABLE 1/2

NATIONAL BUSINESS COMPANY, INC.

BALANCE SHEET
DECEMBER 31, 19——

Assets		(I) *Liabilities*	
Current Assets		Current Liabilities	
Cash	$ 200,000	Accounts Payable ... $ 30,000	
Investments	168,750	Accrued Taxes	110,000
Accounts Receivable ...	200,000	Accrued Wages,	
Inventories	150,000	Interest, etc.	5,000
	$ 718,750		$ 145,000
Property, Plant and Equipment		Long-Term Liabilities	
Cost $615,000		6% First Mortgage ..	100,000
Less Reserve for Depreciation. 300,000			
Net Property	315,000	(II) *Stockholders' Equity*	
		Capital Stock (25,000	
Intangibles		shares, no-par value)	300,000
Patents	0	Retained Earnings ..	488,750
Good Will	0		
		Total Liabilities and	
Total Assets	$1,033,750	Stockholders' Equity .	$1,033,750

bilities the value of the capital stock and the retained earnings. In a sense, the corporation *owes* these sums to the owners of the corporation itself. But the two items together, being the difference between the supposed value of what the company owns and the sums owed to out-siders, represent what is called the "net worth" of the company—that is, the worth of the company to the stockholders. In this balance sheet, the net worth is called "Stockholders' Equity."

The size of the retained earnings is determined by the amount added to this item (or subtracted from it) year by year, as shown by the annual income statements. The value of the stock is whatever value was assigned to it when it was issued, often what the original stockholders paid for it. It is called "stated value"; it may be very different from what the present stockholders actually paid for their shares or from the amount the shares could be sold for.

One other characteristic of the balance sheet as a whole deserves special attention. If the corporation transacts business which changes any item on the balance sheet, this change will affect some other item or items on it; as a result, the two sides will remain in balance. Suppose, for example, the corporation pays a debt and thus reduces Accounts Payable on the liabilities side. The money with which it pays may be taken out of cash, and so will require a corresponding reduction on the assets side. Or suppose the corporation invests in new machinery and thus increases the asset Property, Plant, and Equipment. The money to buy the machinery must be obtained somewhere. If the money is borrowed or is raised by the sale of new stock, liabilities will be correspondingly increased. If the money is obtained from a fund set aside for such purposes and temporarily invested, a reduction in investments will offset the addition to assets represented by the purchase of the machinery.

At the end of the year, when the surplus from income is transferred to retained earnings on the liabilities side of the balance sheet, the change will be balanced on the assets side by an increase either in cash or in some investment in plant or securities for which the surplus was used.

The balance sheet is an example of what is called "double-entry bookkeeping," in which a transaction must be entered twice, once as a debit and once as a credit.

We shall now comment on some of the specific headings.

ASSETS

Current assets are cash and items that, in the normal course of business, will be turned into cash within one year. Cash includes currency in the office or safe and bank deposits that can be drawn out at will. United States Government securities (listed as "Investments" in the balance sheet shown), in which businesses invest, can be sold on any business day; there is always a market for them, and the price obtainable seldom changes rapidly. Government securities are regarded as the nearest thing to cash; business firms hold them to earn some interest on money that they are not likely to need right away. Accounts Receivable represents bills that have been sent out to customers and which will ordinarily be paid within a few months. The sum shown is already diminished by a "Reserve for Bad Debts"—a percentage which the experience of the company shows may be uncollectible. So far, so good; the assets represent dollars readily available, except during a financial crisis.

We must pause, however, on Inventories. Inventories consist of the stock in trade of the company, sales of which constitute its major source of revenue. In the case of a manufacturing company, inventories would consist of materials, goods in process, and finished goods awaiting sale. Obviously they are worth something, but the accountant always takes a risk in estimating how much. If prices should rise, they would be worth more when they are sold than they are at present. The opposite would be true if prices should fall. Possibly, because of a change in customers' demands, some of them could not be sold at all. To be on the safe side, the accountant follows the common practice of valuing inventories at cost value or at market value, whichever is *lower*. Other methods are sometimes used.

Conservatively valued, securities, like inventories, will be set down either at cost or at market, whichever is lower.

Property, Plant, and Equipment is set down at cost. The item is the sum of a long list of purchases, such as land, buildings, machinery, trucks, and other equipment, made at various times. Each of these items, except probably land, wears out in the course of time. Or it may be superseded by a better building or machine before it wears out—it may thus become "obsolete." Therefore, from the cost of each building, machine, or other item is subtracted annually a reserve for depreciation, which has been accumulated with the idea that when the piece of property has become useless, it will be valued at zero and so will not appear among the assets. Look back at the income statement and you will see that one of the expenses deducted from annual income is "Depreciation." The Reserve for Depreciation deducted from Property, Plant, and Equipment on the balance sheet is the sum of all the annual charges for depreciation which have been made to date.

The question of how much to charge off for depreciation year by year may be answered in many ways. A machine depreciated quickly may still be useful long after it has become "worth" nothing on the balance sheet. A machine which soon becomes obsolete may not have been fully depreciated by the time it has to be discarded for one of better design. Or by the time the funds accumulated by depreciation charges need to be used to replace a machine, the money laid aside may buy a new and greatly improved machine worth much more to the company than the old one was.

Even if depreciation accurately represents the situation, the value of the plant as stated may be much higher than it would sell for if the company should go out of business. This item on the balance sheet is, therefore, scarcely a precise estimate. The "value" is highly uncertain. Actually, the value depends largely on how successful the company is and what policies it follows.

Intangibles such as Good Will are supposed to cover the company's name and reputation, plus a trained organization, which is obviously valuable yet is difficult to evaluate in dollars. The same may be true of patents or trade secrets. Some companies include them as assets with an estimated value; others do not, listing them as shown in the balance sheet shown. Both practices can be defended under appropriate circumstances.

LIABILITIES

Current liabilities correspond with current assets, because they represent debts that will have to be paid within one year. Accounts Payable represents the bills received for materials or supplies already bought. Taxes have to be paid by certain dates; the company knows in advance approximately what they will be. Accrued Taxes on this balance sheet covers taxes for all or part of the previous year and should be charged against it, even if not yet payable. Some wages, interest, or other expenses are likewise accrued at the close of business on December 31. Suppose, for example, December 31 falls on a Wednesday, and wages are paid every Friday. The firm would, on December 31, owe the wages for work done on Monday, Tuesday, and Wednesday.

The reason that current assets and current liabilities are separated from other assets and liabilities is that, if the business does not meet its obligations to suppliers, government, or employees when they are due, its credit will suffer and it may even get into serious difficulties. Our imaginary company is very well situated in this respect. It has more than enough cash to pay all its outstanding bills, even without selling any of its investments, collecting any of the money owed to it, or selling any of its inventories.

The ratio between all its current assets and its current liabilities, commonly called the "current ratio," is almost five to one. How big the current ratio has to be for safety depends somewhat on the circumstances and largely on the nature of the business. A company whose business consists in buying daily newspapers at wholesale and selling them at retail, for example, would not need nearly so much cash in relation to its volume of sales—that is, so large a current ratio—as a piano manufacturer, since the latter deals in an expensive product which takes a long time to manufacture and may take a long time to sell.

There is little to be said about the remaining liabilities. Obviously the mortgage is a debt which the company owes to the bank. It will have to be repaid—either on a certain date in the future or at so much every year. Bonds issued by big concerns are similar forms of long-term debt— many of them are actually secured by mortgages.

The entries under Capital Stock and Retained Earnings have already been explained.

The stockholders should be well pleased with the performance of this company. Presumably those who bought shares when they were issued by the company paid $300,000 for the 25,000 shares they bought, or an average of $12 a share. Those who still retained this stock are receiving, with their annual dividend of $2 a share, 16⅔ percent on their original investment. In addition, the company has accumulated $488,750 of retained earnings, mostly reinvested in the business. This should make it worth much more than the original stockholders paid. The total net worth, according to the balance sheet, is $788,750. This makes each share theoretically "worth" about $31.50—though whether the shares would actually be sold and bought for that amount depends on unknown conditions. However, the $2 dividend per share is slightly more than 6 percent on the "net worth" which each share represents—under many circumstances not a bad yield for a company in good condition which presumably has experienced a rapid growth and might still grow.

To illustrate some points discussed in this chapter and also to give students practice in understanding the working of a balance sheet, the following problem is submitted. Note that there are numerous correct answers. The test of the answers will be whether they are reasonable under the circumstances and whether the changes in the balance sheet are internally consistent.

For a case study giving more details about interpretation of financial accounts, see Chapter 29.

PROBLEM

You are president of a small corporation. You are concerned about the business situation because orders have been falling off and you expect prices to drop. Your balance sheet at this time shows the following:

Current Assets		Current Liabilities	
Cash	$25,000	Accounts Payable	$40,000
Investments	10,000	Accrued Taxes	6,000
Accounts Receivable	35,000	Accrued Interest	4,000
Inventory	50,000	Bank Loan	50,000

(a) What do you do? Show the current assets and current liabilities as they would appear after you had carried out your plan. Why is your situation improved?

(b) If other firms should follow your example, what would be the effect on production and employment?

(c) The other assets and liabilities of your corporation are:

Assets			Liabilities	
Other investments		$ 30,000	Mortgage on property	$ 35,000
Property, Plant, and			*Stockholders' Equity*	
Equipment			Capital stock	
Cost	$200,000		Preferred	25,000
Less Res. for			Common	100,000
Depr.	40,000			
Net Property		160,000		

What are your company's retained earnings?

(d) After the changes in (a) have been made, you feel that business conditions will improve and you buy new machinery costing $50,000. You raise the money by selling your other investments, issuing $15,000 new common stock and borrowing $5,000. Draw up your balance sheet as it will now stand. What will be the effect on production and employment of the action you have taken?

2 / GOVERNMENT INCOME

ACCOUNTS /

Many things that people need or desire nowadays they cannot purchase from a business concern—things like an army, a navy, or an air force, social security, soil conservation. Some services the government must supply because no private company could make a profit selling them; some governmental functions could not be entrusted to any management not representing the people as a whole; and some, like the post office, roads, and public schools, have been turned over to government because the people's representatives decided that a public agency was needed to do the job properly.

Unlike a private business, government is not concerned about making profits; it can even operate at a loss for considerable periods without incurring any great danger of passing out of existence. Unlike a private business, too, government does not have to depend mainly on purchases by individual citizens for what it sells; it has the power to raise revenues by taxation. If it has to borrow, it can, as a rule, borrow larger sums at lower interest rates than any private business could. Government, like private businesses, keeps careful accounts and must know whether its revenues exceed its expenses.

In the United States, the President is directed by law to submit to Congress every January a financial report of past operations and a budget of estimated revenues and expenses based on the administration program for the coming fiscal year (beginning July 1). This report is called the "Budget Message." It is drawn up by a highly skilled Bureau of the Budget, which is part of the executive office of the President. Congress, under the Constitution, has the sole right to decide how much shall be spent and for what, as well as the right to say how the tax revenue shall be raised. If Congress votes to spend more money than it votes to levy in taxes, the Secretary of the Treasury has to borrow whatever is needed to make up the deficit. Borrowings by the Treasury in preceding years, if still not repaid, constitute the national debt. Most state and local

13

governments have accounting provisions roughly similar to those of the federal government.

The importance of governmental accounts and of the policies based on them is indicated by the fact that in 1954, a recent fairly typical year, federal, state, and local governments spent about $96 billion, whereas all the consumers in the United States spent (after paying their taxes) about $234 billion. In other words, what the citizens authorized the governments to provide for them cost about three eights as much as what they paid for commercially sold goods and services. Of course, this proportion is much higher when, as in 1954, expenses for military purposes are high, at least in comparison with previous periods of peace.

THE FEDERAL BUDGET

Here is a summary of the income account of the United States Government for the fiscal year ended June 30, 1959, together with the budget estimate for the year ended June 30, 1960, as presented in the Budget Message to Congress in January, 1960.

Individual income taxes, it will be seen, yielded the largest single item of revenue and provided more than half the total. Next came corporation income taxes. Excise taxes—that is, taxes on cigarettes, gasoline, new automobiles, and the so-called "luxury taxes"—yielded the third highest revenue. Excise taxes are paid to the government by the producers, but are added by them to the prices paid by the consumers. Employment taxes are the sums collected from employers and employees for the payment of unemployment insurance and the like. Estate taxes are taxes on estates left by persons who die. Gift taxes must be paid on gifts made to individuals and to organizations not exempt from taxation on the ground that they are philanthropic and, hence, do not make profits. The recipient must pay the tax. Customs revenues come from tariff duties on imports.

Before listing its receipts, the government excludes certain amounts. One such item is the sum collected for old-age pensions, which it turns over to a trust fund accumulated for that purpose. Another is the sum collected and turned over to a retirement fund for railroad employees. These sums are not listed under Expenditures. Finally, there must be deducted refunds made to taxpayers who have paid more in taxes than they legally owe.

Under Expenditures, "major national security" dwarfs all the others. This item covers Army, Navy, Air Force, Atomic Energy Commission, and military aid to foreign nations, as well as smaller items. Next in order of size is interest (on the debt). Not far behind comes veterans' services and benefits. Since the debt was largely incurred for war or defense purposes, these three items are attributable mainly to past or (possibly) to future wars. All the rest of what the federal government

TABLE 2/1

FEDERAL RECEIPTS AND EXPENDITURES
YEAR ENDED JUNE 30, 1959, AND ESTIMATE FOR
YEAR ENDED JUNE 30, 1960
(in millions of dollars)

Description	1959	Estimate 1960
BUDGET RECEIPTS		
Individual income taxes	$ 36,719	$40,306
Corporation income taxes	17,309	22,200
Excise taxes	8,504	9,100
Employment taxes	321	333
Estate and gift taxes	1,333	1,470
Customs	925	1,176
Miscellaneous receipts	3,160	4,015
Total, budget receipts	$ 68,270	$78,600
BUDGET EXPENDITURES		
Major national security	$ 46,426	$45,650
International affairs and finance	3,780	2,066
Veterans services and benefits	5,174	5,157
Labor and welfare	4,421	4,441
Agriculture and agricultural resources	6,529	5,113
Natural resources	1,669	1,785
Commerce and housing	3,421	3,002
General government	1,606	1,711
Interest	7,671	9,385
Allowance for contingencies	......	75
Adjustment to daily Treasury statement basis	......	......
Total, budget expenditures	$ 80,697	$78,383
Budget surplus (+) or deficit (−)	$−12,427	$ +217

spent amounted to barely more than $20 billion, or somewhat less than one fourth of all its expenditures.

Many people think that their income taxes are too high. Yet if expenditures attributable to national security were continued, abolishing everything else the government pays for—including interest on the debt, veterans' services, all services to civilians, the President, the Executive Departments, Congress, and the Federal courts—would make possible a cut of less than one half in the total individual income taxes.

The budget estimates for the fiscal year ended June 30, 1960, showed much the same proportions, both for revenues and for expenditures.

The income account for 1959 turns up with a deficit—somewhat small in relation to total revenue. During the years of World War II, the federal government had a huge deficit. In 1947, 1948, and 1951, it had a small surplus; in all other postwar years through 1954, there was a deficit; for several years thereafter, a small surplus.

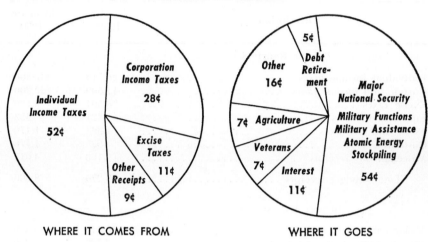

Fig. 2.1.

THE CASH BUDGET

It is generally believed that if the government spends more than it receives in taxes and in direct remuneration for its services, the budget will be unbalanced, with all the consequences, desirable or undesirable, of such a situation. A "budget" is commonly understood to be the account similar to the one presented and explained above. Yet, if one is concerned with the effect on the total economy of government finances, this budget may give a false impression, since it does not cover either all the tax receipts of the treasury or all the money disbursed by the government. Specifically, it deducts from receipts the social security and railroad retirement contributions made by employers and employees to old-age pensions, and it does not show among its expenditures the payments made to the beneficiaries of old-age pensions and assistance. These two totals usually do not, in any one year, balance each other, and the difference may be large enough materially to alter the impression left by the regular budget concerning any gap between government receipts and expenditures.

Another type of income and expenditure account for the federal government is called the "cash budget." It covers everything the government takes in from the public and everything it pays out (excluding loans in both cases). These totals are somewhat larger than those in the regular budget. As we have seen, the regular budget deducts from receipts the taxes it collects for old-age pension and railroad retirement.

The regular budget, moreover, does not include in its expenditures the benefits paid during the year for these purposes. The money actually comes from the public and is paid out to it—by an agency set up separately within the government. The cash budget does include these items.

The table below shows cash receipts and cash expenditures of both

TABLE 2/2

GOVERNMENT CASH RECEIPTS FROM AND
PAYMENTS TO THE PUBLIC, 1946–1961
[in billions of dollars]

Period	Total			Federal [1]			State and local [2]		
	Cash re-ceipts	Cash pay-ments	Excess of re-ceipts or of pay-ments (−)	Cash re-ceipts	Cash pay-ments	Excess of re-ceipts or of pay-ments (−)	Cash re-ceipts	Cash pay-ments	Excess of re-ceipts or of pay-ments (−)
Calendar year:									
1946	52.9	50.9	2.0	41.4	41.4	([3])	11.4	9.5	1.9
1947	57.4	50.7	6.7	44.3	38.6	5.7	13.1	12.1	1.0
1948	60.0	51.8	8.2	44.9	36.9	8.0	15.1	14.9	.2
1949	57.9	59.8	−1.8	41.3	42.6	−1.3	16.6	17.1	−.5
1950	60.4	61.1	−.6	42.4	42.0	.5	18.0	19.1	−1.1
1951	79.1	78.3	.9	59.3	58.0	1.2	19.9	20.2	−.4
1952	92.6	94.2	−1.6	70.9	72.6	−1.7	21.7	21.6	.1
1953	93.9	99.7	−5.9	70.6	76.8	−6.1	23.2	23.0	.3
1954	93.3	95.3	−2.0	68.6	69.7	−1.1	24.7	25.6	−.9
1955	98.4	100.2	−1.8	71.4	72.2	−.7	26.9	28.0	−1.1
1956	110.2	105.2	5.0	80.3	74.8	5.5	29.9	30.4	−.5
1957	116.8	116.5	.2	84.5	83.3	1.2	32.3	33.2	−.9
1958	115.7	124.5	−8.8	81.7	89.0	−7.3	33.9	35.5	−1.5
1959 [4]	124.3	133.4	−9.1	87.6	95.6	−8.0	36.7	37.8	−1.1
Fiscal year:									
1946	54.2	70.2	−16.0	43.5	61.7	−18.2	10.7	8.5	2.2
1947	55.6	47.5	8.1	43.5	36.9	6.6	12.1	10.6	1.5
1948	59.6	50.2	9.4	45.4	36.5	8.9	14.2	13.7	.5
1949	57.6	56.3	1.3	41.6	40.6	1.0	16.0	15.7	.3
1950	58.2	61.5	−3.3	40.9	43.1	−2.2	17.3	18.4	−1.1
1951	72.5	65.2	7.3	53.4	45.8	7.6	19.1	19.4	−.3
1952	88.7	88.9	−.2	68.0	68.0	([3])	20.7	20.9	−.2
1953	93.9	99.1	−5.2	71.5	76.8	−5.3	22.4	22.3	.1
1954	95.6	96.1	−.4	71.6	71.9	−.2	24.0	24.2	−.2
1955	93.5	97.5	−4.0	67.8	70.5	−2.7	25.7	27.0	−1.3
1956	105.8	101.6	4.2	77.1	72.6	4.5	28.7	29.0	−.3
1957	113.3	111.8	1.5	82.1	80.0	2.1	31.2	31.8	−.6
1958	114.9	117.9	−3.0	81.9	83.4	−1.5	33.0	34.5	−1.5
1959	116.8	131.2	−14.4	81.7	94.8	−13.1	35.1	36.4	−1.3
1960 [5]				94.8	95.3	−.5			
1961 [5]				102.2	96.3	5.9			

[1] For derivation of Federal cash receipts and payments, see *Budget of the United States Government for the Fiscal Year ending June 30, 1961.*

[2] Estimated by Council of Economic Advisers from receipts and expenditures in the national income accounts. Cash receipts consist of personal tax and nontax receipts, indirect business tax and nontax accruals, and corporate tax accruals adjusted to a collection basis. Cash payments are total expenditures less Federal grants-in-aid and less contributions for social insurance. (Federal grants-in-aid are therefore excluded from State and local receipts and payments and included only in Federal payments.)

[3] Less than $50 million.

[4] Preliminary.

[5] Estimate.

Note: Detail will not necessarily add to totals because of rounding.

Sources: Treasury Department, Bureau of the Budget, Department of Commerce, and Council of Economic Advisers.

federal and state governments for the years 1946–1961. On the basis of
these figures, the federal government, in 1959, had a cash deficit of nearly
a billion dollars more than that shown in the conventional budget. The
only years in which the cash budget has been balanced since World
War II are 1947, 1948, 1949, 1950, 1956, and 1957. The states have
usually spent more than they have received.

The cash budget is the one we must consult if we are interested in
whether the government is, on balance, adding to or subtracting from
the cash income of the people by its operations. In 1959 it did add
$13 billion. This is a sizable amount in comparison either with total
government expenditures or with everybody's income. Those who
thought that their taxes were high and that the government expenditures
which made the taxes necessary were excessive, may be startled to learn
that the federal government did make a net contribution to private
money incomes on the whole.

What these people are likely to forget is that everything the government spends—by paying contractors, employees, and others—becomes part
of the incomes of the recipients, just as does everything business spends.
If the government actually pays out more than it takes back, it is
increasing incomes by just that much.

Of course, what we are looking at here is only the *money* incomes
received. Consumers might have had more of what they wanted for their
households, rather than the services the government provided, if their
taxes had been reduced, if the government had spent correspondingly
less, and if the productive capacity thus released had been employed to
produce whatever each consumer could have bought with his tax relief.

GOVERNMENT CAPITAL ACCOUNTS

Unlike a business concern, the government does not regularly prepare and publish a balance sheet in which its assets are listed on one
side and its liabilities on the other. If it did so, it could put under assets
its cash and inventories, its investments, and its immense property in
land and buildings; it could put under liabilities all that it owes—that
is, the public debt. One might, in that case, arrive at an estimate of the
government's "net worth" by subtracting the liabilities from the assets.
But the account would be of little use for ordinary purposes, since the
government has no stockholders and does not exist to make profits. And
the "value" of government property might be even more difficult to
determine accurately than the value of private inventories, plants, and
equipment. How, for example, would one judge the value of aircraft
carriers or of land that nobody wants to buy? However, it is quite possible that, in the future, a government balance sheet will be developed.

Of course, governments do keep, in separate accounts, lists of all
their property. They also keep very careful accounts of their debts.
These are necessary in order to know when and how much interest and

principal must be paid to those who have lent money by buying government securities.

The total amount of debt of the federal government shown in Table 2/3 is increased by a budget deficit and decreased by a surplus. Many argue that a large debt is a danger to the country and that it should be reduced as rapidly as possible—perhaps even paid off entirely. How can we tell whether a national debt is dangerous or whether it is

TABLE 2/3

FEDERAL BUDGET RECEIPTS AND EXPENDITURES
AND THE PUBLIC DEBT, 1929–1961
(in millions of dollars)

Period	Net budget receipts [1]	Budget expenditures	Surplus or deficit (−)	Public debt at end of year [2]
Fiscal year:				
1929	3,861	3,127	734	16,931
1930	4,058	3,320	738	16,185
1931	3,116	3,577	−462	16,801
1932	1,924	4,659	−2,735	19,487
1933	2,021	4,623	−2,602	22,539
1934	3,064	6,694	−3,630	27,053
1935	3,730	6,521	−2,791	28,701
1936	4,069	8,493	−4,425	33,779
1937	4,979	7,756	−2,777	36,425
1938	5,615	6,792	−1,177	37,165
1939	4,996	8,858	−3,862	40,440
1940	5,144	9,062	−3,918	42,968
1941	7,103	13,262	−6,159	48,961
1942	12,555	34,046	−21,490	72,422
1943	21,987	79,407	−57,420	136,696
1944	43,635	95,059	−51,423	201,003
1945	44,475	98,416	−53,941	258,682
1946	39,771	60,448	−20,676	269,422
1947	39,786	39,032	754	258,286
1948	41,488	33,069	8,419	252,292
1949	37,696	39,507	−1,811	252,770
1950	36,495	39,617	−3,122	257,357
1951	47,568	44,058	3,510	255,222
1952	61,391	65,408	−4,017	259,105
1953	64,825	74,274	−9,449	266,071
1954	64,655	67,772	−3,117	271,260
1955	60,390	64,570	−4,180	274,374
1956	68,165	66,540	1,626	272,751
1957	71,029	69,433	1,596	270,527
1958	69,117	71,936	−2,819	276,343
1959	68,270	80,697	−12,427	284,706
1960 [3]	78,600	78,383	217	284,500
1961 [3]	84,000	79,816	4,184	280,000

[1] Gross receipts less refunds of receipts and transfers of tax receipts to the old-age and survivors insurance trust fund, the disability insurance trust fund, the railroad retirement account, and the highway trust fund.

[2] Excludes guaranteed obligations. The change in the public debt from year to year reflects not only the budget surplus or deficit but also changes in the Treasury's cash balances, the effect of certain trust-fund transactions, and direct borrowing from the public by certain Government enterprises.

[3] Estimate.

[4] Preliminary; subject to minor changes.

Note: Detail will not necessarily add to totals because of rounding.

Sources: Treasury Department and Bureau of the Budget (except as noted).

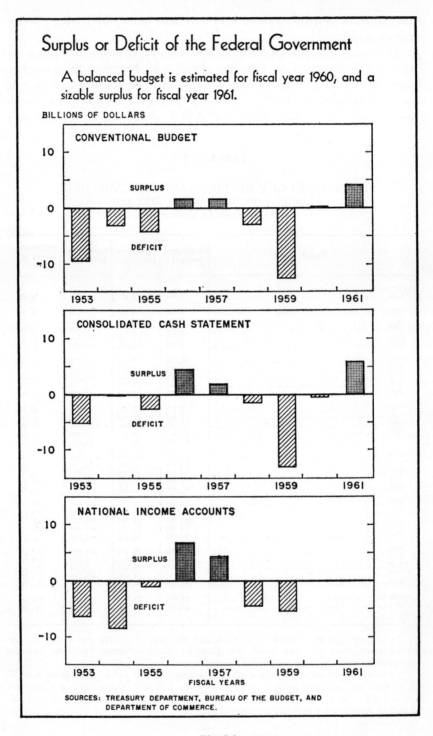

Fig. 2.2.

too large? This question involves more than may appear on the surface. Let us look briefly at some of the problems involved.

Some may fear that the government might become bankrupt, so that its obligations would be worthless. In that case those who had lent the government money by buying bonds would not be repaid, and it could not borrow any more money. But such a lamentable outcome would not occur so long as the government could raise enough money by taxation to pay the interest due on the bonds, in addition to its other expenses. You will notice that the share of the federal government's income paid in interest is not a large one, compared with all its other expenditures. Apparently, no difficulty in this score is yet in sight.

Another theoretical possibility is that the government would have to use so much of its revenue in interest on the debt that it could not afford other and more desirable expenditures. But this involves the broader question as to how large a part of the income of the people and of business the government can take in taxes without impairing the welfare of the people. One test of this question is—how large a part of the national income does government income account for? If national income grows, government spending can grow at the same rate without causing any great difficulty. We shall be better able to look into this matter after we have learned more about the national income in subsequent chapters.

There are other important questions relating to the size and nature of the national debt, but we are not prepared to discuss them at this point. Among such questions are these: Under what circumstances should the debt be reduced, and under what circumstances should it be increased? Can a large government debt lead to inflation by increasing the money supply, and if so, how? Does the national debt tend to change the distribution of income by taxation of poor people in order to pay interest to rich bondholders, or does it work in the opposite direction?

PROBLEM

(a) Assume that Congress had decided to reduce taxes with the result that individual income tax receipts for the fiscal year ended June 30, 1959, were 10 percent lower than they had been in the previous year, and that corporation income tax receipts were 20 percent lower. Assume that no other items of federal income or expenditure changed from 1958 to 1959.

What would the total federal debt have been on June 30, 1959?

(b) *In addition to the above change,* assume that, because of bad conditions, many elderly people decided to retire and that, as a result, government had had to pay an extra $1.2 billion in old-age pensions during the fiscal year ended June 30, 1959. What would have been its net cash contribution to the incomes of the public during that year?

All the information necessary to answer these questions is contained in Chapter 2.

3/ PERSONAL ACCOUNTS / Any individual

may keep an income and expenditure account on much the same principle as the accounts of business or government. Obviously, an individual's account is less complicated. To keep such an account for any accounting period, a person would list first all money received and then all expenditures; subtract one from the other; and come out with a surplus to be added to savings, or a deficit, to be carried over to the next period.

Such an account may be kept weekly or monthly. At the end of the accounting period, if the figures are accurate, the balance obtained by subtracting expenditures from income should, of course, equal the cash on hand.

Why go to all this trouble? Why should anyone account to himself for the way he receives and spends his money? Many do not bother to do so. But many find that they have a tendency to spend more than they receive; or, if they come out with a surplus, it is not so much as they want to save. Perhaps equally important, an individual may not be making the best use of his money, since he may have to deny himself something which he regards as extremely rewarding, without realizing that he is spending more than is necessary on something else. The way to attack the problem is to start by *measuring,* just as businesses and governments do, in order that intelligent judgments may be made on the basis of reliable knowledge based on experience. In other words, measuring and accounting by an individual may help him to allocate his resources better, just as it may help a business or a government do so.

USE OF BUDGETS

If the individual classifies the major purposes for which he spends his money—such as rent, food, clothing, amusements, and other items—and finds the total under each classification for a month, or perhaps for a year, he may be able to rearrange his expenditures more satisfactorily. This is "economizing." Popularly, economizing means spending less. As

22

an economist uses the term, it may mean, indeed, spending less for some things but, at the same time, spending more for others. One of the basic functions of economic management, whether for individual, household, business, or nation, is to *allocate* to the most desirable uses the resources available.

The way to do this, many have learned, is to make a budget for the future, based on a classified measurement of past expenditures. A good budget facilitates changes in spending habits, without leading to the disappointment involved in spasmodic efforts to attempt the impossible.

Ways of making such changes are exactly what the President proposes to Congress in his budget message. In addition to the statement listing past receipts and expenditures, such as that shown in Chapter 2, he includes a forecast for the coming fiscal year, in which he makes detailed and classified estimates of future receipts and expenditures, all carefully considered in advance and recommended to Congress for appropriate action. Many business concerns also use budgets in planning their future.

Once a plan for spending is made and recorded in a budget, it is of little use unless one keeps a current record of income and expenditures for comparison with the budget. Then it is possible to tell how close one comes to the mark. Very few governments, businesses, or individuals hit the bull's-eye; and often it is necessary to revise the budget because of unforeseen circumstances. Nevertheless, it is better to have a plan and check performance against it than to float along on uncertainties.

CHECKING ACCOUNTS

A checking account offers a ready substitute for a personal income account. Money received and deposited is recorded in the checkbook. The major bills are paid by check and recorded on the stubs; only enough is drawn out in cash to supply pocket money. By going over the checkbook, the depositor may see where his money comes from and how most of it is spent. If, in addition, he finds it desirable to pay cash regularly for marketing or other shopping, he may specify on stubs of the checks drawn the purposes for which the money has been used.

Unless a minimum sum is always kept in the checking account, banks usually make a small charge for handling the checking accounts (or, as they are called in technical banking language, "demand deposits"). But this charge may be worth paying because of the convenience to the depositor and the added safety of not having to worry about money which may be lost or stolen if carried about or left at home.

PERSONAL BALANCE SHEETS

A person who owns stocks, bonds, houses, insurance policies, and other valuable papers may also keep a "capital account" or balance sheet on exactly the same principles as the business balance sheet. His assets, or what he owns, are listed on one side, and his liabilities, or what he owes, on the other. The difference is his "net worth." It is seldom worth while for anyone to keep such an account unless he has considerable personal property, although everyone who owns anything except cash assets should at least keep a list of such possessions. It will help him to judge whether he is making the best use of his savings, and would be of great convenience to his family or other heirs if he should die.

If everyone did keep a balance sheet, even though he owned no "investments" in the ordinary sense of stocks and bonds, one kind of information of importance to the whole national economy would appear. Let us consider this example.

Suppose A buys an automobile on the installment plan, as millions do every year. On the assets side of the balance sheet, he would enter the value of the new car. If he turned in an old car in part payment, it would naturally cease to be listed as an asset. However, since he acquired a new car, his total assets would be increased by the value of the new car. The amount that A had borrowed from the finance company or the bank to finance the purchase of the car would be entered on the liabilities side and would thus increase A's liabilities. (The total of the monthly installments would be somewhat more than the cost price of the car, as it would include interest, finance, and other charges, as well as the cost of the car itself.)

The following simplified balance sheets illustrates the process.

TABLE 3/1

A'S BALANCE SHEET BEFORE PURCHASING CAR

Assets		Liabilities	
Cash	$ 300	Accounts Payable	$ 50
Books, Clothing, etc.	250	Net Worth	1,400
Automobile	900		
	$1,450		$1,450

A'S BALANCE SHEET AFTER PURCHASING CAR

Assets		Liabilities	
Cash	$ 300	Accounts Payable	$ 50
Books, Clothing, etc.	250	Principal of Finance Loan	1,200
Automobile	2,100	Net Worth	1,400
	$2,650		$2,650

A, by borrowing $1,200 to buy a new car, has increased his expenditures, and thus the payments that provide income to others, by $1,200.

He has done this without adding anything to his own income or decreasing his immediate expenditures for other things. If all potential purchasers do as A does, such borrowing and spending will certainly tend to increase other people's incomes by a very large amount. A, however, is no better off financially. Although his assets have increased, so have his liabilities; his net worth remains the same.

Now, suppose that B, who has exactly the same income as A and starts with exactly the same balance sheet, saves $1,200 out of his income. Suppose also that B decides to get along with his old car, thus adding the $1,200 to his cash. His balance sheets would look like this:

TABLE 3/2

B'S BALANCE SHEET

BEFORE SAVING

Assets		Liabilities	
Cash	$ 300	Accounts Payable	$ 50
Books, Clothing, etc.	250		
Automobile	900	Net Worth	1,400
	$1,450		$1,450

AFTER SAVING

Assets		Liabilities	
Cash	$1,500	Accounts Payable	$ 50
Books, Clothing, etc.	250		
Automobile	600	Net Worth	2,300
	$2,350		$2,350

B's second balance sheet shows that the car has depreciated $300 while B was saving the $1,200; nevertheless his net worth has increased, unlike A's, because he has incurred no new debts. Yet, instead of spending and adding $1,200 to the income of others, B is holding $1,200 in cash, unspent. If all potential purchasers act as B does, much less will be spent (and received) in the aggregate than if they all acted as A did. (B, however, may now buy a new car without paying so much for it as A did, since he will not have to pay interest on borrowed money.)

Naturally, the same principle applies to the purchase of houses, furniture, or anything else people may buy.

It is extremely unlikely that the whole population will at one time be composed of A's or of B's. But it is just as unlikely that the debt-financed spendings of the A's will at any one time be exactly offset by the new savings of the B's. The result is that the action of consumers as a whole will tend either to expand or to contract the total of incomes.

INCOME TAX ACCOUNTS[1]

Keeping of personal accounts in one form or another has been greatly stimulated in recent years because a large portion of the population is subject to the federal income tax. To make a correct tax payment to the government, the taxpayer must, of course, know what his income is. In addition, the income tax law allows many taxpayers to subtract from their actual incomes a variety of expenses or other deductions before arriving at the figure on which the tax must be paid. Without records of past income and expenditure, it would be difficult for the taxpayer to know how much he legally owes, and even more difficult for him to prove to the government that he has paid the proper amount if it should question his return—as it sometimes does.

The income tax law is so frequently changed and has become so complicated that no one who must pay a substantial sum should attempt to prepare his return without careful study of the latest regulations—or perhaps advice from the tax authorities, a lawyer, or a professional accountant. Yet the main principles usually remain the same year after year and may be illustrated by a look at a recent form (1040) for individual tax returns.

The first page of the form is a summary, containing three main divisions.

Exemptions. Nobody need pay a tax on the first $600 of his income (or, if he is over 65 or is blind, on the first $1,200). In addition, the taxpayer is entitled to an exemption of $600 for a dependent wife, each dependent child, and other dependent relatives with incomes of less than $600. The total of such exemptions may be subtracted from income before taxes are calculated.

Income. Under this heading is listed the total of salaries, wages, and other income earned during the year. If the taxpayer has been employed, the employer will already have withheld an amount for payment to the government as income tax. The withholding is figured according to a formula which is the same for everybody, and may be more or less than the taxpayer legally owes. The amount withheld by the employer, however, must be included here, as part of total compensation. From the total, the taxpayer may subtract sick pay. He may also subtract expenses incurred in connection with his work for an employer, provided the employer has not reimbursed him for them. The total, after such deductions as are allowed, is called "adjusted gross income" (line 11).

Tax Due or Refund. For the convenience of a person with an income below $5,000, the government provides a table on which he can locate his income and immediately find out how much he owes, without

---

[1] The student should have a copy of Form 1040 for reference.

any further figuring. This table allows for a deduction of about 10 percent of gross income to cover certain types of expenditures. If these expenditures exceed 10 percent of income, the taxpayer will not gain by using the table; it will be to his advantage to calculate his tax, as people with larger incomes do.

A person with an income of $5,000 or more can take a "standard deduction" of 10 percent of his income, but not more than $1,000. If his actual allowable deductions are greater than this amount, it will pay him to itemize them.

Allowable deductions include contributions to religious or philanthropic organizations; interest paid on borrowed money (including the interest in installment payments); taxes paid to state and local governments (such as sales taxes, property taxes, state gasoline taxes); medical and dental expenses (up to a limit); expenses for a baby sitter if one is required because the mother is employed; losses from fire, storm, accident, and other hazards which were not compensated by insurance; and other things. Clearly, the total of allowable deductions may be large, and it is well to make sure that none have been overlooked. But if the taxpayer claims such deductions, he must be prepared to prove that he really had the expenses; for this purpose it is well to keep canceled checks, receipted bills, and the like. The space for itemized deductions is provided on page 2 of the return.

The taxpayer figures what he has to pay in the "Tax due or refund" section, if he does not use the table for persons with income less than $5,000.

First he enters the tax calculated on page 2 of the return. Then, if he has received dividends, he may subtract a limited credit. He may also subtract a limited credit for retirement income which he may have received. Both are calculated on page 4 of the return.

Many persons make money in some occupation of their own, which is not a business in the ordinary sense. This "self-employed" income must be added (or subtracted if it incurs a deficit).

Finally, the taxpayer subtracts the amounts withheld as tax by the employer, or previously paid, quarterly, during the year by the taxpayer himself. If not enough has been paid, he sends the remainder with the return. If too much has been paid, he is entitled to a refund. It may either be applied to next year's tax or may be returned to the taxpayer. He may indicate his preference in the space provided.

A student who works part of the year should remember that he or she is often entitled to such a refund. He may have earned less than $600 during the year, for example, and yet the employer has withheld taxes from his pay, calculated as if he were a permanent employee. Or he may be entitled to deductions or credits on some other ground. *But he will receive no refund from the government unless he proves that he is entitled to one by filing a return.*

Now let us turn to the other pages of the return, on which calculations are made that finally are summarized on page 1.

Page 2 contains the space for recording itemized deductions, and the space in which to calculate taxable income, by subtracting deductions and exemptions from gross income (see the section headed "Tax Computation").

Page 3 contains schedules on which the taxpayer records various forms of income other than wages and salaries. Some of them are self-explanatory. Others, like the income from a business, require the taxpayer to fill out a separate schedule or statement. Anyone who has to do this will probably employ an expert to help him.

A table furnished by the government in a separate pamphlet of instructions enables the taxpayer to find the tax on his taxable income. The rate of tax is a "progressive" one; that is, the larger the income, the higher the rate.

Page 4, on which the taxpayer figures the credit to which he may be entitled on dividends or retirement income, has already been mentioned. The details of these calculations need not here be explained.

Anyone who has inspected the complexity of this return (Form 1040) and has a simple kind of income coming from one or two sources, would probably be glad to have the government calculate for him what he owes. This he may do by using another form, 1040A.

The taxpayer using either of these forms must enclose slips received from his employer, showing how much the employer has paid him during the year and how much the employer has withheld for taxes.

QUESTIONS

Suppose that you subtracted all your expenditures during a year from all the income you had received during that year, and found that you had some money left. If you now compared this remainder with the remainder of the previous year, you would learn whether you had saved anything. (In economic terms, saving is income not expended.) If the remainder of the most recent year were larger than that of the previous year, your savings would be positive; if it were smaller, your savings would be negative, or "dissaving." Note also that "income" does not include money borrowed. New borrowing is "dissaving"; repayment of borrowings is "savings."

1. What, if any, difference does it make to the general economic welfare whether you spend former saving for current purchases, deposit it in a savings bank, or keep it in a strongbox or safe-deposit vault? Would your reply vary according to circumstances?

2. If you should draw up a balance sheet for yourself, what item or items would be comparable to "inventory" in a business balance sheet? Under what circumstances would you be wise to enlarge this item? Under what circumstances would you reduce it? What effect would either of these courses exert on production and employment, if consumers generally acted as you did in this respect?

4 / THE FLOW OF PAYMENTS / Businesses,

governments, and individuals all receive money and all pay it out. Business receipts come from payments by governments and individuals. Government receipts come mainly from taxes. Individual receipts come from wages and salaries, interest and dividends, and other payments made by businesses, governments, or other individuals. Clearly, the income flows around from one to another of all these recipients and purchasers. Can this complex flow be pictured in any diagram? If that is possible, even in oversimplified form, we may obtain a mental image of the money economy as a whole.

To begin our examination of the flow, we must break in somewhere. Let us start with consumers, since everybody is a consumer and the purchases of consumer goods and services form the largest of the major classifications of spending.

Step 1. The tank (or receptacle) at the top of Figure 4/1 represents personal incomes from which come the expenditures by individuals either for taxes or for purchases. Taxes flow down the pipe into the government tank. Spendings flow to the retailers of goods and services—stores, landlords, and others.

Step 2. Retailers in turn pay taxes and buy from distributors. They purchase from wholesalers, railroads, truckers, and others. Sometimes, of course, they buy direct from manufacturers, in which case this step is omitted.

Step 3. Distributors pay taxes and buy from manufacturers. Sometimes they buy from primary producers; in which case this step is omitted.

Step 4. Manufacturers pay taxes and buy from primary producers—mines, farmers, and other producers of raw materials.

Obviously, this is an incomplete picture, for two main reasons. First, it does not show where consumers get the money they spend. Second, it does not show what government does with its money (it does not keep it). Figure 4/2 supplies these deficiencies.

29

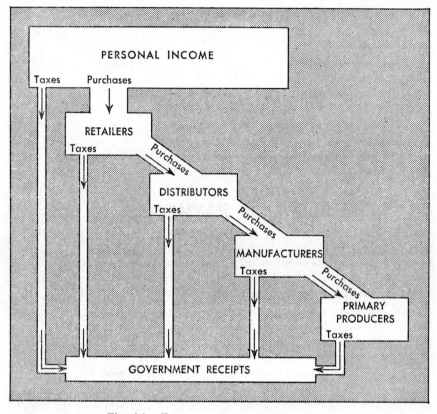

Fig. 4.1.   FLOW OF SPENDING AND TAXATION.

All business concerns pay salaries to employees. They also pay profits to owners. Government compensates public employees and pays social security benefits, pensions, and other benefits. The pipes leading from the business and the government tanks to personal income indicate these flows.

Government buys supplies from business concerns, as well as paying individuals. Pipes flowing from the government tank indicate these purchases.

To complete the circuit, all that has to be done is to connect the personal income with the personal expenditure (plus taxes). Both are, of course, identical with regard to the flow of money, provided savings and borrowings are disregarded. The omission of savings and borrowings is the most serious flaw in Figure 4/2.

WHAT HAPPENS TO SAVINGS

Individuals, businesses, and governments save. They also borrow. If you save, you refrain from spending money you own. If you borrow,

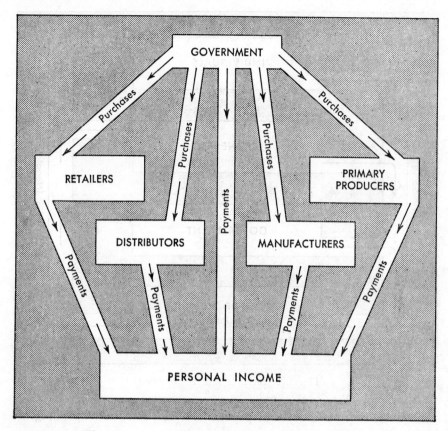

Fig. 4.2. FLOW OF INCOME AND GOVERNMENT SPENDING.

you spend money without owning it. Savings may be spent in the future and, when spent, will add to your current spendings. Borrowings have to be repaid in the future and, when repaid, will diminish your current spendings. Savings and borrowings are therefore opposites. One has a plus sign; the other, a minus sign. For this reason, borrowings are often called by economists "negative savings."

If you keep saved money in your pocket, in a strongbox, or in some other hiding place, you are taking something out of the flow of money and hence diminishing the receipts of others. If you later spend the saved money, you are then restoring to the flow what you took out of it.

If you deposit saved money in a bank, someone else may borrow it from the bank—to build a house, for example. If you buy a government bond with your savings, you are, of course, lending the money directly to the government. If your saved money is borrowed and spent by the borrowers, what you take out of the stream is spent by the person or persons who borrow it, and the total income flow is neither smaller nor larger. In this case, savings are canceled by negative savings.

But the total savings of everybody are not usually equal to the total borrowings by everybody. Sometimes they are larger; sometimes smaller.

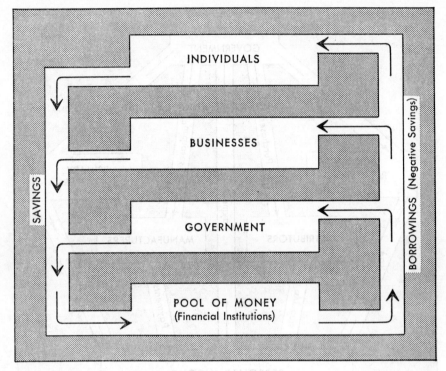

Fig. 4.3. SAVINGS AND BORROWINGS.

Therefore, the total stream of payments is usually either expanding or contracting.

To picture the flow of savings and borrowings, Figure 4/3 shows savings going into what may be called a "pool of money," and borrowings are shown coming out of it. This pool may be thought of as the whole array of banks, insurance companies, and other financial institutions.

It is easy to see how less money may flow out of the money pool by borrowing than flows into it in savings. It is not so easy to see how *more* money can flow out of the money pool than flows into it—at least for very long. We shall learn more about both processes when we examine money and banking.

FLOW OF GOODS AND SERVICES

The flow of goods and services does not, of course, go round and round, like the flow of money. It starts with the primary producer and flows to the consumer. When the good or the service gets to its final user, its flow stops. In any particular transaction, the flow of goods or services is in the opposite direction to the flow of money; it is what the money is paid for. I pay the grocer 24 cents; he gives me a quart of milk.

Goods and services constitute the *real* income of any person or community. So far, we have been speaking in terms of money, but only because money is a common measure of many kinds of goods and services. It is also the medium of exchange used in buying and selling these commodities and a store of value when it is saved. But, in economic thinking, we should never forget that the basic consideration is what happens to *real* income and *real* wealth. Later we shall see that although money is the best common measure economists have been able to find, it has serious flaws as a measure. And we shall examine some of the methods of compensating for those flaws.

QUESTIONS

1. Although expenditures must give rise to income, is it equally true that all income received must be spent?

2. Can anyone spend more than he receives in income? If so, how does he get the money?

3. If a recipient of income does not spend all he receives, how does the remainder get back into the income stream, if it does get back?

5 / MEASURING EVERYONE'S

INCOME / By measuring income and outgo, the businessman derives information useful in his business, government learns how better to manage taxing and spending, the individual can allocate his resources to greater advantage. All of us are affected by what businessmen do, what policies government follows, how individuals spend or save their money. Is there any way in which to keep tabs on the income and outgo of *all* of us, which so greatly influences the welfare of *each* of us?

There is such a way, and it is called "national income accounting." This kind of bookkeeping deals with the sum of all incomes within a given nation. National income figures for a series of years reveal whether the people of a nation are improving their economic welfare or the reverse. They also show important facts about changes in the distribution of income among various parts of the population. Moreover, the information so obtained may be put to use in many ways—even in a concerted effort to change for the better the behavior of the national economy as a whole.

The United States Department of Commerce, with its access to the huge array of statistics collected by the government, keeps the national income accounts for the United States. Not all the figures are complete; there are gaps in the information which make estimates necessary. Nevertheless, the totals built up are so large that minor errors do not make much difference in the use of the figures for policy-making or analysis. In a private concern, a cashier who was short several hundred thousand dollars would soon land in jail, but a mistake of even a billion dollars in government accounts would be but a fraction of 1 percent of the total value of production or income in the entire United States.

34 **RIDER COLLEGE LIBRARY**

GROSS NATIONAL PRODUCT

We have seen that every person, business, or government agency receiving income derives it from the spending by other persons, businesses, or agencies. Income flows around continually. As received, it is regarded as income; as spent, it is regarded as expenditure. This constant flow makes it logical to measure income both as it is received and as it is spent. If all receipts and all expenditures are listed, the two totals should, theoretically, be equal. This fact makes possible the use of double-entry bookkeeping to check the progress of the total product of a nation (measured by its value in dollars) and the amount distributed in income to those who produce it. This account is called "Gross National Product or Expenditure" (GNP). The title recognizes that income can be measured in both ways. Table 5/1 shows the major categories, under which are listed the items of expenditure (in the right column) and the items of income received by those who derive income from production (in the left column).

TABLE 5/1

GROSS NATIONAL PRODUCT OR EXPENDITURE

Product	*Expenditures*
(Measured by receipts)	Personal Consumption Expenditures
Compensation of Employees	
Net Income of Unincorporated Business	
Rental Income of Persons	Gross Private Domestic Investment
Interest	
Dividends	
Undistributed Profits of Corporations	Government Purchases of Goods and Services
Taxes on Profits	
Indirect Business Taxes	Net Foreign Investment (may be plus or minus)

The following table shows GNP (as measured by expenditures) for 1929–1959.

TABLE 5/2

GROSS NATIONAL PRODUCT OR EXPENDITURE, 1929–1959[1]
(in billions of dollars)

Period	Total gross national product	Personal consumption expenditures	Gross private domestic investment				Net exports of goods and services [1]			Government purchases of goods and services					
			Total	New construction	Producers' durable equipment	Net change in business inventories	Net exports	Exports	Imports	Total	Federal				State and local
											Total	National defense [2]	Other	Less: Government sales	
1929	104.4	79.0	16.2	8.7	5.8	1.7	0.8	7.0	6.3	8.5	1.3		1.3	(³)	7.2
1930	91.1	71.0	10.3	6.2	4.5	−.4	.7	5.4	4.8	9.2	1.4		1.4	(³)	7.8
1931	76.3	61.3	5.5	4.0	2.8	−1.3	.2	3.6	3.4	9.2	1.5		1.5	(³)	7.7
1932	58.5	49.3	.9	1.9	1.6	−2.6	.2	2.5	2.3	8.1	1.5		1.5	(³)	6.6
1933	56.0	46.4	1.4	1.4	1.6	−1.6	.2	2.4	2.3	8.0	2.0		2.0	(³)	6.0
1934	65.0	51.9	2.9	1.7	2.3	−1.1	.4	3.0	2.5	9.8	3.0		3.0	(²)	6.8
1935	72.5	56.3	6.3	2.3	3.1	.9	−.1	3.3	3.3	10.0	2.9		2.9	(³)	7.1
1936	82.7	62.6	8.4	3.3	4.2	1.0	−.1	3.5	3.6	11.8	4.8		4.8	(³)	7.0
1937	90.8	67.3	11.7	4.4	5.1	2.2	.1	4.6	4.5	11.7	4.6		4.6,	(³)	7.2
1938	85.2	64.6	6.7	4.0	3.6	−.9	1.1	4.3	3.2	12.8	5.3		5 3	(³)	7.5
1939	91.1	67.6	9.3	4.8	4.2	.4	,9	4.4	3.5	13.3	5.2	1.3	3.9	(²)	8.2
1940	100.6	71.9	13.2	5.5	5.5	2.2	1.5	5.4	3.8	14.1	6.2	2.2	4.0	(³)	7.9
1941	125.8	81.9	18.1	6.6	6.9	4.5	1.1	6.0	4.8	24.8	16.9	13.8	3.2	(³)	7.8
1942	159.1	89.7	9.9	3.7	4.3	1.8	−.2	4.9	5.1	59.7	52.0	49.6	2.7	0.2	7.7
1943	192.5	100.5	5.6	2.3	4.0	−.8	−2.2	4.5	6.8	88.6	81.2	80.4	1.5	.6	7.4
1944	211.4	109.8	7.1	2.7	5.4	−1.0	−2.1	5.4	7.5	96.5	89.0	88.6	1.6	1.2	7.5
1945	213.6	121.7	10.4	3.8	7.7	−1.1	−1.4	7.4	8.8	82.9	74.8	75.9	1.0	2.2	8.1
1946	210.7	147.1	28.1	11.0	10.7	6.4	4.9	12.8	7.9	30.5	20.6	18.8	4.5	2.7	9.9
1947	234.3	165.4	31.5	15.3	16.7	−.5	9.0	17.9	8.9	28.4	15.6	11.4	5.4	1.1	12.7
1948	259.4	178.3	43.1	19.5	18.9	4.7	3.5	14.5	11.0	34.5	19.3	11.6	8.2	.5	15.2
1949	258.1	181.2	33.0	18.8	17.2	−3.1	3.8	14.0	10.2	40.2	22.2	13.6	8.9	.2	17.9
1950	284.6	195.0	50.0	24.2	18.9	6.8	.6	13.1	12.5	39.0	19.3	14.3	5.2	.1	19.7
1951	329.0	209.8	56.3	24.8	21.3	10.2	2.4	17.9	15.5	60.5	38.8	33.9	5.2	.3	21.7
1952	347.0	219.8	49.9	25.5	21.3	3.1	1.3	17.4	16.1	76.0	52.9	46.4	6.7	.3	23.2
1953	365.4	232.6	50.3	27.6	22.3	.4	−.4	16.6	17.0	82.8	58.0	49.3	9.0	.3	24.9
1954	363.1	238.0	48.9	29.7	20.8	−1.6	1.0	17.5	16.5	75.3	47.5	41.2	6.7	.3	27.7
1955	397.5	256.9	63.8	34.9	23.1	5.8	1.1	19.4	18.3	75.6	45.3	39.1	6.6	.4	30.3
1956	419.2	269.9	67.4	35.5	27.2	4.7	2.9	23.1	20.2	79.0	45.7	40.4	5.7	.3	33.2
1957	442.5	284.8	66.6	36.1	28.5	2.0	4.9	26.2	21.3	86.2	49.4	44.3	5.5	.4	36.8
1958	441.7	293.0	54.9	35.8	22.9	−3.8	1.2	22.6	21.3	92.6	52.2	44.5	8.1	.5	40.5
1959 [4]	478.8	311.4	70.3	40.3	26.1	3.9	−.7	(⁵)	(⁵)	97.9	53.6	45.8	8.1	.4	44.3

[1] For 1929–45, net exports of goods and services and net foreign investment have been equated, since foreign net transfers by Government were negligible during that period.

[2] This category corresponds closely to the major national security classification in the *Budget of the United States Government for the Fiscal Year ending June 30, 1961*.

[3] Less than $50 million.

[4] Preliminary estimates by Council of Economic Advisers.

[5] Not available.

Note: Detail will not necessarily add to totals because of rounding.

Source: Department of Commerce (except as noted).

Let us look, first, at the items in this account that cover all the expenditures. Specific figures for a recent year (1957) are listed.

The following table includes, naturally enough, what individuals spend, what businesses spend, and what federal, state, and local governments spend. It also includes an item to cover foreign trade. (Since the method does not change from year to year, any year will do as an illustration.)[1]

TABLE 5/3

GROSS NATIONAL PRODUCT OR EXPENDITURE, 1957
(in billions of dollars)

1. Personal consumption expenditures	$284.4
2. Gross private domestic investment	65.3
3. Government purchases of goods and services	85.7
4. Net foreign investment	4.9
Total	$440.3

1. "Personal consumption expenditures" covers the goods and services bought by individuals during the year. The total is made up of the items shown in Table 5/4.

TABLE 5/4

PERSONAL CONSUMPTION EXPENDITURES
(in billions of dollars)

Durable goods		
Automobiles and parts	$17.1	
Furniture and household equipment	17.3	
Other	5.5	
Total		$ 39.9
Nondurable goods		
Food (including alcoholic averages)	$66.4	
Clothing and shoes	24.6	
Gasoline and oil	10.2	
Other	36.7	
Total		$138.0
Services		
Housing	$35.4	
Household operation	15.8	
Transportation	9.0	
Other	46.4	
Total		$106.5

[1] Totals of the figures in Tables 5/3–5/8 differ slightly from the totals for similar categories in Table 5/2, since revisions were made for 1957 after these tables were published. The differences, however, are relatively so small as to be unimportant for the purposes of this discussion.

"Housing" does *not* mean the buying of houses. It does mean rent paid by those who rented their dwelling places, and what is called "imputed rent"—that is, what the owner of a house would have to pay in rent if he did not own the house.

2. "Gross private domestic investment" covers the expenditures which private business concerns made within the United States (as distinct from investment abroad) for goods expected to be of use in their businesses, such as their investment in plant and machinery. It does *not* cover the spendings which a business income statement includes as "cost of goods sold" (see Chapter 1). Goods sold to consumers or to government are omitted to avoid double counting in total GNP, since they are covered by the expenditures of consumers and government, which are separately listed in the gross national product account.

The main subheads of the $65.2 billion gross private domestic investment are as follows:

TABLE 5/5

GROSS PRIVATE DOMESTIC INVESTMENT
(in billions of dollars)

New Construction	
Residential (Nonfarm)	$17.0
Other	19.5
Total	$36.5
Producers' durable equipment	27.9
Net change in business inventories	1.0

Note that provision for the expenditures for the *building* of new houses appears in this section. From the business point of view, these expenditures represent investments, whether the houses are to be sold to individuals or are to be rented.

"Other" business construction consists of factories, warehouses, stores, and farm buildings.

"Producers' durable equipment" consists of machinery, trucks, and the like.

"Net change in business inventories" requires some explanation. We have just seen that business expenses for making goods to be sold to consumers are *not* included in gross national product; to do so would duplicate consumer expenditures for the same goods. But when a business inventory is enlarged, that is, when there is an *addition* of goods, and the increase is not offset by consumers purchases in the year for which the account is drawn up, the addition to inventory must be included. The same logic applies to a *decrease* in inventory.

A further refinement must be explained. Accounts as kept by business concerns may show a rise in the *value* of inventory, caused by a rise in the prices of the goods on hand rather than by an increase in the actual quantity of goods. A price rise is not a real increase in national product. An adjustment is therefore made to accommodate changes in inventory value caused by rises (or falls) in prices.

3. "Government purchases of goods and services" totaling $85.7 billion is subdivided as follows:

TABLE 5/6

GOVERNMENT PURCHASES OF GOODS AND SERVICES
(in billions of dollars)

Federal		
National defense	$44.3	
Other	5.5	
Less: Government sales	−.4	
Total		$49.4
State and local		36.3

4. "Net foreign investment" is the difference between the value of exports and the value of imports. If foreigners buy more from the United States than Americans buy from foreigners, the excess represents debt of foreigners to Americans, unless the surplus is paid for in international money—that is, gold. A good debt (from the point of view of the debtor) is an investment (from the point of view of the creditor). A more detailed treatment of the international account is included in Chapter 21.

NATIONAL INCOME

Gross national product is measured, we have seen, by all that is paid in a year for goods and services by "final users." To the recipients of these payments, the money must, one would think, constitute income. Simon Kuznets, an economist who has done much to develop national income measurements, defined the national income as "the net product of, or net return on, the economic activity of individuals, business firms, and the social and political institutions that make up a nation." This definition assumes that the product equals the "return on" economic activity. Notice, however, that Kuznets speaks of *net* product," whereas the figures we have just been examining are called *"gross* product." Apparently there is something to be subtracted from gross product in order to find the net product.

A clue to what has to be subtracted may be obtained from the definition of national income offered by the Department of Commerce, which compiles the figures. National income is, says the Department, "the aggregate earnings of labor and property which arise from the current production of goods and services by the nation's economy." The key word here is *current* production.

Everything consumers buy in a year is certainly current production. But what about business? When business concerns buy buildings or machinery, some of the expenditures pay for additional capacity to produce, and this is certainly part of the national income for the year. But some of the building and or a piece of equipment may be bought only to replace old and worn-out facilities for production. Theoretically, such spending does not increase national income at all, if we think of income as the actual product for final use. If old facilities were not renewed and replaced, the national income could not remain the same; it would decline.

Therefore, from gross national product the statisticians subtract a sum to cover this part of business spending; it is called "capital consumption allowances." The figure is derived from the total of the items found on business income statements and balance sheets which are labeled "depreciation." On a business income statement, such charges are deducted from revenues before the figure for income is arrived at.

Net national product is the remainder obtained when capital consumption allowances are deducted from gross national product. In 1957, capital consumption allowances totaled $37.7 billion, and net national product, $402.6 billion.

Since net national product (measured by the expenditure made for it) should equal net national income, let us see if the income figures for 1957, as totaled by the Department of Commerce, really do equal the net product. The totals for income can be derived from statistics largely independent of those used for expenditure. The following table (5/7) shows how the total income is distributed between earnings for work and earnings of capital.

TABLE 5/7

NATIONAL INCOME BY TYPE OF INCOME, 1957
(in billions of dollars)

Compensation of employees	$254.6
Business and professional income	
(with inventory valuation adjustment)	31.4
Income of farm proprietors	11.6
Rental income of persons	11.8
Corporate profits	
(with inventory valuation adjustment)	41.9
Net interest	12.6
Total	$364.0

This total, $364 billion, *is* less than the $402 billion net national product for the same year. Before investigating this apparently illogical difference, let us see what the items in the national income table mean.

"Compensation of employees" means wages and salaries, plus any supplementary payments for maintenance, pension funds, social insurance, compensation for injuries, and the like.

"Business and professional income" covers the profits of unincorporated businesses like small retail stores, and the income of lawyers, doctors, and any others who practice their professions as independent enterprises.

"Income of farm proprietors" is, of course, the profit made by owning or renting farmers.

"Rental income of persons" covers the rents received by individual owners of land, buildings, houses, and the like. Rental income received by corporations is covered by the following item.

"Corporate profits" are the profits as reckoned *before* the payment of income taxes or excess-profits taxes.

"Net interest" is the total of interest received by individuals, less the total of interest they pay. Interest paid or received by businesses is covered in the business and the corporate items.

There is, however, one large omission—the interest paid to holders of federal securities. This item is omitted because such a large part of the government debt, on which interest is paid, was incurred for war purposes that it is not regarded as representing investment in production which could properly be considered as enlarging the national income. The same omission is made in Table 5/2, showing gross product or expenditure. Government spending in that table comprises, it will be seen, "purchases of goods and services" and does not include payment of interest.

Interest on government securities is much like another group of payments excluded from both product and income tables—called "transfer payments." What individuals receive in social security payments is excluded from their income as recorded in the tables, just as it is excluded from the total of government expenditures in the gross national product account. The reason is that the government collects this money and later passes it out, or *transfers* it, without any production having occurred as the direct result of either payment.

SOURCE OF THE DIFFERENCE BETWEEN NET NATIONAL PRODUCT AND NET NATIONAL INCOME

Personal spendings are included in the product or expenditure table (5/2); personal income (in its various forms) in the income table (5/7). Business spending is included in the first table; business income, in the second. At first, it may seem strange that although government spending is an item in the expenditure table—and a large one—there is no corresponding item for government income in the income table. This item may possibly account for the apparent discrepancy between spending and income. Are there, in the income table, items which account for all the current revenue received by government?

All the kinds of income received by individuals in payment for either labor or capital engaged in current production are included in the items of the income table. From what they receive, these individuals have to pay income and other taxes to the government. Therefore, the government revenue derived from persons is all accounted for in the income table.

Business profits—including what businesses have to pay as taxes on profits—are totaled in the income table. These taxes, too, form part of government revenue. But businesses pay many other taxes that they treat as expenses and routinely deduct in reckoning their profits. These are not included in Table 5/3. Such taxes are property taxes paid to localities, tariff duties on imported products, excise taxes on the value of their products, and others. These "indirect" business taxes do not appear in the income table, although the money derived from them is spent by the government and is listed as part of the government purchases of goods and services in the product table. This item is a large source of the difference.

Two other minor corrections must be made to complete our double-entry check. First, government pays subsidies to governmentally owned enterprises that lose money (the postal service, for example). On some of its enterprises, government makes money. The net result of these transactions either diminishes or increases governmental capacity to buy goods and services, without regard to the tax revenue which it received from individuals or businesses. This result must therefore be eliminated from the product table to make it agree with the income table. Second, there are "transfer payments" made by business concerns which involve no real production. These appear in the spending listed in the product table but not in the income table, since they are accounted for by businesses before profit is reckoned.

Now we are in a position to see what the remaining statistical discrepancy is.

TABLE 5/8

RELATION BETWEEN GNP, NET NATIONAL PRODUCT, AND NATIONAL INCOME
(1957; in billions of dollars)

Gross National Product	$440.3
Less capital consumption allowances	37.7
Net National Product	**$402.6**
Plus Subsidies less current surplus of Government enterprises	+ 1.3
Less indirect business taxes	−37.6
Less business transfer payments	− 1.6
Statistical discrepancy	− 0.7
	38.6
National Income	$364.0

The total of expenditures, it will be seen, is still slightly greater than the total of corresponding income. The remainder is attributable to a "statistical discrepancy," inevitable where such large aggregates of figures are concerned, since not every error in the sources can be checked.

WHAT ABOUT SAVINGS?

A question frequently raised by those examining national income figures is, where do savings enter this picture? The product or expenditure table shows all that is spent; the income table, all that is received; but "savings," or money not spent by the receivers, is not mentioned in either one.

The spending of business for investment comes partly from its own savings—that is, the profits not distributed to stockholders. The rest of what business invests in houses, plant, equipment, or inventory comes from borrowed funds. The government likewise spends not only the revenue it derives from taxes but also borrowed money, whenever it has a deficit. Most of the income not spent (saved) finds its way to the borrowings by business, government, or individuals. It does so directly if the saver buys government securities, bonds issued by business concerns, or mortgages on houses. The money entrusted to banks, insurance companies, and other financial institutions may be used by these institutions for loans to business, government, or individuals. The income, which is the source of savings, is included in the income table; the investments or government expenditures which depend on borrowing are included in the product or expenditure table. Thus, savings are accounted for without specific listing in the tables.

Table 5/9 summarizes this situation for each year from 1939 through 1958.

It will be seen that the algebraic total of private savings and government surplus or deficit equals the total of investment, with a small statistical discrepancy.

It may seem a strange coincidence that, in any year, the total of savings in a nation almost exactly equals the total of investment. Could not someone hold out of his income a sum which, instead of investing directly or entrusting to a financial institution, he hides under his mattress? Yes, indeed—and many do so occasionally. This tends to diminish future incomes, just as the spending of borrowed money by anyone tends to increase future incomes.

But income and product tables are records of what has occurred in *past* periods; the table for any one year tells us nothing about tendencies for the future. In any such table, logically drawn up, total income by assumption equals total product. Income must be either spent for consumer goods and services or saved. Product, as measured by expenditure, must consist either of consumer goods and services sold or of investment goods. Since the amount spent for consumer goods must equal the

TABLE 5/9

FINANCIAL SAVING BY INDIVIDUALS, 1939–1959[1]
(in billions of dollars)

Period	Total	Currency and bank deposits	Savings shares [2]	Securities				Private insurance reserves[4]	Noninsured pension funds	Government insurance and pension reserves[5]	Less: Increase in debt		
				Total	U.S. savings bonds	Other government[3]	Corporate and other				Mortgage debt[6]	Consumer debt[7]	Securities loans[3]
1939	4.24	2.99	0.08	-0.83	0.66	-0.87	-0.62	1.72	0.05	1.30	0.50	0.81	-0.23
1940	4.23	2.87	.26	-.43	.86	-.84	-.44	1.85	.05	1.30	.85	1.01	-.20
1941	10.51	4.77	.42	2.64	2.75	.38	-.50	2.14	.08	1.86	.82	.69	-.11
1942	29.28	10.93	.27	10.33	7.98	2.34	.01	2.49	.12	2.55	.10	-2.96	.27
1943	38.69	16.18	.57	14.14	11.14	3.25	-.26	2.85	.20	3.92	-.38	-1.03	.58
1944	41.39	17.53	.85	15.71	11.80	4.59	-.68	3.21	.60	4.96	-.05	.14	1.38
1945	37.33	18.98	1.10	9.93	6.85	4.23	-1.16	3.46	.93	5.14	.22	.48	1.48
1946	14.06	10.57	1.23	-1.43	.96	-2.40	(9)	3.42	.30	3.55	3.60	2.32	-2.34
1947	6.47	2.00	1.28	2.42	2.01	-.28	.69	3.64	.30	3.49	4.62	2.81	-.76
1948	2.76	-1.83	1.30	3.12	1.60	.40	1.12	3.75	.40	3.57	4.72	2.41	.43
1949	2.21	-1.36	1.61	2.39	1.46	.20	.73	3.71	.60	2.34	4.12	2.64	.32
1950	.82	3.50	1.67	.90	.25	-.07	.71	3.92	.90	1.09	7.29	3.64	.22
1951	11.11	5.90	2.28	.54	-.47	-.42	1.43	4.06	1.35	4.24	6.58	.99	-.30
1952	13.14	7.02	3.34	3.51	.09	1.26	2.16	4.84	1.51	4.40	6.51	4.36	.60
1953	10.88	4.73	3.97	3.44	.20	2.01	1.23	5.00	1.84	3.24	7.29	3.65	.40
1954	9.47	5.37	4.79	.37	.60	-.91	.68	5.21	1.93	2.63	9.01	.96	.86
1955	7.14	3.29	5.23	6.41	.26	3.92	2.23	5.54	2.08	3.10	11.83	6.09	.60
1956	14.10	4.68	5.37	5.20	-.09	3.30	2.00	5.54	2.41	3.57	10.28	3.14	-.75
1957	17.68	5.10	5.21	6.56	-1.91	5.29	3.18	5.12	2.68	3.19	7.76	2.49	-.07
1958	16.17	10.26	6.51	.59	-.52	-1.80	2.92	5.23	2.78	.67	9.32	.10	.45
1959 [10]	16.00	5.60	6.90	10.60	-1.80	11.00	1.40	5.30	3.40	1.90	12.50	5.60	-.40

[1] Individuals' saving, in addition to personal holdings, covers saving of unincorporated business, trust funds, and nonprofit institutions in the forms specified.

[2] Includes shares in savings and loan associations and shares and deposits in credit unions.

[3] Includes U.S. Government issues (except savings bonds), nonguaranteed Federal agency securities, and securities of state and local governments.

[4] Includes insured pension reserves.

[5] Includes social security funds, state and local retirement systems, etc.

[6] Mortgage debt to institutions on one- to four-family nonfarm dwellings.

[7] Consumer debt owed to corporations, largely attributable to purchases of automobiles and other durable consumer goods, although including some debt arising from purchases of consumption goods. Policy loans on Government and private life insurance have been deducted from those items of saving.

[8] Changes in bank loans made for the purpose of purchasing or carrying securities.

[9] Less than $5 million.

[10] Preliminary.

Note: In addition to the concept of saving shown above, there are other concepts of individuals' saving, with varying degrees of coverage, currently in use. The personal saving estimates of the Department of Commerce are derived as the difference between personal income and expenditures. Conceptually, Commerce saving includes the following items not included in Securities and Exchange Commission saving: Housing, farm and unincorporated business investment in inventories and plant and equipment, net of depreciation, and increase in debt. Government insurance is excluded from the Commerce saving series. For a reconciliation of the two series, see Securities and Exchange Commission *Statistical Bulletin,* July 1959, and *Survey of Current Business,* July 1959.

The Federal Reserve Board's flow-of-funds system of accounts includes capital investments as well as financial components of saving and covers saving of Federal, State and local governments, businesses, financial institutions and consumers. While the Federal Reserve Board's estimates of consumer saving in financial form are similar amount received for such goods, the amount *saved* must equal the amount received for investment goods. Savings must equal investment simply because the amount of savings is estimated by subtracting expenditures from income.

DISPOSABLE INCOME

One other total in the national income figures often quoted is of special importance to consumers and to those business or financial institutions which deal with consumers. This is the total of income which consumers may either spend or save. It is derived (1) by *subtracting* from the consumer income, as found in the national income tables, the amount which individuals have to pay in taxes, and (2) by *adding* to that figure what individuals receive in interest on federal government bonds and in "transfer payments." Transfer payments are government payments for unemployment insurance, old-age annuities, and other benefits, which are collected from the public in contributions but which involve no production in their circuit from the citizens and back again to the beneficiaries. Since such payments are not payments for production, they do not logically belong in the tabulation of national product or income. They do, however, belong in "disposable income" of individuals.

USE OF NATIONAL INCOME FIGURES

Gross national product figures are usually the first to become available after any given period, and hence are widely used to indicate improvement of business conditions or the reverse. They are, however, a pretty rough measure. Net national income totals are a much better measure of such things as growth or decline in production, spending, or distribution of income.

Both kinds of figures in their raw state reflect changes in prices as well as changes in actual product and income. The people do not gain anything when gross national product, or national income, rises because of soaring prices, if the actual output does not increase. Corrections for price changes are therefore in order, to reveal *real* income or *real* product.

Such corrections involve statistical methods. In Chapters 6 and 7 a few elementary facts about such methods are described.

In subsequent chapters we shall discover a number of the uses to

---

to the Securities and Exchange Commission estimates of individuals' saving, there are some statistical and conceptual differences in the two sets of data.

Revisions for 1947–59 in the consumer credit statistics of the Board of Governors of the Federal Reserve System have not yet been incorporated into these estimates.

Detail will not necessarily add to totals because of rounding.

Source: Securities and Exchange Commission.

which measurements of national income are put. The large totals given
in this chapter are made up of many minor classifications, which may
also be very revealing. It is possible to break down total income and
expenditure in many different categories—by industries, localities, occupations, size of income, and other groups.

Before going on to other matters, however, it is useful to fix in our
minds some of the basic characteristics of national income accounting by
operating with the figures.

PROBLEMS

1. Using the figures for 1958 in Table 5/2 as a basis, draw up a
similar entry for 1959, using the following assumptions.

(a) No change occurs either in the total amount of production or in
the prices received for the products.

(b) Because of increasing demand for United States products, foreigners buy more from us, so that net exports change from $1.2 billion
to $2 billion.

(c) Government deficit decreases to $5 billion.

There may be a number of correct answers to this problem. After
drawing up your table for 1959, describe in words what the changes you
have made in the figures mean to consumers and to business.

2. Compare the figures you prepared in Problem 1 with the actual
figures for 1959, and explain why the actual outcome differed from that
based on the above assumptions.

6 / STATISTICAL MEASURES / We have thus

far examined some measurements used in economics, but they have been rather direct—like the total dollar value of incomes or of savings in any given year. But there is much still to be known, which cannot be conveniently reckoned or discussed in the same way. In this chapter we shall examine some of the devices more frequently used to make informative data easier to handle or to interpret. Such devices are, in a sense, a sort of shorthand. Mathematically, they are grouped under the name of "statistics."

SAMPLING

We hear a great deal these days about sampling studies—in predicting elections, in analyzing markets, in testing the quality of factory products, in discovering how income is distributed among various classes, and so on. Samples are used when it is either impossible or too costly in money and time to gather or inspect *all* the items which are to be treated statistically. If the sample selected is reasonably representative of the entire lot being investigated, estimates may be based on the sample. This is just what a shopper does when she takes a small piece of material as a basis of comparison before she buys several yards. The sample is not so certain a test as an inspection of every square inch would be, but sampling is much more convenient.

The most important consideration in sampling is to obtain what is called a "representative sample." If a small sample of cloth is cut from a bolt in the store, it is probably fairly representative of the whole bolt. However, if you taste an apple from the top of a basket, there is perhaps less assurance that your sample is representative. A small sample will do for testing of a large number of items, called a "universe" or a "population," if there is good assurance that what you are sampling is homogeneous (distributed in the same fashion throughout the universe) for the quality for which you are sampling it. For example, you do not need

47

a large sample to assure you that adult members of the human race, as a rule, have variations in height and weight differing from those of dogs (though, of course, exceptions can be found). If you used as your sample just four or five individuals, it might be that your sample was exceptional in this respect. If you increased a little, the number of individuals in your sample, the probability of error would rapidly decline.

If the universe or population were known or suspected to be not homogeneous in respect to the subject of your investigation, then you would classify it before sampling, to be more nearly certain of finding a representative sample of each part or section. For example, you might take one apple from the bottom and one from the middle, as well as the top, of a basket. In sampling a human population, you would, of course, find distinctions of sex, age, education, locality of residence, and many other differences, any one or more of which might be relevant to your problem.

If you had finally decided that it was desirable to take samples from various subclassifications (called "strata") of the universe or population to be examined, you would still face the problem of how to select the particular items constituting the sample, so that they might be as representative as possible. Relying on pure chance, or "random" sampling, is an approved statistical procedure. To take random samples is not so easy in practice as it might appear. If any element of human choice is involved in the process, biases or distortions of choice, of which the statistician is not aware, may appear in the results. To assure that the choice is truly random, therefore, a good deal of ingenuity has been devoted to devising of methods.

Once a sample is obtained, mathematics depending on the principles of probability may be used to determine what is the probability of accuracy of the statistics derived from the sample in representing the universe (its "probable error"). Knowledge of the range within which the truth may lie enables the statistician to judge whether the sample is of practical use in any given situation. If, for example, the results of a national election sampling poll were found to have a probable error of 20 percentage points, the poll would be useless in estimating the outcome of a presidential election in the United States, since majorities of popular votes are almost invariably smaller than that. If, on the other hand, the probable error were 1 or 2 points, the poll would be informative of the majority preference of the universe or classifications sampled, except in a very close election.

AVERAGES

In speaking of either a universe or a sample as a whole, it is often convenient to know its "central tendency"; that is, a value about which all the data will be evenly distributed. Averages are measures of central tendency. The simplest and most commonly used average is the "arithmetic mean." It is derived by finding the sum of all the figures to be averaged, and then dividing the sum by the number of separate figures. This procedure is probably familiar to everyone. For example, tests in school are usually a sample of a student's performance. If a student's grade is to be determined by the arithmetic mean of three tests, on one of which he received 81, on another 87, and on the third 90, his final grade is computed as follows:

$$\begin{array}{r} 81 \\ 87 \\ 90 \\ \hline 3 \,) \; 258 \\ \hline 86 \end{array}$$

This method of averaging, however, is misleading as a measure of central tendency in certain situations. It works best when the numbers to be averaged are within close range. But suppose you wished to find out the rate of pay in a small establishment and were told simply that there were two weekly wage levels—$150 and $30. The arithmetic mean would be $90 a week ($180 divided by 2). Then suppose you discovered that in the two scales, the salary of the president, $150, was averaged in with the wages of three employees, at $30 each. Although the statement of the wage-scale average would be mathematically correct, it would scarcely represent the actual situation. Now suppose that, in an office, there was one employee at $100, one at $95, one at $85, and one at $80; the arithmetic mean would be the same. This situation differs from that described above; yet the mean alone does not show the difference.

$$\begin{array}{r} \$100 \\ 95 \\ 85 \\ 80 \\ \hline 4 \,) \; 360 \\ \hline \$ \; 90 \end{array}$$

To deal with a situation of this kind, statisticians use other kinds of averages, which are discussed in the following sections.

The Weighted Average.   To obtain the weighted arithmetic mean, you multiply each salary or wage by the number receiving that salary or wage, and divide the total of these products by the number of employees.

Payment	Number Receiving (or Weight)	Payment Times Weight
$150	1	$150
30	3	90
		4) 240
		$ 60

The weighted arithmetic mean of $60 is a much more enlightening figure than the arithmetic mean of $90, though in each case the basic data were the same. The weighted arithmetic mean is used, of course, for data of many kinds.

Even a weighted average, however, may not tell all you want to know, especially if a large number of instances are involved—for example, thousands of employees of a big company, with wages ranging from a minimum right up to a high maximum.

To understand the situation in such instances, you may need to know how often a given figure appears and what the range is between the highest and the lowest. In order to acquire this information, you arrange in order all the figures with which you are concerned, from the lowest to the highest or vice versa. This is called an "array."

The Median and Other Positional Measures of Central Tendency. If the statistian has an array of all the items to be averaged, the middle point of this array—that is, the point above which there are as many items as there are below—is called the "median." (If the number of items in a series is odd, the median will be the item in the very middle; if the number of items is even, the median will be halfway between the two items that are nearest the middle—one above it and one below it.)

The median is called a "positional" average. This average is often better than a mean for use with a series of items in which the numbers of items in the lower groups are relatively large and those in the upper groups relatively small (or vice versa). For example, relatively large numbers of families in the United States have incomes below the arithmetic mean; relatively few families have incomes above it. Such a series is described as "skewed," that is, lopsided. To judge the welfare of the people by the arithmetic mean would conceal this central tendency. The median, however, will take it into account, for there are as many families below it as above it.

In the following array of incomes, the median would be $2,500, whereas the arithmetic mean would be $3,008.33:

$$
\begin{array}{r}
\$ \ 1,000 \\
1,025 \\
1,050 \\
2,000 \\
2,500, \text{ median} \\
3,000 \\
4,000 \\
5,500 \\
7,000 \\
\hline
9)\ \ 27,075 \\
\hline
3,008.33
\end{array}
$$

Other positional measures are often used in analyzing such data as income distribution. For example, if an array of incomes is divided into four parts, so that there are four equal groups of income recipients, the mean (or the median) income may be obtained for each of the four groups, from the highest group to the lowest. Or, the array may be divided into ten equal parts. Each one of four divisions is called a "quartile"; each of ten divisions, a "decile."

The Mode. Still another type of average is the value which occurs most frequently in a series. Obviously such a value is of importance for many purposes. It is called the "mode."

To find the mode, list all the items in an array, and then see whether any one of the values occurs more frequently than any other. Sometimes in an array of individual items one can easily be picked as the mode. Often, however, though some of the items may be close together, no two will be duplicated or equal duplication may occur in scattered parts of the series. In that case it is better to group the items in the array and then see if you can pick the modal group or class. This will, of course, not represent an exact figure, but merely a modal class.

For example, in a large factory, it might be found that the full-time weekly wage most frequently paid was exactly $65 a week. But if you made an array of the sums actually found in the pay envelopes, which were made up after accounting for overtime or undertime, for withholdings of taxes based on family exemptions, and for other variations, it might be impossible to pick a single mode. If, however, you grouped the wage earners according to their weekly earnings in steps or stages, it might be easy to discover that the most frequent earnings group was that which earned $60 or more, but less than $65. In this case the modal class would be $60–$64.

In some series there is no meaningful mode or modal group. There may be important concentrations of items in entirely separate parts of the array. In that case, it cannot be said that there is a central tendency. It is important, however, to remember that in a series which has a mode, the mode may differ both from the mean and from the median.

THE FREQUENCY DISTRIBUTION

Starting with an array, a table showing how many times each number appears may be drawn up; this is called a "frequency distribution."

When a large number of instances must be considered, as with the employees of a large concern, it is convenient to make the frequency distribution by groups or classes instead of singly. For example, those receiving $30–$39.99 might be put in one class; those receiving $40–$49.99 in the next; and so on up, in ten-dollar steps. It is then possible to see how many employees are in each wage class. With this information, it is easy to calculate what percent of the total number is in each wage class, and to include the percentages in the table.

TABLE 6/1

FREQUENCY DISTRIBUTION OF
WAGES PAID BY A BUSINESS CONCERN

Weekly Earnings	No. in Class	Percent in Class
$ 35–$ 39.99	10	2
40– 49.99	15	3
50– 59.99	30	6
60– 69.99	40	8
70– 79.99	75	15
80– 89.99	100	20
90– 99.99	200	40
100– 109.99	15	3
110– 119.99	10	2
120– 129.99	5	1
	500	100

If you wish, you may make a weighted average of wages for the firm by using the percentages instead of the absolute numbers. To do this, multiply the salary of each group (taking the middle point of the wage class as the typical wage for that group) by the percentage of employees in the group and add up your results. To illustrate, let us consider again the firm in which there was a president with a salary of $150 and three employees who received $30 each. In this case, the president is 25 percent of the four persons involved, while the three in the $30 class are 75 percent of the total number.

$$\$150 \times .25 = \$37.50$$
$$30 \times .75 = \underline{22.50}$$

$60.00, weighted average

In the next chapter we shall discuss the drawing of curves picturing frequency distribution and their bearing on averages.

INDEX NUMBERS

Frequently, it is desirable to compare a figure for one year with a figure covering the same items for another year. You would normally do this by stating that the figure for the second year is higher or lower than that of the first year by a certain percentage. Suppose, however, you want to trace a trend over a series of years. Statisticians have a convenient way of doing this by setting down a series of percentages (100 percent for the first year) instead of the actual figures. Such a series is called an "index," and the number for any one year is an "index number."

The main principle of index numbers is simplicity itself. First you choose a year (or an average of several years) as the basis of comparison. The index number for that year or average of years is 100. Then the index number for any other year is 100 plus (or minus) the percentage change from the base. Thus, suppose in 1956 your income was $1,000 and in 1957 it was $1,100, and you wanted to reckon incomes as a percentage of 1956. The index number for 1956 income would be 100, and that for 1957 would be 110. If, unfortunately, your income in 1960 should be only $750, the index number for that year would be 75. By looking at your index-number table, you could tell at a glance that your income in 1957 was 10 percent higher than in 1956, and your income in 1960 was 25 percent lower than in 1956.

Note that it is necessary always to find the *difference* between an index number and 100 in order to read off the percentage change. This may seem elementary, yet a prominent presidential candidate in a speech before his party convention in 1952 made a ridiculous blunder by disregarding just this point. Comparing the percentage rise of money wages since the prewar period with the rise of retail prices in the same period, he took the whole index number for prices in 1952 as the percentage *change* in prices since before the war, and thus was able to "prove" that wage earners had suffered a dramatic loss in purchasing power. The truth, of course, was just the contrary—they had gained.

Also, if you want to find the percentage change from any year other than the base year, you cannot read it off directly from the index numbers. Suppose, for example, your income in 1956 was $1,000; in 1957, $1,100; in 1960, $1,500. The corresponding index numbers (based on 1956) would be 100 for 1956, 110 for 1957, and 150 for 1960. Now, suppose you wanted to find the percentage increase from 1957 to 1960. It would be incorrect to say that it was 40 percent, just as it would be incorrect to say that $1,500 is 140 percent of $1,100. (If you doubt this, obtain the correct percentage by dividing $1,500 by $1,100.) It would, however, be correct to say that there was a difference of 40 *percentage points,* according to an index based on 1956.

Two other cautions are in order about interpreting index numbers. One is that the choice of the base year often makes a great difference in the impression which the figures give. If, for example, you were looking at index numbers for national income and found that the base year was 1933—the bottom of the worst depression the nation has had in recent decades—you would discount somewhat the high figures for other years. It might be equally misleading to choose as a base year 1929, the year of the frantic boom before the great depression.

The final caution is that the longer a series of index numbers runs, the less representative of the actual situation the later numbers are likely to be. For example, an index of prices based on what consumers of a certain occupational group bought in 1900 would hardly be applicable to purchases of the same group in 1955, since so many more and different things are now bought by consumers.

Now let us look at a few of the more important series of index numbers in common use, to see how they are compiled and how some of the more important problems found in compiling them are solved.

THE WHOLESALE PRICE INDEX

The Wholesale Price Index issued by the United States Bureau of Labor Statistics, covers about 1,000 different commodities at the prices

TABLE 6/2

WHOLESALE PRICE INDEXES, 1929–1959
(1947–49 = 100[1])

Period	All commodities	Farm products	Processed foods	All commodities other than farm products and foods				
				Total	Textile products and apparel	Chemicals and allied products	Rubber and rubber products	Lumber and wood products
1929	61.9	58.6	58.5	65.5	64.2	(2)	83.5	31.9
1930	56.1	49.3	53.3	60.9	57.1	(2)	73.0	29.4
1931	47.4	36.2	44.8	53.6	47.1	(2)	62.0	23.8
1932	42.1	26.9	36.5	50.2	39.0	(2)	53.8	20.3
1933	42.8	28.7	36.3	50.9	46.0	51.2	56.8	24.2
1934	48.7	36.5	42.6	56.0	51.8	53.7	65.8	28.5
1935	52.0	44.0	52.1	55.7	50.4	56.0	66.4	27.4
1936	52.5	45.2	50.1	56.9	50.8	56.4	71.7	28.7
1937	56.1	48.3	52.4	61.0	54.2	59.0	84.4	33.7
1938	51.1	38.3	45.6	58.4	47.4	55.9	82.7	30.8
1939	50.1	36.5	43.3	58.1	49.5	55.8	86.3	31.6
1940	51.1	37.8	43.6	59.4	52.4	56.6	80.2	35.2
1941	56.8	46.0	50.5	63.7	60.3	61.6	86.5	41.8
1942	64.2	59.2	59.1	68.3	68.9	69.3	100.6	45.4
1943	67.0	68.5	61.6	69.3	69.2	69.5	103.3	48.0
1944	67.6	68.9	60.4	70.4	69.9	70.2	102.0	51.9
1945	68.8	71.6	60.8	71.3	71.1	70.6	98.9	52.5
1946	78.7	83.2	77.6	78.3	82.6	76.3	99.4	60.3
1947	96.4	100.0	98.2	95.3	100.1	101.4	99.0	93.7
1948	104.4	107.3	106.1	103.4	104.4	103.8	102.1	107.2
1949	99.2	92.8	95.7	101.3	95.5	94.8	98.9	99.2
1950	103.1	97.5	99.8	105.0	99.2	96.3	120.5	113.9
1951	114.8	113.4	111.4	115.9	110.6	110.0	148.0	123.9
1952	111.6	107.0	108.8	113.2	99.8	104.5	134.0	120.3
1953	110.1	97.0	104.6	114.0	97.3	105.7	125.0	120.2
1954	110.3	95.6	105.3	114.5	95.2	107.0	126.9	118.0
1955	110.7	89.6	101.7	117.0	95.3	106.6	143.8	123.6
1956	114.3	88.4	101.7	122.2	95.3	107.2	145.8	125.4
1957	117.6	90.9	105.6	125.6	95.4	109.5	145.2	119.0
1958	119.2	94.9	110.9	126.0	93.5	110.4	145.0	117.7
1959 [3]	119.5	89.1	107.0	128.2	95.0	109.9	144.8	125.8

[1] This does not replace the former index (1926=100) as the official index prior to January 1952. Data beginning January 1947 represent the revised sample and weighting pattern. Prior to January 1947 they are based on the month-to-month movement of the former index.
[2] Not available.
[3] Preliminary.
Source: Department of Labor.

paid for large-scale or wholesale quantities in the United States. The index number for each year, month, or week is a single figure representing all these prices together. Up to 1952, the base of the index was the typical year 1926. For the years 1952 to date, a new base, 1947–1949, has been used.

How are the prices for hundreds of different commodities combined into a single figure? One possible method, of course, is to add up all the prices per unit (pound, quart, bushel, for example) and then divide the sum by the number of items, thus getting what is commonly called a "simple average"—in statistical terms, the arithmetic mean. But this ' figure would be very misleading, because some of the priced commodities bulk much larger in the national economy than others. For example, a change in the price per bushel of the millions of bushels of wheat sold during a year would count no more in the simple average than a change in the price per pound of some rare metal of which only a small amount was produced.

TABLE 6/2—Continued

Period	Hides, skins, leather, and leather products	Fuel, power, and lighting materials	Pulp, paper, and allied products	Metals and metal products	Machinery and motive products	Furniture and other household durables	Non-metallic minerals (structural)	Tobacco manufactures and bottled beverages	Miscellaneous products
1929	59.3	70.2	(²)	67.0	(²)	69.3	72.6	86.6	(²)
1930	54.4	66.5	(²)	60.3	(²)	68.2	72.4	87.1	(²)
1931	46.8	57.2	(²)	54.1	(²)	62.8	67.6	84.6	(²)
1932	39.7	59.5	(²)	49.9	(²)	55.4	63.4	81.4	(²)
1933	44.0	56.1	(²)	50.9	(²)	55.5	66.9	72.8	(²)
1934	47.1	62.0	(²)	56.2	(²)	60.2	71.6	76.0	(²)
1935	48.7	62.2	(²)	56.2	(²)	59.8	71.6	75.9	(²)
1936	51.9	64.5	(²)	57.3	(²)	60.6	71.7	75.8	(²)
1937	56.9	65.7	(²)	65.6	(²)	67.2	73.4	76.5	(²)
1938	50.5	64.7	(²)	63.1	(²)	65.6	71.1	76.4	(²)
1939	52.0	61.8	(²)	62.6	65.3	65.4	69.5	76.4	(²)
1940	54.8	60.7	(²)	62.8	66.2	66.8	69.7	77.3	(²)
1941	58.9	64.5	(²)	64.0	68.6	71.2	71.3	78.1	(²)
1942	64.0	66.4	(²)	64.9	71.2	76.8	74.1	79.1	(²)
1943	63.9	68.4	(²)	64.8	71.0	76.4	74.5	83.0	(²)
1944	63.4	70.3	(²)	64.8	71.0	78.4	75.9	83.4	(²)
1945	64.2	71.1	(²)	65.9	71.6	78.6	79.1	85.8	(²)
1946	74.6	76.2	(²)	73.9	80.3	83.0	84.2	89.7	(²)
1947	101.0	90.9	98.6	91.3	92.5	95.6	93.9	97.2	100.8
1948	102.1	107.1	102.9	103.9	100.9	101.4	101.7	100.5	103.1
1949	96.9	101.9	98.5	104.8	106.6	103.1	104.4	102.3	96.1
1950	104.6	103.0	100.9	110.3	108.6	105.3	106.9	103.5	96.6
1951	120.3	106.7	119.6	122.8	119.0	114.1	113.6	109.4	104.9
1952	97.2	106.6	116.5	123.0	121.5	112.0	113.6	111.8	108.3
1953	98.5	109.5	116.1	126.9	123.0	114.2	118.2	115.4	97.8
1954	94.2	108.1	116.3	128.0	124.6	115.4	120.9	120.6	102.5
1955	93.8	107.9	119.3	136.6	128.4	115.9	124.2	121.6	92.0
1956	99.3	111.2	127.2	148.4	137.8	119.1	129.6	122.3	91.0
1957	99.4	117.2	129.6	151.2	146.1	122.2	134.6	126.1	89.6
1958	100.6	112.7	131.0	150.4	149.8	123.2	136.0	128.2	94.2
1959 ³	114.3	112.7	132.2	153.7	153.0	123.4	137.7	131.4	94.5

The solution applied by the Bureau *weights* each price according to the quantity sold. First, the price of each commodity in a typical year (or average of years) is multiplied by the quantity produced in that year. The values so obtained for each commodity are totalled, so that the sum is the value of everything produced in that year. Next, each price in another year is multiplied by the quantity produced in the same base year, and the sum of the results is found. Then, it is necessary only to find the percentage change between the respective value totals for the two years in order to obtain the index number for all wholesale prices. The formula for this process is:

$$\frac{\Sigma P_0 Q_0}{\Sigma P_0 Q_0}$$

This type of index number is called a "base year weighted aggregate."

The wholesale price index, one of the most inclusive of all price indexes, is generally used as an indication of widespread price tendencies.

THE CONSUMER PRICE INDEX

An index of retail prices, the Consumer Price Index, is more pertinent than the wholesale price index in indicating the purchasing power of individual incomes, since retail prices do not follow wholesale prices closely. Here again, the problem of weighting arises.

The Bureau of Labor Statistics solved it by a combination of sampling and weighting. It made a budget study of several thousand wage and salary earners in the middle ranges of income. A large number of representative items bought by each of these families in a given year were listed and priced. The resulting costs of the family budgets, averaged, supplied the figure for the base year of the series. The family purchases are, of course, classified in the usual manner—food, rent, clothing, and other items.

To find how retail prices change, articles and services (rent being a payment for service), carefully described and specified in the first study, are priced again. It is not necessary to price every article in the budget, since, as a rule, retail prices of articles of a certain kind move up or down together; however, a large sample is used. Thus, comparative costs of the whole budget and of its main sections may be obtained. The index numbers are published monthly for the whole country and for important geographical sections.

The consumer price index, although informative, has limitations. It cannot be applied accurately to families with incomes much above (or below) those on which it is based, since families with larger incomes buy goods in different quantities from those with smaller incomes. A given family, too, may differ in composition from the typical one used in

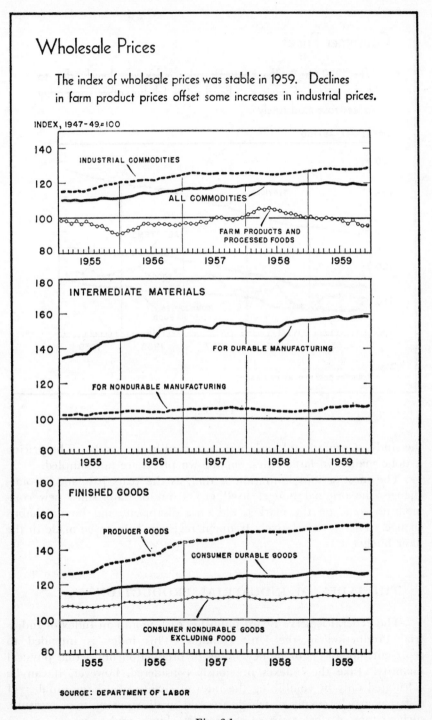

Fig. 6.1.

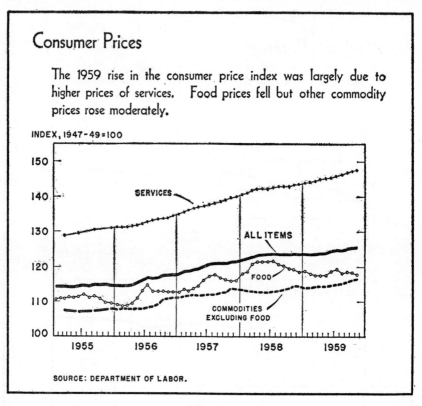

Consumer Prices

The 1959 rise in the consumer price index was largely due to higher prices of services. Food prices fell but other commodity prices rose moderately.

INDEX, 1947-49=100

SOURCE: DEPARTMENT OF LABOR.

Fig. 6.2.

the study. Geographical variations also modify the results. The pricing is done mainly in large cities; small-town prices are not sampled.

The most serious limitation is that, as the years pass and incomes change, the original budget itself grows out of date, since new commodities come on the market, old ones disappear, and buying habits change. Therefore, relatively frequent revisions have to be made in the basic budget.

THE INDEX OF INDUSTRIAL PRODUCTION

The Federal Reserve Board publishes each month an Index of Industrial Production in the United States. This index is intended to represent, not prices or money values of production but actual physical quantity. Like the indexes previously considered, however, it can be calculated only by combining the rates of change of a large number of different articles, many of which are sold in different units of measure, such as tons of steel, pairs of shoes or stockings, and so on.

How is this purpose achieved, without unduly distorting the facts? First, an index is calculated separately for the output of each type of

TABLE 6/3

CONSUMER PRICE INDEXES, BY MAJOR GROUPS, 1929-1959
FOR CITY WAGE-EARNER AND CLERICAL-WORKER FAMILIES
(1947-49 = 100)

Period	All items	Food	Housing		Apparel	Transportation	Medical care	Personal care	Reading and recreation	Other goods and services
			Total	Rent						
1929	73.3	65.6	(¹)	117.4	60.3	(¹)	(¹)	(¹)	(¹)	(¹)
1930	71.4	62.4	(¹)	114.2	58.9	(¹)	(¹)	(¹)	(¹)	(¹)
1931	65.0	51.4	(¹)	108.2	53.6	(¹)	(¹)	(¹)	(¹)	(¹)
1932	58.4	42.8	(¹)	97.1	47.5	(¹)	(¹)	(¹)	(¹)	(¹)
1933	55.3	41.6	(¹)	83.6	45.9	(¹)	(¹)	(¹)	(¹)	(¹)
1934	57.2	46.4	(¹)	78.4	50.2	(¹)	(¹)	(¹)	(¹)	(¹)
1935	58.7	49.7	71.8	78.2	50.6	69.6	71.4	54.6	58.1	67.2
1936	59.3	50.1	72.8	80.1	51.0	70.2	71.6	55.3	59.1	67.0
1937	61.4	52.1	75.4	83.8	53.7	71.3	72.3	58.5	60.8	68.8
1938	60.3	48.4	76.6	86.5	53.4	71.9	72.5	59.8	62.9	69.4
1939	59.4	47.1	76.1	86.6	52.5	70.2	72.6	59.6	63.0	70.6
1940	59.9	47.8	76.4	86.9	53.2	69.8	72.7	59.5	64.1	72.8
1941	62.9	52.2	78.3	88.4	55.6	72.2	73.1	61.0	66.4	74.2
1942	69.7	61.3	81.8	90.4	64.9	78.5	75.1	66.9	69.5	76.3
1943	74.0	68.3	82.8	90.3	67.8	78.2	78.7	73.8	75.3	80.2
1944	75.2	67.4	84.7	90.6	72.6	78.2	81.2	79.0	83.4	82.4
1945	76.9	68.9	86.1	90.9	76.3	78.1	83.1	81.5	86.8	85.7
1946	83.4	79.0	88.3	91.4	83.7	82.1	87.7	87.4	89.7	88.6
1947	95.5	95.9	95.0	94.4	97.1	90.6	94.9	97.6	95.5	96.1
1948	102.8	104.1	101.7	100.7	103.5	100.9	100.9	101.3	100.4	100.5
1949	101.8	100.0	103.3	105.0	99.4	108.5	104.1	101.1	104.1	103.4
1950	102.8	101.2	106.1	108.8	98.1	111.3	106.0	101.1	103.4	105.2
1951	111.0	112.6	112.4	113.1	106.9	118.4	111.1	110.5	106.5	109.7
1952	113.5	114.6	114.6	117.9	105.8	126.2	117.2	111.8	107.0	115.4
1953	114.4	112.8	117.7	124.1	104.8	129.7	121.3	112.8	108.0	118.2
1954	114.8	112.6	119.1	128.5	104.3	128.0	125.2	113.4	107.0	120.1
1955	114.5	110.9	120.0	130.3	103.7	126.4	128.0	115.3	106.6	120.2
1956	116.2	111.7	121.7	132.7	105.5	128.7	132.6	120.0	108.1	122.0
1957	120.2	115.4	125.6	135.2	106.9	136.0	138.0	124.4	112.2	125.5
1958	123.5	120.3	127.7	137.7	107.0	140.5	144.6	128.6	116.7	127.2
1959 ²	124.5	118.3	129.1	139.6	107.8	146.1	150.6	131.0	118.4	129.5

¹ Not available.
² January–November average.
Source: Department of Labor.

commodity. Then, the indexes are combined by weighting each according to the value produced in a base year. The base of the series is the average of the years 1947-1949. The values of mineral products in the index are the price times the quantity sold; the values of manufactured goods used in the index are the sum called by the census "value added by manufacture"—that is, the sales value minus the cost of materials and power.

Two limitations in interpretation of this index must be noted. One arises when totally new products must be added which are not comparable with manufactured products that preceded them—such as tanks made in wartime by a factory previously making automobiles. Another is that even one product like automobiles changes so much during the years that it eventually becomes almost a different article. Virtually no allowance is made in the index for either improvement or deterioration of the product. This objection is not so serious when comparisons are made only over a short period.

TABLE 6/4

INDUSTRIAL PRODUCTION INDEXES, 1947–1959

1947–49=100

Period	Total industrial production[1]	Industry					Market			
		Manufacturing			Min-ing	Utili-ties	Final products			Mate-rials
		Total	Dur-able	Non-durable			Total	Con-sumer	Equip-ment	
1947	99	99	100	98	101	91	99	98	100	100
1948	103	103	105	102	106	101	102	101	105	104
1949	98	97	95	100	94	108	99	101	94	96
1950	113	113	116	111	105	123	112	115	102	114
1951	123	123	130	115	115	140	121	114	142	124
1952	127	127	138	117	114	152	130	116	170	125
1953	138	139	156	122	117	166	138	124	182	137
1954	130	129	138	122	113	178	132	123	161	128
1955	146	145	159	134	125	199	144	136	172	147
1956	151	150	162	139	132	218	150	139	188	151
1957	152	150	162	141	132	233	152	141	189	151
1958	141	139	141	141	120	244	145	140	165	138
1959[3]	159	158	165	155	125	268	162	155	188	157

1957=100

Period	Total industrial production[2]	Industry					Market			
		Manufacturing			Min-ing	Utili-ties	Final products			Mate-rials
		Total	Dur-able	Non-durable			Total	Con-sumer	Equip-ment	
1947	65	66	62	70	76	39	65	70	53	66
1948	68	69	64	72	80	43	67	72	56	69
1949	64	65	59	71	71	46	65	71	50	64
1950	74	75	71	79	80	53	73	82	54	75
1951	81	82	80	82	87	60	79	81	75	82
1952	84	85	85	83	87	65	85	82	90	83
1953	91	92	96	87	89	71	91	88	96	91
1954	85	86	85	87	86	76	86	87	85	84
1955	96	97	98	95	95	85	95	97	91	97
1956	99	100	100	99	100	94	99	99	99	100
1957	100	100	100	100	100	100	100	100	100	100
1958	93	92	87	100	91	104	95	99	87	91
1959[1]	105	105	102	110	95	115	107	110	100	103

[1] Annual indexes (1947–49=100) for 1929–46, respectively, are: 58, 48, 40, 31, 37, 40, 46, 55, 60, 47, 58, 66, 85, 105, 125, 123, 106, and 90.

[2] Annual indexes (1957=100) for 1929–46, respectively, are: 38, 32, 26, 21, 24, 26, 31, 36, 40, 31, 38, 44, 56, 69, 82, 81, 70, and 59.

[3] Preliminary.

Note: The data in this table are the revised series on industrial production. Coverage has been broadened to include electric and gas utility production, in addition to manufacturing and mining. For details, see *Federal Reserve Bulletin,* December 1959.

Source: Board of Governors of the Federal Reserve System.

USE OF INDEX NUMBERS

Suppose you wish to compare index numbers in the same series for two years, neither of which is the base. Let us say that consumer prices have risen from 115 to 140. Prices have risen 25 *percentage points*. To find the actual percentage of rise, you must find what percentage 25 constitutes of the index for the year at which you start your comparison, or 115. Thus, $\frac{25}{115} = .217+$, or approximately 22 percent increase.

Suppose you wish to calculate how much the purchasing power of your income has changed because of rising retail prices. Let us say that in 1940 your income was $1,000, and in 1950 it was $1,250. The index of this income, based on 1940, would obviously be:

1940	100
1950	125

The consumer price index (based on 1947) for these years was:

1940	59.9
1950	102.8

Now divide the index of dollar income (often called "nominal income") by the price index.

Income (in current dollars)		Index of Consumer Prices	Real Income
1940	100	59.9	166.6
1950	125	102.8	111.9

Thus, while your dollar income went up 25 percent, your real income fell by 54.7 percentage points, or approximately 33 percent.

Index of Real Income
(in 1940 dollars)

1940	100
1950	67

CAUTION IN USE OF STATISTICS

Since this is not a textbook of statistical mathematics, the reader cannot learn from it the complexities or the statistical refinements sometimes used by experts. The purpose here is merely to acquaint the student with some of the more elementary principles and terms so that he may understand the more familiar statistical tables found in public documents or other information intended for general use.

One caution, however, deserves more attention, both from laymen and experts, than it sometimes receives. No statistical conclusion is any more reliable than the raw data on which it is based. No amount of mathematical manipulation can make up for mistakes in the basic information which is manipulated.

This does not mean that all statistics must be precisely accurate in order to be useful. The error may be so small that for certain practical purposes it makes little difference. Or, a given set of statistical figures may be good for one purpose but not for another. For example, an elaborate study of the buying intentions of retail consumers was found, after careful testing against the purchases actually made by consumers, to be an excellent indication of *whether* their spending would increase or decrease, but not of *how much*. Another good principle is not to carry out figures to more decimal places than the accuracy of the basic data warrants.

This leads to a second caution. In using statistics, always try to find out what the given series or table is good for and what it is not good for. Skilled experts in economic research often find it necessary to go back to the sources and make new studies, to be sure that the basic material is in suitable form for the particular inquiry they are pursuing.

PROBLEMS

1. From tables in this chapter, calculate how large a percentage increase occurred between 1946 and 1958 in:
    (a) Wholesale prices
    (b) Consumer prices
    (c) Industrial production
Compare the change in the wholesale price index with that in the consumer price index. Do you think this comparison is a reliable basis for judgment concerning changes in the cost of distribution at retail of what consumers buy? Give reasons for your answer.

2. The instructor will collect unsigned slips from the members of your class, on which each states his or her approximate weight. He will then distribute sheets on which these weights are listed in no particular order but are separated by sex, if the class is coeducational. (If the class is large, he will use random samples for this purpose.)
    (a) Draw up an array of these weights for your own sex.
    (b) On the basis of the array, tabulate a frequency distribution.
    (c) What is the arithmetic mean of the students' weights?
    (d) What is their weighted mean?
    (e) What is the median?
    (f) What is the mode?

3. (a) Write down your approximate income for each year 1955–1961. If you had none or if you do not know, use imaginary figures. Then calculate the course of the purchasing power of your income (your *real* income) for these years, assuming that the consumers price index were applicable to your expenditures.

(b) Is the consumers price index roughly applicable to your expenditures? Give reason for your answer.

7/ CHARTS AND GRAPHS / Some people can

comprehend a situation better by looking at a picture of it than by reading words or examining tables of figures. It is also sometimes possible to discover from pictures relationships among quantities which would not be apparent by inspection of the figures alone. Charts and graphs are the pictures commonly used in economic reports and in discussions of economic theory. It is well to be able to interpret them, to know the advantages and disadvantages of various kinds, and to be aware of unwarranted conclusions that a chart may convey.

BAR CHART

One of the simplest ways of comparing visually a small number of quantities is the familiar "bar (or column) chart"—the longer the bar, the larger the quantity. A defect of the bar chart is that if the differences among the quantities being compared are large, the longer bars look top-heavy and occupy too much space; anything like accurate comparison by eye becomes difficult. Figure 7/1 is an example of a bar chart.

The technical name for the bar chart is "histogram." In the technical sense what is being compared is the *areas* of the bars—and since, in ordinary bar charts, the widths of all the bars are the same, it is sufficient to compare only their lengths. But sometimes, in histograms, the widths as well as the heights vary, and this variation involves a comparison of areas, which is often misleading to the untrained eye. (A square having twice the area of another square has, of course, sides less than one and one half times the length of the sides in the smaller one.)

A variation of the bar chart is the "pictograph," which, instead of bars, shows a series of little men, bushels of wheat, machines, or other object, to picture comparative quantities. The objections to such a chart may be the same as those to the histogram.

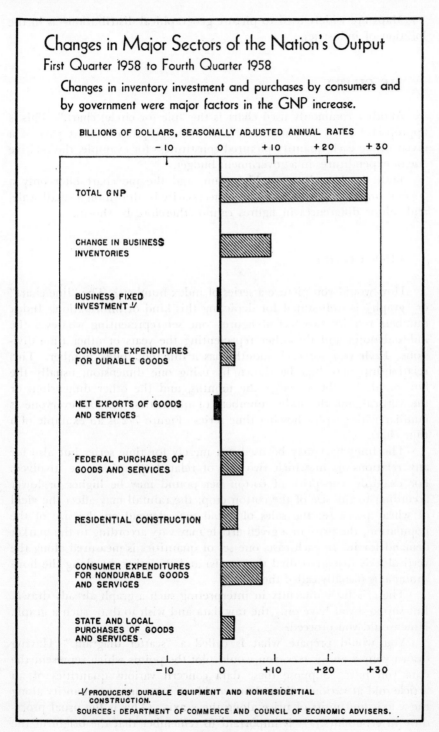

Changes in Major Sectors of the Nation's Output

First Quarter 1958 to Fourth Quarter 1958

Changes in inventory investment and purchases by consumers and by government were major factors in the GNP increase.

BILLIONS OF DOLLARS, SEASONALLY ADJUSTED ANNUAL RATES

– 10   0   + 10   + 20   + 30

TOTAL GNP

CHANGE IN BUSINESS INVENTORIES

BUSINESS FIXED INVESTMENT $^{1/}$

CONSUMER EXPENDITURES FOR DURABLE GOODS

NET EXPORTS OF GOODS AND SERVICES

FEDERAL PURCHASES OF GOODS AND SERVICES

RESIDENTIAL CONSTRUCTION

CONSUMER EXPENDITURES FOR NONDURABLE GOODS AND SERVICES

STATE AND LOCAL PURCHASES OF GOODS AND SERVICES

– 10   0   + 10   + 20   + 30

$^{1/}$ PRODUCERS' DURABLE EQUIPMENT AND NONRESIDENTIAL CONSTRUCTION.

SOURCES: DEPARTMENT OF COMMERCE AND COUNCIL OF ECONOMIC ADVISERS.

Fig. 7.1.

Maps are widely used to picture geographical distribution—as in the location of industries.

PIE CHART

Another commonly used chart is the "pie (or circle) chart." This is appropriate when the intention is to show graphically what part of a given whole each quantity pictured constitutes—for example, the relative size of expenditures in a government budget.

Both the bar chart, or histogram, and the pie chart offer only a general impression, since they must necessarily be drawn on a small scale, and minor differences in figures cannot therefore be shown.

LINE CHART

How would you picture a series of index numbers? The "line chart" or "graph" is well suited for depicting this kind of information. Index numbers require two sets of figures—one set representing whatever the index denotes and the other representing the years or other time divisions. Each year (or each month) has a different index number. This relationship may best be shown by using one dimension, usually the horizontal, for the years or the months, and the other dimension, or the vertical, for the index numbers of quantities. Almost everyone is familiar with graphs showing time series. Figure 7/2 is an example of a time chart.

The line chart may be used not merely for time series but also for any relationship in which two sets of related quantities are involved. For example, the price of cotton per pound may be higher or lower according to the size of the cotton crop; the rainfall may affect the yield of wheat per acre; the sales of bread may depend on the size of the population; the price of a given article may vary according to the market demand for it. In each case, one set of quantities is measured along the vertical axis (usually called the y axis) and the other set along the horizontal axis (usually called the x axis).

There is little difficulty in interpreting such a graph already drawn. But suppose you have only the raw data and wish to draw such a graph. How would you proceed?

You would prepare what is called a "scatter diagram." Having drawn your x and y axes, you would plot the points which represent the data you have. Suppose these data concern various quantities of an article sold at various prices. You would measure units of quantity along the x axis and units of price along the y axis. (This is the usual procedure in economics.) It is important to remember that the origin of the two axes (the point of intersection) must be zero. Now suppose you knew that ten units were sold at $1. You would show this information

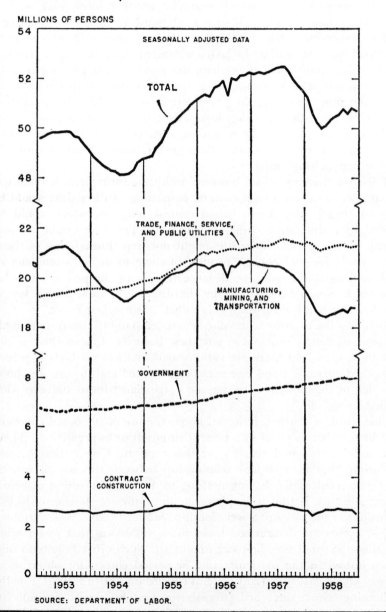

Employment in Nonagricultural Establishments

Manufacturing, mining, and transportation accounted for four-fifths of the 1957–58 decline in employment and for half of the increase since April.

MILLIONS OF PERSONS

SEASONALLY ADJUSTED DATA

TOTAL

TRADE, FINANCE, SERVICE, AND PUBLIC UTILITIES

MANUFACTURING, MINING, AND TRANSPORTATION

GOVERNMENT

CONTRACT CONSTRUCTION

1953   1954   1955   1956   1957   1958

SOURCE: DEPARTMENT OF LABOR.

Fig. 7.2.

by placing a dot ten units to the right along the x axis and parallel to the $1.00 on the y axis; that is, perpendicular to the x axis (see Figure 7/3). All other information about prices and quantities of this article would be shown by other dots, similarly plotted. You would now have your scatter diagram.

One question that might occur is whether any regular relationship existed among these points—for example, whether more were sold at lower prices than at higher. If such a relationship existed and were very regular, inspection might reveal that all the points were on a straight line, which you could draw by laying a straightedge along them. (In this case, the line would start high along the y axis and slope down toward the x axis, since the lower the price, the larger the quantity sold.)

At the other extreme, the points might be so widely scattered that it would be impossible to imagine any regular relationship among them which could be pictured by a line or a curve. This situation would indicate that circumstances other than price eliminated any relationship between price and quantity.

Either of these extremes, however, would be infrequent, if there was good reason to expect a relationship. Inspection of the points would be likely to suggest that there was a central tendency which could be pictured by a line, either straight or curved. This line would not pass through all the points; indeed, it might not pass through any of them. But it would be near enough to most of them to depict a tendency or trend; and, on the whole, the distance from it of the points which lay on one side would be balanced by the distance of those which lay on the other. Such a line, if drawn, is called a "smoothed curve."

It is possible to draw a smoothed curve freehand to illustrate roughly a central tendency. For some purposes, however, this method is not accurate enough, and there are various mathematical methods by which a smoothed curve or trend line may be calculated and drawn. In choosing which of these methods to use, the statistician tries to arrive at what is called a good "fit."

One word of caution, however, about the use of smoothed curves or trend lines either as proof of a present situation or as prediction. There are a number of good reasons for this caution. One is that a good correlation (that is, a regular relationship between two sets of figures) may occur accidentally, having nothing to do with the course of actual events. Another is that a graph on a plane surface, having only two dimensions, can picture a relationship between only two variables, whereas events are determined by so many influences that forces other than those pictured may be more important. Such other influences may be neutralized in the particular case or period chosen for observation, but may knock galley-west any general conclusion drawn from it. Finally, in choosing which smoothed curve is the best fit, the statistician frequently must exercise a somewhat arbitrary judgment. If a different choice were made, predictions or calculations based on it might be very different.

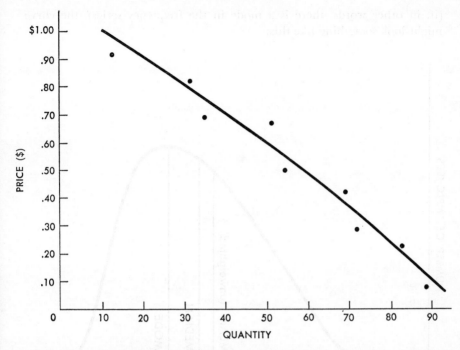

Fig. 7.3. SCATTER DIAGRAM AND CURVE. This diagram shows the relation between prices and quantities demanded.

These cautions do not diminish the importance and usefulness of time series as an indication of past occurrences, provided the figures on which they rest are well chosen and well authenticated. The caution applies to drawing of conclusions about causes or logical relationships which may be based on inspection of all graphs portraying relationships by lines.

THE CURVE OF FREQUENCY DISTRIBUTION

In Chapter 6 we learned how to tabulate a frequency distribution of a set of data and something of its usefulness. Such a distribution may easily be pictured by a graph, in which each subdivision is represented by a column or a bar, the length of which shows the comparative number in that division. A smoothed curve can then be drawn connecting the ends of the bars. A curve depicting the frequency distribution of wages and salaries in a given factory or industry would show, by horizontal measurement from the origin of the axes, the dollars received in any wage classification and, by vertical measurement, the number receiving each wage. If, as is likely to be the case, one wage bracket includes more workers than any of the other brackets, and the number receiving wages either higher or lower than this tapers down from it on each side (if, in other words, there is a mode in the frequency series), the curve might look something like this:

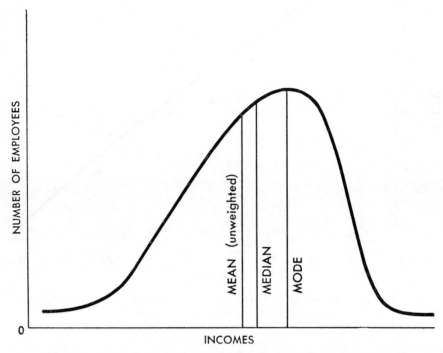

Fig. 7.4. CURVE OF FREQUENCY DISTRIBUTION. This diagram shows the savings by workers in one company.

A curve showing the distribution of income in the United States would have a similar appearance.

In a curve so drawn, the mode would obviously be identical with the height of the curve at its highest point, since this is the wage or income most frequently received. The unweighted arithmetic mean would not coincide with the mode, as it is derived without reference to the number receiving any given amount, simply by dividing all the wages received by the total number receiving them. In this curve it is obvious that more dollars lie in the area to the left of the mode than to the right of it; hence, the unweighted mean would lie to the left. As the statistician would say, the distribution is "skewed." The median would lie between the mode and the mean.

It is a curious fact that, in picturing distribution of a very large series of instances, especially where *chance* plays a role, the distribution curve tends to approach closely a shape representing what is called "normal distribution." The normal distribution, or bell-shaped, curve looks something like an inverted U.

In the normal distribution curve, not only the mode but also the

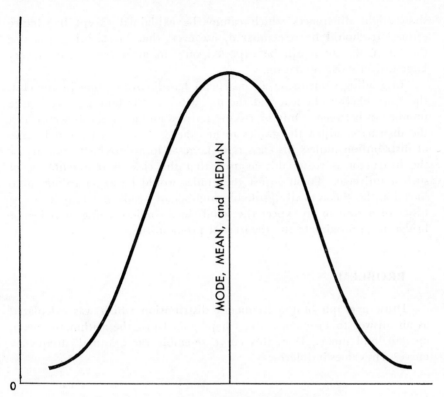

Fig. 7.5. NORMAL DISTRIBUTION CURVE.

median and the arithmetic mean coincide with the perpendicular to the top of the curve, since this is exactly halfway between the smallest and the largest quantities being measured and the areas each side of it bounded by the curve are equal.

One might, for example, expect to find that the frequency distribution of heights or weights in a population as large as that of the United States closely paralleled the normal frequency curve. Or, to illustrate the influence of chance more explicitly, suppose a coin were so evenly balanced that, if tossed, the chance that it would come down heads apparently equaled the chance that it would come down tails. If you tossed such a coin, let us say ten times, it probably would *not* come down heads exactly five times, no more and no less. It might even come down heads ten times or no times. But, in a very long series of sets of ten tosses, there might probably be more instances in which heads appeared five times than otherwise. The next most numerous instances would be those in which heads appeared either six or four times, and so on down. If you plotted the frequency curve of these trials, it would approximate the normal frequency curve.

Astronomers and other scientists use the normal distribution curve to make almost accurate measurements where repeated measurements show slight differences which cannot be explained except by chance errors. It should be remembered, however, that in statistical practice the "normal" curve can be expected only in measurements of a very large universe or population.

In grading students, every instructor has discovered that in any class there are likely to be a few at the top, a few at the bottom, and a large number in between. Only by risking fairness and accuracy, however, can the instructor adjust the grades to fit exactly a smoothed normal curve of distribution, unless his class is so large as to approximate infinity or the instructor is reasonably assured that the class is representative of such a universe. To so adjust the grades would be as hazardous as to look for the theoretically probable number of heads and tails in a few tosses of a coin or to expect the hands in a single evening of poker or bridge to approximate the theoretical probabilities.

PROBLEM

Draw a graph of the frequency distribution which was calculated as an answer to Problem 2 (b), Chapter 6. Draw the arithmetic mean, median, and mode. Does this curve resemble the "normal" frequency curve? How does it differ?

PART II / HOW OUR INSTITUTIONS OPERATE

Now that we have learned something about using the tools of the economist's trade—how to measure by accounts and statistics and how to picture relationships expressed in quantities—let us inquire how our economic institutions operate and what the outcome of their behavior has been.

Since ours is not an economy like that of the single self-sustaining farm, no single person or agency can decide what goods shall be made, what services shall be offered, and how much of each shall be made and offered. It is easy to see how the welfare of a pioneer family depends on the skill with which it fashions its resources and the choices it makes about their allocation among numerous possible uses. With the complexity of our great economic society, we cannot understand how decisions are made about production and use of scarce goods without examining markets and prices. Insofar as resources are allocated to the best advantage through a system of markets and prices, this outcome would seem, at first sight, almost miraculous. Yet such a system is dominant in present-day economies.

We shall have to examine not only this theory but also business organization and practices, the alternation of good times and bad—called the "business cycle," and the banks and other institutions which affect money and its uses. We shall have to look into modern government and its activities, the special problems and practices of farmers and of wage earners, and the impact of foreign trade.

Finally, we shall study the outcome of our economic behavior. What has our kind of economy accomplished in satisfying the wants of those who compose it? What economic growth has occurred? What major problems remain? These are the matters examined in Part II.

8 / MARKETS AND PRICES / A pioneer in the

wilderness might build his own house from logs that he had cut; he might feed and clothe himself by raising his own crops and shooting or trapping game. But such solitary production for use is not characteristic of human societies, even the most primitive. Before the introduction of factories, in farming communities much of the necessary production was carried on by the family or the household, but today man almost universally resorts to trade in order to supply his wants more adequately than would be possible solely by individual or household production.

One family or larger group finds that it has a surplus of some commodities and not enough of others. Skills differ from person to person and resources differ from place to place. The result is that people find it advantageous to trade what they have in excess or can produce more readily for other things that they lack or that others can make better. Trading may be simple swapping or barter. But when many kinds of things are traded or the several producers do not all meet because trading covers a wide area, men habitually use money as a medium of exchange. The relative exchange values of the things traded are then stated in units of money. Money is therefore both a medium of exchange and a measure of value.

Thus, as Adam Smith and others have pointed out, the wants of a whole society can be supplied by buying and selling in free markets, which seem almost miraculously to allocate scarce resources to the most desired uses. Through demand and supply operating upon prices, markets serve as signposts to individual producers of what is wanted and in what quantities. A central planning agency, trying to decide in advance what a whole society should produce and in what quantities, could probably not do so good a job. It does not follow from this statement, however, that we have a perfect market system or that in many instances it could not be supplemented or improved, to the great advantage of the public, by governmental or other nonprofit-seeking intervention.

ECONOMIC GOODS AND FREE GOODS

Economic goods are those scarce enough in relation to the demand so that anyone who controls a supply of any one of them can sell the good in question at some price, high or low. Since the available supply of any economic good is not freely accessible in the quantity any user might like, such goods must be "economized"; that is, they must be allocated among competing uses.

In contradistinction to things that are bought or sold, other substances are commonly called free goods, such as air or sea water. Some of these may be just as useful for production as those ordinarily included under the classical factor, land. Air is used as a raw material for the manufacture of nitrogen and other products; magnesium and other metals are extracted from sea water. The reason free goods are not usually included among the factors of production is that, for the present at least, they are so abundant in relation to the demand that they can command no price, and nobody can control the supply. It is only relatively *scarce* goods and commodities, which can be controlled by sellers, that have a market value.

The main categories of productive resources are usually called "land," "labor," and "capital." (These are also often referred to in economics as the "factors of production"). The remuneration derived from production goes to those who provide these three factors.

"Land," in this theory, means what is generally understood by the word, but also includes anything found on land or under it, such as fish, wild life, standing timber, water, stone, and minerals. In economics, the term is usually synonymous with natural resources.

"Labor" means not only wage labor but also work of any kind which is economically productive, such as that performed by farmers either for sale or for their own use and that of their families, by independent professional persons like lawyers and doctors, by salaried employees—even chief executives—or by the owners of businesses. The term covers human resources.

"Capital" is a term more ambiguous than either land or labor. In a purely physical sense it means the produced instruments and goods used in the process of production, things not intended for immediate consumption. Tools, machinery, buildings, goods awaiting sale, farm animals, railroad tracks, cars and locomotives, ships, airplanes, airports—all such things are real capital or capital goods. But capital is also used to mean capital funds—that is, money devoted to or invested in enterprise. There are markets for goods, markets for land, markets for services (labor), and markets for capital (instruments of production or money capital).

MARKETS AS MEANS OF EXCHANGE

A market may be a particular *place* where goods or services are exchanged for money, and vice versa. An example of such a market is the old-fashioned fairground, where farmers brought their crops to show to possible buyers, and buyers of crops came to see what was being offered for sale and to choose what, if anything, they wished to buy. Often in the same place—as in a country fair—sellers of goods that farmers do not grow display their wares so that the farmers, having sold their produce, might buy things that they want.

In economics, the word "market" is often used to describe not merely a place but the whole process of buying and selling either a single product or a series of products, whether the buying and selling occurs in one place or in many places.

One of the principal concerns of economists has been to analyze systematically what goes on in markets, since it is by means of some sort of market process that prices are determined, wants are satisfied, and earnings (wages, profits, interest) are distributed. Obviously, then, what goes on in markets is of prime importance to the understanding of any society in which trading, the use of money, and production for sale play a large role.

The economic theory of markets, in its crudest and most simplified form, is a part of our folklore; it seems to spring from common experience. Prices, we believe, go up when demand exceeds supply and go down when supply exceeds demand. A high price may curtail demand; a low price may encourage sales. Conversely, a high price stimulates production and a low price may discourage it. Competition among sellers tends to lower prices, while a monopolist may overcharge the buyers. Competition among buyers tends to raise prices, while a monopolistic buyer may pay what he pleases. The ideal situation, resulting in the most all-round satisfaction, is thought to be a free market in which both sellers and buyers compete; this situation leads to fair prices, brings to the top the most efficient producers, and favors economic progress. Competitive and free markets on the whole characterize free private enterprise, and this, among other things, is what has made the United States the richest nation in the world.

The above statements omit many of the details and qualifications that characterize the systematic theory developed by economists. We shall examine that theory in Chapter 9. Before doing so, however, it will be well to take a brief look at a few actual markets in the United States. Do they in fact correspond with the prevailing ideas? Do they have many common features, so that it would be easy to generalize about them?

The Labor Market. When a young man or woman wants a job, he does not, as a rule, bargain much with the prospective employer. He either accepts an offer or turns it down and looks for something else. If he takes a job in an establishment where a union contract governs the position in question, he is paid according to the scale established in the union contract with the employer. If the job in question is not covered by collective agreement, the employer usually has determined in advance what the pay will be, and adheres to his decision. Labor is not a commodity which can be bought, sold, or stored like wheat or coal, and the "labor market" has unique characteristics. Labor itself is largely unstandardized, unlike graded wheat or specified steel.

In such a market, price does not often respond quickly to changes in demand and supply. Of course, an applicant may shop around and take the offer he likes best, and the employer may choose among applicants. But the applicant does not have time or means to see *all* the possible employers; nor do the employers have time to interview all possible applicants. Certainly the remuneration offered—that is, the "price" of labor —seems at any one time to be little affected by market forces.

Wages, as a rule, rise much more readily than they fall. They may tend to fall when the supply of labor is persistently greater than the demand for it, as in a very severe depression—that is, when unemployment is unusually high. Wages usually rise when there are fewer qualified applicants than jobs to be filled—that is, when there is a labor shortage. But general changes in either direction do not come quickly and easily. A higher price for labor—that is, higher wages—does not bring a large or quick increase in the wage-earning population; nor a lower price quickly diminish it—though it may affect the size of the labor force proper—that is, those actively seeking work. Many other considerations enter into the fixing of pay rates—custom, what people think is fair, how much it takes to support a family at a standard of living prevalent in a given community or in the experience of the worker, union contracts, prosperity of the employer or the lack of it, or even minimum wage laws.

The labor market is a huge market affecting directly a large majority of persons in the nation (everybody who has, is looking for, or is offering employment), a market influenced by many forces other than demand and supply, and by demand and supply only slowly and imperfectly. Competition is present in this market, since there are numerous buyers and many sellers—but competition is severely limited. Clearly this is not the kind of market that could readily be accounted for in the short run by a theory expressing an exact mathematical relationship among demand, supply, and price.

The Stock Exchange.   Now let us examine a market at the opposite extreme—the market for shares of stock in business corporations. Almost everyone in the United States who wants to sell or buy a share will either use the stock exchange for this purpose or will make his transaction at the price established on that market. In the purchase and sale of stocks, it is as nearly true as in any other market that all sellers and all buyers meet, at least through their agents, the brokers.

The articles bought or sold are highly standardized. That is, one share of stock of a given corporation is exactly like every other share of the same issue. The purchaser or the seller may choose among a large number of corporations and a large number of issues, but each knows exactly what he is buying or selling—as far as the title of the stock itself can tell him. Therefore, an order of preference can be established; the demand for, and supply of, any given stock can vary according to what people think it is worth. (What people may think it is worth, however, depends on a great many considerations, some of them highly intangible.)

Competition among buyers and sellers seems to be complete and perfect, at least on the surface. Any broker who has an order from a customer to sell shares of a given stock—say, U. S. Steel Common—goes to a certain "trading post" on the floor of the exchange where that stock is dealt in. If the customer has instructed the broker to sell it at "the market"—that is, at whatever he can get for it—the broker announces how many shares he has for sale, and accepts the highest bid from other brokers who have come to that trading post with orders to buy U. S. Steel Common. If the customer has fixed a minimum below which he will not sell, the broker will accept no bid below that minimum; and if no one will bid enough, no sale is made. If the customer is anxious to sell quickly, he will probably instruct the broker to lower the price or to take the best offer he can get.

The stock exchange is engaged in carrying on a continual auction. The price of any one stock varies up or down quickly and easily according to the relationship of demand and supply; nothing else affects it. Relative prices of different stocks can, in turn, reflect the collective valuation that the buying and selling public places on them.

If one limits his attention to what goes on within the stock exchange itself, this market seems to be an almost perfect example of a "free competitive market," where nothing stands in the way of the influence which the relationship between supply and demand is supposed to exert upon prices. Therefore, it should be a suitable market to illustrate a formal supply-and-demand theory. If, however, this theory should be one that implied also an influence exerted by prices upon either supply or demand, the stock market might not be so good an illustration. A high price for an existing stock may, to be sure, bring a larger supply of the shares already issued to be sold. But corporations do not, as a matter of routine, manufacture additional numbers of their shares just to supply a growing demand indicated by a higher price, though sometimes they do so. Nor do investors or speculators necessarily demand fewer shares when prices are high than when prices are low; indeed, frequently the exact opposite is the case. They buy on the basis more of what change in price they anticipate than on the basis of what the present price is. Investors, of course, are not so much affected by speculative motives as are speculators.

The Retail Market. The department store or the mail-order house is an example of a part of the retail market which does not specialize in selling something more or less of one kind, labor or shares of stock. On the contrary, its appeal, particularly that of the mail-order house, lies largely in the fact that it offers for sale a wide array of goods, so that the customer can find much that he wants without looking further. Both therefore profit, not so much from high prices as from a large volume of sales. And both stimulate the idea among purchasers that because of their size and volume, they can offer a better quality of merchandise at lower prices than can smaller specialty shops, and as a rule this idea is correct.

Because department stores offer such a large variety of merchandise, they think much more about the profit arising from their total transactions than about the profit from any one type of goods, such as handkerchiefs, radios, or hammocks. They may actually sell some articles at a loss or at very little profit, merely because their prestige demands carrying a full line and because this policy attracts customers who may buy other things. Indeed, they cannot readily know what they make on any one kind of sale, since it is next to impossible to decide which part of their general cost of doing business (conventionally called "overhead") should be assigned to each kind of article that they stock.

In these circumstances a demand of consumers for more of an article than is on hand is not likely to result in much, if any, increase in price; rather, the management uses its utmost endeavor to obtain more of the same article—and perhaps it may do so at a lower cost, because larger volume may reduce costs of manufacture. In this case an excess of demand over supply may ultimately push prices downward instead of upward, and its effect may be seen almost entirely in an enlargement of the supply.

The department store or mail-order kind of market is therefore about as far removed as possible from the auction market typified by the stock exchange. It is, as a rule, not a market primarily interested in buying or selling any one kind of standardized goods. Prices are set in this market by the seller; there is no dicker or bargain; the individual purchaser pays what is asked or goes without. Yet competition among stores usually leads the seller to fix, or at least to try to create the impression that he is fixing, the lowest possible price. His interest normally leads him to emphasize large volume rather than high prices. Some stores emphasize quality rather than price, but the great effort is to keep goods moving, since large and quick turnover is the chief element in the profit of the concern.

The Steel Market. Still a different type of market is that for basic steel—mostly to be fabricated into a wide variety of goods such as armament, railroad equipment, buildings, bridges and other types of construction, automobiles, machinery, and many other products. Those who buy structural steel—rails, plate, bars, rods, sheets—are not, as individuals, consumers of steel; they use it in their businesses. In the end, the market for steel does depend upon what individual consumers buy or are expected to buy (including what they buy through payment of taxes to their governments). Yet the effect of ultimate consumer demand is both indirect and complicated.

Since the steel industry deals mainly with large purchasers—corporations and governments—it is not greatly concerned with offering price inducements to stimulate individual consumer buying. It assumes that the demand for its product is affected not so much by the price as by the plans of those business concerns or governmental agencies who must have steel at almost any price when they need it and will not buy it, however low the price, when they do not need it.

The practice of the big steel company is to figure what it costs to produce steel, add what it regards as a reasonable profit, and quote a price accordingly. The tradition of the industry is that the smaller producers follow the price leadership of the big ones. If the steel company, large or small, can sell the steel at that price, it sells all it can; if it cannot sell much at that price, it curtails production and lays off employees. The quoted price of steel has varied little between prosperity and depression; on the other hand, the production and employment in steel mills varies widely from one period to another.

It is true that "gray markets" exist in steel when demand is either unusually active or unusually dull. Unannounced price increases or concessions are made when demand changes widely. The big companies maintain their published prices; the smaller companies and wholesalers occasionally charge higher prices when they can and lower prices when demand falls off. But, by and large, the steel market is one in which producers control the supply to maintain a predetermined price. The price is set by the producer; given the demand, he adjusts the supply to meet the demand at the price set, without much upward or downward movement of price.

The Wheat Market. At almost the opposite pole from the steel market is the wheat market. There are relatively few steel producers; there are millions of wheat farmers. Steel companies can shut down or conserve their assets by laying off men when demand falls off. Most wheat farmers live on their farms and are helped by their families; they cannot, therefore, shut down without firing themselves, their sons, and daughters. Steel companies first set their prices and then produce what is ordered; wheat farmers first produce and then sell at whatever prices they can get.

In recent years, government has intervened in various ways to prevent the prices of agricultural staples from falling below certain limits (though not to prevent them from rising as far above these limits as market demand may take them). But before intervention of this kind, the price of wheat and other staples had, unlike the price of steel, extremely wide variations, while the production of wheat changes only slowly in response to changes in demand. Farmers who can grow only or mainly wheat may actually raise more when prices are low, in order to keep up their incomes; farmers who grow several crops may shift to another crop. Production does vary widely with changes in weather conditions, however.

VARIATIONS IN MARKETS

These brief comments on a few actual markets indicate that the ideas with which we began to analyze the market process are greatly over-simplified. One could scarcely start with a simply stated general theory and, by applying it, expect to understand all that takes place in any of these markets, especially in the short run. Detailed study of any one of them would add many more complications. Similar study of other specific markets—and there are many—would show that no two are exactly alike. Is it possible to make any valid theoretical generalizations about markets? In the next chapter we shall examine the most prominent theory that economists have outlined, and see what we can learn from the so-called "law" of supply and demand.

For an illustration of the workings of an actual market and its development, see Chapter 29.

QUESTIONS

1. Give examples of products or services the prices of which are so inflexible that the purchaser either pays what is asked or goes without.

2. Can you give examples of products or services about whose prices the purchaser may engage in considerable bargaining?

3. Can you mention products for which the purchaser must pay the amount on the price tag, yet, in the setting of the price, competition probably occurs among sellers?

4. Do you think that the purchaser customarily regards a relatively high price for a particular article or service as indicative of high quality? Do you think consumers often have the opportunity and ability to test this assumption?

9 / THEORY OF SUPPLY AND

DEMAND / In Chapter 8 we studied a number of markets, all different in detail. If we should survey the separate markets for all the kinds of goods and services, we would hardly find two exactly alike. Yet if we are to think intelligently about such general ideas as supply and demand and their effect on price and production, we must find a general principle which applies at least in some degree or in some way to markets in general.

Such unifying principles, common in all branches of science, are called "theories." Without theories, we could make little sense of the world we live in. Examples of theories which most of us accept as a matter of course and which are put to everyday use are the germ theory of disease, the theory of gravitation, the theory of light refraction (which comes into play every time we take a snapshot or look through a pair of eyeglasses). The fact that such theories are not applicable in all cases does not prevent us from using them when they do help us to understand. Some diseases are not caused by germs, but those that are may be prevented by sanitation or inoculation. The laws of gravitation discovered by Isaac Newton do not apply accurately in astronomical distances; however, though superseded by principles discovered by Albert Einstein, they are good enough for most practical purposes. Scientists have been puzzled as to whether light rays are carried by waves or a series of impulses, but the classical theory did enable man to make lenses that work.

To devise a theory covering a large number of different cases, it is usually necessary to begin by making simplifying assumptions, in order to exclude influences other than a few which we suppose to be the most important or to have the most widespread effects. Thus, in market theory, we wish to examine the interaction of demand, supply, and price. We start by excluding other influences that might affect what occurs in buying and selling, just as in developing the theory of gravitation, scientists excluded such influences as resistance of the air. We then devise a principle which seems a reasonable way to account for what occurs. A precise statement of such a theory is called a "hypothesis." A hypothesis, once formulated, must be thoroughly tested by actual experiment or observation before it can be dignified as "scientific law." Any theory, however reasonable or accepted, is open to refutation or revision if observation of what really takes place should prove not to be in accord with the theory.

INTERESTS OF BUYERS AND SELLERS

What concerns buyers and sellers in any market? If we exclude consideration of the influence of factors other than price, such as habit, social prestige, and similar factors, the *buyer,* we may suppose, wishes to know what he needs or desires. And since he has a limited amount to spend, he has to have some order of preference among the things offered for sale. He is also concerned with the price of anything that he is thinking of buying and with its quality. Naturally he favors the lowest price which the seller will take for what he wants.

The *seller,* in all probability, is concerned with getting the highest possible price for what he has for sale. His desire for a high price, however, may be moderated by a number of considerations. He is not likely to charge so high a price that no buyer will pay it. In that case, his work will have gone for nothing. In addition, he may find that the higher the price, the fewer he can sell, and it may be more remunerative to sell more at a lower price than fewer at a higher price.

A market may consist of just one buyer and one seller, and just one kind of goods may be for sale. In that case, how much is bought and sold and how much will be paid for it, will depend on how the considerations mentioned above influence the actions of the buyer and the seller. Presumably, there is a maximum price above which the buyer will not buy and a minimum price below which the seller will not sell. If the buyer's maximum is below the seller's minimum, no sale will take place. This would probably be the case of a student considering the purchase of a Rolls-Royce car (priced in the neighborhood of $20,000). If the buyer's maximum is above the seller's minimum, we can suppose that the outcome will result from a process of dickering or bargaining.

If there are more than one buyer and more than one seller, a degree of *competition* enters the situation. If the buyer is energetic and prudent, his search for the best quality and the lowest price should lead him to examine the wares of all the sellers. The seller's search for the greatest gain should lead him similarly to sound out the desires of as many buyers as possible. Each must also pay attention to the competition with himself. If there are few goods for sale and many willing buyers, any one buyer may have to complete a transaction quickly at a high price or go without what he wants. He may not be able to drive a shrewd bargain. If, on the other hand, there are few or reluctant buyers and many willing sellers with large stocks to sell, the sellers will probably have to make concessions if they are not to be left with goods on their hands.

THE MATERIALS FOR A HYPOTHESIS

The statements in the immediately preceding section probably sound reasonable to the reader. They are handed down by tradition, seem logical, and are based on what any of us might possibly deduce from what he thinks is his own experience and observation. But they are not yet economic theory; still less a theory validated by systematic and careful observation and applicable to the world we live in. They first need to be woven into a hypothesis, or a system of consistent hypotheses, which can be tested by observation of the actual behavior of buyers and sellers in the present economic order.

It is already clear, however, what sort of relationships such a system of hypotheses would seek to explain. It would have to do with the effects of demand and supply on price and with the effects of price on demand and supply. It would probably also have to include some influences other than demand or supply affecting prices—for example, competition or the lack of it.

Apparently, an active demand favors the existence of higher prices, and an abundant supply favors the existence of lower prices. This is an idea familiar to all of us, without any study of economics.

Now let us proceed to state a hypothesis.

Simplifying Assumptions. Let us begin by making assumptions that will simplify the task of analysis, even though in some markets such assumptions may be contrary to fact, and even though any hypothesis based upon them may have to be modified if it is to be applied as an explanation of what really happens.

The first assumption is that we are considering what happens only in a relatively short period. This period, let us say, is so short that during its span the buyers' incomes and tastes will not greatly change, new products will not come on the market, producers will not be able to enlarge their plants or introduce new technical improvements. Their costs for any given output will not change. Economists usually call such a period the *short run*.

The next step is to define exactly what we mean by demand and supply.

Demand. Demand arises, according to the hypothesis, from the wants of individuals, whatever those wants may be. At this point we are not concerned with questions about how wants are determined; such considerations may be introduced at a later stage, if necessary.

In economics, however, demand does *not* mean merely a desire to have something. It also means ability to buy a product at a given price, that is, "effective demand." A person who wants something but has no money with which to buy it obviously cannot affect what goes on in a market.

If regularities of buying behavior depending solely on price are to be established, we must imagine a purchaser whose buying behavior might be reliably foretold if we knew the price of what he was demanding. Economic theorists have assumed, for the purpose of the theory, that there is such a paragon of reasonable behavior, sometimes known as the "economic man," who is completely rational, who recognizes his own material interest, and who has full knowledge of the situation.

With these assumptions, it is possible to draw a graph which illustrates the demand of one person for one kind of article in the short run. A specific article is generally used as an illustration—eggs, apples, loaves of bread. This is a hazardous practice, because if the demand of any one real person for any one real commodity could be charted from actual observation, the resulting curve might not comply with the assumptions made. Let us therefore retain for this graph a rigorous anonymity. And let us remember that it is not intended to be a picture of something that has occurred—as if we could read it off a meter, as the gas company reads the consumption of gas—but rather of what we should expect to occur, granted our assumptions.

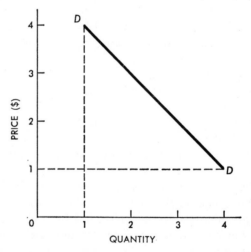

Fig. 9.1. DEMAND BY ONE PERSON FOR ONE KIND OF ARTICLE.

(Any reader who has difficulty in understanding this graph may refer back to Chapter 7.)

If a horizontal line is drawn from any point on the curve over to the vertical axis, it will show a price which the purchaser may be charged. If a vertical line is drawn from the same point down to the horizontal axis, it will show the quantity he will buy at that price.

Thus, according to this imaginary curve, our individual buyer will take 1 unit if the price is $4 apiece. At lower prices he will buy more and more until at the price of $1, he will buy 4 units.

There is usually more than just one buyer for articles of any one kind. At any rate, the simplified hypothesis assumes many buyers. If there were many buyers, we might add up all their demands at each price and thus derive a curve showing the demand in the market at any possible price. Though there would be variations among the individual demands, buyers as a group would presumably buy more at low prices and less at high prices. A graph similar to that for the individual would illustrate this assumption. It would probably differ somewhat from the first curve, however.

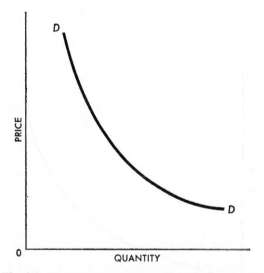

Fig. 9.2. MARKET DEMAND FOR ONE KIND OF ARTICLE.

Note that the curves of demand, both for the individual and for the market, *slopes down to the right,* on the assumption that the lower the price, the greater the demand. This probably is usually the case, but there may be exceptions.

Supply. The hypothesis must embody simplifying assumptions about supply, just as it does about demand. Supply must, of course, refer to just one kind of article—the same kind illustrated in the demand curve. This supply must mean, moreover, *the amount offered for sale* at various prices in the market in question, not the total amount in the world or in the warehouses of the suppliers. This assumption is necessary if we are to exclude from consideration all variations of supply except those arising from differences in price. For example, if a formerly scarce article should become abundant because of an improvement in the technology of production, the change in supply could not logically be pictured in the same curve intended to show the differing quantities which would be offered for sale according to the level of the market price. Furthermore, such a change could not occur in the short run, as previously defined.

With these assumptions, we are in a position to draw a typical supply curve that may logically be superimposed on the same graph that contained our typical demand curve. If there are a large number of sellers and if they compete with one another in the same market, no one of them will have the power to fix the price charged to the buyers; he will have to accept the market price or else not sell his goods at all. We may suppose, however, that more units will be offered for sale at a higher price than at a lower one. For example, if prices are low, some producers may be unable to produce and come out even, because their costs are higher than those of other producers.

If, as in the case of the individual purchaser, we add up the supplies offered by all sellers in the market at each possible price, we may thus derive an imaginary supply curve that looks something like this:

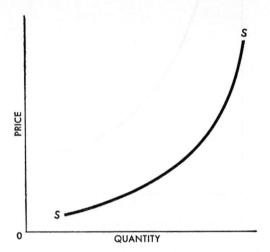

Fig. 9.3. MARKET SUPPLY FOR ONE KIND OF ARTICLE.

This curve, it will be observed, *slopes generally upward*—that is, it depicts the supposition that the higher the price, the more will be offered for sale. Near the top, its slope approximates the vertical, since presumably the total possible supply is limited in the short run. Above a certain price, no more can be put on the market, no matter how high the offering price may be. Near the bottom, the curve approximates the horizontal; this implies that if the price dropped below a certain point, the article could not be offered for sale, since it would not be possible for anyone to deal in the article if he had to give it away.

Supply, Demand, and Price. We are now in a position to put our graphs of supply and demand together to see what meaning we can derive from them. (This graph illustrates the so-called "law" of supply and demand.)

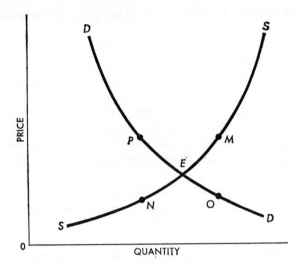

Fig. 9.4. MARKET SUPPLY, DEMAND, AND PRICE FOR ONE KIND OF ARTICLE.

The curves *D–D* and *S–S*, it will be noted, are the same ones drawn separately in our previous graphs of demand and supply. Where these curves intersect, at *E*, the quantity demanded exactly equals the quantity supplied. The price asked by sellers also exactly equals the price offered by buyers. Obviously, at this point (*E*) sales will be made, provided all the assumptions depicted in the graph are fulfilled in fact. The combination of this price and this quantity is unique; it does not appear anywhere else in the graph. The graph would seem to imply that, if the curves were of such shape and in such a position that they did not intersect at all, no sales would be made, since buyers would not be willing to pay any price that sellers would be willing to charge.

The graph also implies that no sales will long be made at any point other than *E*, on either of these curves. If the quantity offered were on any point of the supply curve (*S–S*) to the right of *E*, a point which we may call *M*, the price would be higher than purchasers on the whole would pay for that quantity, and so competition among sellers would quickly reduce the price. If the quantity offered were at any point to the left of *E* on the supply curve, a point which we may call *N*, the demand of the purchasers would be so great as to raise the price quickly and so increase the quantity offered.

If the amount demanded by buyers were at the right of *E* on the demand curve (*D–D*), a point which we may call *O*, the price that they would offer for this quantity would be less than would bring the requisite supply to market. They could buy *some* at this price, but not so much as they would offer to buy at it, and their competition for a relatively scarce supply would raise the price. If the amount demanded by buyers were at the left of *E* on the curve *D–D*, say at a point which we may call *P*, the price offered for that quantity would be so high as to tempt sellers to

offer more than could be sold at that price; competition would then reduce the price.

The intersection of a supply curve and a demand curve therefore
marks an "equilibrium" price—the only point at which demand and
supply are equal. Just as a pair of scales wavers up and down when something is being weighed, demand and supply may waver about this equilibrium price, but they will, according to the hypothesis, always tend to
settle at this price. Sometimes the equilibrium price is called the
"normal" price. This price is seldom the actual price found in any
market, but it is a *norm* which the market price tends to approximate. So
runs the theory.

Note that the notion of an equilibrium price, or normal price, de-
pends on the assumption that there is competition both among buyers
and among sellers.

Changes in Demand and Supply. One of the important simplifying assumptions made in the foregoing analysis was that demand and
supply were affected by nothing else than price, so that the amount
bought and sold on the market varied only according to the price. Higher
or lower demand or supply accordingly would mean merely a higher or
lower point on a particular curve or schedule.

There are continual changes, however, in both demand and supply
which arise from sources other than changes in price; these changes do
not have such noticeable effects in what economists, for lack of a better
term, call the "short run," but over a longer period they are frequently of
major importance. Incomes change, as do styles, tastes, and requirements,
so that the money which consumers are willing to spend for any one kind
of article at a given price may be less or more at one time than at
another. Technological changes play an important role in these variations. The introduction of farm tractors, for example, decreased to the
vanishing point the demand for work horses, and this, in turn, decreased
the demand for hay.

Similar developments affect supply in ways quite different from the
consequences of a rise or fall in prices. Producers are continually changing their work orders according to their estimates of future market conditions; businessmen are getting into or going out of particular lines of
business; new products come into production; and technical processes
change. If one should try to plot a graph of demand and supply like that
illustrated on page 89 by obtaining data from an actual market, provided such data were obtainable, the graph might well be out of date by
the time it was plotted.

A shift in either demand or supply not depending on the short-run
price situation in any market—that is, a change similar to those mentioned
in the immediately preceding paragraphs—must be pictured by drawing
an entirely new pair of curves. If, for example, the total demand for a
given article increased, so that at a whole series of prices the demand
would be greater than before, the whole demand curve would have to be

placed higher on the graph and further to the right. On the graph below, let us represent the old demand curve by D_0–D_0 and the demand
curve after the above change by D_1–D_1.

If a general reduction in demand for any one kind of article occurred, fewer would be bought at any given price. This situation would
be pictured by a shift of the whole demand curve downward and to the
left. We may call this new demand curve D_2–D_2.

If the whole market supply were enlarged so that more could be
bought at any given price, the supply curve would naturally show this
by a shift of the supply curve downward (representing lower prices) and
to the right (representing larger quantities). We may illustrate this condition in the graph by a line like S_1–S_1.

Or if the market supply were diminished so that there were less to
be obtained at any given price, the curve would naturally shift upward
and to the left, thus showing fewer at each price. This curve may be
called S_2–S_2. All these possibilities are illustrated in Figure 9/5.

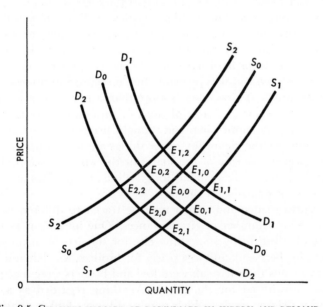

Fig. 9.5 CHANGES UPWARD OR DOWNWARD IN SUPPLY AND DEMAND.

The new equilibrium points are identified by E, with subscripts representing first, the demand curve, and second, the supply curve. Thus,
$E_{1,2}$ is the intersection of a higher demand curve, D_1–D_1, with a supply
curve representing a diminished supply, S_2–S_2.

Elasticity and the Slope of the Curve. Suppose a store manager
were thinking of making a reduction in the price of an article—say, shirts
—in order to sell more. Would he gain or lose by doing so? That would
depend on *how many* more he could sell at any one reduction in price.
What he presumably wants is the largest possible *sales revenue* (unless he

is simply selling off surplus stock). The revenue from the sales of any article is, of course, the price multiplied by the number sold.

Suppose, for example, he had been selling 1,000 shirts a month at $5; the revenue would be $5,000. If, as a result of reducing the price to $4.95, he could sell 1,500 shirts a month, his revenue would obviously rise considerably—to $7,425. But if, by this reduction of five cents a shirt, he sold only ten shirts more than before, he would lose a little revenue—the extra $49.50 he would take in by selling the ten additional shirts would be less than the $50 he would sacrifice by selling the original thousand at five cents less apiece.

The relationship of changes in demand to changes in price is called "elasticity of demand with respect to price." (There may be also "elasticity of supply with respect to price.") If changes in price do not greatly affect demand, the demand is less elastic with regard to price than if changes in price do greatly affect demand. The word "elastic" carries its own image—a demand which easily stretches or shrinks according to price is highly elastic; one which remains almost the same is less so.

A few examples of low or high elasticity follow. If you own a car and can readily afford to operate it whenever you have use for it, your demand for gasoline will not depend much on variations in the price of gasoline. If you are a habitual cigarette smoker and ration yourself to, say, one pack a day, you will probably buy no more and no less regardless of the price, unless it rises or falls more than a few cents a pack. But if you were a speculator in shares of stock or bushels of wheat, you would probably try to buy more when you thought prices were low. In the case of the gasoline or the cigarettes, other things are more important to you than the price; in the case of the shares or the wheat, price is almost the only consideration. Your demand for gasoline or cigarettes would be less elastic than your demand for shares.

Differences in demand which may be traced to differences in price may arise from a number of circumstances. One important factor is the possibility of substituting something else for the article in question. At high prices for beefsteak and low prices for broilers, the demand for steak is likely to be less than if steak were low and broilers were high; one can readily be substituted for the other. Anything regarded as a luxury— that is, an article or service which potential buyers find it relatively easy to forego—will usually have a demand more elastic in relation to price than anything which purchasers feel they must have if they can possibly afford it. An article which we want in relatively fixed but small amounts —for example, salt—the cost of which does not constitute a large part of the budget, is not likely to meet a very different demand in response to changes in price.

If you were to draw a graph illustrating the elasticity of demand for any article, it would of course indicate the number sold at each of a whole series of prices. If demand increased rapidly with small price reductions, the demand curve would naturally slope very gently to the right—since prices are shown on the vertical, or y, axis, and quantities are shown on the horizontal, or *x*, axis. But if large price reductions brought only small increases in demand, the curve would slope down very sharply. (*D–D₁* is more elastic; *D–D₂* is less elastic.) This statement applies, however, only to reductions of price from *D*, the point of intersection.

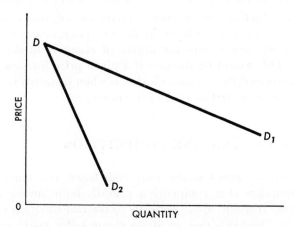

Fig. 9.6. DIFFERENCE IN ELASTICITY OF DEMAND.

In a graph showing a demand curve, the revenue obtainable at a given price is represented by the area of a rectangle formed by drawing a horiztontal line from the price axis to the curve, and then a vertical line to the horizontal axis. The area of the rectangle is, of course, the price

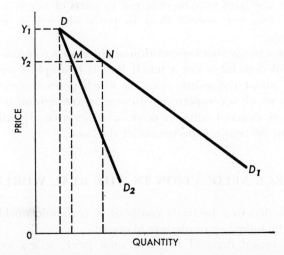

Fig. 9.7. In this graph, the original price is represented by Y_1, the price after the reduction by Y_2. With little elasticity in demand, the revenue obtained after the reduction is shown by the rectangle with its upper right corner at *M*, which is but little larger than the rectangle with its corner at *D*. Compare this with the rectangle with its corner at *N*.

multiplied by the quantity. Let us try this out on the inelastic and elastic curves shown in the previous graph. Suppose we make the same price reduction in both cases. The two rectangles formed by using the elastic curve D–D_1 show that there is a substantial increase in both demand and revenue at the lower price. But the two rectangles formed by using the inelastic curve D–D_2 show that the demand is so little increased by this price reduction that revenue is increased but little if at all.

A demand might be inelastic in the low price ranges but elastic in the higher price ranges; and the degree of elasticity might increase as prices rose. This would be the case if a given price increase (in dollars and cents) decreased the demand much less when it started in a low price range that when it started in a high price range.

SUPPLY, DEMAND, AND COMPETITION

The theory presented in this chapter is based, one must not forget, on the assumption that competition prevails both among sellers and among buyers. It would apply perfectly to the real situation only if competition were "perfect"—that is, if no single seller could exercise any appreciable control over the total supply in the market, and if no single buyer could exercise control over the demand.

There are many markets in our economy in which competition is far from perfect. We shall briefly look into them later. Insofar as such markets exist, the law of supply and demand of course works haltingly or imperfectly. The distribution of goods, of services, of income, and the allocation of resources may be different in parts of our economy where competition does not prevail than in parts where it is more closely approximated.

This is not to say that competition ought always to prevail. The law of supply and demand is not a moral law; it is simply a description of what occurs under the assumptions on which it rests—one of the most important of which is competition. Insofar as competition is not perfect, such things as demand, supply, price, and resource allocation will be different from the results expected under the "law."

RESOURCE ALLOCATION IN THE REAL WORLD

Theoretically, in a perfectly competitive economic world, we might expect that the following results would occur:

Since increased demand tends to raise price, sellers would be encouraged to offer for sale the articles or services for which demand is large or rising. Since the producers who offered the best qualities at the lowest prices would have the largest sales, the more skillful or efficient would tend to survive and prosper. The net result would be that scarce resources would be allocated generally according to the desires of consumers.

To a large extent this is what does occur in any market economy, even if it is far from being purely competitive. We do rely on private enterprise and markets for production and distribution of a very large share of the goods and services that make up our national product or income. Even though there are in this economic sector many departures from complete competition, it does act—though imperfectly—to make a reasonably satisfactory allocation of resources to the goods and services which it provides.

This is, however, only part of the story, and those who describe our economy solely as a "free enterprise, competitive, market economy" are distorting the actual situation. Important exceptions exist, many of them adopted in the private interest of business organizations and many others adopted for the purpose of serving the interest of the people of the nation or large sections of them. We shall have to examine these exceptions in order to understand the operation of our economy as a whole and to render any intelligent judgment as to its performance in desirable allocation of resources. We must therefore consider such matters as these:

1. Business organization and practices
2. Money and its regulation
3. Role of government
4. Labor organizations and institutions
5. Agriculture and its problems
6. Consumer behavior
7. Role of foreign trade.

For an example of the operation of demand and supply in two actual markets, see Chapters 28 and 29.

QUESTIONS

1. If a common necessity like food should become so scarce that everyone could not have all he wanted, who would get the food under each of the following market conditions?
   (a) A free competitive market.
   (b) Maximum prices below the equilibrium level, under governmental price control but with no other restriction.
   (c) Prices controlled as in (b) and an effective rationing system.

2. Would you expect elasticity of demand to be comparatively high, low, or medium for the following articles? Explain your reasons in each case.
   (a) Diamonds
   (b) Structural steel
   (c) Pepper
   (d) Used cars in good condition
   (e) Porterhouse steak
   (f) Medicines prescribed by physicians
   (g) Records of classical music

10 /   BUSINESS ORGANIZATION   /

SOLE PROPRIETORSHIP

Anyone may start a business with no legal formalities, unless the business requires a license of some kind—for example, vending on the streets, trucking, plumbing, or doctoring. The individual owner of a business assumes full responsibility for it.

If the business succeeds, the owner is entitled to the profit; if it loses money, he still has to pay the bills it has incurred. In collecting these charges, creditors have a right to lay claim not only to whatever the owner has put into the business but also, if that is insufficient, to any or all of his personal possessions—house, savings account, and the rest. If the business fails and is forced to cease operations because the owner cannot pay, he may ask a court to declare him bankrupt. Bankruptcy can free him from future obligation for existing bills he cannot pay. He may legally start again with a clean slate, but with impaired credit.

PARTNERSHIP

A business enterprise frequently demands more capital than a single individual can supply; also the varying skills and associations of two or more persons may strengthen the chances for its success. For this reason the partnership is a common form of business organization. Partnerships are formed by agreement among the partners. (The Ford Motor Co. started as a partnership.)

A partnership agreement is a legal contract and, as such, is subject to the law of contracts. If any partner should violate the agreement, the others may ask for a court order compelling him to desist from the violation; they may also sue him for damages. Partnership agreements usually specify what each partner is to contribute to the business, what his special duties (if any) are to be, and what share in profits each shall have.

The law of contracts does not depend in the main on any statute passed by a legislative body, but on what is called the "common law"— a tradition of Anglo-Saxon justice built up by a long series of court decisions in equity cases. A court of equity adjudicates disputes between persons and, as such, is distinguished from a court in which a government official prosecutes a supposed offender for violation of a statute passed by a legislative body.

The legal obligations of each partner toward those who sell goods and services to the business are exactly the same as the obligations of a single owner. Each partner is liable for all the debts of the business. This "unlimited liability" was formerly believed to strengthen the credit of a partnership, especially if one or more of the partners possessed a good deal of wealth aside from his interest in the particular business. The fact that J. P. Morgan and Co., once a leading private banking firm, was for years a partnership doubtless added something to its prestige. All law firms are partnerships, they are not permitted to incorporate.

If one partner dies or resigns, a new agreement has to be drawn. If new partners are admitted to the firm, the agreement must be appropriately modified. A partnership does not automatically survive changes in ownership or participation; affirmative and appropriate action must be taken in each instance if the partnership is not to be liquidated when an existing partner resigns or dies.

CORPORATION

Unlike the individual proprietorship or the partnership, the corporation is legally a creation of the "sovereign"—that is, the state or government. It exists by virtue of a charter which grants it privileges not available to unincorporated businesses and which may impose special obligations on it in return.

Most early corporations were formed to carry out purposes important to the government; the Virginia Company was chartered by the British crown to colonize North America. Corporations of this kind were frequently granted monopolies as an inducement to persons with money to risk the large sums of capital necessary for a great enterprise. Later, canal and railroad corporations were granted the right of eminent domain, by virtue of which they could take, at a reasonable compensation, any land needed for rights of way whether or not the owner wished to sell—a privilege ordinarily belonging only to government itself. In addition, such companies frequently were subsidized.

The most important privilege granted to incorporated companies, however, turned out to be that of "limited liability," which every incorporated business now possesses. The corporation itself is regarded by the law as a person; unsatisfied creditors can levy on anything it owns. But those who become owners by buying shares in the corporation risk only the money they put into the company. If it should be unable to pay its debts, they might lose what they had invested in it but not their other property. The corporation usually notifies the public that it has this privilege—in Britain by the abbreviation "Ltd." following its name; in the United States by "Inc." if the word "corporation" does not appear in its title.

This distinction from a partnership is important to the owners of a corporation, and by the same token it is almost a *sine qua non* in raising capital for a big business such as a railroad or a steel company. Large amounts of capital must often be collected from hundreds if not thousands of investors, who are willing to risk a moderate sum in any given business enterprise but are not willing to stake all their properties in a venture in which they take no active part (as partners usually do) and concerning whose affairs they can know only what the management tells them.

Another advantage of the corporation over the partnership, as far as the investor is concerned, is that its charter fixes the form of its government. Owners may usually vote for members of the board of directors, having one vote for each share of ownership. The directors appoint the executives of the business. Owners may come and go through purchase and sale of stock, but the corporation itself is immortal, so long as it can pay its bills and taxes or is not voluntarily dissolved. If a partner dies, the partnership is automatically dissolved; when a stockholder dies, the estate of the deceased simply steps into his shoes.

In return for the privileges granted to corporations by their charters, few duties are exacted by the state, except sometimes in the case of public utilities. Ordinarily, all the corporation is compelled to do in return for its charter is to pay an incorporation fee and other taxes, and to observe the terms of the charter in regard to elections of officers, stock issues, and the like.

When the corporate form of business organization first came into use in the United States, the charter of each corporation was granted only by a special act of Congress or a state legislature. Most of the corporations were large institutions owning canals, railroads, or banks. Later, when the advantages of the corporate form were more clearly understood by ordinary business, states began to pass general incorporation laws, under which corporate charters could be obtained from administrative bureaus by compliance with certain broad conditions and by payment of a nominal fee.

Today not only big concerns but also most partnerships and many individually owned enterprises have changed to corporations. In this way risks can be segregated. A man with several interests can incorporate each one. A man of moderate means can start a small business without risking everything he has.

One corporation may legally own another unless the effect is substantially to lessen competition or unless such ownership is specifically forbidden in the industry in question. Many corporations which find it desirable to have a separate plant or division to make materials or parts or to do some other specialized job, incorporate it separately and control it by owning its stock. Sometimes a new and risky venture undertaken by an established corporation is itself incorporated.

Many large corporations whose names are nationally known do not make or sell anything but act as "holding (or owning) corporations" of other incorporated companies, which attend to the actual manufacture or sale. A corporation that is wholly owned by another is called a "subsidiary corporation." Companies owned by holding corporations are frequently also called "operating companies." A familiar example of the holding corporation is American Telephone and Telegraph Co., which owns or has a controlling interest in the stock of local and regional companies that operate the telephones and collect the payments from subscribers.

Most American corporations are chartered by one or another of the states rather than by the federal government, even if they do a nation-wide or interstate business. Under the United States Constitution a business incorporated in any state can freely do business in any other; though, if it does an interstate business, it is of course subject to any applicable federal laws regulating commerce and to laws of the states in which it operates.

The privilege of incorporation does not extend to lawyers or doctors, in the practice of their profession.

COMBINATIONS AND THE LAW

Most states in the union, and the federal government itself, have passed statutes forbidding monopolistic practices, or "combinations in restraint of trade." These laws are based on the almost universal belief that a monopolistic seller has an unfair advantage over competitive buyers, and that a monopolistic buyer has an unfair advantage over competitive sellers. They are also in accord with the classical economic theory that a system based on private enterprise and free markets will not serve the general good unless competition prevails.

Soon after the Civil War large industrial concerns in the United States began to restrict competition by voluntary agreements among themselves. These agreements sometimes set prices, limited output, divided the market among competitors geographically or otherwise, and pooled profits according to agreed shares, no matter how much or how little any one competitor earned in a given year. Such agreements, however, usually did not work well because some member of the combination would violate the provisions in his own interest. In that case the only remedy open to the others was to sue the violator for damages arising from breach of contract. But the equity courts would not award such damages, because of the tradition of the common law that contracts in restraint of trade are contrary to the general good and therefore cannot be enforced.

In order to get around this obstacle, businessmen intent on limiting competition sought other devices. One widely used was the "trust." The trust has long been a perfectly legal and respectable institution for safe-guarding heirs against mismanagement of an estate left by a parent or other relative. The property is placed under the control of trustees, who are given the right to manage it according to provisions set forth by the owner in the deed of trust. What could be more simple than for competi-tors to place the shares of their several companies under the control of a single group of trustees, instructed to manage all the businesses concerned and distribute the income to the owners?

Trusts used for purposes of business monopoly were outlawed by many states, as well as by the federal Sherman Act of 1890, commonly called the Sherman Antitrust Act. This law forbade "every contract, combination in the form of trust or otherwise, or conspiracy, in restraint of trade or commerce among the several states." Anyone who "shall monopolize, or attempt to monopolize, or combine or conspire . . . to monopolize any part of the trade or commerce among the several states" may legally be prosecuted under the criminal law, enjoined by a federal court to desist from monopolistic practices, or sued for triple damages by any private person who suffers injury. But the law proved to be diffi-cult to enforce.

An attempt to strengthen the law resulted in the Clayton Act of 1914, supplementing the broad language of the Sherman Act, which often had been nullified in effect by judicial interpretation in particular cases. The Clayton Act outlawed specific practices such as interlocking director-ates (by which several companies would be linked because their boards of directors were partly composed of the same persons); price discrimina-tion among buyers (sometimes used to penalize those who did not buy exclusively from one firm); exclusive selling contracts; "tying contracts" (which forced a customer who wanted to buy one product from a pro-ducer also to buy something else, made by the same company, which he might not want). But it forbade these practices only when they tended substantially to lessen competition or promote monopoly, and this situa-tion again left the door open to judicial interpretation.

In 1914 Congress also set up the Federal Trade Commission to inves-tigate and forbid "unfair methods of competition" which had been used in the past by large concerns to harass weaker competitors. But when, after investigation and hearings, the Commission ordered firms to "cease and desist" from such practices, appeals to the courts frequently resulted in voidance of the orders by judicial decision.

In some industries conditions do not favor the existence of dominant large concerns. Where numerous and competing firms prevail, a common practice is to organize associations of the competitors for mutual benefit, known as "trade associations." The trade association has no police powers over its members except through expulsion for violation of its codes. It renders many services, including statistical information and advice on accounting practices. But in some cases these services may approximate monopoly in the sense of restricting price competition—as when the association publishes standard prices, which are observed by tacit agreement; or installs standard accounting systems according to which the actual costs of individual firms are ignored and, instead, uniform costs for the industry are used in submitting estimates or rendering bills. It is the business of the Federal Trade Commission to prevent, by "cease and desist" orders, "unfair methods of competition" forbidden by the federal law. In a "trade practice conference" with any industry it can work out a code which forbids practices adjudged "unfair" for that industry.

HOLDING COMPANIES USED FOR MERGERS

Even before the Sherman law was enacted, companies had begun to merge through the device of the holding corporation. A new company would be formed to own the several merging companies; the stockholders of the latter would exchange their shares for the shares of the holding, or "parent" corporation, on a pro-rata basis.

The Clayton Act forbade holding companies to acquire the stock of subsidiaries when the effect was substantially to lessen competition or to promote monopoly. Yet it was not easy to prove in court that such mergers had a monopolistic purpose. Their promoters argued that they were interested in achieving economies through large-scale operation, or that they wished to assure themselves of a continuous supply of desirable materials or to strengthen their organizations in order to be in a better position to raise capital for expansion. Did monopoly exist when a merger controlled not 100 percent of a market but 50, 70, or even 90 percent?

Court decisions held that mere size was not forbidden by law; that the holding company as a form of organization was not outlawed; that Congress could not have intended to forbid "reasonable" restraints of trade if those restraints were incidental to some other benefit to the public.

Agreements among business competitors to fix prices are *per se* contrary to law. Such agreements are just as unlawful for many small competitors as they are for a few big ones. The courts have held them illegal regardless of the degree of price fixing or the benefits which may follow. The only exceptions have been created by specific statutes, such as the law permitting farm cooperatives to act as sellers for the members or the emergency price fixing allowed by the National Industrial Recovery Act during the depression of the early 1930's (subsequently declared unconstitutional). There is additional legal confusion about the policies of mergers (or industries dominated by a few concerns). Here arise problems of size; of "price leadership," in which a price announced by a dominant concern is adopted by others; the "rule of reason," mentioned earlier; and the degree of control exercised by a large concern. What is "reasonable" restraint exercised in any specific case? Here no simple criteria of judgment have been developed.

The government in its attempt to curb monopoly also suffered from political influence on the executive or prosecuting authorities, and the fact that appropriations for the purpose left the Department of Justice without sufficient funds for the long and expensive litigation which could be financed by big corporations in their own defense. During wars, too, the government had to depend on existing companies, many of them large, to fill its orders for munitions and supplies, and could not fight them at the very moment when it needed their cooperation.

MONOPOLIES SANCTIONED BY LAW

Monopolies or monopolistic practices of some kinds are sanctioned by law and in many cases are even created by government in the public interest.

Some monopolies cannot be dissolved under the law. Among these are monopolies resulting from possession of secret processes or unique skills, which the possessors cannot be compelled to share. Ownership of limited sources of raw material (for example, sulfur) is also not illegal in the United States. A company which grows big without using illegal methods may obtain a virtually monopolistic position.

In granting a patent, the government deliberately awards a monopoly —for seventeen years—to the inventor. The purpose of this grant is to encourage technical progress. Nobody would begrudge the inventor the sole right to profit from his ingenuity for a limited period. The inventor may, of course, sell his patent. If he does so, it usually falls into the hands of an existing corporation. Indeed, companies with industrial research laboratories expect any patents based on ideas developed by their employees to be turned over to the company.

Any owner of a patent may license its use by others. Companies in the same field owning valuable patents may thus license their patents to one another, on the basis of an understanding that no one else be admitted to such a patent pool or cross-licensing system. Such devices may easily become the unifying factor in an industrial monopoly, far removed from the original purpose of rewarding an individual inventor for his originality. Courts may in such cases decide that the antitrust laws are being violated, patent or no patent, but the issues are far from clear.

What about the seventeen-year patent limitation? If only one patent were involved, the termination of the patent period might end the whole monopoly exercised by corporations owning the patent or licensed under it. But when numerous patents are involved, they usually are of different dates and new patents representing variations or improvements are almost invariably taken out before the old ones expire. The expiration of a single patent is not of much use to a possible competitor when a monopoly is built on a whole system of patents, continually changing by addition of new methods and devices. There has been much agitation for change of the patent law to avoid abuses of this kind.

Legal monopolies for long periods are customarily granted by franchises to companies engaged in communication or transportation, water systems, supply of electrical power, and other public utility. In such cases the public interest is served by the absence of competition. It would be a costly nuisance if everyone had to subscribe to the service of fifteen or twenty telephone companies in order to be sure of communicating with anyone he might want to call. Streets are not wide enough to accommodate innumerable bus lines on the same routes or a multiplicity of water mains. Besides, the cost would be prohibitive. A single company selling electrical power in a given community can distribute it much more cheaply than numerous companies, each of which would have to set up its own cables and wires. In such cases the place of competition in keeping prices down and service up is filled by public regulatory commissions or other authorities. If these do not work well, outright public ownership may be substituted.

Exemptions from the laws against combination are sometimes granted in instances where unlimited competition is felt to be so injurious to the competitors as to be contrary to the public interest. This was the case, generally, with labor organizations, which long suffered because antitrust laws were applied to them. Another instance is the effort by government to maintain prices of farm products above the level which would result in a free, competitive market. Farm organizations have more (though not complete) immunity from antitrust laws than do labor organizations. Retailers have been protected in many states by laws authorizing maintenance of retail prices set by the manufacturers of certain types of products, though such laws are falling into disuse. The chief argument in favor of retail price maintenance legislation is that it protects the small retailer against extinction because of the competition of large chain stores, department stores, discount houses and the like. Whether this price maintenance imposes too great a burden on the consumer is a much-debated question.

The Webb-Pomerence Act exempted associations of corporations from the antitrust laws in selling abroad. Most foreign countries do not have such laws, and combinations or cartels are dominant in many branches of international trade. The theory was that American business must be allowed to enter combinations for the sole purpose of selling abroad if it were to have a fair share of foreign trade. Unfortunately, however, agreements of this sort have often had the practical effect of limiting foreign competition with big companies in the United States.

BIG BUSINESS AND SMALL

Few important American industries have been subject to complete monopoly, at least for very long. The cases usually cited are the original

Standard Oil Company (before it was dissolved into a number of companies under the Sherman law); the United Shoe Machinery Company (which did not sell its machinery but rented it to shoe manufacturers, and only to those who would use its complete line); and the Aluminum Company of America (before World War II, when the government, because of its great need for aluminum, encouraged competitors, and even built new plants and rented them to two competing companies, who subsequently bought the plants).

The situation prevalent in some important industries is that a few big companies are responsible for a large percentage of the product, while there are a rather limited number of smaller competitors. One measure of concentration in manufacture, frequently cited, is shown in the following table, based on the United States Census of Manufactures for 1947.

TABLE 10/1

PERCENTAGE OF SHIPMENTS BY FOUR LEADING CONCERNS
IN SELECTED INDUSTRIES WITH OUTPUT OF
$500 MILLION OR MORE (1947)

	Percent of Shipments (by value)
Primary Aluminum (3 companies)	100
Small-Arms Ammunition	99.9
Telephone Equipment	95.7
Electric Lamps	90.8
Locomotives	90.7
Cigarettes	90.4
Petroleum and Coal Products	88.2
Steam Engines and Turbines	87.6
Linoleum	80.3
Tin Cans and Other Tinware	77.8
Rubber Tires and Tubes	76.6
Distilled Liquors	74.6
Biscuits, Crackers, Pretzels	71.5
Steelworks and Rolling Mills	44.7
Petroleum Refiners	37.3
Plumbers' Supplies	34.7
Woolen and Worsted Goods	28.1
Footwear (except rubber)	27.9
Bread and Other Bakery Products	16.4

This table clearly shows a wide range in concentration even in big manufacturing industries. (Such measures of concentration are rather rough, since not all the firms concerned may make strictly identical products.) If similar statistics were available for distributive industries, they would probably show a still wider range; there are many more small retailers than small manufacturers, although nationwide retailing concerns with large volume of sales are prominent.

A picture of concentration in manufacturing industries as it existed in 1935 is shown in the following figure. This sort of chart is known as a "scatter diagram." It indicates what percentage of the total output in each of 136 industries was turned out by the four leading firms in the industry, and what percentage of the total employees in the industry these four employed.

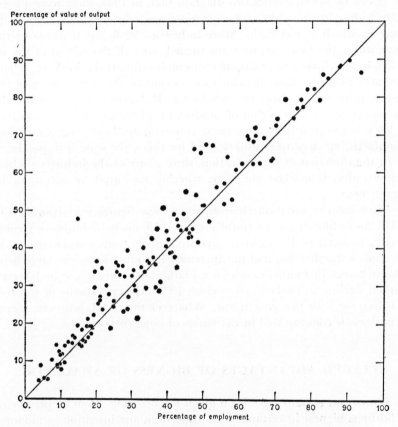

Fig. 10.1. CONCENTRATION OF EMPLOYMENT AND OUTPUT IN LEADING FOUR FIRMS, 136 MANUFACTURING INDUSTRIES, UNITED STATES, 1935. (Gideon Rosenbluth, "Measures of Concentration," *Business Concentration and Price Policy*, p. 91. Published by Princeton University Press [1955] for the National Bureau of Economic Research.)

In this figure, each dot represents the four leading firms. Let us look, for example, at the dot at the extreme upper right, which lies almost on the diagonal line. Looking across at the vertical axis, you will see that in this industry the four turned out about 90 percent of the product. Looking down at the horizontal axis, you will see that the same four employed about 90 percent of the workers in the industry.

At the extreme lower left, you will find a dot representing another industry. In this industry it appears that the four leading firms turned out about 4 percent of the product and employed a slightly smaller percentage of the employees. Between these two extremes are scattered the dots representing the other industries covered by the data.

These 136 industries are half of all the industries listed by the National Resources Committee—every second one on its list, so that the sample is representative.

It can be inferred from this diagram that, in 1935, there were a good many industries in which concentration was relatively low, as well as many in which it was high. More industries lie below than above the point where the four leading firms turned out half the output of the industry in which they were situated, or employed half the workers. There were still plenty of cases in which the output or the employment of the leading firms was far from overwhelming. If, however, one thinks of the percentage of the total value of product of all manufacturing industries which was turned out by the leading concerns, or of the percentage of all manufacturing employees who worked for them, the scale is tipped heavily in the direction of concentration, since many of the industries where concentration is marked are large, whether measured by output or by employment.

How has the situation changed since these figures were compiled in 1935? According to a study (published in 1955) made by Professor George Stigler, formerly of Columbia University, in the twenty years covered in the study concentration had not increased in industries where large firms exist, whereas in industries where no large firms exist there had been a marked decline in concentration since 1935. Other students of the subject disagree with this conclusion. Whatever the trend, however, plenty of business is concentrated in the hands of large corporations.

ALLEGED ADVANTAGES OF BIGNESS OR SMALLNESS

Numerous reasons have been given for bringing about or preserving of business bigness in certain areas, aside from any intention to monopolize markets. Big companies may compete; bigness is not identical with monopoly. Yet big companies may exercise more control over prices than small ones.

1. Economies of Scale. A mass-production industry which requires large investment in plant and machinery—for example, petroleum refining, or automobiles—is not profitable for really small concerns. New competitors of established companies cannot hope to survive unless they can assemble enough capital and skill to operate on a relatively large scale. In almost any industry, however, the largest companies are not always the most efficient.

2. Advantages in Marketing. In modern mass markets, many consumers habitually buy products with an established brand name. It takes huge expenditures in advertising and merchandising to establish and maintain widespread acceptance of this name, and only relatively big companies can afford such expenditures. Cigarettes are an example. Almost any moderately small firm can afford the necessary investment in cigarette-making machinery; the big problem is to sell a cigarette hitherto unknown to the public. It would be very difficult to introduce a new brand "on a shoestring."

3. Advantage in Technical Advance. In rapidly advancing technical fields—chemicals, plastics, or electronics—research and development of new products play an important role. Big companies with extensive research laboratories, with facilities for testing and perfecting new devices or commodities, and with capital to risk in training work forces and in trying out markets may have an advantage over small concerns. Nevertheless, many inventions are made by individuals, and improvements are frequently introduced by relatively small firms.

Mergers. Large concerns are often created by mergers. Varied motives, aside from monopolistic control, exist for mergers, such as (1) the desire of financial promoters to profit by selling the securities of a holding company for high prices on an active and rising stock market; (2) the desire of the merged companies to improve their market position or to gain economies of scale; (3) the desire to gain balanced production by supplementing the sales of one product by sales of others, so that slack seasons may be filled in or risks minimized; (4) the desire of a company which is losing money to save what it can by merging with a stronger one, which may be able to salvage its business; (5) in times of high income taxes, the desire of a highly profitable company to reduce its tax load by absorbing an unprofitable firm; (6) the desire to benefit sellers of a corporation by making it possible for them to take their profit in capital gain rather than in income (capital gains are taxed at a lower rate than incomes in the upper brackets).

REASONS FOR PREVALENCE OF SMALL FIRMS

In industries where large numbers of small firms prevail, numerous circumstances may contribute to that result.

EASE OF ENTRY. The capital necessary to start a profitable business may be small where mass production is not the rule and expensive equipment need not be bought. For example, shops making women's garments may rent their machinery and set up business in one floor of a building. Frequent style changes place a premium on style origination rather than on large-scale, standardized production.

LOCAL NATURE OF A MARKET.   The nature of a market, like that for pastry and cake, may lead to the existence of a large number of small concerns. The same logic applies to dry-cleaning establishments and the like.

AVAILABILITY OF SUFFICIENT NATURAL RESOURCES.   The availability of natural resources in widely scattered localities may favor relatively small, competitive operations. This is one of the reasons for the prevalence of the family-sized farm in the United States and for the existence of numerous independent bituminous coal mines and oil wells. It is in expensive oil refining and in industries based on processed coal products that the big concerns dominate.

Small Concerns in Big Industries.

Industries in which the big producers assemble many materials or parts frequently contain numerous smaller firms, from which the big companies buy their "bits and pieces." This is the case in the automobile industry. The biggest companies can, and sometimes do, set up their own subsidiaries for this purpose, but sometimes they find it more advantageous to depend on the decentralized management of independent concerns, in which the owners have special skills and personal interests. Somewhat the same logic applies also in distribution or servicing, as in gasoline and service stations, automobile dealers, garages and similar businesses.

Small Optimum Size.

Because large-scale operation or mass production is more economical in some instances, it should not be inferred that the bigger a business is, the more efficient it is. The task of good management becomes increasingly difficult as size increases and problems become more complex. Human capacities are limited. A very large concern must resort to a good deal of routine and may become the prey of bureaucratic red tape. Where personal attention to detail is important, where originality or personal initiative is at a premium, a very large concern may be at a disadvantage. This is especially the case when a business can achieve all the practicable economies of scale due to technological developments without becoming gigantic.

Where monopolistic control does not exist or cannot prevent the rise of smaller competitors, concerns so large that they exceed the optimum size may lose a large part of the market to firms which are more efficient because they are smaller or because they have the advantage of more aggressive and imaginative executives.

Just as specific industries rise and decline, so specific firms are born, grow, and then remain static or decline while others grow. Though at any one time a few firms may hold a dominating position in an industry, the identity of the dominant firms may change from time to time. An industry may be of the sort where concentration grows easily; in that case it may—up to a point—become more highly concentrated. Or it may be of the sort in which concentration is difficult or may easily go too far, in which case concentration is likely to be absent or to decline. The

American economy is a rapidly changing and developing one, in which not only has technological advance occurred at an accelerating rate but also business organization and control have undergone many changes. This process is likely to continue. What is most to be feared in the interest of public policy is rigid barriers to experimenting and to desirable change, whether imposed by government authority or by private aggregations of power.

SOCIAL AND POLITICAL DANGERS OF BIGNESS

The problem of big business has many aspects other than the economic. As has many times been pointed out, there is a difference in nature, not merely in size, between a small business run by one or a few men who own it and a large corporation with widely distributed ownership. In the latter, the many scattered stockholders possess the legal right to elect directors who in turn appoint the executive officers of the concern; but the stockholders seldom exercise this right as individuals or know enough about the affairs of the company to do so intelligently. Customarily they do not attend annual stockholders' meetings but, by signing proxies, delegate the privilege of voting to some insider. The active management consists of professionals whose duties and powers are very great.

The corporation becomes, in essence, an institution whose policies exert important effects, for better or for worse, on the public welfare. Corporations are often run by self-perpetuating oligarchies. Their political influence may be great; their decisions and practices can affect labor, consumers, and the whole cultural climate of the nation. Management employees may become enmeshed in bureaucracy or be concerned more with promotion and advancement of social status than with the interests or ideals which theoretically should influence individual citizens of a free democratic society. Sociologists have pointed out numerous ignoble tendencies, such as superficial conformity, which often seem to rule the lives of administrative employees of big business.

See Chapters 27, 28, 29, and 31 for illustrations of the influence of business organization on actual industries, competitive or otherwise.

For a case study of an industry in which concentration leads to "price leadership" by a big concern, see Chapter 29 on the proposed Bethlehem-Youngstown merger.

QUESTIONS

1. The corporate form of business organization has many advantages.

(a) Can you imagine why the leading American investment banking firm, J. P. Morgan & Co., remained an unincorporated partnership for many years?

(b) Can you guess why the law does not permit law firms or physicians to incorporate?

2. In some industries the size of establishment necessary for efficient operation is so large that relatively few companies can do the bulk of the business. Can you guess why, aside from any fear of antitrust laws, the larger firms in such industries often maintain prices high enough to permit less efficient competitors to remain in business? Among possible reasons, consider such conditions as the following:

    (a) Little elasticity of demand

    (b) Wide variation in demand between prosperous and depressed business conditions

    (c) Rapid growth of demand over a period of years

    (d) A capacity for production by the industry as a whole which exceeds demand except in the most highly prosperous periods

11 / THEORIES OF BUSINESS

BEHAVIOR / In Chapter 9 on demand and supply it

was assumed that in the market for any one article the seller would supply a given quantity at any given price; the higher the price, the greater the supply, and vice versa.

Since active demand tends to pull prices up and slackening demand acts to push prices down, the response of suppliers (sellers) to changes in price is one of the major forces in allocating the use of scarce resources according to the wants of consumers. This is easy to see, from the standpoint of the operation of markets as a whole. The individual firm, however, has its own role to play in the allocation of resources. For purposes of simplification, we may assume, as economic theorists do, that the executive of each firm strives to maximize profits (or minimize losses if losses are unavoidable), that he acts in a perfectly rational manner, and that he knows the essential facts on which rational action must be based. Then how would he decide exactly how much to offer for sale?

So far we have not examined closely what factors would determine the judgment of a businessman concerning how many of any given article to make and put on the market. What economic forces lie behind the supply? The theory that deals with this question is usually known as the "economics of the firm."

COST

Presumably every businessman wants to make (or buy) his products at a cost lower than the price at which he can sell them. He does not always succeed in doing so, but if he should long continue to lose money on every article he sold, he could not pay his bills. His contribution to market supply, therefore, is limited in some way by his cost of production. Cost obviously has much to do with the market supply. Let us begin our analysis with a look at the nature of costs.

111

In order to simplify the matter, economists customarily make the following assumptions.

1. We are here concerned with the costs entering into only *one kind of article*. Actually, most businessmen make or sell numerous kinds of articles, but as we must think of demand in terms of a specific article and its price, so we must think of supply in terms of the cost of the same article and the profit to be made in selling it.

2. Although businessmen are influenced by many considerations in making their decisions—desire to build up public favor, to stabilize and enlarge their enterprises, or even to serve the public welfare—for present purposes it must be assumed that their decisions about production of any one article are made solely on the basis of the profit they can make in selling that article. They are supposed to be concerned solely, as the economist says, with "maximizing profit."

Fixed and Variable Costs. *Fixed costs,* often called "overhead," are costs that must be incurred by a business no matter how much or how little a business produces or offers for sale. The firm, let us say, rents a building; the rent it is obligated to pay is a fixed cost. If the firm owns the factory, it has to pay taxes on it and charges off depreciation as well. Interest on mortgages or long-term bond issues is fixed. Repairs and upkeep of machinery and equipment, which go on whether anything is produced, are fixed costs (though much of these do vary with production). So is fire insurance. Salaries of the officers of the concern and the permanent staffs are fixed costs.

The question may arise, cannot a firm enlarge its plant, install new machinery, or do other things which would increase fixed costs? Or cannot the firm decrease its fixed costs by getting rid of some of its executives and staff or renting out part of its building? Yes indeed; so-called "fixed" costs seldom stay fixed for very long. To use the term at all, we must postulate a relatively brief period in which such changes cannot take effect—say, somewhere between a month and a year.

A period short enough to justify application of fixed costs is ordinarily called by economists the "short run." In the "long run" no costs are fixed, though some change more slowly than others.

Variable costs are those which disappear if output ceases. They differ according to the amount of production or other business done. Every unit of output contains materials which have to be bought; the more the units produced, the greater are the payments for material. To a large extent the same principle holds true for the cost of productive labor. If much is produced, workers are on the job for more hours a week and so they earn more. A large gain in production may require the hiring of extra workers. If sales are small, workers may be called in for only part time or may be laid off altogether. Salesmen's commissions are variable costs.

Any cost which remains the same or about the same, regardless of the amount of business done may be classified as a fixed cost; any cost which does not exist where nothing is produced may be classified as a variable cost.

The Break-Even Point. One usefulness of this distinction is easy to see. Clearly the firm will not make any money unless its revenue from sales is greater than such costs as material and labor. It must sell its product at a price that will provide more than enough revenue to cover its variable costs. It must also sell enough to cover its fixed costs as well, before a profit on the whole operation will begin to appear. The quantity of sales which will cover both variable and fixed costs is commonly called the "break-even point."

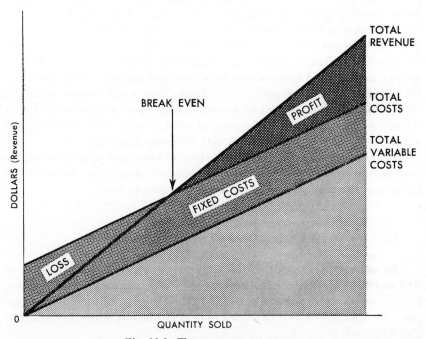

Fig. 11.1. THE BREAK-EVEN POINT.

If a firm has a large investment in buildings and machinery but pays relatively little for material and productive labor—that is, if its fixed costs are high relative to its variable costs—it has more to lose from small sales than a firm which has relatively low fixed costs. The firm with the large investment in plant and equipment can lose large amounts of money quickly when sales are below the point where fixed costs are covered. A firm, however, which has relatively little expense except that involved in paying for materials and productive labor can, by cutting its purchases and laying off workers when sales fall off, more easily minimize its losses when business is bad, since it has fewer expenses that continue, regardless of how much is sold. In other words, its break-even point is lower than that of a firm with high fixed costs.

If a firm sells enough to exceed its break-even point, the more goods it can make (and sell at a profit), the larger will be the difference between its costs and its revenue from sales and the more profitable it will be. At least, so it would seem. Many businessmen assume that this is the case and try to sell as much as they can, regarding their profit as being limited, in the short run, only by the utmost capacity of their plant.

There are, however, other things to consider. One is the price at which the product can be sold. Will the firm have to reduce the price if it is to sell a larger quantity? The other is the cost of producing each unit sold. Will the unit cost differ if production varies? And if so, will cost change up or down, according to the quantity produced? Let us assume for the moment that the businessman in question does not worry about the selling price but thinks he can sell at existing market prices as many as he can make. Let us also assume that the prices of materials and wages do not change as a result of any changes he may make in quantity produced. This is the way a businessman presumably thinks if he is subject to uncurbed competition in selling and buying. He knows what his materials can be bought for; he knows how much he can expect to charge for his product; and he knows that he alone cannot affect either the cost of what he buys or the price of what he sells. If he does not buy, someone else will; if he does not sell, someone else will.

In other words, to begin our analysis of costs and profits, we are assuming the existence of a perfectly competitive market, although we know well that such a market is, in fact, not easy to find.

UNIT COSTS IN A COMPETITIVE MARKET

In order to make calculations of cost more precise, it is helpful to find out how an increase in the output of tons of coal, suits of clothes, bushels of wheat, or other commodity affects the cost of each unit of output. In other words, it is necessary to deal not merely with *total costs* but also with *costs per unit*.

Fixed Unit Costs. Let us suppose that a firm has to pay fixed costs —taxes, salaries, insurance, and the like—amounting to $1.2 million a year. If it produces in that year only one unit of product, its fixed cost per unit produced will be $1.2 million. If it produces two units, its fixed unit cost will be $600,000. The more it produces, the lower its fixed cost per unit will shrink. If it produces 1.2 million units, its fixed unit cost will be only one dollar.

Variable Unit Costs. If the labor, materials, and other variable costs entering into the production of this article cost $100 for each unit produced, then the variable unit cost, one might think, would be $100 if one unit is produced, $100 if two units are produced, and $100 if a million units are produced.

Variable unit costs, however, remain the same only within certain limits. They will be somewhat higher if the factory produces very few units than they will be as the factory approaches normal operation. Then they will cease to fall. They will probably continue at about the normal level until the factory nears the upper limit of output of which it is capable. Then variable unit costs are likely to rise.

Let us suppose that the factory, in order to produce at all, has to run the work in process through ten different operations, and for these operations it will require a productive labor force of at least a hundred employees. (The smallest amount of materials, labor, and the like required to turn out one unit of output is called a "unit of input.") If only one unit of output is being made, each of the ten teams or groups of workers will have to stand around doing nothing until the work reaches them or after it leaves their part of the shop. Nevertheless, they all have to be paid. This situation will lead to high labor cost for producing only one unit. As more units are produced, the factory approaches the point where the smallest number of employees required to make anything at all will be kept busy. The labor cost per unit will shrink accordingly. After that point is passed, the labor cost per unit will remain approximately the same as output rises until the utmost capacity of the factory is in sight.

As production nears capacity, more breakdowns are likely to occur and machinery has to be repaired more often. Perhaps the supply of the better-trained and more efficient labor will be exhausted, and it is necessary to hire workers who are slower and make more mistakes. The speeding-up process may affect the quality of the product; there is more spoilage. The task of management becomes more difficult because of the pressure and because the work is not well done. More delays occur in the delivery of material. Eventually, output cannot be increased at all by the hiring of more men, as there will not be machines enough for them.

The slackening of output per unit of input at some point near capacity is called the "principle of diminishing returns."

The traditional short-run theory of the firm assumes that this principle is at work in most businesses. At the low end of the production scale, variable unit costs are higher than they are when more is produced, because when production is low, fewer units of output come from the smallest possible input. Above the very low level of output, variable unit costs remain about the same. The firm can perhaps expand its output many times before it reaches the point at which the addition of more units of input will not proportionally increase units of output. Then diminishing returns will take over, until the point is reached where nothing more can be produced, no matter how much is spent on such things as materials and productive labor. Note that the principle of diminishing returns applies only to variable costs, not to fixed costs; and that it applies only to a plant which does not enlarge its capacity by installing new machinery or better technological methods.

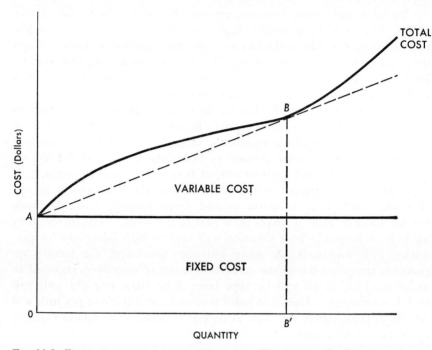

FIG. 11.2. FIXED, VARIABLE, AND TOTAL COSTS. Fixed cost, the lowest
band, remains the same at any level of output, assuming
capacity of plant is not changed. Variable cost rises rapidly
at lower stages of production; then rises less rapidly until
maximum capacity is approached. The point of diminishing average returns is reached at B, where a line drawn
from A tangent to the total-cost curve touches that curve.
Beyond B the curve of variable cost rises more rapidly than
at levels of output less than B'.

Let us see how costs would operate in the case of a hypothetical firm
in which these assumptions hold true. Let us assume these facts:

1. Total fixed costs are $1,200,000.

2. The cost of a unit of input is $1,000.

3. Ten units of output can be made with each unit of input, up to
the point of diminishing returns. Beyond that point the number of units
of output per unit of input becomes smaller.

4. The point of diminishing returns is found above a production of
800,000 units.

In this table, fixed unit costs (column 4) are derived by dividing the
figures in column 3 (total fixed costs) by column 2 (units of output).
Variable unit costs (column 6) are derived by dividing column 5 (total
variable costs) by column 2 (units of output).

The figures in column 3 (total fixed costs) are the same no matter
how much or how little is produced, according to the definition of fixed
costs. The consequence is that the more the units produced, the less the
fixed cost of each unit. This is apparent in column 4.

TABLE 11/1

COSTS OF HYPOTHETICAL FIRM AT LOW LEVELS OF OUTPUT

(1)	(2)	(3)	(4)	(5)	(6)	(7)
Units of input	Units of output	Total fixed costs	Fixed unit costs	Total variable costs	Variable unit costs	Average cost per unit of output
1	1	$1,200,000	$1,200,000	$1,000	$1,000	$1,201,000
1	2	1,200,000	600,000	1,000	500	600,500
1	3	1,200,000	400,000	1,000	333	400,333
1	4	1,200,000	300,000	1,000	250	300,250
1	5	1,200,000	240,000	1,000	200	240,200
1	6	1,200,000	200,000	1,000	166	200,166
1	7	1,200,000	171,428	1,000	143	171,871
1	8	1,200,000	150,000	1,000	125	150,125
1	9	1,200,000	133,333	1,000	111	133,444
1	10	1,200,000	120,000	1,000	100	120,100
2	20	1,200,000	60,000	2,000	100	60,100
3	30	1,200,000	40,000	3,000	100	40,100
4	40	1,200,000	30,000	4,000	100	30,100

The figures in column 5 (total variable costs) are derived by multiplying the cost of a unit of input, which we assumed to be $1,000, by column 1 (the units of input).

The figures in column 7 are the sum of those in columns 4 and 6.

We assumed that, with each unit of input, 10 units of output could be produced. From this fact two consequences follow, both revealed in the table. One is that the variable unit cost shrinks rapidly between 1 unit of output and 10 units of output; for output over 10 units, it remains the same. The other consequence is that, upwards of 10 units of output, the output changes by 10 units at a time, since the firm cannot add or subtract less than one unit of input.

So much for the explanation of Table 11/1. Now lets us see what, if anything, we can learn from it.

The most important observation is that the average cost of making each article (that is, the sum of fixed and variable unit costs) is less, the more the firm produces; and more, the less the firm produces. These facts are demonstrated by the table, at least for low levels of production.

By adding columns 4 and 6, we see that the cost of production for only one unit is $1,201,000, and that, at higher levels of production, the cost is less, the average cost of each of 40 units being $30,100.

It is easy to see that this reduction in average cost with increased production will go on as more and more units are produced, since fixed unit costs are gradually less as production is larger, and variable unit costs (above an output of ten units) remain the same. That is, average cost will be less at least until capacity output is approached and diminishing returns set in. The figures for the middle ranges of operation may be omitted. (Diminishing returns are defined as a fall in physical output per unit of input.)

Now let us see what happens at high levels of output. By assumption, each additional unit of input ordinarily raises output by 10, but diminishing returns begin after an output of 800,000 is passed (Table 11/2).

TABLE 11/2

COSTS OF HYPOTHETICAL FIRM AT HIGH LEVELS OF OUTPUT

(1)	(2)	(3)	(4)	(5)	(6)	(7)
Units of input	Units of output	Total fixed costs	Fixed unit costs	Total variable costs	Variable unit costs	Average costs
79,999	799,990	$1,200,000	$1.50+	$79,999,900	$100.00	$101.50+
80,000	800,000	1,200,000	1.50	80,000,000	100.00	101.50
80,001	800,009	1,200,000	1.4999+	80,001,000	100.0001+	101.50+

Adding the 80,000th unit of input raises the number of units of output by 10, as at large levels of output. But if production is increased by adding the 80,001st unit of input, only 9 additional units of output are obtained, because the firm is too close to its capacity to operate most efficiently. Fixed unit costs keep on falling, though not so rapidly as formerly. Variable unit costs start to rise slightly. These changes in costs are but small fractions of a cent. Nevertheless, they indicate an important tendency.

At an output of 800,000, the firm operates at its highest point of efficiency in terms of cost—its lowest average cost per unit of output is $101.50. In physical terms, the output per unit of variable input has begun to *fall* sufficiently to offset the continued increase in output per unit of fixed input.

In this particular table, average costs turn up at the precise point when variable unit costs begin to rise. This will not necessarily be the case with every firm. It is a consequence of the fact that above an output of 800,000, the reduction of fixed unit costs with additional units of output has become so small that the rise in variable unit costs outweighs it. Nevertheless, it is not important whether what is called the "point of least costs"—lowest average costs—is reached as soon as variable unit costs begin to rise, or somewhat later. What is important is that, at the point of least costs, the firm is operating most efficiently in terms of fixed and variable costs combined. It is turning out the most units of output possible per units of fixed capital, materials, and labor combined. In other words, it is making the best use of the country's resources of which it is capable—that is, the best use as judged by consumers' market demand.

Now let us add the element of price, to see how all this turns out in

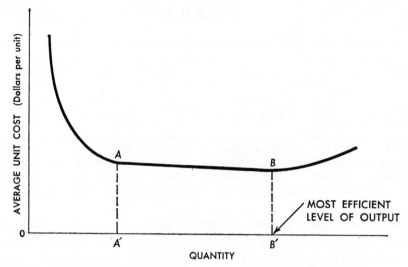

FIG. 11.3. AVERAGE COST. Average unit costs, the sum of fixed and variable unit costs, fall rapidly with increased output at low stages of production. At point *A* they flatten out and change little as output increases, until variable costs begin to rise (because of diminishing returns) enough to exceed the steady fall of fixed unit costs. *B'* is load of output at which the plant is operating most efficiently.

terms of profit. If the price is not at least as high as the lowest average cost at which the firm can operate—$101.50—it cannot even cover its costs at any level of output. It may operate at a loss rather than close down entirely, since the loss will be less if it has some income rather than none; fixed costs have to be paid in any event as long as the firm remains in business. But it cannot, of course, remain in business indefinitely if it continues to lose money.

Let us see what would happen if the selling price were $110.

In Table 11/3, total expenditure (column 3) is obtained by adding total fixed cost and total variable cost (from Table 11/2). Total revenue (column 5) is the product of units of output multiplied by the price. When total expenditure is subtracted from total revenue, the profit is seen to be highest at the production level of 800,000. At this output the firm nets $6,800,000. Its profit is $1,000 less at the next lower level of output, and $900 less at the next higher. The firm therefore has a financial incentive (on the short run) to produce as many as 800,000, but no more—in other words, to operate at the level of output which is, for it, the most efficient level.

Now, suppose the price were slightly higher—say, $120. Then, total revenue at an output of 800,000 would be $96,000,000 and profit correspondingly higher, or $14,800,000. At the next stage of output, 800,009 units, the total revenue at $120 per unit would be $96,001,080. Subtracting the cost of producing these units $81,201,000 (from Table 11/3), we find a profit of $14,800,080. The $80 added profit would provide an in-

TABLE 11/3

PROFIT OF HYPOTHETICAL FIRM AT HIGH LEVELS OF OUTPUT

(1)	(2)	(3)	(4)	(5)	(6)
Units of input	Units of output	Total Expenditure	Price	Total Revenue	Profit
79,999	799,990	$81,199,900	$110	$87,998,900	$6,799,000
80,000	800,000	81,200,000	110	88,000,000	6,800,000
80,001	800,009	81,201,000	110	88,000,900	6,799,100

centive for the firm to turn out 800,009 units. Thus, prices sufficiently above least cost would lead the firm to produce more, even though it had exceeded its most efficient level of output (in the sense of least cost per unit). But as long as the plant was not enlarged, there would be a point at which total profit would shrink with added output.

As long as the firm, by adding more output, obtained revenue from the added unit greater than the added cost of producing that unit, there would be a financial incentive to increase output. The higher the price, the further above the point of least costs—the most efficient point—this incentive would persist.

SUPPLY IN THE COMPETITIVE MARKET (SHORT RUN)

Up to this point we have been considering only one firm supplying goods. But since the market is assumed to be competitive, there would be other firms—probably many of them. The whole supply of the market would be the sum of the output of all the firms. So far, all we know is that in the short run any one of these firms would strive to produce enough to cover its least costs, assuming that the price were high enough to cover these costs. If the price were enough higher than that, it would supply more so long as its profit grew by doing so.

In any competitive industry, it is almost certain that the "least costs" of each firm will not be the same. Some firms will be more favorably situated than others with regard to access to materials. Some will have plants closer to the "optimum size" than others (see Figure 11/4). Some will be better managed than others. Some will have a more highly productive labor force or better machinery.

Even the most efficient seller will not long continue to market the article unless the price is high enough to cover his costs. If the price should be enough higher than this, he would be induced to increase his output. A higher price might also be sufficient to cover the least cost of the next most efficient sellers, and so induce them to begin operations. The higher the price, the more the competitors will offer for sale. Less

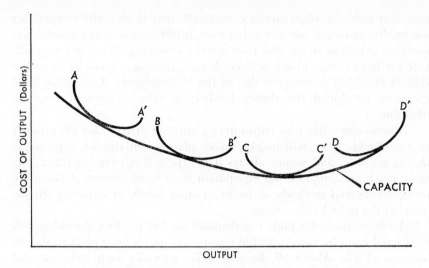

FIG. 11.4. VARYING EFFICIENCY OF FIRMS ACCORDING TO SIZE. The large
curve represents the least costs of firms according to capacity.
The small curves represent the costs of individual firms.
Firm CC' is of the most efficient size.

and less efficient producers will be called into action as prices rise. Thus,
the supply offered by all the sellers would correspond with the assumption in our previous analysis of supply and demand in a competitive
market—the higher the price, the greater the supply; the lower the price,
the smaller the supply.

From the standpoint of the whole market, however, at least one assumption about costs will have to be changed. No one competitor, we
supposed, could affect the price of what he bought, no matter how much
or how little he purchased. Consequently, we have assumed, in analyzing
the costs of a single firm, that the cost of each unit of input (consisting of
such things as materials and labor) would be the same for a low level of
output as for a high one. But for all the firms in the industry taken together, this assumption might not be true, especially if the industry were
a large one. For example, if only one clothing manufacturer in the
United States were operating, the textile mills would scarcely feel the
effect of his demand for material, no matter how little or how much he
ordered. But if all the clothing manufacturers were busy, the prices of
materials could easily rise. This factor would increase unit costs in
clothing manufacture and decrease profits at any given price of clothing.

SUPPLY IN A COMPETITIVE MARKET (LONG RUN)

The short-run analysis customary in textbooks (including this one)
must not be understood as a description of what actually occurs, even in
a purely competitive market for a single kind of article. The logic on
which it is based is correct. Even this logic, however, rests on the assump-

tion that only the *short run* is considered; that is, that the competitors are neither reducing nor increasing their investment in plant, machinery, or other overhead items, and thus are not changing their total expenditure for fixed costs. This is seldom, if ever, the case, especially in such a rapidly changing economy as that of the United States. Economists have therefore developed the theory further, to take account of long-run planning.

Almost any seller who encounters a growing demand for his product at a profitable price will quickly make plans to enlarge his capacity, if that is possible—and almost always it is. He will enlarge his plant, buy more machinery, replace old equipment with more efficient devices, improve managerial methods, or resort to other means of satisfying the demand at the price he can charge.

A competitor who finds the demand for his product shrinking will trim fixed costs by every possible means, so long as he expects to stay in business at all. Above all, he will strive to make such technical and managerial improvements as to increase the units of output per unit of input, thus reducing not only his fixed unit costs but his variable unit costs as well.

In such conditions it is difficult if not impossible to separate fixed unit costs from variable unit costs and to find a volume of production corresponding with least costs. Probably most competitive businessmen never even attempt such separation except in making day-to-day decisions about how much to produce or decisions about the best size of a new plant. Few if any costs are in reality fixed for very long; variable unit costs are jumping up and down. The executive is not a leisurely mathematician; he feels more like a circus rider standing on the backs of two horses and driving a dozen others. He tries to sell all he can, often shading the price if he has to do so to get the order; at the same time he tries to fill the orders at a margin of profit. Sometimes he succeeds, and sometimes he does not. He is beset by changes in taste, development of new products, outbreaks of war and of peace, changes in taxes and other legislation, geographical shifts of population, and hundreds of other circumstances to which adjustment is required.

In spite of all this confusion, the economic theorist insists, there exists at any one time a point of least costs for any firm, even if the managers do not know what it is. Those who cannot sell at prices high enough to cover these costs incur losses. Even if the price just covers their least costs, they will lose money if they cannot sell enough at this price to attain the level of production at which unit cost is lowest.

The economic theorist also points out that if anything like pure competition is to exist, the way must be open for new competitors easily to enter the industry. In other words, the gates must not be barred by patents, by monopolistic practices of any sort, or even by difficulty of obtaining the necessary capital. When entry into the industry is easy, if profits are being made in the selling of any product, new firms will be organized to supply it and more will enter the industry until the profit incentive no longer beckons.

The competitors may discover that their assumptions about costs and prices do not operate in the market for their product as a whole. Since no one of them apparently can influence the price, no matter how little or how much he offers for sale, he is likely to act as if the price will remain the same at high levels of production as at low levels. The tables and the reasoning in this chapter are based on that assumption. Nevertheless, the assumption is not true of the market as a whole. The action of all sellers striving for increased output at the same time is likely so to increase the supply as to drive prices down. Thus, as output in the whole market increases, the individual seller may be caught between rising costs for his units of input and falling revenue per unit of output. He will be lucky if the sales revenue does not fall to or below his point of least costs.

Thus we come to the conclusion extolled by economic theorists that "free, competitive, private enterprise" would always be tending to the point where no profits can be made. That is, there would be no profit in the proper economic sense. The business might earn enough to pay the going rate of interest on the capital invested in it, and to pay the managers (including any company owner or owners) the market value of their services. In ordinary corporate accounting, these costs, or "implied costs," are often not specified as such but rather are lumped under net income. But, theoretically, pure competition always tends to the absence of true economic profits for the producer.

CONSUMERS' COMPETITIVE ELYSIUM

For the consumer, however, pure competition would be a sort of earthly paradise. The consumer gets anything he wants to buy at the lowest cost at which it can be produced, without contributing toward any true profit to the less efficient producers. His demand will allocate to the production and distribution of each article he wants to buy exactly the right amount of materials, labor, capital, and other resources needed to fulfill his demand—at a price which will just about cover the cost. If at this price his wish for a particular article is sufficiently satisfied so that he would rather utilize the rest of his money to acquire other things, he will by his spending allocate the nation's resources to the output of these other things, in proportion to their importance to him. If his desire for any one kind of article is at any time strong enough so that he will pay more than the least cost of producing it, the producer will make a corresponding profit. But this profit will induce the existing competitors (and perhaps new ones as well) to increase their output until the price again approximates the point of least costs of the most efficient firm.

Thus the equilibrium price of the purely competitive industry is continually approximated; it is the same as the equilibrium price of the purely competitive market. Having established the circumstances under which an equilibrium must logically appear, the economic theorist is in a position logically to account for absences of equilibrium in the real world, by noting departures from the assumptions necessary for the existence of an automatic equilibrium.

In the real world, consumers' heaven cannot be found on earth, and pure competition exists seldom, if at all. The impulse of businessmen, who want large and stable profit, to escape or curb competition in some way is quite understandable.

ESCAPES FROM COMPETITION

Most businessmen do not need to be convinced by an intricate theory that if they had to submit to the rigors of unlimited competition, they could make little or no profit. They feel it in their bones.

In most cases the businessman has little hope of becoming the sole seller or the sole buyer in any market—that is, hope of being completely monopolistic. Even if the law does not stand in his way, competition of some kind is usually unavoidable. But there are many stages between pure competition and pure monopoly, and firms have been ingenious in seizing one or more of these vantage points.

A specially favorable location is important for merchants; good sites for stores or even for some factories are frequently limited in number in regions where the greatest advantages lie. A mild form of monopolistic advantage is achieved by the firm that establishes a reputation for superior products, reliable dealings, or conveniences offered to customers. Many persons prefer to deal with such a firm even though they know that they might find a somewhat lower price by shopping around. In the case of consumers' goods, the label of a leading firm often lends prestige to the buyer.

Such opportunities for gain by no means eliminate all possible competition, yet they do enable those who possess them to attract purchasers by means other than offering the lowest money price—for identical articles. The businessman usually considers such an exclusive advantage as part of the competitive struggle itself, but in the strict sense of price theory it is a means of lifting his head somewhat above the floodwaters of "pure" competition. The purchaser is, to be sure, buying something of worth to him even when he buys the prestige or reliability of a name or the ease of shopping in a convenient location; nevertheless it does not follow that other competitive sellers have an equal chance of offering these inducements.

PRODUCT DIFFERENTIATION— MONOPOLISTIC COMPETITION

One common method of introducing some monopolistic advantage into a highly competitive market, in which there are, as a rule, many competitors, is to sell, not just bacon, sugar, salt, canned vegetables, tea, tooth paste, or a common drug that might be bought wholesale by the pharmacist and prescribed by a physician, but to sell substantially the same thing in a distinctive package, tube, or bottle, under a proprietary name or with the manufacturer's label. Expensive advertising is employed by each producer to impress on the customer's mind not only the name or label but also the belief that this particular product is different from, and superior to, all others intended for the same uses. Such differences may be real, or they may be imaginary.

The product may or may not actually be superior, but the great economic advantage won by the seller who succeeds in differentiating his product is that, since nobody else can legally use his brand name or trademark, he has achieved a monopoly of all goods sold in a particular package and under a particular label. Even though the contents might not differ in the slightest from the contents of a package, tube, or bottle sold without a brand name or under another name, the seller goes a long way to eliminate the competition with which he would have had to deal if consumers went into the store and asked simply for a certain amount of bacon, sugar, salt, tooth paste, aspirin, or what have you. A price correspondingly higher can be (and is) charged for the brand name.

Without prompting from sellers, consumers themselves differentiate among different lots of commodities of the same kind. They do so habitually in the supermarket when they inspect fresh vegetables and fruit, but in doing so they favor no particular producer. The competitive farmer who sells fruit or vegetables cannot set his price; he has to sell at what the market offers, and he makes more (or loses less) by selling all he can than by withholding any of his supply.

Monopoly enters the picture only when a well-publicized brand name acts as a substitute for consumer inspection and comparison. The branded product may actually be superior and may offer the consumer the advantage of being able to rely on uniformity of excellence in choosing what he likes best. Commercial morals or sagacity are not at issue. The point is merely that monopoly of any product, even though substitutes may readily be chosen, offers the producer a chance to escape the grim prospect of pure competition and so to make a true economic profit. This chance lies in his ability to name the price at which he will sell his own product.

The usual term for competition among producers who make products to satisfy essentially the same wants, though each of the products is differentiated from the others, is "monopolistic competition."

OLIGOPOLY

Oligos—the Greek word for "few"—indicates the meaning of "oligopoly" as distinguished from "monopoly." Instead of one seller, there are a few dominant sellers. Precisely how few sellers there must be to constitute oligopoly is impossible to state in general terms; oligopoly exists if each seller, in setting its prices, is affected by what it thinks the other seller will charge.

In some industries the same firms may practice both oligopolistic competition and monopolistic competition. This practice prevails, for example, in the automobile industry. This industry consists of a few companies, each of which sets the prices for its annual models on about the same levels as those set by the other companies (and usually sticks to these prices), and each of which strives to differentiate its products from those of its rivals by styling, minor differences in construction, and extensive advertising of brand names..

The precise theories about pricing in monopolistic competition or oligopolistic competition are too advanced for a beginning text. We must be satisfied with the main distinction that any approach to monopoly gives the producer some control over the selling price, the amount produced in the market, or both.

Chapters 28 and 29 illustrate aspects of the theories discussed in this chapter.

QUESTIONS

1. Consider the situation of a manufacturer of books. No matter how few or how many copies of a given book may be printed, it must be set up by compositors. Unless only a few copies are needed, electroplates (or plates) are made from the type. Before the presses can begin to roll, the plates must be put through an expensive process called "make-ready," to assure that the impressions will be clean and clear.

Identify each of the following items of expense as fixed or variable:
- (a) Depreciation and taxes on the plant of the manufacturer, or rent if he does not own it
- (b) Depreciation on his equipment
- (c) Insurance
- (d) Salaries of executives and office staff
- (e) Labor and materials used in setting type and making electrotypes
- (f) Labor used in running presses
- (g) Paper and ink

2. Would the book manufacturer be likely to charge the same amount for the first or second thousand copies of a given book as for additional thousands?

3. Would a book publisher be as well satisfied by selling 2,000 copies each of one hundred different books as by selling, at the same price per copy, 40,000 copies each of five books?

4. Would you expect that a point of diminishing returns would be reached in the production and sale of any book, regardless of the number of copies sold?

12 / MONEY AND BANKS / The most primitive
method of trade consists in the direct exchange of one kind of goods or
services for another. In early times in America, the owner of a gristmill,
in which grindstones were powered by a water wheel, would grind grain
for the neighboring farmers, taking his pay in part of the grist from the
mill. This, in turn, the owner of the mill could use, so far as it was
superfluous for his own food, to buy skins from trappers, iron implements
from the blacksmith, or anything else that had value.

Virtually all societies that engaged in trading found, sooner or later,
that one kind of commodity was being exchanged more frequently than
other kinds, not so much for final use by most of those who accepted it as
for use by them in making payments for other things that they needed.
Invariably, of course, this "medium of exchange" was something that was
regarded as having value throughout the trading area; otherwise the
seller might not accept it. In many, though not all, cases, the commodity
was something not generally used to satisfy an immediate physical need,
such as food; as food, being a necessity, would not likely be retained in
order that purchases might be made with it. Often the value of the
commodity used as the medium of exchange would lie in its attractive-
ness or its use for ornamental purposes, such as feathers among primitive
tribes; Indian wampum, made of colored shells and beads; or precious
metals, such as gold and silver, or semiprecious ones, such as copper and
nickel, used almost universally.

Once something comes into use as a medium of exchange, it serves at
the same time as a "measure of value." In early Virginia, when tobacco
was used as money, the market value of other things was, of course,
known by the amount of tobacco required to buy them. In other parts
of the colonies where, as sometimes was the case, beaver skins were used
as money, the worth of an article was expressed by the number of skins
it would cost.

Those who sold commodities naturally tried to store for future use
some of whatever was acceptable as money. Thus, a third important
function of money appeared—it became a "store of value."

The functions by which money of any kind may be recognized are

127

therefore these: (1) a medium of exchange, (2) a measure of value, (3) a store of value. Such money may also serve as a standard for deferred payments and a medium of loans.

MONEY IN THE MODERN WORLD

Such articles as skins, feathers, or tobacco are not very satisfactory in serving the three functions of money. As media of exchange they are inconvenient to carry around and may not be widely recognized as valuable; as measures of value they are not reliable because their qualities or sizes are not uniform; as stores of value they are subject to spoilage or decay.

Probably because of such faults in other substances, the precious metals became widely preferred by people engaged in trading or in accumulation of money. As media of exchange they were convenient because they were scarce and desirable enough to embody large value in relatively small compass; and they were acceptable throughout most of the trading world. As measures of value they were even more satisfactory, because they are chemical elements, the relative purity of which can be established by analysis: gold of a certain fineness is the same the world over and can be precisely measured by weighing it. As stores of value, precious metals are not subject to decay or rust; if not worn by use, they will remain unspoiled through centuries.

Gold or silver can be assayed and weighed by those skilled in doing so, but only people who possess these metals in considerable quantities can afford the time and the expense of having them tested. Furthermore, when such tests were made, some assayers or goldsmiths were bound to be dishonest or careless. Therefore, rulers who wished to encourage trade by providing a reliable medium of exchange for general use began to mold or stamp out coins. The stamp of the king or other sovereign on the coin was a guarantee to all that it was of a certain fineness and weight; coins of the realm thus became universally acceptable among its subjects.

The traces of this origin of modern metallic money still survive in the language. After silver became the principal form of money in Britain, pennies were made of silver and called "sterlings." They were guaranteed by Edward I in the thirteenth century to be of a certain fineness (925 fine); hence today we still speak of "sterling silver" as the material in articles consisting of nearly pure silver. The basic unit of money in Britain is still the "pound sterling." This signifies, historically, 240 silver sterlings, which presumably weighed one pound. (There is no coin worth a pound, even today.)

Another prevalent kind of money consists of paper, bearing various kinds of inscriptions. A widely used form of paper money is a *promise to pay to the bearer on demand*—that is, to pay whenever the holder of the paper wants it—a certain amount of metallic money. This is known as a "note." Sometimes those who issued paper of this sort in the early days were merchants known to possess ample wealth and trusted to keep their promises—that is, their "credit" was good. The person to whom the note was offered was willing to accept it instead of the coin because (1) it was more convenient to carry around, (2) he could be sure of redeeming it whenever he wanted to do so, and (3) he could be reasonably certain that others would accept it in payment, since their confidence in the merchant would be as firm as his. If a note certifies that the metal is on hand with which to redeem it, it is a "certificate." Governments frequently issue certificates and notes.

A note made out to a specific person rather than to "the bearer" is not, properly speaking, money, because it is customarily not passed around from one person to another and consequently is not used as a medium of exchange. Such a note, however, may be exchanged for money if the recipient's credit is good and if he endorses it.

HOW THE GOVERNMENT CREATES MONEY

According to the Constitution of the United States, the federal government has the sole right to "coin money and regulate the value thereof." A miner or anyone else who wishes to convert gold or silver into money may offer the metal for sale to the government.

Under present law, the government *must* accept all gold offered and pay $35 an ounce for it; it pays the seller by check. Any monetary gold which comes into the possession of a bank must be turned over to the government.

The government is not obliged to buy unlimited amounts of silver; as a rule, it buys only as much as is needed for circulation, paying the seller either in minted silver dollars or in *silver certificates.*

Look at the printing on a dollar bill. On the face it bears the label "Silver Certificate," at the top. It further bears the legend "This certifies that there is on deposit in the Treasury of the United States of America one dollar in silver payable to the bearer on demand." To the left of the picture of George Washington is this inscription: "This certificate is legal tender for all debts, public and private." This means that if the dollar bill is tendered in payment, it cancels any debt for a dollar, whether the creditor accepts it or not. By these promises and assurances, the government makes the dollar bill worth just as much as a silver dollar.

Some bills of higher denominations are also silver certificates; most of them are, traditionally, based on gold. But did you ever see a gold coin or a gold certificate? If by some remote chance one should turn up, it should be taken at once to a bank and turned in for some other form of money unless the holder wishes to keep it as a collector's item, since possession is otherwise contrary to law. All monetary gold (ever since the 1930's) must be held in the United States Treasury, and nobody is entitled to hold even a gold certificate except a federal reserve bank. Federal reserve banks will be discussed in Chapter 13.

Study a ten-dollar bill or one of higher denomination. Almost all such bills are labeled "Federal Reserve Note." Federal reserve notes are issued by federal reserve banks. They are not certificates, exchangeable for an equal amount of gold or silver in the United States Treasury, but merely bank notes which are promises to pay. What do they promise to pay? The legend reads, "The United States of America will pay to the bearer on demand ten dollars"—not silver, not gold, but merely ten dollars of any kind. The small print at the left of the portrait reads, "This note is legal tender for all debts, public and private, and is redeemable in lawful money at the United States Treasury or at any Federal Reserve Bank." The note is thus guaranteed by the government, but the government does not have nearly enough gold and silver combined to redeem all federal reserve notes. If you try to redeem one, you might ask for and might get silver. But you will get no gold (which legally backs federal reserve notes) and you are likely to get only other federal reserve notes.

Occasionally a bill bears the notation "United States Note." All $2 bills are of this kind. This is a note issued directly by the United States Government, not through a bank. Such notes were originally issued during the Civil War to pay expenses of the federal government, but they were not redeemable in gold. The popular name for them was "greenbacks." The government originally intended to retire them after the war was over, but powerful political forces, which wanted to expand the money in circulation, argued against this course, and eventually a compromise was reached by which the amount to be kept in circulation was limited to about $300 million.

A government can issue so much irredeemable paper money that it becomes nearly worthless. The Continental Congress did so during the American Revolution—hence the phrase "not worth a Continental." More recently, other governments have done so. At present, however, United States notes make up so small a part of the total circulation that they are universally accepted at face value. Of course, the note that may come into one's possession is not the very same piece of paper printed during the Civil War; it was issued to replace one which became worn out and was destroyed.

Thus, neither United States notes nor federal reserve notes can be redeemed in gold; both are universally accepted at their face value. The fact that no one can exchange them for gold seems to make no difference. We shall discuss this matter further in Chapter 13.

KINDS OF MONEY

To understand the relative importance of the various kinds of money in circulation among the general public, exclusive of banks, let us consult a recent tabulation.

These figures fluctuate from time to time, but the relative importance does not greatly change. Here we see that demand deposits are more than three times as large as all currency, and that the total of federal

TABLE 12/1

MONEY IN CIRCULATION, JULY 31, 1960
(in millions of dollars)

Coins	
Silver dollars	$ 488
Subsidiary silver coins...............................	1,555
Minor coins	562
Treasury Certificates and Notes	
Silver certificates, etc................................	2,395
United States notes..................................	100
Miscellaneous	156
Federal Reserve Notes...............................	28,652
Total	33,908
(Compare this total with the amount of demand deposits in banks on which checks are drawn for most payments.)	
Demand Deposits	125,970

reserve notes is five times as large as that of all coins and other currency combined. These facts emphasize the predominance of the banking system as a source of money.

BANKS

In early days a person with money that he wished to keep safe from loss or robbery would often deposit it with a goldsmith or a merchant, with the understanding that he could have it back when he wanted it. Such merchants or goldsmiths, having a large store of money on hand began to make loans to those who needed it. Sometimes they lent only their own money, but often they lent as well money deposited with them. Thus began the practice of commercial banking—which involves receiving deposited money on the one hand and lending or investing money on the other.

Eventually, institutions known as banks were founded by profit-seeking investors for this specific purpose. A bank makes profits by charging interest on loans, or by receiving a return on its investments. Sometimes banks also charge the depositor for taking care of his money, but this practice long ago fell into disuse except in cases where the deposit is so small that a charge is necessary to pay the expenses of handling it.

Why does a bank dare to lend or invest money belonging to others, which it may have to pay back to the depositors at any time on demand? This apparently risky procedure rests on the experience of bankers that *all* depositors will almost *never* want to withdraw *all* their money at the same time. In the course of daily business, new deposits are usually made as fast as old ones are withdrawn. Therefore the bank finds that it normally has in its possession a large amount of money available for loan or investment. Naturally, the bank lends only to persons or business concerns whose credit it regards as good, and lends usually for short terms, so that there will be an incoming stream of repayments to match outgoing loans. When the bank invests, it invests mainly in government bonds or in securities of private corporations for which there is almost always a demand by other investors; thus, if the bank needs money, it may sell these securities quickly at any time with little or no loss.

Another practice of banks ever since the early days of banking still further enlarges their capacity to lend or to repay depositors. The bank would print notes (known as "bank notes") which were promises by itself to pay; these were passed out instead of actual coin to depositors who withdrew their deposits or to borrowers from the bank. For many years in the United States, such notes were printed by individual banks and were good only to the extent that the individual bank could redeem them. In recent years, bank notes have been issued only by the Federal Reserve System, which is a governmental agency.

Because people generally had confidence in the ability of banks to redeem their notes, bank notes became widely circulated and thus were added to the supply of money. Bank notes differ from most paper money in that they are not *certificates;* that is, there is not a dollar's worth of gold or silver held by the bank to back up each dollar's worth of note issued. Just as banks discovered that they almost never were compelled to pay back all the depositors' money at once, and so could lend or invest it, they also learned that holders of their notes almost never asked to have them redeemed all at once in gold or silver. The bank was safe enough under ordinary circumstances if it kept in reserve an amount of metallic money which was only a fraction of its total note issues and deposits—a fraction ranging, say, from 10 to 25 percent, according to circumstances. Money held by a bank to meet possible withdrawals by depositors and redemption of notes is called its "reserve."

Of course, any bank is in danger if depositors or holders of its notes begin to lose confidence in its ability to meet its promises to pay, since the reserve is only a fraction of the amount necessary to repay everybody. When people withdrew money because of fear that they could not get it if they were not among the first to withdraw, the result was a "run" on a bank.

Although banks habitually promise to pay out more than they keep in reserve, they never, if they are honestly and prudently run, incur obligations as large as their total assets. Previously, in case of a run, a bank would sometimes find it impossible to sell quickly enough, and so turn into cash, its investments such as bonds, banking premises, and other assets. To avoid disaster, it would close its doors before all creditors were satisfied. If loss of confidence in banks and consequent desire for cash occurred on a nationwide scale, there would be either a general closing of banks or what was called a "suspension of specie payments" enforced by the government—"specie" being the precious metal or metallic coin which acts as a reserve for the banks' obligations to depositors and noteholders. In such a case, of course, money other than bank notes was almost unobtainable for the time being. Crises or panics of this sort have occurred on numerous occasions in the United States. This situation has been greatly improved since 1933 by new banking legislation and insurance of deposits—up to a certain limit—by a governmentally sponsored agency.

BANK DEPOSITS AS MONEY

Most business obligations and many personal ones are paid not by coin or printed paper money of any kind but by check. A check is simply an order to the bank where a firm or an individual keeps a deposit to transfer the amount stated on the check to somebody else. The recipient of the check may take it to a bank and ask for cash in exchange. If he takes it to the same bank on which the check is drawn, the bank simply hands out the cash and then deducts the amount from the depositor's account on its books. If the recipient of the check cashes it at another bank, it is soon returned to the drawer's bank, which then (by a roundabout route) pays the money back to the bank which cashed the check, and deducts the amount from the drawer's account. The recipients of most checks, however, do not cash them at all but simply deposit them in their own accounts. Thus, the check becomes a transfer of deposits from one account to another.

In this way, deposits serve the purposes of money. They constitute a medium of exchange just as truly as silver dollars or paper bills. They are also measures of value and stores of value. Because of the greatly increased use of checking accounts in contemporary civilization, bank deposits have in fact become by far the largest element among the media of exchange. Although they are not money in the strict historical sense of the word, they are to all intents and purposes the same as money and are generally lumped with it in economic analysis. When payments are made by check and the recipients deposit these checks in bank accounts from which they subsequently make payments by check, the circulation of receipts and payments occurs by a bookkeeping process carried on by the banks at the direction of their customers. Thus, little by little, the passing about of precious metals as a medium of exchange has receded into the background, and its place has largely been taken by an intricate bookkeeping process.

BANKS "CREATE" MONEY

If a businessman comes into a bank to borrow money, the bank does not necessarily take cash out of the till and hand it over to him. Rather, it simply adds the proceeds of the loan to his deposit account and makes corresponding adjustments on its books. He then may draw out cash if he needs it, but for the most part he uses the loan by drawing checks, which in turn are deposited by the recipient either in the lending bank or in another. For the banking system as a whole, the greater part of bank deposits thus arises from bank loans. The larger the total volume of loans from banks, the larger is the total volume of deposits.

The amount of loans that any given bank can make is limited by the size of its reserve. It must, we have seen, have a reserve big enough, as shown by experience, to meet such demands as its depositors may make for cash. This will be only a percentage of its total deposits. (There are legal limits fixing the percentage below which banks must not allow their reserves to fall.) Thus the whole banking system can lend more money than the banks have; and if their reserves are in excess of the required amount, the system can actually "create" new money (in the form of deposits) by the simple process of making loans. How this process works out is explained in more detail in Chapter 13.

When anyone borrows from a bank, he signs a note promising to repay the loan, either on demand or, more frequently, after a stated number of months. Often loans are secured by "collateral"—that is, securities or valuable goods belonging to the borrower which the bank has the right to sell if the loan should not be repaid. In any case, however, the bank makes loans only to those who it believes, on the basis of experience, can be trusted to repay according to their promises. Thus, bank loans are based on credit (from the Latin *credo,* "I believe"). The ability of borrowers to repay depends mainly upon their future earnings —that is, their ability to create goods or services of economic value. Thus deposit money created by bank loans is, by and large, matched by future economic value to be created by the borrowers.

This state of affairs is revealed by the balance sheet of a bank. Its deposits are liabilities (as shown in Table 12/2)—what it owes to depositors. The notes signed by borrowers become assets of the bank, just as do any bonds or other types of promises to pay, which it may buy. Thus, when the liabilities of a bank grow because it increases its loans, its assets grow by exactly the same amount because of the notes signed by the borrowers, which are added to its assets.

Any interest collected on loans also becomes a part of a bank's assets; such additions are matched on the liabilities side of the balance sheet by additions to undivided profits.

Just as a matter of terminology, it may be useful to remember that interest deducted from the principal of a loan before the proceeds are added to the deposit account of the borrower is called "discount."

BALANCE SHEET OF A BANK

To illustrate some of the principles discussed, let us study a much oversimplified balance sheet of a small, imaginary bank. This bank, let us say, is compelled by law to keep a reserve equal to not less than 15 percent of its deposit liabilities, and has loaned all that it legally can under this requirement.

TABLE 12/2

FIRST NATIONAL BANK
BALANCE SHEET, JUNE 30, 19—

Resources		Liabilities	
(1) Cash on Hand and Due from Other Banks	$150,000	(5) Deposits $1,000,000	
(2) Investments U.S. Govt. and Other Securities.	100,000	(6) Undivided Profits....	50,000
(3) Bank Building and Equipment	100,000	(7) Capital Stock	100,000
(4) Loans and Discounts.	900,000	(8) Capital Surplus	100,000
	$1,250,000		$1,250,000

Note that the left-hand side, which is headed "Assets" in the balance sheet of a business concern, is called "Resources." This word is used because a large part of the money at the disposal of the bank really belongs to depositors rather than to the bank itself. This money constitutes the resources which the bank is permitted to use; to call it an asset might imply that it was actually the bank's property. Some banks, however, overlook this fine distinction and simply use the word "assets."

1. This is the bank's reserve. Years ago the reserve would have been called simply "cash," meaning gold, coins redeemable in gold, or other United States currency. Today most banks are compelled by law to deposit in federal reserve banks all their reserves except such cash as is needed from day to day, and so the reserve item would be called "Cash on Hand and Due from Other Banks."

2. Investments are, of course, securities bought by the bank.

3. This item is self-explanatory.

4. The item "Loans" stands for the promissory notes which borrowers have left with the bank.

5. The deposits in the bank, which the depositors may draw out, constitute the bank's chief form of indebtedness.

6. This undivided profit was earned from interest on loans and investments; it has not yet been paid out to stockholders and therefore is, in a sense, a debt of the corporation to them.

7. The "value" of the capital stock is what the stockholders paid for their shares.

8. Capital surplus was also paid in by the stockholders, to provide an additional element of safety in meeting obligations to depositors. No

doubt this money was used mainly to build up the initial reserve—that is, it was left in the bank's vaults as cash.

KINDS OF BANKS

The kind of bank we have been considering in this chapter is called a "commercial bank." Only commercial banks accept deposits that may be drawn out on demand, or make short-term loans.

Another type of bank is the "savings bank," which accepts deposits intended as savings for an indefinite period and not for payments for current needs. The depositor can himself withdraw his savings, but he cannot transfer them to others by drawing checks. Legally, the savings bank may require advance notice by the depositor before he makes withdrawals; in practice, it usually does not do so. The savings bank pays interest on deposits; commercial banks are not allowed by law to pay interest on demand deposits. Commercial banks may, however, accept savings deposits on which they pay interest (often called "time deposits") and many of them do so.

The funds of savings banks are not available for short-term loans, but are usually invested in bonds or mortgages, which are supposed to be unusually safe because they are secured by property of a value higher than the amount loaned by the bank. Savings banks, unlike commercial banks, cannot create deposits by making loans; it is therefore literally true that what they lend has first come to them for safekeeping. Some savings banks are "mutual"—that is, they share their profits among their depositors.

Trust companies were originally formed to handle estates, accepting money "in trust" and investing it for the owner. As a rule, however, trust companies do a general banking business as well.

Commercial banks chartered by the federal government are known as "national banks"; other commercial banks are chartered by the several states. All national banks are subject to rigid supervision and inspection by agencies of the federal government; state banks are supervised according to state laws, which vary from state to state.

Many other financial institutions exist which accept savings or make loans—insurance companies, savings and loan associations, installment finance companies, for example—but they need not be considered here because their relationship to the money supply is somewhat more remote than that of the commercial banks.

QUESTIONS

1. Before the American colonies became independent, the legal currency was English money, but the colonists often found this hard to come by. On one occasion Massachusetts issued notes redeemable in unsettled

land owned by the colonial government. Land at the time was the chief form of wealth.

Issues of these notes led to a serious inflation, with rapid rise of the prices of commodities. Can you offer a possible explanation?

2. The Constitution authorized the United States Government to issue coins and fix their value. By authority of the Congress, the dollar was established as the legal monetary unit, having the value of, and exchangeable for, a certain weight of gold and a certain weight of silver. The ratio was roughly the same as the relative market values of the two metals. (Such a monetary standard is known as "bimetallism.")

Since gold was the scarcer metal, the principal coinage—dollars, half dollars, quarter dollars, and dimes—consisted of silver. Later, these coins began to disappear from circulation. Can you guess the reason? Can you imagine what was done about the situation?

3. Before the present Federal Reserve System was adopted, each bank could issue its own notes, redeemable in gold or silver. Seldom if ever, however, did any bank have in its possession enough of these precious metals to redeem more than a minor percentage of its outstanding notes. Why do you suppose people accepted these notes from the banks and one another at face value?

On several occasions the banks found it necessary to "suspend specie payments"; that is, to stop paying out gold or silver to depositors or to redeem their notes. What do you suppose led to these monetary crises?

13 / FEDERAL RESERVE AND
GOVERNMENT / In the United States there are,

and have long been, a large number of local banks. The people of this country have always feared private monopoly control of the money supply, and so, by legislation have prevented mergers of banks outside local regions, or even the establishment of branches. The only exceptions to this rule exist in states where state-chartered banks are allowed to do a state-wide business. The doors are kept open for all who wish to set up new and competing banks, provided they can raise the necessary capital and meet the legal requirements.

A system of many independent banks, however, sometimes failed to provide enough money when it was most needed, as in a panic, and sometimes provided too much money so that it expanded the purchasing power of the public more rapidly than goods and services were being produced. The Federal Reserve Act, passed in 1913, with subsequent amendments, set up the Federal Reserve System primarily to influence the supply of money in the public interest. The Federal Reserve System also carries out other important functions, such as acting as the fiscal agent for the federal government, facilitating the collection and clearing of checks, and conducting extensive research and publishing the results.

KEY TO THE SYSTEM

As we have seen, the principal form of money is bank deposits. Deposits may be enlarged by the banking system through an expansion of loans or diminished by a contraction of loans. The quantity of bank deposits which any bank may carry depends on the size of its reserve. The key to control of the amount of money in circulation therefore rests on control of bank reserves.

The Act set up twelve federal reserve banks, one for each of twelve

138

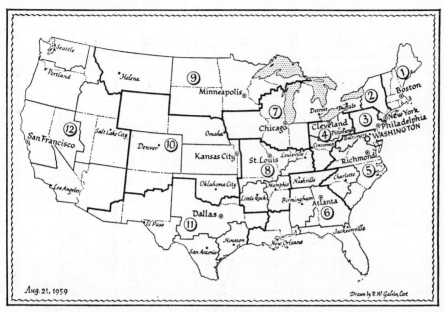

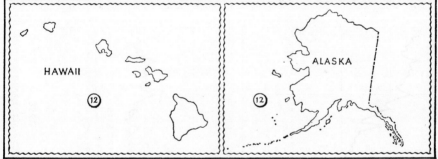

Legend

▬▬ Boundaries of Federal Reserve Districts ▬▬Boundaries of Federal Reserve Branch Territories

✪ Board of Governors of the Federal Reserve System

◉ Federal Reserve Bank Cities   • Federal Reserve Branch Cities

Fig. 13.1. Boundaries of federal reserve districts and their branch
    territories.

regions of the country. Each of these reserve banks is a "bankers' bank"—
that is, it accepts deposits from, and may make loans to, any bank in its
district which is a member of the system. Most banks are members of the
system, since the law compels all national banks to enter it and permits
state banks to do so.

The essential feature of the System is that *each member bank is compelled to deposit its reserve in the federal reserve bank of its district,*

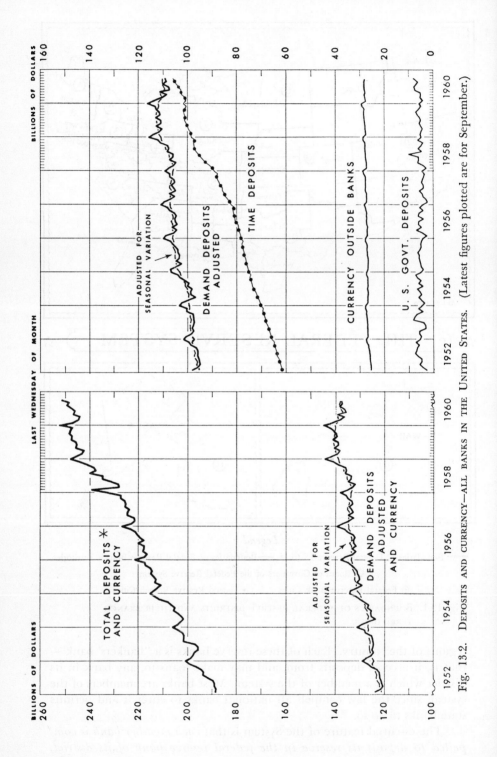

Fig. 13.2. Deposits and currency—all banks in the United States. (Latest figures plotted are for September.)

retaining only such cash as may be necessary to carry in the till for daily needs. Deposits in the twelve reserve banks by the member banks are identical with the reserves of the member banks. The reserve banks can influence the volume of these deposits just as the member banks can influence the volume of deposits held by the general public. Indeed, the power of the reserve banks over the quantity of deposits (reserves) belonging to the member banks is far greater than the power of the member banks over the quantity of deposits belonging to the public. Thus the Reserve System holds a key to the quantity of deposit money which the public can circulate in the form of checks or currency.

Figure 13/2 shows the increase in the total money in circulation including demand deposits and currency, between 1952 and 1960—about $120 billion to more than $140 billion. ("Demand deposits adjusted" means merely that seasonal fluctuations have been eliminated from the curve.) The amount of total deposits (plus currency) is much larger because it includes time deposits (savings) also.

Figure 13/3 shows how loans and investments of banks which are members of the Federal Reserve System increased in the same period— about $112 billion to about $160 billion.

Taken together, Figures 13/2 and 13/3 indicate how deposits grew as bank loans grew, since money would usually appear either in the deposit of the borrower or in the deposits of those to whose order he draws checks.

METHODS OF CONTROLLING RESERVES

There are three principal means by which the federal reserve banks influence the reserves of the member banks.

1. Varying of Discount Rate. The discount rate is the interest rate at which reserve banks may lend to the member banks. Such loans are, of course, added to the member banks' deposits in the reserve banks, that is, to their reserves. The member bank will lose money by borrowing unless it charges its own customers higher rates for loans than it has to pay to the reserve bank. When the discount rate is raised, it may be under pressure to raise its own rates if it is lending the borrowed money, and customers may therefore be discouraged from borrowing. The opposite result may arise from a lowered rate.

2. Changing of Required Reserve Ratio. The federal reserve banks have the legal power to specify (within limits) what minimum ratio between reserves and deposits must be observed by the various classes of member banks. A lowering of this ratio has the effect of allowing banks to increase loans to their customers; a raising of the ratio curbs the extension of loans.

Thus, if the required ratio is 10 percent, a bank with a reserve of

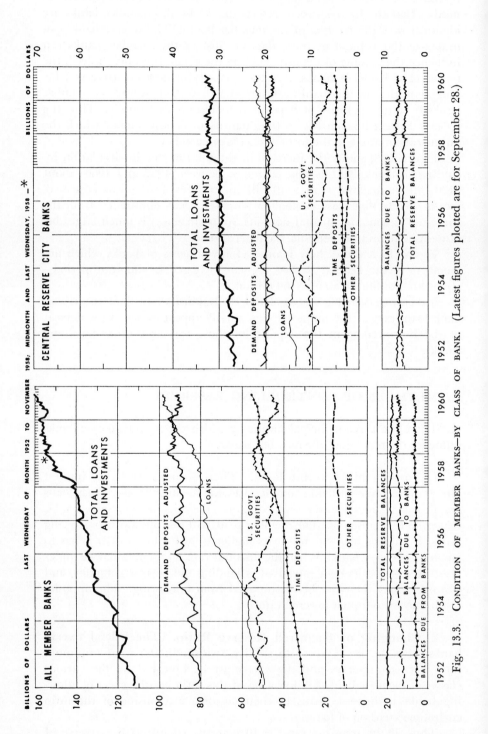

Fig. 13.3. CONDITION OF MEMBER BANKS—BY CLASS OF BANK. (Latest figures plotted are for September 28.)

$1 million may carry deposits up to $10 million. If the minimum ratio is increased to 12 percent, the same $1 million of reserves would permit deposits only up to $8.3 million; if the ratio is reduced to 8 percent, the deposits might be increased to $12.3 million. To reduce deposits of its customers, the bank would have to restrict new loans while old ones were being paid off. To increase deposits, it could make more new loans than were being repaid.

3. Open-Market Policy.   The reserve banks invest in United States Government securities such of their resources as are not used in making loans to member banks. Indeed, with minor exceptions, these are the only investments they are permitted to make. Therefore they almost always have on hand a large stock of government securities, which they may buy and sell at will. When the federal reserve banks *buy* securities, they automatically *increase* the reserves of member banks; when they *sell* securities, they automatically *decrease* the reserves of member banks. This apparently mysterious power is not magic, but operates through ordinary market mechanisms. It works this way:

(a) A federal reserve bank buys in the open market, say, a $1,000 government bond. The seller of this bond receives a check from the bank for $1,000. He deposits the check in the member bank in which he keeps his account. The member bank promptly endorses the check and presents it for payment to the reserve bank which signed it. The reserve bank just as promptly pays up by adding the $1,000 to the deposit account of the member bank, thus increasing its reserve by $1,000.

(b) A federal reserve bank sells, say, a $1,000 bond. The purchaser pays for it by giving the reserve bank a check for $1,000 drawn on a member bank where he keeps his account. The reserve bank promptly makes the member bank pay up by deducting $1,000 from its deposit in the reserve bank—that is, from its reserve.

The open-market policy of the twelve federal reserve banks is deliberately used for its effect on the reserves of member banks. Instead of changing the required *reserve ratio,* as in method 2, it changes the size of the reserves themselves.

USE OF THE THREE METHODS OF RESERVE CONTROL

1. *Raising or lowering the discount rate* can be effective in influencing member banks in regard to borrowing from the reserve banks only when the member banks need to borrow. They will not need to borrow if they already have more reserves than are required to back up their customers' deposits. Occasionally most member banks have had excess reserves.

Even when member banks cannot increase loans to their customers without borrowing from reserve banks, they are usually reluctant to borrow; when they borrow, they do so only for short periods and only if there is no other way of obtaining the money. A reserve bank is not obliged to lend and usually scrutinizes carefully the purpose of the loan. The borrowing bank must furnish collateral for the loan—usually either short-term government securities or short-term notes from its own customers. Other collateral such as mortgages may sometimes be used, but a higher rate is charged on loans secured by it.

In these circumstances, variation of the discount rate is not so much a direct change of economic incentive for borrowing as a signal by the Reserve System of its attitude toward member-bank borrowing. If the rate is raised, the reserve banks are saying in effect that credit should be tightened and that they are reluctant to lend. If the rate is lowered, the signal is given that easier credit policies are to be encouraged.

2. *Changing the required reserve ratio* affects every member bank in the system the moment the change is made. If a bank already has loaned all that it can under the old ratio, an increase of reserve requirements will force it to borrow immediately from its reserve bank or to sell securities and deposit the proceeds. If, on the other hand, the bank has excess reserves, the excess will immediately be reduced or perhaps extinguished. Should the Federal Reserve authorities reduce the reserve requirements, the whole system will at once be flooded with additional lending power.

This method is therefore a drastic one and is used infrequently.

Banks in larger cities must maintain a higher reserve ratio than those in smaller localities. In New York and Chicago, called "central reserve cities," the highest ratio obtains; in other large cities, called "reserve cities," the next highest ratio; all other banks, called "country banks," have the lowest ratio. The limits within which the Federal Reserve authorities may change the ratios are as follows:

	Range—Percent of Reserves to Deposits
Demand deposits	
Central reserve city banks (New York and Chicago)...	13–26
Reserve city banks (60 cities)	10–20
Country banks (all other member banks)	7–14
Time deposits, savings, all member banks	3–6

3. *Open-market policy* does not depend on the desire or willingness of the banks to borrow, as does changing of the discount rate; it changes the size of bank reserves at the initiative of the Federal Reserve authorities themselves. This method, however, is not so drastic as changing the required reserve ratio, since it can be applied in small degrees as well as large, and does not affect every bank at once but requires time to work through the system. It can be altered day by day as conditions change.

MULTIPLE EFFECT OF RESERVE CHANGES

Any change in the size of bank reserves—or required reserve ratios—can change the total of bank deposits by several times the change in reserves. How much the change amounts to depends on the ratio required. Let us take a simple example. Suppose a federal reserve bank buys $100 worth of government securities. The seller receives a check, which he deposits in a member bank. That bank's total of deposits owed to customers is thus increased by $100. At the same time, the member bank, by endorsing and collecting the check from the reserve bank, increases its reserve by $100.

Suppose banks are required to keep an average reserve equal to 20 percent of the deposits owed to customers. The required reserve against the new deposit will be $20; the bank will thus have excess reserves of $80. This, one might think, would permit it to make new loans of five times $80, or $400, to be added to the deposit accounts of the borrowers. The bank could safely do so if it were sure that the new borrowers would not withdraw the money, thus depleting its reserve, or that they would make withdrawals only by checks which the recipients would deposit in the same bank. In other words, the bank could make the loans if it were the only bank in the country. But, of course, there are thousands of other banks, and any money lent may be paid out by the borrowers and deposited elsewhere. Therefore the bank lends only $80—the same amount as its increase in reserve.

If the bank lends only as much as the amount by which its reserve is increased, how is it that the banking system as a whole can expand loans—and thus expand deposits—by five times as much as the increase in bank reserves (at a required reserve ratio of 20 percent)? To see how this may be done, the effects of the original transactions must be traced through the other banks which may benefit by withdrawals from this one. This process is shown in Table 13/1.

Thus, although the system as a whole reacts to an increase in reserves amounting to $100 by an increase in deposits of $500, no one bank has lent at any one time more than 80 percent of the additional amount of deposits it received. The total increase in reserves, $100, instead of remaining in one bank, has been distributed among many banks, and the total amount they lend as a result, $400, plus the original increase in deposits of $100, equals an increase in total deposits of five times the increase in reserves.

SELECTIVE CONTROLS

One other method of curbing the volume of bank credit, and hence of circulating purchasing power, does not operate on all bank credit through reserves but selectively on particular kinds of credit. The Fed-

TABLE 13/1

THE MULTIPLYING CAPACITY OF RESERVE MONEY IN BANK TRANSACTIONS[1]

Transactions	Amount deposited in checking accounts	Amount lent	Amount set aside as reserves on deposit at reserve banks
Bank 1..................	$100.00	$ 80.00	$ 20.00
2..................	80.00	64.00	16.00
3..................	64.00	51.20	12.80
4..................	51.20	40.96	10.24
5..................	40.96	32.77	8.19
6..................	32.77	26.22	6.55
7..................	26.22	20.98	5.24
8..................	20.98	16.78	4.20
9..................	16.78	13.42	3.36
10..................	13.42	10.74	2.68
11..................	10.74	8.59	2.15
12..................	8.59	6.87	1.72
13..................	6.87	5.50	1.37
14..................	5.50	4.40	1.10
15..................	4.40	3.52	.88
16..................	3.52	2.82	.70
17..................	2.82	2.26	.56
18..................	2.26	1.81	.45
19..................	1.81	1.45	.36
20..................	1.45	1.16	.29
Total for 20 banks......	$494.29	$395.45	$ 98.84
Additional banks..........	5.71	[2]4.55	[2]1.16
Grand total, all banks...	$500.00	$400.00	$100.00

[1] Assuming an average member bank reserve requirement of 20 percent of demand deposits.

[2] Adjusted to offset rounding in preceding figures.

eral Reserve authorities always have the right to limit loans secured by shares of stock, and occasionally have been temporarily granted the right to limit consumer credit and mortgage loans.

The speculator in stocks can make $25 by paying $100 in cash for a share and later selling it at $125 (if its price rises that much). But he can make $50 if he can use his $100 cash, plus a loan of $100 from a broker, a dealer, or a bank, to buy two shares of the same stock. It is customary for brokers and banks to lend money to speculators, secured by the collateral of the stocks they buy. In this case the loan of $100 would be secured by two shares—worth, when the loan was made, $200 in all. The loan would pay for half the purchase, leaving the speculator to put up the margin, or 50 percent. The percentage of the purchase that the purchaser must pay in cash is called the "margin." The Federal

Reserve authorities have the right to specify minimum margins and thus to set maximum percentages of speculative loans. This power is used to curb stock-market speculation when the Board believes it may be dangerous to the economy as a whole.

Everything looks rosy to both speculators and lenders as long as the prices of shares are going up. Indeed, the more money speculators use to buy stocks, the faster stock prices rise. But prices do not rise forever; the moment they start to fall, speculators who borrow money begin to get into trouble. The more the rise has been based on loans, the more trouble they get into. Lenders take over the collateral from borrowers who cannot repay, and sell the shares to recover their money. This sends stocks down and gets more borrowers into trouble, who must surrender their stocks pledged as collateral, which in turn must be sold, thus further depressing the market. In the end, lenders themselves may not be able to sell the stocks for enough to make up for the defaults of borrowers, and the whole financial structure of the country may tremble. This is what occurred in the crash of 1929.

Margin requirements are established under Federal Reserve Regulations T and U. Before World War II, margin requirements were 40 percent; during the war, they were raised to 50 percent and later to 75 percent. Since the war, they have varied between 50 percent and 100 percent.

Under Regulation W the Federal Reserve System has, from time to time, fixed the minimum amount of cash required from purchasers of goods on the installment plan and the maximum duration of the loans—the restrictions varying according to the nature of the article bought. Ordinary charge accounts were also limited for a time, as were single-payment loans. These measures helped to curb inflation when consumer goods were scarce because the nation's productive capacity was needed for war supplies. On June 30, 1952, Congress removed power over consumer credit from the Federal Reserve, although many believe that the banking authorities should always have this power.

Under Regulation X the Federal Reserve could specify the maximum amount that could be borrowed on real estate mortgages, the maximum period the loan could run, and the minimum periodic payments to amortize the principal of the loan. The aim was to prevent inflation in real estate credit. This power ceased in September, 1952.

During the Korean crisis voluntary credit restrictions were also promulgated by the Federal Reserve authorities.

RESERVES OF THE FEDERAL RESERVE BANKS

For years the United States was on the gold standard—which meant that its money was backed by gold and could be exchanged for it; consequently gold or its equivalent was the chief constituent of bank reserves. When the Federal Reserve System was formed, all banks that entered it were obliged to deposit their reserves in federal reserve banks, and all banks which have joined it since have been under the same obligation. A bank which now receives any monetary gold must at once deposit it. The federal reserve banks therefore came into possession of much of the monetary gold in the country, and it legally constituted their reserves.

During the depression of the 1930's, the United States went off the gold standard. This meant that henceforth nobody could draw gold out of a bank or exchange either bank notes or United States currency for gold. The federal reserve banks were compelled to deposit their gold in the United States Treasury, receiving in return gold certificates (or a credit for gold certificates). Today, the reserves of the reserve banks consist, in theory, of gold certificates. A reserve bank cannot, however, pay out gold certificates either to another bank or to anyone else to whom it may owe money.

The formalities of a metallic reserve are still observed. The gold certificates are listed as assets in the balance sheets of federal reserve banks. Legally, these certificates are regarded as reserves against the obligations of the reserve banks. These obligations consist mainly of two elements—(1) deposits in the reserve banks, most of which are the reserves of the member banks, and (2) federal reserve notes, which are issued by the federal reserve banks and form the major part of the supply of paper money. The fact that nobody can draw out deposits in gold or can redeem federal reserve notes in gold seems to make no practical difference in the value either of deposit money or of bank notes.

According to present law, reserves of the reserve banks must constitute at least 25 percent of their deposit and note obligations in combination. This law—which might, of course, be amended by Congress—thus sets an upper limit to the supply of money. But the limit has never been reached or even approximated in recent years. For example, the actual reserve ratio of the federal reserve banks on August 31, 1960, was 40 percent, as against the required 25 percent. On the basis of their existing reserves, the federal reserve banks could on that date have increased member bank reserves by 80 per cent. And if this increase were passed on by the member banks to the money supply of the public in the ratio of 5 to 1, the total money supply could have been increased by 800 percent—or eightfold (160 percent times 5).

FEDERAL RESERVE BALANCE SHEET

Now let us examine a balance sheet of the twelve federal reserve banks combined.

The most important items in this balance sheet are, among the assets, gold certificate reserves, discounts for member banks, and United States Government securities; and, among the liabilities, federal reserve notes and member bank reserve accounts. The reserve ratio at the bottom is the percentage that the reserves (gold certificates and other cash) are of the federal reserve notes and deposits combined.

TABLE 13/2

COMPARISON OF BALANCE SHEETS OF FEDERAL RESERVE BANKS[1]
(in millions of dollars)

Account	1920	1930	1940	1953	1960
Assets					
Gold certificate reserves.....	[2]2,060	[2]2,941	19,692	21,339	18,709
Other cash	264	220	229	298	429
Discounts for member banks.	2,687	251	3	420	405
Other discounts and advances	----	----	1	15	----
Industrial loans	----	----	8	2	----
Acceptances purchased	260	364	----	----	32
U. S. Government securities.	287	729	2,184	25,886	27,762
Federal Reserve notes of other Reserve Banks	31	22	27	167	443
Uncollected cash items......	637	585	914	4,503	4,917
Miscellaneous assets	28	89	88	197	313
Total assets	6,254	5,201	23,146	52,827	52,009
Liabilities					
Federal Reserve notes.......	[3]3,553	1,663	5,965	26,808	27,621
Deposits:					
Member bank— reserve accounts	1,781	2,471	13,837	20,064	17,735
U. S. Treasurer— general account	57	19	482	799	481
Foreign and other deposits	23	28	1,712	888	636
Deferred availability cash items	519	564	774	3,134	4,209
Miscellaneous liabilities	19	11	5	26	42
Total liabilities	5,952	4,756	22,775	51,719	50,725
Capital Accounts					
Capital paid in.............	100	170	138	265	402
Surplus	202	275	179	612	775
Other capital accounts......	([4])	([4])	54	231	106
Total liabilities and capital accounts	6,254	5,201	23,146	52,827	52,009
The reserve ratio (percent) .	43.3	73.7	90.6	43.9	40.3

[1] As of Dec. 31, 1920 and 1930; Dec. 24, 1940; Dec. 23, 1953; and Aug. 31, 1960.

[2] Prior to enactment of the Gold Reserve Act of 1934, the amount reported under this item included gold owned by federal reserve banks.

[3] Includes $217 million of federal reserve bank notes, which are no longer issued.

[4] Included in "miscellaneous liabilities."

The balance sheet is given for five years—1920, 1930, 1940, 1953, and 1960. The changes that have taken place in the size of various items are indicative of much financial and economic history.

Gold reserves increased markedly between 1930 and 1940, mainly because during this decade much of the gold in other nations was shipped to the United States, partly for safekeeping and partly in payment of exports of goods and services that foreign nations had no other means of buying. Imports of gold exceeded exports of gold by nearly $16 billion in the period 1934–1940.

Discounts for member banks (that is, loans to them) was, in 1920, the principal means of supplying these banks with reserves and currency. By 1930 the depression had begun to hit the banks severely and they could borrow less; hence the reserve banks bolstered the member banks' reserves by buying government securities, which show a marked increase.

By 1940 the reserves of the member banks had been so increased by inflowing gold that they did not need to borrow; they had large excess reserves. The reserve banks had, in the meantime, seen the banks through the crisis of 1931–1933 by buying large amounts of government securities; it was in these three years that gains before 1940 in government holdings mainly occurred.

After 1940 the reserve banks accumulated government securities rapidly to support their prices while the government was engaged in heavy war borrowing. This policy came to a temporary end in 1951; by 1953 the banks had begun to borrow more than during the previous decade.

Increases in other items in the balance sheet reflect the country's expanding economy and the rising price level since 1930.

It will be noted that among the deposits are accounts of the United States Treasury and foreign banks. These are small, however, compared with deposits (reserves) of the member banks.

Obviously what, in practice, limits the money supply is not the size of the reserves of the federal reserve banks or the minimum reserve ratio applied to them, but the deliberate policy of the Federal Reserve authorities. The gold reserve, though still in existence, is like a sort of archaeological relic; observance of its form has become a ritual. The actual control lies in management, and actual money payments consist mainly in bookkeeping transfers.

After the System was formed, all bank notes, which previously had been issued by the separate national banks, were exchanged for federal reserve notes as soon as they reached a reserve bank. Thus, most of the old bank notes gradually disappeared. When a bank needs federal reserve notes or other currency to give to its customers, it can obtain it from a federal reserve bank by the simple expedient of charging it against its deposit account in the reserve bank—that is, against its own reserve.

STRUCTURE OF THE FEDERAL RESERVE SYSTEM

The member banks of the Federal Reserve System are private, profit-making enterprises. How is it that the government can exercise so much control over them, and how is that control organized? The national banks, which were compelled by law to join the System, were granted their corporate charters by the federal government under special conditions established by act of Congress, and have been subject to federal regulation ever since their establishment in the 1860's. State-chartered banks, which may choose to become members of the System, must, if they join, accept the regulations established by the System. In addition to this basis of legal authority, the government is granted by the Constitution sole power over the issuance of money, and of course banks are closely involved in that function.

Each of the twelve reserve banks established by the Federal Reserve Act is technically "owned" by the member banks of its district, which under the law contributed its capital. This ownership, however, is narrowly circumscribed in its powers. Dividends payable to the owners are limited by law to 6 percent. The reserve banks are instructed by the law to guide their own activities not by the profit incentive but by the need for regulation of the money supply in the public interest. Each reserve bank has nine directors, only three of whom may be bankers. Three must represent business or agricultural interests. These six are elected by the member banks of the district. The other three members represent the public interest directly and are appointed by a central authority in Washington—the Board of Governors of the Federal Reserve System. The directors of each federal reserve bank elect the president (the active executive) of that bank, but the Board of Governors must approve or disapprove the choice and the salary paid to him.

At the top, the Board of Governors is a purely governmental organization. Like Supreme Court justices, its seven members are appointed by the President of the United States and confirmed by the Senate. Their terms are staggered, so that no one President can "pack" the Board with his own appointees. Not only is the Board safeguarded against any political influence that might be exerted by a President, but it is also far more independent of Congress than most other governmental agencies, since it never has to ask Congress for any appropriations with which to pay its expenses. These are paid out of the earnings of the reserve banks—and their earnings are ample. Congress, of course, retains the power to change the legislation under which the Board operates.

Under the law, the Board of Governors has authority over all the important functions of the System which affect general credit policy. It reviews and determines discount rates set by the reserve banks. It determines minimum reserve requirements of the member banks. The important open-market policy is determined by an Open-Market Committee, on which the Board of Governors has a majority. All seven members of the Board are members of the Committee, whereas the twelve reserve banks are represented by five members. The Board of Governors also determines selective credit controls exercised by the System, such as margin requirements for speculative loans.

The Federal Reserve System is thus a curious and ingenious organization, which combines private and public interest, decentralization, and centralization. At the bottom, member banks compete with one another for profitable business. They decide to whom they will lend and how much. (Nobody can force them to lend if they do not wish to do so.) They manage credit at the "grass roots." Above the member banks are the reserve banks, in which they have a voice, but which influence the over-all effect of their policy by control over their reserves. Over the member banks and the reserve banks, in turn, stands a public, non-partisan agency entrusted with determining the policies executed by the reserve banks. Through bank examiners, it also supervises the accounts and the practices of the member banks.

CRITERIA OF POLICY

When do the Federal Reserve authorities decide that more money is needed, and when do they decide that growth of the money supply should be restricted? Their decisions are based partly on experience, partly on theory.

Demands for loans from the banks normally increase at certain seasons of the year—for example, at harvest time, when farmers are paid for their crops; during the fall while retail stores are building up their inventories in preparation for Christmas shopping; when income taxes have to be paid. Thus, signals from the banking system itself have long been recognized and expected; preparations to satisfy them have become routine. After each of the seasonal peaks of demand for credit, loans are repaid, currency returns to the banks, and reserves become ample.

Long-term changes in the demand for credit also occur. As production and trade grow, more money and deposits are required by the public in order to carry on day-by-day transactions. The banking system must furnish the means of payment. But there may come a time when the supply and use of money grows faster than production and trade. In this case the demand for money indicates that the urgency of purchasers in buying goods and services is growing faster than the supply. In a market system, free to respond to the relationships of demand and supply, an excess of demand boosts prices. Under such circumstances the Federal Reserve authorities are likely to decide that the public interest would be best served by restricting the supply of money in use; that is, by limiting bank reserves so that banks will be forced to curb the growth of loans.

This general principle is easier to state than to apply. The central banking authorities may have difficulty in deciding whether the growth of demand may not stimulate more production. They may fear that a restriction of credit would interfere with normal economic growth and would even contribute to a drop in business activity (as it did, for example, in 1921), for which they would be blamed. In any case, they are not pledged to maintain prices at all times without change. The problem is to allow enough freedom to a dynamic and changing economic order, without stimulating damaging price inflation. But, at any rate, once the banking authorities have decided to curb bank loans, ample means are available by which they may execute their policy.

When, on the other hand, demand for goods and services is not active enough to keep the labor and equipment of the nation fully employed, the banking authorities naturally do not wish to restrict the ability of the banks to extend loans. At times of widespread unemployment, there is a clear indication that they should make credit easy. It is easier then to choose the correct policy than in times of business activity. But the correct policy is much harder to execute, at least by central banking policy alone. No matter how large bank reserves may be, businessmen may be reluctant to borrow because they think business prospects are not good. Or the banks themselves may distrust the ability of applicants for loans to repay. The Federal Reserve authorities have no power to force people to borrow or banks to lend. At such times, as in the later 1930's, the member banks may hold large excess reserves while unemployment persists. In the late thirties, the banking system held an ample *supply* of money; the difficulty was that business *demand* for it was lagging.

GOVERNMENT INFLUENCE ON THE MONEY SUPPLY

During great wars, government is unable to collect enough in taxes to pay its war expenses. The result is that its cash budget (see Chapter 2) is heavily unbalanced; it is passing out to the public more money than it is taking in. This situation leads to an increased public demand for goods and services, while the supply of goods and services available for civilians is restricted by military requirements. The result is war inflation—that is, rapidly rising prices.

In the Revolutionary War and the Civil War, government printed the money which it had to spend, over and above its receipts. In more recent wars, government did not create "fiat" money in this way; instead, it borrowed. But it had to borrow so much that it could not get enough merely by borrowing the savings of the public; the banking system had to create much of the extra money. This presents a difficult problem to Federal Reserve policy. It must support the government's need for money; at the same time it must try to restrict price inflation. But it cannot at the same time make credit easy for the government and tight for everybody else. At least, it cannot do this with any of the three major general controls it has over reserves; and it does not have enough selective controls to accomplish the result, even supposing efficient controls could be applied without throttling the war effort itself.

During World War II, price increases were limited by direct price control and rationing. Banking policy entered the picture only to the extent of limiting consumer credit and building loans. The result was that people received more money than ever with which to buy; but since they were not allowed to buy at will, they were forced to save much more than usual. The moment governmental rationing and price controls were removed after the war, they used these savings to buy goods they wanted; consequently, the price inflation suppressed during the war occurred after it.

When there is no war, government sometimes has a cash surplus and sometimes a cash deficit. When government has a surplus, it is decreasing the quantity of money in the hands of the public; when it has a deficit, it is adding to the public's money supply. Obviously, if government works at cross purposes with Federal Reserve policy regarding the supply of money, it may counteract that policy. When, however, government and Federal Reserve follow the same monetary policy, that policy is greatly strengthened, particularly during periods of depression and unemployment. Then, as we have seen, the Federal Reserve authorities can make the money supply in the banks abundant, but they cannot compel the banks to lend or business to borrow. Government, however, can spend on public works and other projects at such times, borrowing the money from the banks.

During periods of high employment and rising prices, the government can greatly aid a restrictive banking policy by maintaining a cash surplus or at least a balanced cash budget. Even so, however, there may be a conflict between Treasury policy and Federal Reserve policy if the national debt is large and has to be continually refunded—that is, if government securities which reach the maturity date have to be paid off and new securities have to be issued to take their places. In such a case, the Treasury is likely to favor a large and steady demand for its securities, since that means it can sell the new issues without paying so much in interest to the lenders. It may rely on open-market buying by federal reserve banks to maintain the demand for its new issues and to keep their price up, and this is equivalent to keeping the interest down. But every time the federal reserve banks buy securities in the open market, they increase the reserves of member banks and thus loosen credit. Since there already is an inflationary tendency, this influence will counteract what is usually thought to be good Federal Reserve policy. A controversy of this very sort occurred after World War II. The laws governing the structure of the Federal Reserve System were expressly designed to keep it independent of the President and his appointees, because such conflicts between the Secretary of the Treasury and the Federal Reserve System were foreseen. The only good solution, however, is that both should work together in the public interest. Even so, Federal Reserve and governmental policy combined may not be sufficient to curb rising prices unless the private sectors of the economy—especially big business and organized labor—cooperate with the effort.

Chapter 30 illustrates the role played by the Federal Reserve System and government in an actual inflation situation. Recent shrinking in the gold reserve is discussed in Chapter 31.

PROBLEM

A commercial bank receives $1,000 in monetary gold from abroad, deposited in payment for exports. Assume these facts:

(a) Legal minimum reserve of federal reserve banks is 25 percent of member banks' deposits and federal reserve notes.

(b) Legal minimum ratio of reserve to deposits for a commercial bank is 20 percent.

(c) The bank referred to has no excess reserves.

1. What is the maximum amount by which, as a result, the total money supply of the country can increase? Show your procedure step by step.

2. If the Federal Reserve authorities wished to discourage increase of money as a result of receipt of gold from abroad, what could they do?

14 / THEORIES OF MONEY AND

INCOME / In Chapter 9 we inspected the theory developed by economists to account for the price of any one type of commodity—the traditional theory of supply and demand. There is another, and more comprehensive, kind of price variation.

The demand for *all* salable articles and services is greater at one time than at others; so is the supply. Moreover, all prices, in the aggregate, tend to rise or to fall. This changeability of total demand and total supply bears on two vitally important problems of any society. One is the problem of business cycles—the alternation between prosperity and depression. The other is the problem of the conditions favoring long-term economic growth. What conditions of demand, supply, and price favor an improvement in the material level of life, and what conditions tend to prevent or retard that improvement?

These questions involve, among other things, consideration of money. How can we conceive the total demand in any or all markets, and how can that demand be measured? Obviously, only by the amount of money people are willing to spend. Although total supply also varies, for the time being variations in demand as represented by money will be considered. We have discovered that there is a continuous flow of money through the economy and that both the Federal Reserve System and government can influence the flow. Now we are ready to take a look at the theory put forward to explain variations in the amount and spending of money and to account for the effects of the variations.

THE QUANTITY THEORY

As long ago as men began to theorize about economics, the belief was developed that when the total quantity of money increased, prices in general would rise. If people had more money to spend, they would

156

offer more for the things they wanted, and the sellers could charge more. One instance, noted by Adam Smith in *The Wealth of Nations* (1776) as well as by others before him, was the long-continued rise in prices throughout Europe which followed the Spanish conquests of Mexico, Peru, and other new-world colonies in the sixteenth century. The gold and silver brought back by the conquerors flooded European markets with coins, and prices tended to rise as long as this flood continued. At least, this was the impression; statistics were so scanty and unreliable that nobody knew exactly how much the circulation of money had increased or how much the general average of prices had risen.

Many times common experience seemed to verify the quantity theory. When money was easy to get and people were spending freely, prices would rise; when money was scarce and people had little to spend, prices would fall. Scarcity of money was especially inconvenient when it seemed to hamper the growth of a new country like the North American colonies or, later, the United States itself. But overabundance of money was inconvenient for those with fixed incomes or employees who could not easily increase their pay, because it meant a high cost of living to them. The quantity theory in its crude form lay behind many hot political controversies about the issuance of money, and this theory was accepted by many economists.

Later, economists saw that the theory, to be logically valid, required more exact statement. In the first place, a large quantity of money could have no effect on prices if it was hoarded—that is, not spent—and little effect if it was spent slowly. In the second place, the supply of goods and services had to be considered. If supply increased as rapidly as the money spent, the two forces would equalize each other and prices would not increase. If there were to be a watertight theory of aggregate demand, aggregate supply, and average price, the interdependence of all three factors would have to be shown, just as with the theory of supply, demand, and price for any single article.

An equation intended to embody just this relationship was eventually formulated in the early part of the twentieth century by Simon Newcomb and developed by Irving Fisher. The simplest form of this "equation of exchange" is shown below.

$$MV = PT$$

In this equation:

M represents the total quantity of money, including not merely gold and silver but also paper money of all kinds (such as bank notes) and bank deposits which can be spent by drawing of checks.

V represents the average velocity of the circulation of money. Multiplying V by M, you should get, according to Fisher, the total sum that changes hands in any given time. Thus, if there were in existence $10 billion and if all of it circulated from hand to hand on the average of once every month, $10 billion a month, or $120 billion a year, would be spent.

P represents the average of prices.

T represents the number of all transactions taking place, that is, the total number of instances in which something is bought and sold. Multiplying *P* by *T*, you get, according to Fisher, the amount of money that changes hands in any given time. For example, if the average price of everything sold were $1 and if 10 billion transactions a month occurred, $10 billion must change hands in a month, or $120 billion in a year. Since both *M V* and *P T* equal the same thing, that is, the amount of money that changes hands in a given time, they must equal each other.

Now, as in any equation, a change in any one factor must be balanced by some equal change in one or more of the other factors. For example, suppose the quantity of money is doubled while the velocity of its circulation remains the same. Then, on the left side of the equation, you have $(2M)V$. This implies that some factor on the right side of the equation must double. If no more goods and services were offered on the market, there could be no increase in *T*, the number of transactions. The inevitable result would be a doubling of average price $(2P)T$. The equation thus becomes:

$$(2M)V = (2P)T$$

This is merely a mathematical restatement of the old theory that a doubling of the money supply means a doubling of price, *other things remaining equal.*

It is easy to vary the equation to describe crudely other observed situations. For example:

$$MV = (\tfrac{1}{2}P)\,(2T)$$

The quantity of money and velocity do not change; but prices are cut in half and as a consequence transactions double. Or, transactions double and as a consequence prices are cut in half. Such a situation could arise in a rapidly developing nation, if its production grew while its money supply did not.

$$MV = (2P)\,(\tfrac{1}{2}T)$$

A doubling of prices brings about a halving of sales; a reduction in sales by one half brings about a doubling of prices.

Actual changes in aggregate supply, demand, and price would, of course, probably be more complicated than those shown in these illustrations, since all four factors at once might be involved; but if the equation represents the facts accurately, all such changes must result in a balance. As a matter of fact, it has been difficult to accumulate the data necessary to test the mathematical accuracy of the equation. In particular, those who first used the equation were unable to estimate velocity, which has been found to vary widely in recent years. The Federal Reserve System tries to adjust the quantity of money to agree with the requirements produced by changes in the other factors.

THE GOLD STANDARD

In the development of economic theory about money and the practice based upon it, the quantity theory had a competitor which often became mixed up with it—the idea that good money had a market value of its own, an "intrinsic" value. Any kind of money which varied from this value was said to be, in some degree, spurious and a fraud on the public.

A gold coin—for example, a twenty-dollar gold piece—was required to contain a certain weight of gold of specified fineness. The government stamp on this coin was a guarantee of the weight and fineness of the gold contained in it. The coin was therefore universally acceptable as being worth twenty dollars. Some governments, being in need of extra money, had deliberately debased their coinage by adulterating the precious metal or by shading the weight of coins. This practice was clearly reprehensible—it was a form of cheating. From time to time, nearly all governments had issued paper money which they promised to redeem in the precious metal on demand. If they were prepared to fulfill this promise, well and good. But if they could not do so, then they were just as guilty of cheating as if they had actually debased their coinage.

When the practice of commercial banking arose, banks as well as governments issued money in the form of paper notes which they promised to redeem in government coins on demand. The value of these notes depended on the ability of the banks to fulfill their promises.

When the metal on which coins and paper money are based consists of gold, and when gold is allowed to circulate freely whenever people would rather have it than paper money—that is, when all paper money is fully redeemable in gold, the "gold standard" obtains. If, in any nation, money is based on silver, that nation is on the "silver standard." When —as in the United States at the beginning and during the greater part of the nineteenth century—money is based on both gold and silver in a certain ratio to each other "bimetallism" is the theoretical basis of money.

A nation which adhered firmly to a gold or a silver standard came to be known as one in which the money was "sound," or one which had "hard money." Experience seemed to show that when a nation departed from this practice by issuing irredeemable currency, as the United States and other nations did during important wars, its currency would fall alarmingly in value. That is another way of stating that prices suffered a marked increase, since the real value of a dollar falls when it will buy less. When the metallic standard was abandoned and prices rose, adherents of a metallic standard often assumed that the price rise was caused by the fact that the currency would no longer buy so much gold or silver. Gold still held its "intrinsic value" as money, but the spurious paper currency no longer represented that value.

A rise in prices when irredeemable currency is issued is perhaps better explained by the Irving Fisher equation ($MV = PT$). When a nation is on the full gold or silver standard and administers it honestly, the total amount of money (including deposit money) depends on the amount of gold or silver in its possession. That is, the volume of money is automatically limited, in some ratio, by the metallic base. In that case, no deliberate increase in the supply of money can take place by the easy process of printing additional paper money. But whenever the tie to the metallic standard is cut, and the issuance of paper money depends only on the will of government or banking authorities, the money issued may be in such large quantities that the volume of money increases faster than production and prices rise drastically. This process came to be called "inflation." Inflation is the blowing up of a monetary balloon no longer tied to earth, so that prices might rise out of sight.

The Fisher equation can also explain rises and falls in prices even when no irredeemable paper money is issued, changes in prices which depend on changes in the quantity of gold or silver.

International aspects of the gold standard will be discussed in Chapter 28.

THE CONFLICT IN POLICY

According to Irving Fisher and many other economists, a major objective of public policy should be to avoid marked rises and falls in average prices resulting from inflation and deflation. "Stable money" expressed their aim. In order to keep P, average prices, from changing, it was necessary to control one or more of the other factors in the equation of exchange. In a private-enterprise economy, it did not seem possible to do much about V, the velocity with which money is spent, since that depends on the habits of a host of individual buyers. Nor was it possible to do much about T, the number of transactions, for the same reason. But government and the banks could deliberately influence M, the quantity of money.

The advocates of stable money therefore urged that the quantity of money be increased when a falling price tendency appeared, and be decreased when a rising price tendency appeared. Changes in quantity would thus counteract changes in prices. As a result, the dollar would be "sound," in terms of the commodities it could buy.

The means which Irving Fisher recommended to change the quantity of money was simply to vary the legal weight of the gold dollar. Since the United States was on the gold standard, a decrease in the weight of each gold coin would automatically make a given quantity of gold worth more dollars and so increase the quantity of money. That would, Fisher thought, push prices up. To increase the weight of the dollar would correspondingly depress prices.

Any proposal deliberately to vary the amount of money in order to stabilize prices outraged the stalwart adherents of the gold standard. If a man made a contract to pay a certain amount of dollars (dollars being redeemable in gold), it did not seem fair or honest that, at the time of payment, he should be required to pay with dollars perhaps worth more in gold than when he made the contract, or perhaps worth less. Furthermore, to give to government officials the power to vary the quantity of money gave them the power to inflate. Government officials were politicians. There were always powerful forces in the country who wanted higher prices—speculators, farmers, many businessmen. So long as the quantity of money was automatically controlled by the amount of gold, politicians could not do anything about it. But once they were given the power to "manage money," as this new theory suggested, they were pretty sure to abuse it or to use it unskillfully—so thought the "hard money" men.

The reply of those who believed in managed money was that it was unfair and dishonest to make contracts payable in dollars which might become worth more or less in purchasable *goods* than when the contracts were made. Since experience had shown that under the gold standard prices could and did, on the average, vary widely over a period, a choice had to be made between maintaining the worth of the dollar to a given amount in gold or to a given amount in bread, clothing, rent, and all the other things people bought. As for politicians, why did we have a government at all if we could not trust officials to manage important matters? The legislation prescribing managed money could be carefully phrased to safeguard the public ends in view.

VARIATIONS IN THE INCOME-SPENDING FLOW

Monetary theory in its early stages had to do mainly with sources of the money supply and regulation of the quantity available. Clearly, this is only part of the story. Anyone who wants to understand the ups and downs of economic activity or the long-term growth of an economy must examine the ways that money gets into or out of circulation and the reasons for variation in its circular flow.

In Chapter 4 the circular flow of payments about the economy was described. Money received by an individual, a business concern, or a governmental unit is paid out again; it is received by some other individual, business, or government. This flow can roughly be measured at several points. The manner and result of such measurements was described in Chapter 5 on national income accounting.

If no dollars were ever added to or subtracted from the money flow and if the velocity of the flow never changed, apparently the total demand (in dollars) would never change. But both experience and statistical measurement show undeniably that it does change—and often by considerable amounts. By what theory may such changes be explained?

The earlier theories of supply and demand offer no adequate explanation of this kind of change. Indeed, taken literally, they imply that since in a free market system the economy is always approximating an equilibrium, in such a system there would be no important depressions or booms. Violent irregularities in income would result from absence of competition or from other interferences with the free market. For example, long-continued or severe unemployment would indicate that the price of labor—that is, wages—was not low enough to stimulate the demand for labor. If workers would only accept low enough wages, the tendency to equilibrium would eliminate unemployment.

This type of theory departs from actual experience so far that it is not of much practical use, at least in explaining business cycles. For example, it completely ignores the fact that when wages are reduced in depressions, the purchasing power of labor is reduced accordingly.

THE THEORY OF INCOME VARIATION

A more recent theory to account for unemployment and income variation is associated with John Maynard Keynes, who elaborated it in his *General Theory of Employment, Interest and Money* (1936). Keynes put together ideas of many of his predecessors, and the theory has been subject to modifications and development since he presented it. Only a brief summary of this type of theory can be discussed here.

A crucial question is, how does money leak out of the flow of income and spending so that the flow becomes smaller, and how is money added to the flow so that it becomes larger?

Any person or other economic unit receiving money may either spend it or not spend it. What is spent flows on and becomes a receipt by other units. What is not spent is held out from the income stream, at least temporarily.

Money received and not spent is often called "savings." If savings are kept in a strongbox (in cash) or are hoarded in any other way, the money is withheld from circulation and so diminishes the volume of the income-spending stream. This is true of savings hoarded by an individual, of business profits not paid out to stockholders and not invested, of money received by government in taxes or other current income and not paid out again to meet governmental expenses.

The income-spending stream is not decreased by the total amount saved, if all that is saved is not hoarded. If an individual deposits his savings in a savings bank and the bank lends the money on mortgage to a builder, the savings will presumably be spent for building and will re-enter the flow in that way. If an individual puts his savings into insurance and the insurance company buys a corporation bond with the money, the corporation may expand its plant with the proceeds, thus spending the money. If a corporation uses its own savings to buy machinery, the savings are spent and become income for those who sell and make the machinery. If a government with a cash surplus increases its spending or reduces its taxes so that what it spends more nearly balances what it takes from the public, it diminishes the amount it holds out of the income stream by the amount of reduction in its cash surplus.

If, however, those who use money for investment do not spend so much for factories, houses, machinery, and the like as savers lay aside, the income stream shrinks and a recession occurs.

How can more be invested than is saved? The extra money can come from that which has previously been hoarded. Or it can come from money derived from the banking system through expansion of credit. It can also come from printing and spending of new currency by government. Instead of printing extra money for the purpose, however, the United States and Britain usually borrow when they wish to spend more than they receive in current income. In present practice, therefore, the two main sources of money used in such a way that it enlarges national income are (1) "dishoarding" and (2) expansion of bank loans either to private spenders or to government.

The two basic Keynesian equations of national income in any accounting period are simple ones resting on the above logic. The first says that all income is either spent or saved.

$$Y = C + S$$

Y means national income. C is the total amount spent for immediate use (consumption). S is the total of savings. This equation looks at income as it is dispensed.

The other basic equation looks at income from the point of view of the payments received, which constitute income.

$$Y = C + I$$

Y, national income, equals the total amount received for the making and handling of consumption goods and services (C), plus the total amount received for the provision of investment goods (I).

By combining the two equations algebraically, we get:

$$C + S = C + I, \text{ or, eliminating } C, S = I$$

This equation means that, for any accounting period, savings equal investment. A study of any national income account set up in double-entry form will show that the figures accord with this statement. But is not the heart of the Keynes theory that savings may be either larger or smaller than investment?

This apparent contradiction is explained by supporters of Keynes as follows: What people in the aggregate *intend* to save at any one time may, and usually does, vary from the amount which people in the aggregate *intend* to invest. But a study of the aggregate figures for a whole accounting period reveals, according to the theory, that what actually has been saved in any one period can be no larger or no smaller than what actually has been invested.

The inequality is between *intended* saving and *intended* investment. Looking forward, or, as economists say, *ex ante*, if intended investment is less than intended saving, national income must fall because total expenditures have declined. If intended investment is greater than intended saving, national income will rise. People begin by reducing their spending and so reduce the total income, or by increasing their spending and so increase the total income. But when total income is reduced, savings are reduced because they are directly dependent on income. Conversely, savings rise when total income is increased. Actual saving must equal actual investment in any past period because, by definition, actual saving and actual investment are both the same thing—they are that part of total flow of income or output that is not consumed. In short, the mechanism that brings saving and investment into equality (*ex post*) when they were unequal (*ex ante*) is a change in the national income.

It is difficult to verify this theory, as it is to verify the theories which preceded it. There seems to be no way of measuring intended savings and intended investment, since economic behavior can scarcely be measured before it has occurred. Actual savings, too, are very difficult to measure even after they have been made; most national income accounting does so chiefly by assuming that savings constitute the difference between income and spending for consumption. But such a residual should be checked by direct measurement.

THE THEORY OF CONSUMPTION AND SAVING

The mere descriptive logic showing how changes in the national income may arise from discrepancies between intended saving and intended investment is incomplete without theories to account for the division of income between saving and investment. Let us begin with saving.

The classical theory held that the amount saved is dependent in large part on the inducement offered to the saver through interest. Keynes believed saving is a habit which has little to do with the rate of interest. Saving varies rather with the size of the income. People with large incomes save more than people with small incomes. Keynes called the percentage of national income saved the "average propensity to save" and the percentage spent for consumption the "average propensity to consume." When used in mathematical equations, these terms become "savings function" and "consumption function."

Since people with large incomes save more than people with small incomes at any one time (a generalization supported by statistical evidence), Keynes inferred that when the average of incomes rises, the average propensity to save will rise. He also assumed that when incomes did not change much, the total amount saved would not greatly vary. Both these assumptions are open to question, at least in the United States in recent years.

Attempts to predict future economic conditions have made serious errors by using the Keynes assumptions about the predictability of the consumption function. Since people, on the average, always spend much more than they save, even a minor mistake in estimating the consumption function will lead to a much larger percentage error in estimating the savings function. For example, if it is estimated that people will spend $90 out of every $100, saving $10, and they really spend $88, saving $12, the error of slightly more than 2 percent in estimating the consumption function means an error of 20 percent in the predicted savings function.

REASONS FOR BUSINESS INVESTMENT

To use money profitably, a businessman has to obtain a larger return than he pays to those who supply the money. Obviously, at any given interest rate, a variation in the return he expects may change his decisions about investing in new equipment, buildings, or inventory. It is the difference between the interest rate per dollar and the expected return per dollar invested that counts, not the interest rate alone.

If a manufacturer buys a new machine, he will expect it to pay for itself in a given number of years. The revenue he derives from its operation must be enough to pay the interest on the money he has to tie up in order to buy it, plus enough to repay the amount he has to spend for the machine itself. If he thinks that the market for his product will keep the machine busy, and that he can sell the product for a price high enough to make the investment profitable, he will buy the machine; otherwise he will not do so.

Suppose a businessman who does not think the investment of borrowed money will be profitable already has idle money of his own and does not need to borrow in order to make a new investment, could he not make the investment profitably? No, because he could lend this money at the same rate of return that he expects to earn by tying it up in new plant and equipment.

If he does not even lend, except perhaps by buying readily salable and reliable securities, it will be because he is so pessimistic about the immediate future that he wants to keep his money in cash so that it will be available at a moment's notice. People who keep money in cash rather than invest it are exercising, according to Keynes, "liquidity preference"—that is, they are keeping their funds liquid. Liquidity preference results in hoarding and so holds money out of the income-spending stream.

THE INVESTMENT MULTIPLIER

Since, according to Keynes, saving habits are fairly steady and are not much influenced by the same forces that determine the amount of investment in new capital goods, the aggregate amount of intended saving may be less or greater than the aggregate amount of intended investment. If intended saving is less than intended investment, savers will be holding less out of the income flow than investors are putting into it, and aggregate income will expand.

The theory of the investment multiplier is supposed to explain *how much* aggregate income will expand as a result of any given addition to investment.

An investment of, say, $1 billion will theoretically expand national income more than $1 billion. Why? Suppose the billion is spent in putting up new factories. It will be paid out to the building contractors and therefore will bring income for them. This already increases total income by a billion. The contractors will pay the money to their workers and the producers of materials. On this second step, $1 billion is added to the incomes of those who receive it. Already we have a $2 billion addition to aggregate spending. But the increase does not stop there. The workers and material makers will spend the money, those who receive this money will also spend it, and so on. Since the money flow is supposed to be circular, going round and round, any addition to the quantity flowing will add to incomes all the way around the circle.

But as long as people save anything, they will not spend all they receive. Therefore, the addition to income will diminish at each step of receiving and spending. It might be inferred that the total addition to income will be determined by the average fraction of a year's total income being spent (that is, not saved) at the time the new investment is made or, in other words, by the average propensity to consume. But, according to Keynes, this assumption would be erroneous. When the income of a person is increased, he spends a smaller fraction of it than before, and therefore saves a larger fraction. And when national income is increased for any year, all the people in the nation spend a smaller fraction of it than before. What actually affects the total addition to income as a result of any given addition to total investment is the fraction of the *additional* income which is spent. This fraction is called the "marginal propensity to consume."

Now we are ready to conclude: by what must we multiply the addition to investment in order to discover how much it will increase national income? Let us say that $\frac{4}{5}$ of the addition to national income caused by an additional investment would be spent during a year—in other words, that the marginal propensity to consume is $\frac{4}{5}$. The amount of the additional income that would be saved is therefore $\frac{1}{5}$. Stand this fraction on its head (invert it) and you get 5. Five is the "multiplier." An additional investment of $1 billion in a year would increase national income for that year by $5 billion.

Putting all this in the approved technical terms: the investment multiplier is the reciprocal ($\frac{5}{1}$) of the complement ($\frac{1}{5}$) of the marginal propensity to consume ($\frac{4}{5}$).

The logic of this proposition may be tested by the following procedure. At the first step, the recipients spend $\frac{4}{5}$ of the extra amount they get as the result of an addition to investment. Four fifths of $1 billion is $800 million. At the second step, the recipients get $800 million and spend $\frac{4}{5}$ of it, or $640 million, and so on. If this process were followed through to the end, adding up all the incomes at each step until there was nothing more to add, a final sum of $5 billion would be obtained. But the process would be endless, because by this arithmetical process there would always be something more to add. By an infinite series of steps, the sum would be approaching $5 billion as a limit. The application of calculus could prove that the final sum is $5 billion.

The multiplier works just as logically downward as it does upward. A *contraction* in investment should produce a larger contraction in national income, which can be determined by the use of the appropriate multiplier.

So thought Keynes.

THE KEYNESIAN EQUILIBRIUM

According to classical monetary theory, savings tend to equal investment because they represent supply and demand in the money market, and both, like supply and demand in any market, vibrate closely about an equilibrium price. Since interest is the price charged for loans, the equilibrium price in this case is the "natural" rate of interest.

The great practical difference between Keynes and the classical theorists who preceded him is that Keynes thought that equilibrium could arise at a low level of income—in other words, under depressed conditions when unemployment is prevalent; whereas the classical theory led to the belief that the equilibrium toward which the money market tended would occur only when the economic system was in a state of health and every employable person who wanted a job could get one.

This difference led to wide differences in policy. The old theory assumed that unemployment would disappear if only market forces were left free to work without government intervention. The new theory implied that unemployment might continue indefinitely unless government did intervene. The Keynes theory of equilibrium is, therefore, perhaps the most important part of his doctrine.

When economic activity and employment show no marked tendency either to expand or to contract, general equilibrium must exist. At this point, according to the theory, intended savings must equal intended investment, because a difference between them would cause an upswing or a downswing. Such an equilibrium can exist when unemployment is prevalent and income is low, because, no matter how low the interest rate, businessmen may not expect much profit from increasing their investments.

THE KEYNESIAN PRESCRIPTION FOR
FULL EMPLOYMENT

If the economy suffers from unemployment, the reason, according to Keynes, is that business is not investing enough to maintain a high level of activity.

One possible remedy is to reduce the interest rate and keep it low. Government and the central banks, combined, can depress interest rates. Low interest rates may be particularly effective in maintaining economic growth over a long term, but interest rates cannot be varied sufficiently over the short term to avoid economic fluctuations. If businessmen's expectations are optimistic, they will borrow at a high rate; if demand is shrinking, they will not invest, no matter how low the rate.

A more powerful remedy is for government to pour money into the economic system as a substitute for the lacking private investment. It can do this by spending for a large number of valuable purposes such as public works, housing, unemployment relief, farm relief, and education. But even if the money is used wastefully, it may stimulate investment in the private sector of the economy.

The money which government spends should not be taken from the private sector in ways that will decrease private spending or investment. The money must not, in other words, be taken as taxes from consumers with small incomes. By reducing taxes which bear heavily on low incomes, government may stimulate consumer spending. It may tap idle private funds—hoarded money—either by taxation or by borrowing. Still more efficiently, it may, by borrowing from the banking system, get money that no spender or investor had before; it may increase the total amount in circulation by an expansion of borrowing based on bank credit.

Government spending of borrowed money to relieve depression is called "deficit spending," because the government has a deficit when it spends more than it raises in taxes.

As government spends more, the recipients of the money spend more. The multiplier goes to work, just as it does in the case of private investment. Demand increases in the markets. This increase should, according to theory, induce businessmen to invest more, because it should enhance their expectations of profit. According to the original theory, a moderate amount of government deficit spending can "prime the pump" so that private enterprise will continue to operate as it should without any more governmental stimulation. This did not seem to work very well in the depression of the 1930's. But if pump priming does not work, huge amounts of governmental deficit spending will greatly increase employment, as is demonstrated during a war. Indeed, in modern war, so much is spent that demand becomes greater than total possible supply and the consequence is a rapidly rising price level.

THE KEYNESIAN REMEDY FOR INFLATION

The Keynesian theory does not approve governmental deficit spending, once full employment is achieved. It does not look with favor on an inflationary price rise, which must be the result if there is increased spending even after the temporary limit of national production has been reached.

The remedy for inflation is not, according to the Keynesians, an increase in the basic interest rate, since if this had any effect at all, it would be to discourage new investment—and new investment is necessary to keep production expanding and the economy growing. The Keynesians do approve *selective* controls over credit in specific markets where credit expansion might result in a mere rise of prices—as in loans to finance stock-market speculation.

The basic remedy offered is that the government should save instead of spend, thus taking money *out of* the income stream to balance the excess poured in by private spenders. This means that the government should, in periods of inflation, have a cash surplus. Government should use this surplus, so far as possible, to retire its securities in the hands of the banks.

DEFLATIONARY AND INFLATIONARY GAPS

The word "income," as used so far in this chapter, has meant merely income in money. If the general price level falls, the same money income will buy more; if the price level rises, it will buy less. Changes in *real* income may thus come from price changes as well as from changes in money received.

There is little point in increasing money income if at the same time prices rise by the same amount. The main purpose in increasing money income is to stimulate production and employment by creating more demand when the existing resources of the nation are not fully utilized. If unemployment is high, an increase in money income may not cause any marked or general rise in prices, because the increase will put the unemployed to work and so bring about an increase in supply equivalent to the increase in demand constituted by the additional spending. But when the labor force is fully employed, the supply cannot further be increased except by the relatively slow process of increasing output per man-hour through technological progress.

According to theory, for any given price level and for any given level of productivity, there is a national income which is just large enough to maintain full employment and no larger. This is called a "full employment income." A leading objective of social policy with regard to income is, roughly, to bring income to the full employment level and keep it there.

If anyone wanted to estimate how large a full employment income is at any one time, he would have to know, first, the size of the total labor force; second, the percentage of the labor force employed; third, the existing national income. Then he would try to estimate how much the national income would have to be increased, assuming no change occurred in the price level, in order to bring employment up to the desired level. Employment can never be exactly equal to the labor force, since some people are always changing jobs, some are laid up by illness, and some are out of work for other reasons.

When national income in money is not large enough to maintain full employment at the existing price level, the difference between the existing investment and the amount necessary to induce a full employment income is often called the "deflationary gap." When income is too large to maintain full employment at the existing price level, and as a consequence prices are rising, the amount by which investment exceeds the amount necessary to maintain a full employment income is called the "inflationary gap." Elimination or prevention of both deflationary or inflationary gaps is generally thought to be the chief aim of monetary and governmental fiscal policy.

The study of money and income did not stop with Keynes. Like all great economists, he greatly stimulated theory but did not have the final word. His hypothesis remained to be tested by observation and measurement of economic experience. Like other hypotheses, his may be improved or even abandoned if it does not fit the facts.

The depression in the 1930's seemed to indicate that the "multiplier" did not work as Keynes expected. Government deficit spending—supposed to be equivalent to new investment as a stimulus to recovery—did not stimulate enough new private investment and a continued rise in national income, sufficient to wipe out unemployment. Some followers of Keynes ascribed the failure to the lack of confidence by businessmen and concluded that the Keynesian remedies would work only if and when the business community understood and approved them, so that business executives would anticipate more profitable business and would increase investment accordingly.

After World War II, the chief problem has been, for most of the time, not to maintain a high level of employment but to avoid inflation. Large governmental expenditures for such purposes as reconstruction and defense have stimulated rising national income and rising profits, which have been accompanied by rising prices. This has been the case even in nations, like the United States and the United Kingdom, in which the government cash budget has been balanced by heavy taxation and the central banks have followed a conservative policy. It seems to be practically impossible to raise investment just enough to maintain full employment, without any appreciable price increase, and then to hold that position without further price increases. Some economists have raised the question whether it is possible, in our economic order, to maintain full employment and at the same time to avoid inflation.

The new situation has given rise to theoretical re-examination of the problems of monetary management, government fiscal policy, and private sources of financing.

1. The private financial institutions of the United States have been so far expanded outside the commercial banking system by the growth of insurance companies, finance companies, private pension funds, and other such institutions, that Federal Reserve monetary management is no longer sufficient to moderate an investment boom when it is necessary to control inflation, even if government cooperates with the effort through

its fiscal policy. And it is much more difficult politically for government to retain a surplus in good times than a deficit in bad times.

2. Federal Reserve restriction of credit does curb desirable and necessary activities like housing construction, borrowing by states and subordinate governmental units for schools, and small business operations, while at the same time it does not curb important inflationary forces like big business investment or installment buying by consumers. In the United States, it is argued that specific credit controls would be better than a general rise in the interest rate. In Britain, the Labor Party advocates a substitution of direct controls over investment and prices rather than reliance on central bank policy.

3. Some theorists believe that the traditional anti-inflationary policies will not work as long as labor is free to demand—and often to enforce—rises in wages more rapid than increase in productivity, thus raising costs of production and leading employers to increase their prices. Some urge that labor organizations and employers should voluntarily curb increases in both wages and prices; others contend that employers could forego price increases even when wages rise, since in so doing they would stimulate sufficiently enlarged sales to maintain adequate profits and thus would help to maintain continued economic growth.

Whatever the justification for any of these positions, all would seem to indicate that even a combination of central banking and governmental fiscal policies aimed at stabilizing the economy, powerful as they may be, are not sufficient, at least with the measures so far employed, to achieve the results desired.

Material relevant to this chapter will be found in Chapter 30.

QUESTIONS

1. During a major war, so many men and goods are required for military purposes that there is likely to be a shortage in the supply of ordinary consumers' wants. At the same time, payments of profits, salaries, and wages are likely to be higher than in peacetime because of labor shortages and full employment. Under such circumstances, explain what would happen to the four factors of the "equation of exchange" in each of the following courses of action.

(a) The government raises all the money it has to spend either by taxation of incomes and profits or by borrowing in such a way that the funds loaned are deducted from the current incomes of the people.

(b) The government obtains the money it has to spend by borrowing from banks or issuing securities bought by banks or accepted by them as collateral for loans to the purchaser of the bonds.

(c) The government raises part of the money it requires as in (a) and part as in (b). It also establishes effective price and wage controls and effective rationing of consumer goods and allocation of scarce materials used by industry.

(d) Under procedure (c) what would happen to savings?

2. Assume, as many economists do, that the purchase of houses or durable consumer goods by families is a form of investment. Most families borrow to finance such purchases and pay off the debt by installments. According to the reasoning of John Maynard Keynes about the effect on national income of investment which exceeds saving and of saving which exceeds investment, what should be the result to the national economy of periods when installment debt grows rapidly, followed by periods when it either ceases to grow or grows slowly?

Do you think that Keynes' belief that the larger the family income, the greater the percentage of it saved, would be materially affected by the prevalence of installment buying among families of low and medium incomes?

15 / BUSINESS CYCLES / For centuries mankind

has been accustomed to years of plenty and years of scarcity. Even in primitive agricultural societies good crops or poor crops brought either abundance or hunger. After the extension of markets and the growth of transportation gave rise to cities and stimulated trade and production for sale, alternation between good times and bad times was frequently felt, trade booms and declines occurred without much relationship to the vagaries of weather or crops. No known society in which business enterprise is prominent has escaped these ups and downs.

MONETARY AND INCOME THEORIES

After the middle of the nineteenth century, economists began to recognize that the alternation of prosperity and depression was a recurring phenomenon that deserved more systematic attention. Much of the discussion of the subject attributed the irregularity to monetary and price phenomena. This line of thought eventually culminated in the brilliant *General Theory of Employment, Interest and Money,* by John Maynard Keynes, which explains depressions as caused by a failure of investment to equal savings (see Chapter 14).

There were, however, numerous other suggestions, such as that advanced by the Austrian economist Schumpeter (later a professor at Harvard) that the fluctuations of business could be explained by the spasmodic occurrence of basic technological changes—especially inventions—which would temporarily stimulate investment. Others suggested wavelike movements of confidence or foreboding which influenced business judgments. A large variety of theories was developed, not all of which, as Wesley Mitchell observed, might be substantiated by the facts, some of which might be true as far as they went but were not sufficient guides to understanding of the whole phenomenon, and many of which were mutually inconsistent. Nevertheless, it was generally acknowledged that

173

the phenomenon was not just a sporadic or occasional one but a recurring cycle of good and bad times.

Wesley Mitchell's Approach. Wesley Clair Mitchell, acknowledged as the greatest authority on the business cycle in the United States if not in the world, spent much of his working life in planning and carrying out a major attack on the problem. He began his attack not by first announcing, and then trying to test, any one theory but rather by studying in detail the actual cyclical behavior of the economy in the past. A large body of statistical time series had become available before Mitchell began his intensive work, and many more were added during its course. He enlisted the aid of skilled experts in the organization which he headed, The National Bureau of Economic Research, and the findings published from time to time informed and stimulated many other workers in the field. He died before completing the task he had laid out for himself, but did lay a substantial foundation on which succeeding students of the subject have built.

First of all he set down the following working definition of what he was studying, based upon such information as was already at hand.

> Business cycles are a type of fluctuation found in the aggregate economic activity of nations that organize their work mainly in business enterprises: a cycle consists of expansions occurring at or about the same time in many economic activities, followed by similarly general recessions, contractions, and revivals which merge into the expansion phase of the next cycle; this sequence of changes is recurrent but not periodic; in duration the shorter type of business cycles varies from more than one year to ten or twelve years; they are not divisible into shorter cycles of similar character with amplitudes approximating their own.

Let us pause to examine some of the implications of this definition, all of which were substantiated by research.

Cycles are found in "aggregate economic activity." Before Mitchell's study, it had become customary to identify cycles by one or at most two or three measurements, such as employment, physical production, or prices. Mitchell substituted a wider concept which included many economic activities.

Cycles are found in nations that practice "business enterprise." They occur wherever business enterprise exists, and are associated with this type of economic organization. This is the phenomenon under examination, not any fluctuations that might accompany central direction of an economy, or a system of self-sustaining agriculture.

A cycle is one complete round of up and down movements. In order to understand it, we must study all its phases, not simply depressions. And each cycle merges into the next. In other words, we are never in a flat calm or on a plateau; we always are on the way up or on the way down.

This sequence of changes is recurrent but not periodic. This means that although cycle follows close upon cycle, the cycle is not of any regular duration or magnitude, like the phases of the moon or the paths of the planets around the sun. We can predict that these changes will follow in order, but we cannot apply any mathematical formula to spot the time of the next depression or predict its severity. Hundreds had attempted such predictions and had met with miserable failure.

Cycles of the sort Mitchell studied are not divisible into shorter cycles with similar magnitudes. This means that although there may be longer tides than business cycles in general economic activity, there are no shorter ones of equal size or importance. For example, some evidence exists that in the United States there are twenty-year fluctuations in important economic activities; Mitchell was not considering these but only those that in the past have lasted more than a year and less than twelve.

The next move was to study the historical records to see when booms and depressions had occurred in the past. High points and low points were identified by the writings of financial and economic commentators, which were checked against such statistical records as existed. These studies were summarized in a table tentatively showing the trough and the peak of each cycle in the United States from 1854 to 1939. In these eighty-five years, there were twenty-one complete cycles of varying lengths.

Having established the historical turning points, or "reference dates," the researchers could reconstruct the course of any available statistical series within each reference cycle. Before doing so, they eliminated seasonal influences from each series. In this way, the study observed what occurred in some hundreds of separate economic activities during each of several cycles. They could then discover whether there was any regularity of cyclical behavior of the various series in all the cycles covered.

In all, nearly 800 statistical series were studied. Naturally, more data are available for later years than for earlier. Of the statistical series, 13 covered general business activity, 135 had to do with finance, 168 showed prices of commodities and services, and 478 indicated the flow of commodities, services, and income.

SOME IMPORTANT FINDINGS

The more important findings of statistical studies are these:

1. About nine tenths of the statistical series available show a relationship with the general business cycle; the others reveal no cyclical movement at all.

2. Those that do have a cyclical rhythm, however, vary widely in the extent to which they conform with the general movement, as well as in the timing of their turning points.

3. At every phase of the cycle, some activities are going down while others are going up. It is a bunching of downward trends that cumulates in a general recession, and a bunching of upward trends that characterizes a general revival.

TABLE 15/1

CHARACTERISTIC DIRECTION AND AMPLITUDE OF 26 "COMPREHENSIVE" SERIES DURING A BUSINESS CYCLE

SERIES NUMBER	SERIES	Trough to first third	First to middle third	Middle to last third	Last third to peak	Peak to first third	First to middle third	Middle to last third	Last third to trough	NUMBER OF BUSINESS CYCLES COVERED	Rise	Fall	Rise	Fall
		TYPICAL DIRECTION OF MOVEMENT DURING A BUSINESS CYCLE[1]									PERCENTAGE OF CONFORMING MOVEMENTS DURING SPAN OF STAGES IN WHICH SERIES IS SAID TO		AVERAGE AMPLITUDE[2] OF MOVEMENTS DURING SPAN OF STAGES IN WHICH SERIES IS SAID TO	
		EXPANSION				CONTRACTION								
1.	Bond sales, N.Y. Stock Exchange	+	−	−	−	−	−	+	+	14	86	79	35.0	14.7
2.	Railroad bond prices	+	+	−	−	−	−	−	+	19	65	74	7.4	3.8
3.	Commercial failures, liab., *inverted*	+	+	+	−	−	−	−	+	14	86	93	74.5	57.8
4.	Common stock prices	+	+	+	−	−	−	−	+	16	94	82	26.8	20.2
5.	Shares sold, N.Y. Stock Exchange	+	+	+	−	−	−	−	+	16	94	88	40.6	36.2
6.	Corporate security issues	+	+	+	−	−	−	−	+	8	100	75	46.9	46.1
7.	Construction contracts, value	+	+	+	−	−	−	−	+	7	86	75	43.2	30.4
8.	Deposits activity	+	+	+	−	−	−	−	+	16	94	88	14.3	16.7
9.	Bank clearings, N.Y.C.	+	+	+	−	−	−	−	+	18	100	89	30.8	26.6
10.	Incorporations, number	+	+	+	−	−	−	−	+	19	84	80	26.9	10.2
11.	Bank clearings, outside N.Y.C.	+	+	+	−	−	−	−	+	14	100	79	25.5	12.8
12.	Bank clearings, total	+	+	+	+	−	−	−	+	14	100	86	29.2	20.4
13.	Imports, value	+	+	+	+	−	−	−	+	16	94	75	26.1	18.9
14.	Industrial production, total	+	+	+	+	−	−	−	−	5	100	100	35.2	32.5
15.	Fuel and electricity production	+	+	+	+	−	−	−	−	5	100	100	25.5	14.6
16.	Pig iron production	+	+	+	+	−	−	−	−	16	100	100	54.2	44.9
17.	Railroad freight ton-miles	+	+	+	+	−	−	−	−	6	100	88	27.8	25.1
18.	Factory employment	+	+	+	+	−	−	−	−	6	100	100	21.8	22.8
19.	Factory payrolls	+	+	+	+	−	−	−	−	5	100	100	36.3	39.9
20.	Income payments, total	+	+	+	+	−	−	−	−	4	100	50	22.6	17.6
21.	Corporate profits	+	+	+	+	−	−	−	−	4	100	100	168.8	174.6
22.	Commercial failures, no., *inverted*	+	+	+	+	−	−	−	−	16	75	88	22.3	26.1
23.	Department store sales	+	+	+	+	−	−	−	−	4	100	75	17.6	9.1
24.	Wholesale trade sales, value	+	+	+	+	−	−	−	−	3	100	100	17.7	19.1
25.	Wholesale commodity prices	+	+	+	+	−	−	−	−	11	82	91	8.7	8.9
26.	Railroad bond yields	−	−	+	+	+	−	−	−	19	74	65	3.7	6.2

[1] A plus denotes rise; a minus denotes fall. Series 3 and 22 are inverted here. [2] Expressed as percentage of mean value during a cycle.

Source: Arthur F. Burns, *The Frontiers of Economic Knowledge,* p. 123 (Princeton, N. J.: Princeton University Press, 1954).

4. There is a tendency for the same series to behave in the same way in each cycle. For example, some series usually lead the general movement and some usually lag behind it. Some, however, show more consistent behavior than others, and even the most consistent has occasional lapses.

Such findings, when examined in detail, are useful in various ways.

FORECASTING

It may help forecasters to know that the cyclical movements of farming have little relation to business conditions in general. It will be relevant, however, that prices of bonds and stocks usually lead the general activity of business, as do total liabilities of business failures, the latter usually by months. Liabilities of business failures, of course, increase before business contraction and decrease before revivals. Orders for machinery, business buildings, and other equipment usually go up (or down) in advance of more general movements.

If the forecaster knows the usual sequence of the series which lead most consistently, those which coincide, and those which lag—there are about 40 or 50 of these "sensitive" indexes—and can discover what direction these series have been taking in the recent past, he can make a pretty fair guess at whether we are on the upward sweep of the wave, near its crest, or on the way down. Of course, such guesses have to be modified by any special circumstances of the time.

One of the hazards in attempting to forecast the future on the basis of the recent behavior of a few sensitive indexes is that it is difficult to determine from current figures whether a cyclical turning point has actually occurred or not. Most indexes wobble up and down all the time; they do not rise smoothly to their apex and then curve over and drop steadily, like a waterfall, until they reach the bottom. If the stock market, for example, has been falling for a few weeks, it may turn up again and, with minor variations, maintain an upward trend for several months.

Another device which may help in such judgments is based on the observation that in every phase of the cycle, high or low, some individual series are going up while others are going down, and that the general cyclical movement is merely a reflection of the bunching of rises or falls in a large number of series. If a calculation is made which shows what *percentage* of a number of representative series is rising at any one time, the point at which this percentage starts to rise from its trough precedes by several months the bottom of the slump as traced by an index representing the movement of all the series regarded as a whole.

For example, suppose that when business is on the downgrade, out of 100 representative economic activities 75 are falling while 25 are rising. Suppose that in the following month 72 are falling while 28 are rising. Obviously, business in general will still be on the downgrade, but there will be 3 more activities which have started upward than in the previous month. If in the third month 70 are falling while 30 are rising, the premonitions of general improvement will have been increased. When the point is reached where 50 are falling and 50 rising, the bottom of the trough will have been reached for all the series considered together. But months before that, the *percentage* that are rising will have been growing. An index which reflects the *percentage that are rising* will precede the general movement, both upward and downward, by a fairly long time. Such an index over a period of months should be helpful in forecasting a turning point in the cycle. It is called a "diffusion index." Of course, no confident predictions can be made on such a mechanical basis. It needs checking with observation of circumstances of the time.

Anyone interested in the fortunes of a particular business or industry will be helped by knowing whether the business usually conforms with the general movement, and if it does, whether it is affected greatly or slightly. For example, retail sales of food and some other perishable consumer goods are little affected, telephone service hardly at all. But machine tools are violently affected, steel production falls and rises sharply, as do capital goods in general. There is also wide cyclical variation in sales and production of consumer durable goods, such as automobiles and furniture.

PRICE BEHAVIOR

It is significant that in the case of any given commodity which is greatly affected by the cycle, if production does not vary much, prices will vary greatly, and vice versa. Steel and automobile prices, for example, vary relatively little over the cycle, but their output rises and falls drastically. Retail prices vary much less than wholesale and lag considerably behind them. Also, some cycles are marked by much more violent movement of prices than are others.

STRATEGIC FACTORS IN STABILIZATION

For attempts to dampen down business fluctuations, it will be important to know that the element of the economy which shows the greatest instability is business inventories. Particularly dangerous is speculative increase of inventories in anticipation of higher prices.

Indeed, a speculative furor in commercial buildings, land, common stocks, or inventories is likely to be followed by a serious crash, particularly if the speculation is financed by bank credit. It did not take Wesley Mitchell's research to discover this common generalization, but there is confirmation for it in Mitchell's figures.

Next to business inventories, the most unstable of the important cyclical factors are private investment in other capital goods and consumer purchase of durable goods. These facts point to the importance of stabilizing investment both by business investors and by individual consumers.

IMPLICATIONS FOR THEORY

Does this type of research confirm or refute any theoretical formulation about the business cycle, old or new? It does refute some, such as Jevons' idea that the cycle arises from variation in crop yields, for these are not closely correlated with business-cycle movements. It throws doubt on theories which stress spasmodic causes outside the business order, such as political changes or natural disasters, since these could scarcely recur with sufficient frequency or regularity to bring about the observed cyclical movements.

The classical theory that the economy would hover about an equilibrium point if not disturbed by interference with free markets has no counterpart in Mitchell's findings. He discovers no equilibrium; what appears to be normal is rather continual change. The kind of abstraction he makes from the facts is a "typical cycle."

The results of the study do not confirm the theory of Karl Marx that there is a tendency for depressions to become steadily more severe; no such trend is observable in the figures. Neither does it confirm, as of the time of this writing—the late 1960's—the optimists that depressions are becoming milder and that we need never beware of another. Both mild and severe depressions are found in the past.

What about Keynes' theory that cyclical movements are linked with disparity between savings and investment? The figures do reveal that investment is an important factor of instability, and that its variations precede general movements. But the figures do not show whether savings are at any moment less or more than investment; there are no figures to indicate what "intended savings" are. The facts also indicate one factor largely ignored in Keynes' discussion—the importance of the variability of consumers' purchases of durable goods, largely financed not out of savings but on credit.

No general theory of business-cycle causation has yet emerged from analysis of the time series. This analysis does show how, once started, an expansion spreads over the economy, how the expansion slackens as one activity after another turns downward until a majority start down and recession begins. It shows the same process in reverse as the trough is approached and eventually revival becomes evident. The analysis answers many questions that begin with "how," "when," or "in what order," but it answers no "why."

Detailed study of such a complex phenomenon as the business cycle diminishes any expectation that a single *cause* can ever be discovered. Many variables are simultaneously at work; their interaction is what apparently leads the economy to behave as it does. The situation is not like that of a supposedly healthy human body suddenly invaded by a deadly microbe, the elimination of which is expected to restore health. It is not like that of a machine designed to operate efficiently, which goes haywire because a cogwheel breaks or a short circuit occurs. The alternation of ups and downs appears to be as natural to an enterprise economy as the alternation of storms and clear skies is to the weather.

It does not follow, however, that nothing can be done to diminish the cycles or to avoid severe depressions. Unlike the weather, the behavior of the economy is not the resultant of impersonal forces, uncontrollable by man. It is the result of human behavior, susceptible to alteration by intelligence based on knowledge. The enterprise economy, moreover, is mixed with an important nonenterprise element—governmental activity, which does not characteristically show rhythmic fluctuations and may in some instances be made to fluctuate in opposition to the fluctuations of the private sector of the economy.

Though analysis of the cycle probably will not reveal a "cause," it can readily lead to the discovery of points at which deliberate intervention may change the outcome, whatever the origin of the disturbance.

STABILIZING POLICY, MONETARY AND FISCAL

The policy of attempting to dampen the cycle, on which the United States Government has embarked, now uses three major types of intervention—monetary and fiscal management, "built-in stabilizers," and encouragement of stabilizing policies in the private sector of the economy.

Monetary and fiscal policies of the government have been described in previous chapters. The Federal Reserve authorities, by restricting the expansion of credit when an inflationary price rise is threatened, can do something to prevent the total of demand from exceeding the available supplies of goods and services. The Federal Reserve System also has specific control over credit extended to purchasers of shares on the stock market, and thus can do something to curb credit-based speculative excesses in Wall Street. Government, by maintaining a balanced cash budget in time of business activity and by skillful debt management, can reinforce Federal Reserve anti-inflation policy.

At times the Federal Reserve also has had the legal power to restrict consumers' installment buying by specifying minimum down payments and maximum terms of installment loans, thus curbing demand for consumer durable goods when inflation is threatened. This power may be renewed.

Both Federal Reserve and government can act in reverse to check recessions—the banking authorities, by making it easier for banks to expand loans; the government, by spending more than it collects in taxes.

Not only will a (cash) budgetary surplus in time of threatened inflation aid the effort to curb overexpansion of private credit, but its direct effect on incomes of individuals and businesses will also help to curb an aggregate volume of spending which grows faster than the physical output of goods and services and thus stimulates rising prices. If the federal "cash" budget shows a surplus, the government is taking more money from the public than it is paying out; this means that the government is draining excess purchasing power from the economy just as the spillway of a dam can be adjusted to keep the water behind it at the desired level. It should be remembered that if this policy is to be most effective, not only the federal government but also state and local governments should participate in it. On the contrary, when the cash budget has a deficit, governments are spending more money than they take in, and so enabling consumers and business to spend more than previously. This plan can be a powerful weapon against depression.

Built-In Stabilizers. The "built-in" stabilizers are those already embodied in various public institutions, which work automatically in a countercyclical fashion, without new legislation. They strengthen the compensatory fiscal policy of government—that is, spending less than is collected in taxes during good times and spending more than is collected during bad.

The most prominent of these stabilizers are the income tax and the tax on corporate profits. Without any change in rates, both taxes take a larger percentage of the national income in good times than in bad. Many individual taxpayers rise into higher tax brackets with prosperity and fall into lower ones with depression. Profits rise and fall by greater percentages than national income as a whole. Outgoing payments by the government, however, not only do not shrink in depression but are also likely to be increased. The net result is that when more purchasing power in the hands of the public is needed, the government is likely to be paying out more than it takes in, and the actual disposable income of consumers falls less than their total income. In prosperity, however, government budgets may more easily be balanced because consumers and business are paying more in taxes.

Another built-in stabilizer is social security, particularly unemployment insurance. Since the insurance funds are built up by a tax on payrolls, they take in more money when employment expands and less when employment shrinks. They pay out more money, however, when unemployment is prevalent. Government assistance and relief agencies of all kinds also operate on much the same principle.

Numerous actions to vary government spending can be taken without any new basic legislation. Purchase programs, such as stockpiling strategic materials, could be speeded up or relaxed. Letting of new contracts for authorized construction could be hastened or retarded. Government or governmentally guaranteed lending agencies could expand or restrict their operations. Examples are the Commodity Credit Corporation, which supports crop prices by holding surpluses off the market, and the Federal National Mortgage Association, which purchases mortgages to help finance housing.

A recent expert study of the probable effect of the built-in stabilizers under conditions as they were in the early 1950's estimates that in a two-year recession, which might bring unemployment of 8 million and a price drop of 9 percent, the stabilizers would counteract perhaps as much as 40 percent of the slump.

Since the built-in stabilizers do not require new legislation, they go to work promptly whenever an economic change occurs and so help dampen the cycle before drastic measures become necessary; they are in this sense preventive as well as remedial.

One element of built-in stability, though it is not actively counter-cyclical, is that government employees do not suffer part-time employment, layoffs, or wage and salary cuts during recession. This factor exerts growing influence, with the relative increase of government employment. Indeed, this same influence is exerted by the fact that government spending as a whole is a large part of all spending. Private service industries, like the telephone industry, also suffer little from recession, and employ an increasing part of the labor force.

Discretionary measures to influence private spending or investment can be taken by a number of governmental agencies. The credit agencies that insure home loans may stiffen terms and interest rates when shortage of materials or labor threatens an inflationary rise in building costs, and relax them when the construction industries are on the downgrade.

Non-Built-In Governmental Action. In times of recession or unemployment, government deficit spending may be particularly effective in checking downswing and in mitigating revival. In such times the banks may have plenty of money to lend to borrowers with good credit, but these borrowers may not want to use the money, because their sales are falling and they are restricting, not expanding, their output. Likewise, there may be plenty of savings to be invested, but businessmen are less likely to build new plants and buy machinery while their markets are shrinking. Government, however, not being concerned with sale of products or maximization of profit, can, by spending, put more money in the hands of people who will spend it.

One way in which it can do this is by initiating new public works. This policy, however, may take so long to set in motion, because of the necessity of drawing plans and awarding contracts, that the money is not actually spent until the need for stimulating the economy has passed. Another way is by reducing taxes and thus giving individuals and businesses more to spend. This plan may be put into effect rather promptly, as legislators are almost always ready to vote lower taxes if they can be assured this course is in the public interest.

It is perhaps more difficult to check inflation by governmental action than to check depression. Not everybody is against inflation; many profit from it, and even some economic authorities regard a slowly rising price level as indispensable to economic growth. Yet others point out that even a seemingly small percentage of annual increase in the price level may, like compound interest, build up before many years to an amazingly

high level—certainly enough to discourage individual saving or investment in fixed-yield securities, life insurance, pensions, and annuities. And
there is historical evidence that rapid growth of the United States economy has occurred in periods of gradually falling or stable prices as well
as in periods of rising prices.

Even those who verbally oppose inflation are often reluctant to support the restrictive measures necessary to curb it. Tight money and high
interest rates are not popular among borrowers. Many who favor curbing
government expenditures in general oppose curbing it in projects which
they particularly favor—and every project is favored by somebody. Legislators are not eager at any time to increase taxes, though they sometimes
do so when the military safety of the nation is concerned.

Action by Private Firms. Some influence over the policies of business may be exerted by reports such as those of the Council of Economic
Advisers, as well as by other authorities. Not only do the economists
know much more about business cycles and means of fighting them than
they did a quarter century ago, but this knowledge also is much more
widely shared by the lay public, and especially by many in positions
where business policy is determined.

Although the educational value of the new governmental concentration on stabilization policy is intangible, in the long run this policy may
be more important than direct controls. Wide knowledge of the fact that
there are dykes against economic floods helps to sustain business confidence. Warnings against overconfidence when inflation is threatened, if
issued by responsible authorities and backed by statistics and generally
understood reasoning, may check speculative excesses. One recent important advance in intelligent business behavior is that many corporations
are now scheduling their investment for expansion several years ahead
and are likely to stick to their programs even when recession has begun.
Corporations actually did so in the recessions of 1949 and 1954 and so
helped fairly rapid recovery from these moderate setbacks. The general
practice used to be to expand capacity at the height of booms and to cut
investment drastically during recessions—a practice which, of course, intensified the cycle. Many firms still do this, but a more stable policy is
making headway.

Additional difficulty is encountered in checking cyclical expansions
and contractions of business inventories. Some alternation of inventory
investment inevitably accompanies changes in consumer demand. Speculative buying to profit from anticipated rising prices and selling to avoid
anticipated price declines (actions which exaggerate the price movements
that are expected) may be diminished by banking and government
policies which curb inflationary price increases and subsequent deflation.

Variations in consumer demand are difficult either to predict or to
eliminate, now that consumers have both money to spend for many things
that are not daily necessities, and access to installment credit in buying
more than they can pay for out of savings. Progress is being made in

forecasting consumer demand, however, by surveys such as those made for the Federal Reserve System by the Michigan Research Center.

Responsible students of the subject do not expect that the business cycle can be entirely eliminated. They hope, however, that deep and long-continued depressions may be avoided by prevention of the speculative excesses and consequent financial collapses that usually precede severe slumps, and by prompt application of the policies that can check the spread of recession. At this writing, experience since World War II lends support to this hope. Reconversion to a peacetime economy was accomplished in 1946 without serious interruption of employment, in spite of forebodings. A subsequent (though perhaps needless) inflation was checked before it had bred a collapse. Mild recessions in 1949 and 1954 were outlived, as was a more severe one in 1958. If neither responsible authorities nor the public forgets the lessons of the past, and if both avoid the delusion that the economy has become miraculously "depression proof," they are not so likely to make the mistakes that can lead to disaster.

If, however, serious trouble should arise, more drastic measures may be taken. Meanwhile, the scientific study of the behavior of our economy needs to be vigorously pursued. What has so far been discovered is important and the policies based on it are helpful, but the task is far from finished.

Chapter 30 describes what occurred in the upswing coincident with the Korean War.

QUESTIONS

1. Was the spending by government for waging the war between 1941 and 1945 more than enough, or just enough, to keep the normal labor force employed?

2. (a) How should government spending be financed if it is to stimulate employment during a depression? (b) To what extent were the war expenditures of the United States Government during the early 1940's financed in this way?

3. If government is to relieve unemployment, must it pay for the production of goods and services that cannot be purchased by individual consumers (for example, warships and other military equipment)?

4. What peacetime opportunities exist for government to spend for goods and services that are not offered for sale?

5. (a) When government borrows money to spend, to whom is the debt owed? (b) Is the national wealth directly increased or decreased by this process? (c) What effects may it have on the distribution of income?

16 / GOVERNMENT SPENDING, LENDING,

AND TAXING / The very magnitude of government

as a receiver and spender of income in the United States makes it an
important part of the economic life of the people.

As a receiver of income, any government—federal, state or local—has
to rely largely on its legal right to impose taxes. How much should it,
or can it, take from the individual citizen and private organizations?
What kinds of tax are the fairest, will yield the most, and are the least
damaging to public welfare? Taxation policy is a never-ending source
of difficulty and debate. Other sources of government income arise from
direct payments for governmental services—for example, postal service or
toll-charging public highways. In each case some agency of government
must decide whether the service in question should and can supply net
income to the government, just pay its own way, or be operated at a loss.

If the expenses of government exceed its current revenue, it must
borrow to meet the deficit. This point raises another series of difficult
problems. How can government best raise the money? What will be the
effect of its borrowing on the distribution of income (through collecting
taxes to pay interest and amortization and through the interest paid out)?
Should it, at any one time, borrow by issuing securities which can be
bought by commercial banks, or should it issue savings bonds, which tap
only savings? Should it issue long-term bonds or short-term notes? And,
in general, is the state of the economy such that it needs the stimulation
of governmental excess of spending over revenue, or such that deficit
spending will stimulate an inflationary price use?

Another important consideration concerns what activities government should undertake. Should it take money from the public to pay
for education, and if so, how much? Should it subsidize the merchant
marine? How should it distribute its spending among national defense,
conservation of natural resources, public health and welfare, scientific
research, aid to agriculture, and aid to foreign nations? All such decisions—and many similar ones—exert an important effect on the alloca-

tion of scarce resources in such a way as to serve the welfare—short-term and long-term—of the nation as a whole.

What federal, state, and local governments do must affect in one way or another the growth or decline of the national income, the stability or lack of stability of the economy, the distribution of income, and the allocation of economic resources. This would be true even if governmental activities and powers were never deliberately used to further any general economic purposes.

SIZE AND GROWTH OF GOVERNMENT EXPENDITURE

Chapter 2, on the budget of the federal government, and Chapter 5, on the national income, have shown that what government spends is one of the major elements in the stream of income (in recent years, between one fifth and one fourth). This is particularly true during years of war or heavy military expenditure. Yet the growth of spending by government is not due entirely to wars and their aftermath. After major wars, nonmilitary governmental expenses never go back to the old level and show a long-term growth of their own.

Sketchy estimates indicate that in 1799 federal government expenditures accounted for 1.4 percent of the national income and in 1809 for 1.1 percent.

During the Civil War, federal expenditures rose, but thereafter they never exceeded 3 percent of the gross national product (GNP) until World War I. At that time they touched 23.7 percent—almost one fourth. During the 1920's the expenditures fell to about 3 percent, but never below it.

The great depression of the 1930's brought a striking percentage boost in federal expenditures not merely because of the many activities undertaken for relief of unemployment in industry but also because of the shrinkage of the GNP itself, which was due to the depression. In 1932, before Franklin D. Roosevelt took office, federal expenditures had mounted to 9.2 percent of the GNP. Thereafter, during the 1930's they ranged between 10 and 12 percent except for one year of retrenchment, 1937, when they were 9.6 percent.

World War II, with its gigantic military costs, brought federal government expenditures to 68 percent of the GNP in 1944. In that year, military expenditures alone were 60.5 percent of the GNP. (Nevertheless the total product had grown so much during the war that the amount available for civilian consumption was scarcely less than in 1939.)

Demobilization after the war brought the percentage of federal expenditure down again, but never appreciably below 15 percent of the GNP. In the early postwar years, military expenditures alone fell to about 5 percent of the GNP, but by 1951 they had risen again to 9.2 percent. In 1958, all government expenditures for goods and services were about 17 percent of GNP.

In times of peace, state and local governments have spent much more than the federal government, especially if military expenses are excluded. (See Table 5/2)

In 1929 the civilian expenditures of the federal government were only one tenth as large as those of the states and their subordinate units. Yet the civilian expenditures of the federal government have grown much more rapidly; in 1948 they were more than half those of the states, counties, towns, and cities.

In addition to familiar government activities such as financing roads and schools, the citizens have entrusted to government new functions that demand large expenditure, such as slum clearance; public housing, health services; conservation of forests, water, soil, and other natural resources; reclamation of land for agricultural purposes by drainage and irrigation; flood control; electrical power development; scientific and technological research (including atomic energy); agencies for the extension of credit to agriculture, exporters, and others; statistical and informational services; and regulation of industries and occupations affected by the public interest.

Regarded as a whole, government in the United States is by far the largest single business institution in the world outside of the Soviet Union—though not a business conducted for private profit.

KINDS OF GOVERNMENT EXPENDITURE

In 1954, the employees of governments and governmental enterprises constituted 15 percent of all the nation's workers. The level of salaries and wages paid is correspondingly important, as are the working conditions, security of tenure, and devotion and efficiency of government workers.

At least 38 percent—nearly two fifths—of the nation's expenditures on construction and new equipment were made by federal, state, and local governments in 1954. The nature, location, and timing of public works are correspondingly crucial.

In 1953, it has been estimated, governments owned nearly one fifth of the nation's capital goods (if military equipment is included).

Goods and services purchased from business enterprises by governments totaled $46 billion in 1954. The effect of this demand, of its possible variation from year to year, of its part in allocation of the nation's resources, is clearly a matter of major concern.

Transfer Payments. About one quarter of the nondefense expenditures of government in 1954 consisted of "transfer payments"—that is, such things as benefits to veterans, public assistance to the needy, employee pensions, unemployment compensation, old-age and survivors insurance payments.

The reason for the term "transfer payments" is that the money is collected by the government and transferred to the recipients without any production or consumption on the way. This money is not, therefore, part of the national income in the strict sense, though of course it is a subtraction from the disposable income of those who pay it, and an addition to the disposable income of those who receive it.

Transfer payments involve redistribtuion of spending power by the intervention of government, insofar as the recipients do not individually contribute as much money as they receive. Such redistributions are undertaken in pursuit of social purposes believed desirable. They may have economic effects as well, such as a tendency to stabilize consumer purchasing power over boom and depression.

Not usually lumped with transfer payments but of much the same nature are agricultural price supports or other benefits to farmers, subsidies to the merchant marine, and other subsidies which redistribute income. These, if added to the payments mentioned in the preceding paragraph, would increase the fraction by one fourth of nondefense expenditures in transfer payments.

Interest on the public debt is somewhat like a transfer payment. To be sure, this interest is a commercial transaction, since it is payment for the use of borrowed money. Yet the borrowing does not always involve economically valuable production for civilian purposes. The money for the payment of interest itself is currently collected from taxpayers and directly transferred to holders of government securities. If each owner of government securities paid as much in taxes as he received in interest (in addition to his share of other governmental expenses), interest on the public debt would involve no redistribution of income, but it would be a miracle if this turned out to be the case.

Whether governmental intervention through transfer payments and the like is, in its net result, a redistribution from the rich to the poor or from the poor to the rich is uncertain, but there can be no doubt that such intervention does result in redistribution of some kind. Of course, many needy individuals benefit by particular measures designed to alleviate social maladjustments. Transfer and interest payments by government to individuals account for $1 out of every $14 of personal income.

Government as Banker and Insurer. We have seen in our examination of the Federal Reserve System that the federal government, through the Board of Governors, plays a large role in regulation of the private banking system of the country in order to exert public policy over the money supply. This is one of the most important economic functions of the government. In addition, government operates or sponsors banking institutions for other purposes.

There are twelve federal land banks to assure that ample mortgage loans are available on reasonable terms to farmers. In addition, federal intermediate credit banks supply shorter term credit to enable farmers to carry out production plans. These banks are now owned by cooperative associations of farmers, but government inaugurated them and super-vises them.

A government export-import bank makes loans to foreign countries and domestic businessmen to facilitate the development of foreign trade.

The federal government guarantees loans made by banks and other financial institutions for numerous purposes—for example, housing mort-gage loans to veterans and nonveterans. Through its control of the inter-est rate and terms on which such loans can be guaranteed, the govern-ment can either encourage or discourage activity in the industries concerned. In 1954 such contingent liabilities of the government totaled about $40 billion—about one seventh of the federal debt. The purpose of guarantees of this kind is to permit the extension of credit for purposes considered desirable and for longer terms and at lower interest rates than private financial institutions would consider safe without the guarantee.

Governments or their agencies have administered insurance in num-erous cases—for example, federal deposit insurance, insuring against loss of bank deposits up to $10,000; and state insurance funds, covering em-ployers who are liable to workmen's compensation.

During the depression of the 1930's a federal Reconstruction Finance Corporation was created with broad powers to extend loans to private business, banks, and other business institutions which were in danger of going under. Subsequently, it served many other governmental purposes, especially during World War II. Although it was created in 1931 under the administration of Herbert Hoover as an "emergency" measure, it did not pass out of existence until the 1950's.

Government as Producer. Government produces goods and serv-ices of many kinds. Some of these are available without charge to the individual consumer; some are sold. The postal service, public schools, roads and highways, fire and police departments are time-honored ex-amples. Persons employed in public business enterprises of various sorts constitute about 16 percent of all nondefense government employment. The largest number of federal nondefense employees are in the post office; the largest number of local government employees are in the schools.

Government employees in publicly owned street railways and bus lines constituted one third of all employees in that industry in 1950; those in gas and electric utilities, one fourth. This same year one fourth of medical and health workers were in government employment. Recent additions to the list of governmental enterprises are housing and, in some states, the sale of liquor.

Government as Regulator. Regulation of privately owned indus-try is an important role played by government, though its expense for this is small relative to other public activities.

Among the industries subject to public regulation are railroads, operation of trucks and buses, air transport, communications, gas and electric utilities, water systems, and other industries which are at least partially monopolistic and otherwise "affected by the public interest." In such cases competition cannot be relied upon to bring about fair rates or prices and adequate service.

The financial markets and the issuance of new securities are regulated by the Securities and Exchange Commission.

Regulation aimed at safeguarding the health and welfare of the citizens is applied to such industries as those selling food and drugs. Regulation to protect the workers against disease and accident is applied to mines and factories. Sanitary regulation and inspection covers a wide field in most municipalities. Traffic regulation is a common and obvious activity. Building codes, fire-prevention codes, and others are almost universal.

Occasionally government steps in to protect not the consumer but the producer, as with agricultural price supports, minimum wages, maximum hours, and regulation of collective bargaining practices. In the process of efforts to deal with unemployment, government has established employment offices. It does not exercise a monopoly in this field, but, to qualify for unemployment insurance, any worker must register at a government employment office.

In fields where government does not directly regulate industry, it stands guard through anti-trust legislation to attempt to preserve or restore the competition which is supposed by economic theory to supply automatic regulation in the public interest. The history of its attempt to do so is a complex and checkered one, about the effectiveness of which there is much dispute. But no one would deny that the existence of such laws and of agencies to enforce them can have important economic influences.

KINDS OF GOVERNMENT REVENUE

Fully as important as the way in which the government spends money is the way in which it obtains its revenue from the public.

A minor part of governmental revenue is derived from the sale of goods and services at so much a unit. Postal services, electricity from governmentally owned power stations and transmission lines, water and other publicly owned utilities, tolls on turnpikes owned by state agencies, are examples. In such instances the users pay for as many units as they need or wish to afford, thus allocating the use of resources much as they do in the markets for goods and services offered for sale by private business.

By far the greater part of the public revenue comes from taxation. The principal aim of most taxes is to raise the money necessary for expenditures voted by the elected representatives of the citizens. The ideal policy of taxation is to raise necessary revenue in a way which at once is as fair as possible, yields the most revenue with the least hardship to the taxpayer, and exerts the least injurious effect on the national economy. This raises a number of intricate problems.

Federal Taxation. In the early years of its history, the main source of revenue of the federal government was sale of public lands. About 1815 the protective tariff began to yield substantial amounts, and after the Civil War became the largest revenue producer. Beginning with World War I the personal income tax (established in 1913), supplemented by taxes on the profits of corporations, assumed the leading role.

INCOME TAX. The income tax, though often modified in detail, is based on a plan which has never been altered in general principle. (See Chapter 3.) Incomes below a certain minimum are entirely exempted— by a personal exemption plus additional exemptions for dependents. Those who receive net income above the minimum are subject to taxes on the excess.

The rate of taxation depends on the size of the taxable income. Persons in the lowest bracket pay the smallest rate. For higher incomes, higher rates are charged, rising step by step up the income scale. This kind of taxation is called "progressive." It is based on the theory that the larger the personal income, the larger part of that income can be paid in taxes without undue hardship; the "ability to pay" rises as the income received approaches the higher brackets. It is also based on the theory that those with large incomes derive more benefit than those with small incomes from the existence of a strong government which maintains "law and order" and protects the nation against foreign enemies.

From time to time, many deductions have been allowed in reckoning net taxable income. Numerous kinds of expense incurred in earning the income may be subtracted. In addition, deductions up to a certain percentage of the income are allowed for charitable contributions to tax-exempt nonprofit institutions such as hospitals, churches, and schools; for medical expenses (in part); for uninsured losses to personal property caused by accidents or natural disasters; for alimony paid to a legally divorced spouse; for retail sales taxes; and for many other purposes. Such complications, although introduced in the interest of fairness, place heavier burdens on those who administer the tax and on the time and skill of individuals who make the returns.

Money made from the sale of property such as stocks, bonds, or real estate at a higher price than it cost the seller is in a special category— capital gains. If the property is sold within six months after it is acquired, the seller is regarded as being in the business of buying and selling property (like a stock trader or a real estate operator) and the gain or loss is treated like any other income. If, however, the property is kept more than six months before it is sold, only half the gain is taxable. This provision may be used by persons in high tax brackets to avoid as

TABLE 16/1

THE LARGER THE INCOME, THE HIGHER THE TAX RATE

Taxpayer with One Dependent, U. S. Federal Income Tax, 1959

Net Income[1]	Taxpayer Keeps	Government Takes	Effective Tax Rate[2]
Below			
$ 1,200	$ 1,200	$ 0	0.0%
3,000	2,640	360	12.0
5,000	4,240	760	15.2
8,000	6,584	1,416	17.7
10,000	8,112	1,888	18.9
20,000	15,130	4,870	24.4
50,000	30,400	19,600	39.2
100,000	47,200	82,800	52.8
200,000	66,000	134,000	67.0
500,000	96,000	404,000	80.8
1,000,000	141,000	859,000	85.9
Highest effective tax rate....................................			87.0

[1] Net income means the income remaining after subtracting all allowable expenses in earning that income and all allowable deductions—such as medical expenses, interest paid, charitable contributions, sales, gasoline, property and other taxes paid to states and local governments, accidental damages not covered by insurance, alimony.

[2] The effective tax rate is the percent of net income actually paid by a person with one dependent. Such a person is allowed two "exemptions" of $600 each, one for himself and one for the dependent. A childless married couple with the same net income as an individual with one dependent would pay the same tax. Extra exemptions of $600 each may be taken for additional dependents.

high a rate of tax as they otherwise would have to pay. Sometimes, too, it is worth their while to incur capital losses deliberately in order to minimize tax payments.

Principal arguments in favor of the income tax as a main source of revenue are (1) that it makes nearly everyone conscious that he is helping to pay the cost of government and therefore more ready to oppose extravagance, corruption, or inefficiency; (2) that the tax is as fair as any that can be devised; (3) that the tax acts as an automatic balance wheel for the economy because, without any change in tax rates, tax receipts fall when private income falls and rise when income rises. The result is that the government takes less money from the people at times when their spending power is inadequate to maintain full production and employment, and more money from them at times when large spending may stimulate inflationary increase in prices.

Arguments against the income tax are (1) that it is relatively expensive to collect and enforce; (2) that many succeed in evading it, while attempts to enforce it on all may involve extensive surveillance over private affairs, and perhaps corruption on the part of tax officials; (3) that it imposes a heavy burden of record keeping and paper work on many taxpayers; (4) that, when the rates are high, especially in the upper brackets, it may deprive potential investors of the incentive to take the risks essential for economic progress. For example, at the rates in force in 1955, a person with an income in the highest bracket had to pass over to the government 90 percent of any increase in his net taxable income. Why should he risk his money when, if he makes a profit, he can keep only one tenth of it? In answer to this argument, supporters of the tax point out that a considerable part of income arises from capital gains, subject to lower rates. Also, the risk of loss is often largely compensated by the fact that any reduction of income occasioned by an unsuccessful investment reduces the tax to be paid more than proportionally, because of the progressive rates. Indeed, losses are sometimes deliberately taken to reduce taxes.

CORPORATION PROFITS TAX. Next to the personal income tax, the tax on corporate profits is the largest revenue producer for the federal government. The corporation income tax is based on a certain percentage of the profit. Unlike the personal income tax, it is not graduated; that is, the rates do not increase as the profits increase. There is, however, a lower rate for corporations with profits below a certain minimum.

The reason the corporate profits tax is not made progressive is that the profits in reality belong to shareholders, many of whom may have relatively small incomes. No matter how large the profit of the corporation itself, the owner of a few shares may receive so small an income that it would not be fair to take from him a large percentage of his gains as an owner.

The principal argument for the profits tax is that it is a relatively easy way for the government to add considerably to its revenue. Reputable corporations, which habitually keep careful records, would not find it easy to defraud the government and would be reluctant to run the risk of discovery and punishment. Though there are many small corporations, the task of collecting substantial amounts from thousands of business concerns is much easier than that of collecting taxes from millions of individuals.

Taxes on corporate profits also serve to exercise a stabilizing influence on the economy, as do personal income taxes. Profits rise and fall rapidly with changes in business conditions. Taxes on profits therefore yield widely varying amounts according as business is prosperous or depressed. Through the profits tax, the government collects a large amount when there is danger of too much private spending, and a much smaller amount when there is danger of too little spending.

Two main arguments are directed against the corporation profits tax. One is that it influences business policy through motives irrelevant to business efficiency. A corporation which has to pay a large tax may be led to diminish its recorded profits by means of spending more than it otherwise would for such things as advertising, publicity, or improvements of plant, which may be charged as an expense against current income. It may be led to charge larger percentages of annual depreciation for its plant and equipment. To be sure, larger annual depreciation means that any given asset will be fully depreciated more quickly, but by that time the tax rate may have been reduced.

Yet if there were no tax on corporate profits, tax consideration could still influence corporate policy. Influential stockholders might lead a corporation to reinvest more of its earned surplus rather than increase its dividends, because this action (1) would decrease the amount of their dividend income subject to high personal income taxes, and (2) would make possible larger capital gains by sales of the stock they held. It is generally believed that tax considerations have had an important influence in strengthening the habit of large American corporations of directly reinvesting in their own business a large percentage of their profits rather than distributing more as dividends.

The other argument against the corporate profits tax is that it is "double taxation." The owners of the corporation are, of course, the owners of its stock. These stockholders are taxed once when the corporate profit itself is taxed, and again as individuals on any profits which the corporation distributes to them, since the dividends then become part of their personal incomes. This seems like discrimination against income derived from corporate profits.

Recent researches, however, have indicated that, without the corporate profits tax, many stockholders might have to pay higher taxes than they do. The reason is that if the same amount of money were collected from personal income taxes as is now received from profits taxes, personal income tax rates would have to be raised substantially. The increase would be likely to be made in the lower brackets, since increases in the upper brackets would not yield the requisite revenue. Upper-bracket rates are already high, and those who have to pay them are few relative to the number of those in the lower brackets.

EXCISE TAXES. Excise taxes are collected from producers of specific articles. The rate is based on a certain percentage of receipts from the sale of these articles. In recent years excise taxes have been a major source of federal revenue—next in order to income and profits taxes. They are or have been levied on such goods and services as liquor, cigarettes, new automobiles, furs, jewelry, cosmetics, clocks and watches, and theater admissions.

Excise taxes, unlike income taxes, are probably not really paid by the individual or firm from which they are collected. In times of active demand they are "passed on" to the purchasers by the sellers, who add the tax to the price of the article; thus the tax is eventually paid by the final consumer. In times of restricted demand, excise taxes may be "passed back" to the wage and salary earners in the form of lower wages or unemployment. Therefore, unless excise taxes are on articles bought exclusively by the rich, they are "regressive" not progressive. A regressive tax is one which constitutes a larger percentage of lower income than of higher ones. The lower the income of the purchaser, the larger the bite excise taxes take out of his income. The purchaser may avoid them only by restricting his purchases of the articles in question.

In the case of luxuries such as furs and jewelry, excise taxes may tend to restrict purchases to persons having the larger incomes, but not in the case of commonly used articles such as automobiles, cigarettes, cosmetics, or admission to movie theaters—and it is from these sources that the bulk of the revenue comes.

The principal reason for the imposition of excise taxes is that they constitute an easy source of considerable income for the government. They also incur less "squawk" by the taxpayer, since in many instances he does not realize that he is paying the tax; it is merely included in the price he pays.

A justification for excise taxes in time of war is that an increase in the prices of articles the production of which is not essential for defense limits the demand for these articles and thus leaves more labor and materials for production of war essentials. If such taxes are successful in limiting sales, however, they raise less revenue, since the tax is a fixed percentage of the cost of each unit sold.

In general, excise taxes are undesirable for the very reasons that the personal income tax is desirable. The actual taxpayer often does not know that he is paying them. They are regressive rather than progressive. Insofar as they are levied on commonly used articles, their yield does not vary much between prosperity and depression.

ESTATE AND INHERITANCE TAXES. Taxes on the estates left by persons who die are levied by the federal government on property valued over a certain minimum—in 1952, the minimum was $60,000 for unmarried persons and $120,000 for married. Half the estate may be left, free of tax, to a wife or a husband. The rates are progressive, beginning at a very low percentage and rising to a high one. Estate taxes are deducted from the estate as a whole before it is distributed to the recipients of bequests. The bequest is not counted as part of the taxable income. Some states, however, levy inheritance taxes on the recipients of bequests.

To prevent persons with fortunes from avoiding the estate tax by giving their money to their heirs before they die, a special gift tax is levied on gifts to individuals—though at a lower rate than the estate tax. Sometimes it is difficult for the courts to adjudicate disputes about whether a gift is made for the purpose of avoiding the estate tax.

There are numerous ways of evading at least part, and sometimes all, of the estate tax. Gifts to charitable or nonprofit institutions are exempt from income tax, and so may be made at any time by a person who wishes to reduce the size of his estate in order to fall into a lower bracket or perhaps below the minimum which limits estate taxes. Some ingenious persons have even devised ways of leaving fortunes to charitable foundations from which they can derive an income as long as they live.

Revenue from estate taxes is a minor part of federal and state tax receipts. The purpose of the tax is fully as much social as fiscal. It is regarded as a method of preventing large family fortunes from being passed on from generation to generation and thus increasing the concentration of wealth.

CUSTOMS DUTIES. Customs duties or tariffs are levied on imports of many articles, specified in laws on the subject. For years they have been voted not primarily to raise revenue but to protect domestic producers from foreign competition. Many commodities, such as natural rubber, not produced in the United States are allowed free entry.

Protective tariffs are in effect a tax on the consumer and constitute a subsidy to American producers at the consumers' expense. Since tariffs are not varied according to the purchaser's ability to pay, they constitute, like excise taxes, a regressive tax. The theory of protection is discussed in Chapter 27 on international trade.

SOCIAL SECURITY TAXES. Social security taxes provide for payments of old-age benefits and unemployment insurance. The old-age security tax is levied on both employer and employee, each paying an equal percent on the employee's earnings up to a maximum, above which no tax is paid. The employee's portion of this tax, which is neither progressive nor regressive, is called "proportional," because the rate does not vary with the earnings. It is thought equitable because the money eventually comes back to the wage earner in unemployment or old-age benefits. There are, however, maximum and minimum pensions, the effect of which is to pay back more to some than they have paid in and less to others.

Payroll taxes paid by employers, either to match the employees' contribution to old-age security or to finance unemployment insurance, are generally thought to be "regressive" taxes, since they are charged to business expense and thus must result either in higher prices for the product or in lower wages or both. The consumers or the workers thus pay such taxes in the end, without regard to how much they can afford.

STATE AND LOCAL REVENUE

More than half the revenue of states is derived from taxes on sales and gross receipts of business. There are general sales taxes (such common necessities as food being exempt) ; taxes on gasoline, cigarettes, and tobacco; taxes on insurance companies, public utilities, and other businesses. All of these are regressive taxes.

Many states levy income and profits taxes on a progressive scale. These, of course, are a fairer form of tax, but the revenue from them is limited because the federal income tax takes so large a proportion of incomes. Income taxes are second to sales taxes as a source of state and local revenue.

The third largest source of state revenue consists of license fees for motor vehicles and their operators, for corporations, for dealers in alcoholic beverages, for hunters and fishermen, and for other purposes. These license fees are justified partly because they serve as aids to police measures and partly because they serve to give special benefits to the purchasers of licenses.

States also levy property taxes, severance taxes (as in the case of mines, the products of which are sold outside state lines), and inheritance taxes. The state inheritance tax applies to each separate bequest (charitable bequests being exempt), whereas the federal estate tax is levied on the estate as a whole.

Anyone who receives a bequest which has been taxed by a state can receive a corresponding reduction in the federal estate tax (up to a certain percentage of the estate) by submitting to the federal government the tax receipt from the state. Where states do not collect inheritance taxes, the full federal tax is levied. This reciprocal device permits states to make use of death taxes as a source of revenue, without making the total burden higher than the rates fixed by Congress. It also encourages states to levy the permitted percentage, since their residents would have to pay the same amount in any case.

Subordinate state units—cities, towns, counties—must rely mainly on property taxes, principally on real estate, though many attempts, largely unsuccessful, have been made to collect taxes on personal property as well. Since, with rising expenses of city governments, the revenue from these sources is usually insufficient, cities have resorted to a great variety of other devices, such as sales taxes, licenses, parking fees, automobile-use taxes, and even, in some cases, income taxes, which are not, as a rule, progressive.

GRANTS-IN-AID

Much confusion, inefficiency, and injustice arise from the fact that a great variety of taxes is levied at three separate levels of government. Basic reforms of the tax system are often advocated, but to propose a simplified and logical system that would not compromise the independence of state and local self-government is difficult. Another complication is created by the fact that under the United States Constitution, all powers not expressly granted to the federal government reside in the states. The government at Washington cannot levy a "direct tax" (for example, a tax on real estate); a Constitutional amendment was required to give it the power to collect income taxes.

Nevertheless, the federal income tax has turned out to be such a preponderating tax burden on the citizens that state and local governments are often cramped for funds to meet pressing obligations like adequate support of schools. Legally, state and local governments may, it is true, levy income taxes also, but the rates they can charge must be low in order not to add too much to the federal tax burden.

A device which has alleviated this difficulty in some respects consists of "grants-in-aid." For example, the federal government extends grants-in-aid to states for roads, relief to the indigent, and other purposes. The state governments give grants-in-aid to local communities for education, local roads, and other necessities.

Clearly government redistributes income in one way or another through the ways in which it raises money for public purposes. Since the tax revenue collected by states and local communities is a substantial part of the total, and since so much of this revenue comes from regressive taxes, it is probable that the net effect of taxation in the United States, except when defense expenditures are high, is to lay a heavier burden on the poor, in proportion to their ability to bear it, than on the rich. This statement may seem incredible to those who think of the steeply progressive federal income tax as the chief form of taxation, but most persons are likely to underestimate the burden of hidden or half-hidden levies that drain money away in thousands of driblets.

ALLOCATION OF RESOURCES

Whenever government undertakes any task or project, the money it spends may be paid for the services of employees, office space or buildings, equipment of many kinds, and materials—in other words, for labor, capital goods, and land (or natural resources). Government taps existing and often limited stores of the factors of production which might, if it did not employ them, be devoted to other uses. And in raising the money to pay for the activity, it takes from the public either income or money capital which might, if left in private hands, be spent for other purposes. Thus, government plays a major role in the allocation of the resources available to the economy—a role which is not mainly dependent on the choices of consumers in a free market.

It would be shortsighted and erroneous to suppose, as certain spokesmen for private interests sometimes do, that governmental activities are carried on at the expense of "production" or of consumers. Government, to be sure, is sometimes wasteful, but so are many private undertakings. But government produces many services, and even some goods, that individual consumers could not buy, no matter how much they might want or need them. It performs many public duties that could not prudently be delegated to individuals or private business. Nevertheless, both citizens and public officials, elected and appointed, should bear in mind the important role of government in resource allocation. At least in periods of full employment, nothing it does is really "free," even if the consumer does not buy the product directly. Do we need national defense as much as we want the things we might buy with the taxes necessary to pay for defense? Do we, perhaps, need more and better education than we have, even at the cost of spending somewhat less for automobiles or TV entertainment? It is often easier for the candidate to win votes by promising lower taxes than to take a broad view of the public interest. And it is often easier for him to offer subsidies to special interests than to keep expenses under control so that taxpayers may benefit. Sometimes he advocates both courses at the same time.

In periods of slack employment and underuse of resources, government may expand its activities without diminishing anybody's means to buy goods and services in private markets; indeed, it can increase consumers' real incomes by increased public spending financed by borrowing. But even in such periods, the nation and its public officials would be wise to allocate resources to the most useful and desirable purposes. A time of surplus labor and capital is just the time to undertake projects of the most genuine public benefit.

QUESTIONS

If the large share of the income of the national government devoted to defense could be drastically reduced, how would you wish to see this windfall distributed among the following or other possible uses? Give your reasons.

(a) Reduction of the national debt

(b) Reduction of taxes on profits

(c) Reduction of excise taxes

(d) Reduction of taxes on personal income

(e) Aid to education and scientific research

(f) Conservation of natural resources

(g) Broadening of social security, particularly by addition of universal health insurance

(h) More effective planning and development of metropolitan regions

(i) Encouragement of the arts, performing and visual

(j) More consistent and better planned aid to underdeveloped nations

(k) Aid to depressed regions in the United States

17/ LABOR AND ITS
ORGANIZATION / By "labor" the economist means

not only the manual laborer whose principal means of livelihood is derived from wages. He means anyone—from street sweeper to the President of the United States—who receives an income in compensation for his services. This is true even if he also derives income from any other source —such as profits, interest, or pensions. The businessman who owns and operates his business is part of the labor force of the nation, even though he pays himself no salary. So is the farmer, the doctor, the lawyer, the architect. All these people receive at least part of their incomes by means of producing goods or services; they are neither idle dependents nor the recipients solely of income from ownership.

THE LABOR FORCE

The labor force of a nation is a basic resource of production. At any given stage of what used to be called the "industrial arts" and now is more frequently known as the "capacity to produce per head," a nation in which a large percentage of the population holds jobs is likely to have a higher level of living than one in which a smaller percentage is at work. If, however, the labor force is enlarged by the employment of those who might otherwise be continuing their education, this is a sign of a relatively low level of living.

If a population contains a large proportion of persons who are of working age, it can have a bigger labor force, relatively speaking, than a population more largely composed of children. Countries where both birth rates and death rates are high do have a large proportion of children. A population in which many women earn wages or salaries outside the home will have a larger labor force than one in which more women are confined to households. The fact that mothers and housekeepers do not earn money for their domestic duties does not, of course, imply that

200

their work is any less useful than that of stenographers or factory operatives. They are not counted as part of the labor force simply because
there is no way of measuring the economic value of their services, as there
is for women who receive pay.

The labor force excludes not only housewives but also children in
school, retired persons or others living exclusively on income from investments, those unable to hold jobs because of illness or other disability, and
inmates of penal institutions.

The labor force as defined by the statisticians *does* include the unemployed. If a person is without a job but is willing and able to work,
he is regarded as a member of the labor force.

THE LABOR FORCE IN THE UNITED STATES

According to the United States Bureau of the Census, the labor force
in July, 1955, consisted of more than 70 million persons, nearly 60 percent of the population 14 years old or older. About 4 percent of the
total were in the armed forces; about 4 percent were unemployed. Unemployment later rose to above 5 million (slightly over 7 percent) in the
recession of 1951–1958. These figures, it must be understood, are a rather
rough approximation. Both the size and the composition of the labor
force is continually changing.

One kind of change results from the growth of population. Every
year young people arrive at the legal working age, or, if they are above
the minimum working age, they look for their first jobs. Every year also
some members of the labor force retire or die. If in any year the number
entering the labor force exceeds the number who withdraw from it, the
force will grow in consequence. This has usually been the case in the
United States.

Between 1950 and 1955 the labor force had increased by an average
of about 750,000 a year. The birth rate was higher during the years
1941–1955 than before World War II; therefore the annual growth is
likely to be larger than before 1955, because more young people will be
reaching the minimum legal working age.

Another kind of effect on the labor force results from changes in institutions, laws, or social customs. If the legal school-leaving age is advanced, and if more young people continue their education even beyond
the legal age, growth of the labor force is temporarily retarded by that
much. If more older workers retire, the labor force is curtailed at the
upper end. Both these influences have been at work in the United States
in recent decades and were particularly marked after 1950. On the other
hand, if a larger proportion of women seek paid jobs, the labor force is
augmented by that much. This situation, too, has occurred in the United
States. The tendency was particularly strong during World War II, but
it has lasted over a much longer term. It has more than counteracted the
tendencies which limited growth in the labor force. In 1870 women con-

stituted 14.8 percent of the labor force; in 1940 they made up 24.4 percent of it. Of the women of working age in 1870, 13.3 percent were jobholders or job seekers; in 1940, 25.7 percent of women were in the job market. The increase of women workers apparently continues, especially among married women. In 1955 the labor force contained 12 million working wives as compared with 9.3 million in 1950 and 8.5 million at the peak of World War II.

All these changes taken together have so canceled one another that, for many decades, there has been very little alteration in the percentage of the total population which comprises the labor force.

A third kind of change in the total labor force is seasonal. The force is smallest in January, largest in July. Many men enter the force during the agricultural harvest season. (College students working during their vacations help to swell the labor force in summer.) Men and women contribute equally to the gain between January and June; women seasonal workers outnumber men from September to December (probably because of the approach of the busy Christmas season).

Furthermore, there is a continual turnover in the individuals who actually make up the total labor force. Many persons habitually work for compensation only part of the year. Women enter or leave the labor force because of change in family status, although as a rule more women enter it than leave it. Temporary disability may lead to withdrawal from the labor force and to later re-entry. Therefore, the aggregate figure of those in the labor force at any one time does not begin to cover all those who may seek or find work at some time during the year. The total, including the latter, may be 5 or 6 million larger. Even of those supposed to be in the labor force, not all remain steadily in it during a whole year.

CLASSIFICATION OF THE LABOR FORCE

Though the numbers in various occupations are continually changing, a recent over-all classification throws a good deal of light on the subject.

Military men and women working for Uncle Sam are indeed an important section of our manpower, but they are usually excluded in discussions of labor in the economic sense. The *civilian* labor force, which makes ordinary goods and renders ordinary services, totaled about 65 million in July, 1955.

Of the civilian labor force in 1955, 7.7 million were in agriculture; and this number has had a declining tendency. About 5 million in nonagricultural pursuits were either self-employed or employers—mainly business and professional persons. We now come to the 49.7 million who earned wages and salaries, and the approximately 2.8 million who were unemployed. "Labor problems," as ordinarily discussed, concern mainly the situation of nonfarm employees and of those without jobs.

A special area of labor problems is that of hired farm workers, though they are relatively few in number. Most important crops in the United

States are produced on family-sized farms, with few or no employees. About 4.1 million Americans worked for wages on farms at some time during 1949. Most of these did farm work only for short periods. Somewhat less than a million held agricultural jobs for as long as 150 days.

Of the nonfarm employees, about one third works in manufacturing, though the number varies widely between prosperity and depression. Another third works in transporting or selling goods, in communications, in finance, and in real estate. The remaining third includes mining, forestry, fishing, construction, the professions, and government employees.

In manufacturing, the greatest variation of employment due to the alternation of good and bad times occurs in the industries making durable goods. In prosperous times the durable-goods industries employ about half the manufacturing workers. Iron and steel ranks first in number of employees, machinery (excluding electrical equipment) ranks second, and motor vehicles third. These three industrial giants alone normally account for about one fourth of all manufacturing workers.

Among nondurable-goods industries, which fluctuate comparatively little between prosperity and depression, the biggest industry in number of employees is food products; the next biggest is textile manufacture; the third is the making of apparel.

Aside from the shifts in employment due to temporary business conditions, important long-term changes are taking place in the labor force and are likely to continue. One is a shift of workers out of agriculture into nonagricultural pursuits. This shift has been occurring ever since the early days and has been intensified in recent years, so that, whereas upwards of 80 percent of the labor force were at one time engaged in agriculture, in 1955 about 11 percent were so occupied. There are three chief reasons for this decrease: (1) a population of a given size has a limited capacity for food consumption, (2) technological improvements have tremendously increased agricultural output per person engaged, (3) there seems to be no tendency toward an increase in exports of most crops. To these may be added another reason: most of the good agricultural land in the nation was settled long ago, and over the years the growth of industry, commerce, and other nonagricultural pursuits has offered increasing opportunity for employment.

A second persistent tendency, marked especially since World War I, is a more rapid growth of employment in occupations providing services than there is in mining, manufacturing and other industries producing physical goods. One reason is that technological advance, with its increased output per man-hour, has apparently made more headway in physical production than in the provision of services (for example, in wholesale and retail trade, banking, insurance, real estate, teaching, and medicine. Another reason is that, as the people acquire more income and more leisure and as our civilization becomes more complex, the demand for services of many kinds grows more rapidly than the demand for goods. For confirmation of this fact consult the family budgets in Chapter 22 showing the decreased percentage of consumer spending for such things as food and clothing, and the increased percentage of spending for "miscellaneous"—a classification which includes, among other things, payments for services.

DIFFERENCES IN STATUS IN THE LABOR FORCE

Those who work for wages and salaries differ as much in types of occupation and compensation for their labor as do those who are not employees. One sort of distinction depends on age, sex, or race.

Young men under 25 usually find it more difficult to get jobs than those in older age brackets, and this is especially true when unemployment is prevalent. They are also among the first to be laid off when work forces must be cut. As would be expected, they have the less important jobs and the lowest pay prevalent among men. As a rule, men under 25 change jobs more often in an effort to find a satisfactory berth.

Between the ages of 25 and 44, the risk of unemployment for men decreases, wages rise, and promotions occur. From 45 on, the percentage unemployed increases again, as does the difficulty of finding a new job if the old one is lost. Those who remain employed at steady and good jobs may still continue to receive advances in pay or promotion, although those who have intermittent unemployment are likely to sacrifice income on that account. Above 65, the rate of unemployment declines again, largely because, after this age, many retire and those living solely on pensions or retirement compensation are not regarded as part of the labor force.

Though at any given time middle-aged men are likely to earn more than the young or the old, this does not mean that young men must expect a declining income and status after they pass 45. Real wages have shown a marked rise over the decades, and will probably continue to do so. Most workers would experience this rise even if they never won promotion. The rise in real income has averaged 20 percent every ten years. Illness may cut earnings, to be sure. But there is no reason why an energetic and healthy man should not continue to find economic improvement throughout his working life. If he is forced to retire on a pension, he must, of course, expect a considerable cut in his income unless he has some other source of livelihood.

Women workers are most numerous in clerical occupations; the next largest number are operatives in industry. The third largest contingent are in domestic service, and the fourth in professional services. Three quarters of the women workers comprise these four categories. Next in line are service workers not working in homes. Not as many as 500,000 women employees are in any other one occupation. In no other line of work do women hold a proportion of the jobs as large as their contribution to the entire working force—about 25 percent. Women, as a rule, are not found in jobs commanding the most income, security, or prestige, although slightly more than one tenth of the proprietors, managers, and officers are women.

The average working life of men is approximately twice as long as that of women. Many women work only part of the year; others are intermittent workers. Because of changes in family status, women are more likely to leave jobs or to enter them than men. It may be for this reason that not so many women as men prepare themselves for, or achieve, the more responsible jobs for which long apprenticeship or length of continuous service is often a requisite. Though women who have jobs identical with those performed by men usually receive the same pay as the men, women employees on the average earn only about half as much as men, because of the different nature of their occupations.

Negroes also are concentrated in relatively few occupations, at most of which it is impossible to earn as much as white men may in other occupations. Many of them, principally in the South, are engaged in farming, though only about a quarter of Southern nonwhite males have their own establishments. Incomes of small farmers in the South are notoriously low.

Nonwhite males in 1940 made up 9 percent of all employed males in the nation; yet they constituted 61.6 percent of male domestic service workers, 24 percent of other service workers, and 21.2 percent of laborers —excluding laborers on farms and in mines. Only 1.5 percent of proprietors, managers, and officials not on farms were Negroes, and Negroes were underrepresented in all other occupations—even in factories. The earnings of Negro males averaged about as much as those of white women —that is, half as much as the earnings of white men. The earnings of Negro women were even less. Negroes, like white women, have less stable employment than white men.

Nevertheless, Negroes made great progress in employment opportunity during and after World War II. Many moved from the Southeast to states where opportunities for them were greater; many got jobs in transportation, contract construction, manufacturing, trade, and professions. The proportion of Negroes in occupations covered by social security was increased, between 1939 and 1944, by twice or more in fifteen states outside the Southeast.

Agricultural migratory workers, without regard to age, sex, or race, have the lowest incomes, the poorest living conditions, and the least security of employment among all groups of workers. Their status, however, was improved during World War II because of the scarcity of labor, and much of the improvement has been retained. A large number of the casual farm jobs are filled not by agricultural workers proper but by persons who have other jobs during part of the year and do not need to subsist entirely on their farm wages.

WIDE SPREAD IN WAGE INCOMES

It is customary to think of inequality in distribution of income as chiefly a spread between wage earners and salary earners on the one hand

and the owners of industry on the other. This assumption, of course, is inaccurate. Many who receive income from invested funds, such as those in retirement, have lower incomes than many who depend entirely on income from labor. There is a very wide spread, too, in *annual* incomes received as compensation for work. This diversity arises not merely from difference in rates of pay but almost equally from the amount of employment during the year. Many work only part time from choice, and many suffer layoffs or do daily part-time work because of seasonal or other slack.

Figures tabulated by the Social Security Administration covering employees subject to the compulsory tax for old-age pensions in 1948 show that nearly one quarter of them earned $3,000 or more, while about one eighth earned less than $200. About one fifth earned from $2,000 to $2,999, and another fifth from $1,000 to $1,999. A large majority of employees are covered by social security; in 1948 those omitted were chiefly employees in agriculture and in domestic service.

If male workers only are included, and of these only men who had at least some work in each of the four quarters of the year, then the results showed that nearly half (48.9 percent) earned $3,000 or more in 1948. Another 29.3 percent earned between $2,000 and $2,999. Fewer than one twentieth received less than $1,000 for their work.

Perhaps a better way to show the inequality of earnings is to draw up an array of all the workers for compensation, from the highest to the lowest, and then divide the number into ten parts, or deciles. If all are included, without eliminating any part-time workers, then the average yearly earnings of those in the top decile were, in 1948, about 25 times the average earnings of those in the bottom decile. If those who did not have some work in each quarter of the year are excluded, then those in the top decile earned about five times as much as those in the bottom.

These figures indicate that, in any effort to approach equality in income distribution, a good deal of attention must be given to reducing inequality among employees themselves. It must be remembered also that this inequality is a matter not only of rates of pay per hour, week, or month but also of regularity of employment.

WAGES UP—HOURS DOWN

All the evidence indicates that earners of wages and salaries have, by and large, shared fully over the years in the increase of national income per capita.

Rough estimates indicate that the purchasing power of average hourly pay in the United States increased about 90 percent between 1840 and 1890. The gain was more rapid after 1860 than before. Note that this increase is reckoned not merely in dollars; it also accounts for changes in retail prices and shows the increase in what the dollars would buy. It does not, however, account for the number of hours worked. Regular working hours were somewhat reduced in this half century, and unemployment was often prevalent. Therefore, the gain in *annual* real earnings was irregular and, for the whole period, was less than 90 percent.

Better figures exist for the period since 1890. Estimates of *annual real* earnings per wage earner indicate that such earnings rose about 69 percent between 1890 and 1947. Most of the gain was registered during and immediately after the two world wars. This fact is an indication of the importance of high employment in increasing the incomes of employees. (These figures omit hired workers on farms.)

The most reliable figures are those obtainable from the social security records—which began only in 1938. These indicate not only a marked gain since before World War II but also a decided narrowing of inequality among the workers for pay. The average gain in the purchasing power of annual earnings between 1938 and 1948 was about 40 percent for all workers. This figure takes into account the rise in the cost of living. The gain in income of those in the *lowest* decile was, however, 55 percent, while those in the higher deciles gained less.

The gain in the purchasing power of wage earnings has continued since 1947. Wage rates have advanced more rapidly than the consumer price index, and employment has been high, except for relatively mild recessions in 1949 and 1954 and the more serious ones in 1957–58 and 1960-61. Workers who did not share in the general increase are largely salaried employees, especially those not employed by private, profit-seeking enterprises. Teachers are a conspicuous example.

The greatest sufferers from war and postwar inflation have been persons not in the labor force at all, who are living on fixed incomes (in dollars)—for example, recipients of pensions, annuities, and income from bonds or preferred stock.

While the wage earners were gaining in real wages, they also made marked advances in reduction of the standard working week. A "standard" week consists of the maximum number of hours for which regular rates of pay are received. More hours than the standard in any given week are paid for at overtime or "penalty" rates; fewer hours may be worked when business is dull. In 1840 the prevailing working day for nine industries averaged 11.4 hours; the six-day week was customary. Therefore, the average working week was approximately 68 or 69 hours. In some occupations the twelve-hour day was the rule, and of these, some which for technical reasons operated continuously, like blast furnaces, also had a seven-day work week.

During the fifty years that followed, progress in reducing hours was slow and spotty, in spite of continuous agitation for the short workday. By 1890 the average in twenty-one industries was a ten-hour day; few had yet won even a half holiday on Saturday. The twelve-hour, seven-day week still persisted (in steel it was not abolished until the early 1920's).

The great gains have been made in the twentieth century. The 40-hour week is now standard; indeed, it is the legal maximum without overtime pay according to the laws of the federal and many state governments. Some occupations have gained shorter standard weeks—35 or even

30 hours. The average *hourly* wage is at least four times as high as it was a century earlier (in actual purchasing power). Much of this gain the workers enjoy in shorter hours instead of in higher yearly earnings.

COLLECTIVE BARGAINING AND UNIONS

About one third of the nonagricultural employees in the United States are now members of labor organizations. Unions are prevalent in manufacturing, construction, transportation, mining, as well as in certain service occupations such as acting, radio and television, and music as a profession. Approximately 70 percent of all manufacturing production workers are covered by collective agreements regulating wages, hours of work, working conditions, and numerous "fringe benefits" of interest to the wage earners. Organization is not so prevalent among office workers, service workers, sales and professional people, although unions exist in many of these occupations also. Unions are strong in virtually every other highly industrialized nation.

Collective bargaining through labor organization was won as the result of a long, difficult, and often bitter struggle. Sporadic strikes occurred even in the American colonies before the United States became a nation, but for many years labor organizations themselves were short-lived. The oldest established unions in the United States which are still in existence were organized not long before the Civil War. These are mostly organizations of old and highly skilled crafts like the printing or building trades. Most of the great mass-production industries—steel, automobile, electrical equipment—were not successfully organized until the late 1930's.

The largest "international unions"—that is, unions covering workers in a particular occupation or industry throughout the United States and Canada—are the teamsters (now, of course, mainly drivers of trucks and buses), the carpenters, the automobile workers, the steelworkers, the machinists, and the miners (coal miners). The teamsters, the automobile workers, and the steelworkers each have more than a million members. There are a few more than 200 national or international unions in the United States, most of which are affiliated with the American Federation of Labor-Congress of Industrial Organizations (formed in 1955 by a merger of these two national bodies). The most important of the labor organizations not affiliated with this central national Federation are the four brotherhoods representing the men who operate railroad trains—engineers, firemen, conductors, and trainmen.

The AFL-CIO, the national organization with which most of the national or "international" unions are affiliated, is not a bargaining agency and does not call strikes. It is a rather loose federation, having only the powers delegated to it by the unions affiliated with it. The AFL-CIO holds an annual convention which considers matters important to the labor movement as a whole, passes resolutions stating its position on public issues, and elects officers and an executive council to act between conventions. Subordinate to the AFL-CIO are departments covering various types of industry, such as building trades, metal trades, railroads.

To the central organization the member unions have from time to time delegated certain powers. Among these, perhaps the more important are those (1) outlining the jurisdictional boundaries of the unions, (2) disciplining corruption or unethical practices, (3) carrying on union organizational work either in assisting member unions or in an area over which no member union has as yet been granted jurisdiction, (4) carrying on international functions or relationships with labor organizations in other countries. The AFL-CIO has no power to enforce its decisions about the practices of member unions except by suspending or expelling a member union from the central body and by forbidding others to co-operate with a union subject to disciplinary action. From time to time, the AFL-CIO has suspended or expelled unions for violating its decisions in jurisdictional disputes (that is, seeking members in a trade or industry allocated to another union) or for corrupt practices. In recent years the International Longshoremen's Association and the Teamsters' Union have been expelled.

In most cities and in states, there are labor councils formed on a geographical basis, to which the AFL-CIO unions within the region send delegates. These councils are concerned largely with political and other public questions in their respective areas.

Among the international or national unions affiliated with the AFL-CIO, some have jurisdiction over workers in a separate trade or craft, such as carpenters, plumbers, printing compositors, machinists, printing pressmen; and some cover all the eligible employees within an industry, such as automobile workers, steelworkers, coal miners, textile workers. From time to time, jurisdictional disputes between industrial unions covering an industry and trade or craft unions having jurisdiction over some trades found in that industry have split the labor movement wide open, but on the whole such disputes have been worked out by a series of compromises.

THE COLLECTIVE AGREEMENT

A commonly held idea that unions exist chiefly to conduct strikes may arise from the fact that the headlines announcing these dramatic occurrences are larger than those dealing with other union activities. Unions would not willingly surrender the *right* to strike, because without this threat in the background they might win concessions only with much greater difficulty than they do. Nevertheless, the time actually lost by strikes seldom amounts to more than a fraction of one percent of all the hours worked in the United States in any one year; by far the greater proportion of agreements with employers are achieved without interruptions of production. Some unions have a history of many years of peaceful relations without a major strike.

The aim of union-management negotiations is to arrive at an agreement governing their relationships. The period covered by the agreement is usually a year, though sometimes it is two, three, or more years. These agreements are often called "contracts," but unlike business contracts they are seldom enforced by suits for damages or other recourse in the courts. In reality, they are somewhat more like international treaties, upheld by the good faith of both parties because the signers know they must get along with each other peaceably or suffer accordingly.

One set of clauses in the agreement has to do with wages—specifying either the rates to be paid, the increase (very rarely, the decrease) to be applied to existing rates, or the minimum rates—any of which the employer may exceed if he wishes. Another clause may specify the standard hours of work, the overtime rates, the rates for week ends and holidays, and the special rates for night shifts, if any.

Almost all agreements forbid work stoppages during the life of the agreement and outline the union's responsibility in this respect.

In return for the obligations the union assumes, many agreements contain safeguards of the "security" of the union itself. Such a provision may specify the "union shop." Under this arrangement the management may hire anyone it pleases without regard to union membership, but agrees that any eligible employee must join the union after a specified term of employment. (Managerial employees are, as a rule, ineligible.) Without some such provision as the union shop, union members contend, nonunion workers could enjoy all the privileges won by organization without helping to carry the load, and hostile employers might undermine the union through gradually replacing members by nonmembers.

In a "preferential union shop," the employer must hire a union member in preference to a nonmember if any properly qualified union member is available.

The ultimate in union security is the "closed shop." According to this arrangement the employer may hire only union members. The Taft-Hartley Act—a federal law—made the closed shop agreement illegal, but in some cases where the closed shop is a traditional practice and the union assumes the responsibility for supplying properly trained workers, it survives by tacit consent.

Many agreements specify that union dues shall be collected by management through deduction from pay. This is called the "check-off."

Agreements often specify the rights retained respectively by management and by the union. Managements usually retain jurisdiction over business policies, control of production, hiring and firing (within whatever specific limitations the agreement may provide). Union rights may include forbidding discrimination against any worker for union activity and sometimes for race, creed, nationality, or sex as well. Union rights may also cover safety provisions.

Agreements specify what holidays shall be observed and provide for vacations with pay, if any. Such vacations are a growing practice.

More and more agreements also set up plans for old-age pensions, sick benefits, health insurance, unemployment insurance, and other benefits. The "guaranteed annual wage" is, in the form usually achieved, an extended kind of unemployment insurance. All such "fringe benefits" are, as a rule, paid for by the employer. From an accounting standpoint, the employer regards these payments as part of the wage bill; unions think of them as part of the wage "package." All are, of course, supplementary to public social insurance under federal or state laws.

Finally, the agreement usually includes provisions much more important to the union members, to management, and to successful day-by-day industrial relations than persons not familiar with the subject might suspect. These provisions may set up machinery for the handling of grievances, outline the procedure to be followed in layoffs (for example, to what extent reduced pay because of slack in production shall be shared by curtailed hours of work for all rather than by layoffs), erect safeguards against unfair discharge, specify a procedure for appeal and possibly for arbitration in cases of discharge or discipline, and define the relationship between seniority and promotion.

The continual administration of the agreement is just as important as the words of the document itself. Most of this work falls to shop chairmen, shop committees, and subordinate company executives. Skill and experience on both sides, if built up in this process, eliminate sources of irritation before they have been allowed to grow into serious ill-feeling. The process creates a system of precedents sometimes called the "common law of the industry," which gives all concerned the feeling that they are working under a fair and orderly regime in which legitimate rights are democratically safeguarded.

Collective relations between organized workers and employers are much more than bargaining over economic issues like wages and hours; if successful, they also become a system of constitutional industrial government to replace the autocracy (whether benevolent or otherwise) exercised by a management limited in employment practices only by its own will.

LABOR LEGISLATION

Government takes a hand in the labor market through a large body of legislation built up over the years. There are both state and federal labor laws. The federal laws apply only to employees of firms participating in interstate commerce, but the definition of interstate commerce made by the courts is so broad as to include most important industries and occupations, excepting those which have establishments and markets only within a single state.

The Fair Labor Standards Act (federal) sets the maximum standard work week at 40 hours, requires the payment of a minimum wage of not less than a rate adjusted upward from time to time, and specifies time-and-one-half payment for all hours over 40. It prohibits the employment of children under 16 years of age, with some exceptions. It also sets up control over industrial homework.

For many years, although wage earners in the United States had the abstract legal right to combine and engage in collective bargaining, they had no means of exercising that right except by the economic power which they might possess by threatening or carrying on a strike. But anti-union employers discovered many means of obstructing union organization—including the hiring of spies and "undercover" agents in the labor movement, intimidation, the use of injunctions issued by courts to break strikes, and, occasionally, suing union members for damages under the antitrust laws.

During the 1930's many of these practices were forbidden by federal legislation. The Wagner Act expressly recognized the encouragement of collective bargaining as a national policy. It enumerated a series of "unfair labor practices" which employers were forbidden to use, and placed upon employers a legal obligation to bargain "in good faith" with any organization representing a majority of their employees. A National Labor Relations Board was created to administer the Act. The effect of this legislation was a rapid increase in labor organization and in regularized bargaining between unions and employers. After World War II Congress virtually rewrote the Wagner Act to include the prohibition of certain "unfair labor practices" by unions. The law is known as *The Labor-Management Relations Act of 1947* (the Taft-Hartley Act, a federal law) a complicated piece of legislation regulating collective bargaining, the details of which cannot be adequately described in an introductory book on economics. In general, however, its more important provisions are designed to:

Compel the employer to bargain "in good faith" with an organization which a majority of his employees choose as their bargaining agent; forbid the employer to control or interfere with the organization of such a union; and, where the legitimacy of the bargaining agency is in doubt, provide for elections to determine the majority choice of the employees.

Forbid the employer to discharge employees for union activity.

Withhold the protection of the law from labor organizations whose officers do not take oath that they are not members of the Communist Party.

Forbid the use of union funds for political purposes.

Compel unions to publish reports of their finances.

Outlaw the closed shop and the secondary boycott. (A secondary boycott is a concerted refusal by employees to work for an employer with whom there is no direct dispute, in order to prevent him from using materials made by, or otherwise aiding, an employer against whom there is a strike.)

Permit the federal government to seek a court order stopping a strike which threatens a national emergency, for a specified "cooling-off period," during which a Fact-Finding Board investigates and reports its findings.

Provide for federal mediation of disputes.

Continue the National Labor Relations Board to administer the Act.

The Railway Labor Act of 1926 (federal), covering railway employees, contains provisions similar to those of the Labor-Management Relations Act. It safeguards the right to organize and engage in collective bargaining. In case of a dispute threatening a strike, by consent of both sides the issues may be presented for arbitration to the National Railroad Adjustment Board, whose decisions are binding. If a dispute is not arbitrated, a National Mediation Board attempts to settle it. A strike is forbidden until after the Adjustment Board has made a fact-finding report. This law served as the model for the Taft-Hartley Act, but it does not contain so many restrictive provisions about union action.

The Norris-La Guardia Act of 1932 (federal) instructs federal courts not to issue injunctions interfering with unions' rights to strike or carry on other activities incidental to disputes about wages, hours, and conditions of labor. Labor had long regarded such injunctions as unfair protection of the employer, since a preliminary court order can be issued on the basis of an affidavit presented by only one side without a hearing from the other; and violation of a court order is "contempt of court" and can be punishable, without any trial, by the same judge who issued the order. Proceedings of this kind are not appropriate to disputes between labor and management. The act also outlawed the "yellow-dog contract"—a contract between the employer and each individual employee, binding him, as a condition of employment, not to join a union.

The Social Security Act of 1935 (federal) set up a system of old-age insurance, unemployment insurance, and grants to the states for public assistance to persons in need, the blind, dependent children, and the disabled. The impact of these measures on the economy will be discussed in Chapter 18 on Theories Concerning Labor and Wages.

State laws cover minimum wages, maximum hours, and restriction of child labor in occupations not regarded as interstate commerce—for example, laundries, retail trade, hotels and restaurants, and building service employees. There are also numerous state counterparts of the Taft-Hartley Act. These laws are likely to be even more restrictive of union activities in states where labor is not well organized or politically powerful. State laws forbid the employment of women and minors in dangerous occupations and at night. A great deal of state labor legislation has to do with eliminating working conditions which may lead to accident or many cause injury to the health of the workers. Most states have employee compensation systems, operated on an insurance basis with premiums paid by the employers, to reimburse employees for injuries occurring on the job. All states control their own unemployment insurance systems, under the federal law. Many states have their own old-age pensions, and a few have systems of public health insurance.

All these provisions for regulating employment—the unions and an extensive body of legislation—indicate that our society has not been content with the effects of a completely free market in the purchase and sale of human services, a market concerned with little besides supply, demand, and price.

Considerations involved in modern collective bargaining are illustrated in Chapters 27 and 31.

QUESTIONS

Like other forms of organization designed to exert economic power, trade unions have sometimes been used for personal gain or extortion by corrupt leaders or criminal elements. What attitude would you favor toward such abuses or what remedies would you propose? Consider the following attitudes:

1. The position of some union members that corrupt practices are of no concern to them as long as the leaders obtain for them gains in wages, hours, and working conditions.

2. The proposal that all legal protection should be withdrawn from union organization and collective bargaining.

3. Laws forbidding not only the closed shop but also the union shop, checkoff of dues, or any other device which would interfere with the complete freedom of employers to hire or fire whom they please, or of employees to abstain from union membership.

4. The proposal that the antitrust laws forbidding monopoly and restraints of trade should be fully applicable to unions and should be rigorously enforced against them.

5. The position of the AFL-CIO that unions which violate the code of ethics prescribed by that body must be suspended or expelled by the national organization; and that corrupt practices within unions should be prevented by legal action, although legislation intended to deal with abuses should be carefully drawn so as not to injure the legitimate and honestly conducted labor organizations.

18 / THEORIES CONCERNING LABOR

AND WAGES / Real wages—that is, the actual goods

and services received by anyone who works for pay—are simultaneously being produced by other workers. In other words, the total of wages received by all workers at any given time represents a share of all that is produced. This share comes from the goods and services intended for personal consumption. The more an economy produces per person, the higher wages can be.

There remains the question: what actually determines the share of total national production that goes to wage earners? In the first place, it is clear that nobody can immediately consume that part of the national product which consists of buildings and equipment made for further production—what is ordinarily called "capital goods." Nobody likes for breakfast a steel gear buttered with grease. If an economy with a given total productive capacity devotes a large part of it to making capital goods, the workers will get less, immediately, than those in an economy with the same total output which devotes a smaller part of its resources to making instruments of production and a larger part to making consumer goods and services.

If an economy is planned and to a large degree centrally controlled, the decisions as to how much is to be saved and invested—that is, how much of its capacity is to be used for making instruments or production—can be centrally made. This is the practice in the Soviet Union. It is also the practice in other economies during war, and to a smaller extent, in periods of recovery from the effects of war. When such decisions are made by a central authority, the reasons are usually (1) that it seems desirable to invest more and consume less than would be the case if consumers were given a choice as to how much they would spend for consumption and employers had a choice as to how much they would decide to invest; and (2) that it seems desirable for the time being to concentrate on productive equipment for war or other purposes rather than on equipment which may be used to satisfy the market demands of consumers. Even in an economy not centrally directed, forced investment may be made by government construction financed by taxation.

If investment decisions are not made by a central authority, the question concerning what determines the proportion of income to be saved and invested has no simple answer. It depends on the separate decisions of millions of individuals and firms. (For a discussion of the theory of investment, see Chapter 14.)

The variation of the percentage of net national income in the United States used for new investment decade after decade has not been wide. The average for each decade has approximated 6 or 7 percent. In controlled economies the percentage has often been larger. It is undoubtedly greater in the Soviet Union, though nobody knows exactly how large it is. In Great Britain after World War II, when an urgent necessity existed to build up production rapidly both for exports and for future domestic living levels, the percentage of national income invested has at times been two or three times as large as in the United States.

In any country subject to the business cycle, a smaller proportion of total net income is invested in capital goods during depression than during prosperity.

THE THEORY OF MARGINAL PRODUCTIVITY

Both demand and supply affect the price of wage earners' services (wage rates), as they do prices in any market.

The producer's least cost is at that point at which the addition of another unit of input will cost more than the units already in the production hopper. Now each unit of input presumably contains some labor, as well as other things. The wage cost in each unit of input will obviously play a large role in the decision of the employer concerning how much to produce and consequently how much labor to employ. Thus, in the market as a whole, the unit cost of labor affects the demand for labor, and the demand presumably affects the wage level.

But this reasoning is far too oversimplified to tell the whole story. What determines the unit cost of labor? Surely not merely the wage per hour, as is often taken for granted in popular discussion of these subjects. The productivity of labor is also an important factor. Even at the same hourly wage, more highly productive labor will be cheaper per unit than less highly productive labor. The employer will find that at any given hourly wage he can profitably produce a larger amount with more highly productive labor than with less highly productive labor. The same principle applies to machinery or other units of capital or to natural resources.

The theory of marginal productivity is introduced to account for the division of income among the factors of production—land, labor, and capital. How much goes to rent, how much to wages, and how much to interest? According to theory, the answer depends on the relative marginal productivity of each factor. Each factor enters into any unit of input. The employer will try to combine the factors, in any unit of input, in such a way that the combined cost of the unit is the lowest possible. He will not use more labor if he can get the same output more cheaply by using more machinery. The point at which the quantities of each factor to be utilized will contribute most to efficient production will be the point at which their respective marginal costs—that is, the cost of adding one more unit of any one of the factors—are equal. It will be the point at which it will increase cost to substitute a unit of any one factor for a unit of any other.

The decisions of *all* employers on such questions, since they affect the relative demands for investment, materials, and labor, will help to determine the earnings of labor, of capital (interest), and of the owners of natural resources (rent). The upshot is that the employers' aggregate demand will tend to be greatest for that factor of production which, with the same expenditure, will add most to production at the least expense. The rewards of each factor of production will be proportionate to the relative productivity of its marginal units.

A crude conclusion from this theory, sometimes advanced, is that when wages are too high in a free-enterprise economy, the employers, by substituting machinery for labor, will cause unemployment. This replacement in turn increases the supply of available labor and so leads to a drop in wages. That might be the result for a short term or in a static economy, in which the total demand for products did not increase. But in a dynamic, growing economy, technological unemployment is actually limited to declining or stationary industries and as a rule is transient.

Every technological improvement leads to higher productivity, which in turn increases the real incomes of consumers either through higher wages or through lower prices, so that demand for the products of industry, on the whole, keeps pace with the rise in output capacity. Thus, for each man-hour of work many more units of output are made as time goes on; and the demand for labor taken as a whole (though not necessarily for labor in a particular industry) grows as a result of the increased demand for the products.

Real wages in the United States are the highest in the world and, by and large, have long been so. At the same time, industry in the United States is noted for its avidity for technological improvements which add to productivity. The natural conclusions, under the theory of marginal productivity, would seem to be that (1) high wages constitute an incentive to the employer for the introduction of labor-saving devices, (2) the use of these devices so enlarges demand for their products that more labor than before is needed, and (3) the increased demand for labor raises wages again.

One result of this process is that the wage earners, instead of being regarded as mere elements of the cost of producing something to be sold to nonwage earners, are now regarded also as consumers of many of the

products they make. A century and a half ago, when the factory operatives could not buy much except enough to keep body and soul together,
such wage earners did not offer a promising market to the industries of a
nation. Now, with each successive round of wage increases and each rise
in general standards of living, the expectation of employers that their
markets will grow becomes more rosy. No doubt very few employers have
ever raised wages solely for that reason; on the contrary, many employers
would be glad to keep down the wages they pay while other wages are
going up. But they recognize that this is difficult if not impossible, and
so offer less resistance to rising wages (as long as they do not suffer a competitive disadvantage on that account) than they would if they did not
anticipate growing sales because of the general increase of purchasing
power.

NONMARKET INFLUENCES ON WAGES

Strictly economic calculations are far from being the sole influence on
wages. Labor spokesmen have long emphasized that labor is not a commodity and hence is not subject solely to demand and supply. The relationship between employer and employee is to a large extent a relation
between persons. Human beings are not chattels to be bought and sold
(except in a system of slavery, long ago outlawed in civilized nations). It
is true that the employer buys, and the employee sells, time or services
(for a limited period and purpose), but what such services are believed
"worth" depends largely on ethical considerations, the cultural setting,
and similar intangible factors.

Wage and salary earners have ideas about the standard of living
which they expect to maintain, as do other persons. In a progressive and
highly productive economy, these standards gradually rise. Workers will
not accept pay which they regard as insufficient to maintain the standards
they believe fitting. Most businessmen, too, in the atmosphere of a democratic culture such as that of the United States, do not wish to be stigma-
tized as harsh exploiters of labor; they like to be known as fair, or even
generous, employers, who pay enough to obtain the most efficient and
highly skilled operatives. A majority of the public as a rule supports the
idea that real wages should be at least sufficient to maintain what may
be thought a "decent" standard, or a "minimum of health and comfort."
In the United States at least, this standard increases, and real wages are
expected to rise in order to keep up with it.

In passing, the proper use of the two terms "standard of living," and
"level of living" should be noted. A standard is a test by which to measure. It is an *idea* of what is correct or appropriate. A standard of living
is therefore a generally accepted idea of what goods and services ought to
be within the means of the family or the individual consumer. The level
of living, on the other hand, denotes what actually may be obtained with
any income or class of income. The level of living may or may not coincide with current standards.

These intangible factors operate to keep wages above the level which might result from unrestricted market forces of demand and supply. They may also work to keep wages up, by restricting the *effective supply* of labor at wages which the workers regard as too low, since workers competent to fill certain jobs may decline offers if the compensation seems inadequate.

FLEXIBILITY IN THE LABOR MARKET

Partly because of these intangible factors, wage rates are not very flexible—that is, they do not change quickly in response to changes in demand and supply, although they can go up much more readily than they can go down. This conclusion is supported by a study of wage statistics of the past. Wage-rate reductions are unusual. Even in periods of depression and unemployment, wage rates fall, if at all, much less than either wholesale or retail prices, and the drop of wage rates lags behind the movement of employment, prices, production, or other indications of the state of the economy.

When business is active and improving, increases of *money* wage rates are frequent. If a boom is accompanied by inflationary price increases, however, the rise of money wages may not keep pace with the rise of the consumer price index. Under such conditions there is thus a lag upward.

If, therefore, by "wages," one means the rate per hour paid to those who have jobs, the resultant of the laggard movement of money wage rates has, in the past, often been that *real* wage rates—that is, what can be bought with an hour's pay—achieve their greatest gain in periods of falling prices.

If, on the other hand, one thinks of "wages" as earnings by the month, or year; *real earnings* of the labor force as a whole fall during depression because, although employed workers may be able to buy more than before with an hour's pay on account of the fall in prices, not so many persons are employed and the employed work fewer hours. For example, in the slump of 1957–1958, though wage rates did not fall, unemployment drastically cut earnings in the automobile and other industries most affected. But when employment and business pick up again, any established gain in purchasing power per hour worked will be translated into an increase in *real earnings* because more persons are employed than in depression and they work longer hours. When gains in wage rates are subsequently registered, real earnings are increased on that account also.

So much for the flexibility of wages. What about the elasticity of the supply of, and demand for, labor when its price (wages per hour) rises or falls?

The supply of labor is basically determined, at any given time, by the size of the population of working age. If, as has been the case for years in the United States, immigration is strictly limited, the population of the working age can hardly be increased or decreased by anything except changes in the birth rate or the death rate. The birth rate may respond to high wages by an increase, but the effect on the labor force will not be felt for many years. The death rate certainly does not respond quickly to changes in wages.

A strong demand for labor at high wages may cause more women to enter the labor force and more old persons to remain in it, as during World War II. Low wages and a slump in the demand for labor caused by depression are not likely to lead people to leave the labor force unless they have been discouraged in their attempts at finding jobs. We must conclude, therefore, that while the price of labor has some effect on its supply, this effect is not quickly felt except in unusual circumstances.

Does the price of labor greatly affect the demand for workers? Is it true, as economists suppose it is in most commodity markets, that high prices diminish the quantity that purchasers (in this case, employers) desire to buy and low prices increase their demand?

If so, it is difficult if not impossible to find in the statistics any support for the theory, as far as the total demand for the workers of a nation is concerned. In spite of repeated wage cuts during the depression of the 1930's, unemployment kept increasing. The first sign of genuine revival had no visible relationship with the level of wages, but rather coincided with the settling of the banking crisis and the anticipation of rising prices under a new national administration.

A prevalent theory among economists is that a downturn from the peak of a period of prosperity may be initiated by rising costs (including the cost of labor), which so diminish profit margins as to interfere with the incentive for further expansion. If this situation should occur in a few important industries, the contagion could spread to others, because of reduced spending by those first affected. Such a development is theoretically possible, but to demonstrate that it actually has occurred in any given case would be far from easy. Even rising unit labor costs would not reduce profit margins if the price of the product rose by an equal or greater percentage, as it is likely to do when most prices are on the upgrade.

THEORY REGARDING DIFFERENCES IN EARNINGS

Why is it that some kinds of work are rewarded by much higher pay than others? The answer to this question requires a brief look at the "micro" theory of wages.

Here, the effects of relative demand and supply are clearly in evidence. If the demand for a given product is rapidly increasing, the firms producing it will wish to expand their operations and will need more workers. These firms are likely to offer higher wages as well as other inducements to obtain a sufficiently large working force. If, on the other hand, any firm is subject to declining or stationary demand for its product, and wishes to reduce its staff, it will certainly not increase wages if it can possibly avoid doing so. If it should be forced out of business, the demand for labor in its field of operations would be correspondingly curtailed.

The difference in wages paid to those of different skills and training may be accounted for in part by their relative productivity. A beginner cannot turn out so much as a worker who has had more experience and training, and hence is not "worth" so much. Employers often apply this principle even to experienced workers, by paying piece rates instead of a flat rate per hour. Another prevalent practice is to offer a basic or minimum hourly rate, augmented by some form of incentive payment for output above a standard amount. Piece rates and incentive payments, however, are feasible only when it is possible to measure the output of an individual or team of workers. In cases where quality of the product depends on the care and attention of the worker, time payments are often preferred by the employer, because he does not wish to risk sacrificing quality for quantity.

The differences in pay among workers of various skills and crafts may be due in part to their relative contributions to production—though this difference would be difficult to measure. A much more influential factor in this case is the difference in supply. Those who possess the aptitude and have received the training requisite for the more highly skilled jobs are, as a rule, relatively few in number and cannot so easily be replaced if they should be attracted by more highly paying jobs. Their higher scales are also reinforced by tradition.

The differentials in pay between the operatives on various types of jobs are generally well known; an increase in pay at the bottom of the pyramid almost invariably occasions a demand for an equal increase all the way up the ladder, in order to maintain customary differentials. To upset the traditional hierarchy of pay may cause untold trouble for the employer through dissatisfaction of his older and more highly skilled workers. It should be noted, however, that many times those in the more highly paid occupations have been content to accept an increase in dollars equal to that given the lower ranks, rather than an equal percentage increase. This frequent practice results in closer approximation to equality in the payments to various grades of labor, as time goes on.

Differences Due to Market Obstructions. In the United States, there are geographical differences in wages paid for some of the same types of work. In the Southeastern states the wages of the unskilled and of many semiskilled factory operatives are lower than in the North and the West. For highly skilled workers, however, there is little or no regional difference in wage rates.

These facts may be accounted for partly by the historical background and partly by the relative difficulty with which the less skilled workers move about the country to seek the best opportunities. The Southeast for many years was primarily agricultural. Agricultural workers occupy the lowest rung on the income ladder. Industry, mining, and construction in recent years have been growing rapidly in the South and can attract un-skilled labor or semiskilled factory operatives at lower wages there than must be paid in other sections of the country. The local supply of such labor is large. Skilled labor in the South, however, is not so abundant.

Geographical differences in wages might be expected to disappear quickly if both labor and capital could move easily about the nation—labor, to seek the highest wages; capital, to seek the lowest costs. Un-skilled and untrained workers, however, often do not have the means, the information, or the confidence to migrate. Highly paid skilled workers in the United States, on the other hand, usually have cars or can readily make use of other means of travel. Growing industrial communities in the South which need skilled labor can recruit workers in the North by paying the rates customary in the North. Southern workers with low incomes have been moving north too, but many have stayed behind.

The regional difference in pay, however, is slowly being narrowed. During periods of high industrial employment—as in World War II and after—many Southern workers were attracted to Northern industrial centers by the job opportunities which were open. For many years cotton textile mills in the Northeast have been moving South because of lower wage scales there; but in doing so they are gradually expanding the de-mand for Southern industrial labor and so tend to raise Southern wages. Other Northern industrial concerns are building branch plants in the South as they expand. Some of these firms pay the same wages in all sections, as a matter of policy. They also tend to break down racial barriers which in the past have denied the more desirable types of work to nonwhite workers.

This example confirms the theory that, in any market, inequalities of price will be ironed out if both those who offer the supply (in this case, workers) and those who furnish the demand (in this case, employers) can move about freely and are in a position to accept the best offers. Lack of mobility of both labor and capital have long constituted a barrier to equality of wages for the same kinds of work, but in the United States this barrier is, as a rule, lower than in nations where workers move about less easily. It should be noted that barriers to labor mobility are often social as well as geographic. The democratic traditions of the United States have constituted a powerful agency in the breaking of social bar-riers, though in the special case of racial barriers progress often seems slow.

COLLECTIVE BARGAINING AND MARKET THEORY

The basic theory supporting collective bargaining is that a labor market in which the dealings are between competitive individual workers and employers is not an entirely free market, in which wages can be expected to fluctuate about an "equilibrium" level determined by demand and supply. The individual worker does not have so great a bargaining power as the employer. The wage earner needs a job; as a rule he needs it immediately if he is unemployed, and continually if he is employed. His resources are not great enough to enable him to wait long, to move about in search of the best offer, or to refuse whatever may be offered in the hope of finding something better. The employer, on the other hand, has the financial resources to wait. If one applicant will not accept his offer, he can look around for another. The bigger and more prosperous the employing firm, the greater its bargaining power. If, however, workers join together and bargain collectively, the employer will have difficulty in replacing his whole force if his workers do not like his terms. Therefore the wage earners collectively are able to compel the employer to pay as high a rate as he would have to pay if bargaining power were equal and thus a really free market for labor existed—in other words, if the "equilibrium" rate of wages were approximated.

One type of collective bargaining theory holds that the bargain is limited at both ends—it can succeed only between the lowest the workers will accept and the highest the employer will pay. Within this area, bargaining power determines the share of the value-product that labor can obtain.

A given employer may think he can pay no more than a certain amount and still stay in business, whereas he could do so if he adopted more efficient methods. By exerting pressure for higher wages, unions therefore aid the advance of productivity and stimulate the growth of real national income. The same result is achieved if unions, by enforcing high rates, actually do put less efficient competitors out of business and thus concentrate production in the more efficient sectors of the industry.

If, however, organized labor pushes wages up faster than even the most efficient firms can afford from their existing revenue, one of two results is likely.

If demand for the product is inelastic, the employers may raise prices, increase their revenue, and pay the wages demanded. In this case, the workers concerned will raise their own wages at the expense of other consumers, who will suffer a decline in real income because of the rise in prices, coupled with inability to increase their own compensation proportionately. If demand for the product is elastic, the employers may pay the wages demanded by raising their prices, but only at the cost of diminishing the demand for their product and thus the employment of those who receive the increased wage rates. In this way organized workers may "price themselves out of the market."

Some unions—particularly some in the building trades though not as a rule those in manufacturing industries—restrict more efficient methods of production or compel the employer to hire unnecessary workers with the aim of retaining their craft status or minimizing technological unemployment. This, in effect, obstructs the possibility of higher wage payments through improved productivity. In such a case, the higher wages are certain to be obtained either at the cost of other workers as consumers or at the cost of ultimately diminished employment for the workers in question. In the long run, organized workers are likely to discover that practices restricting more efficient methods substantially restrict their job opportunities. This, however, is not the practice of most unions. Some unions, on the contrary, actively aid employers to adopt more efficient methods so that they may pay higher wages and increase employment opportunity.

MONOPOLY AND MONOPSONY IN BARGAINING

In view of the fact that the courts for many years regarded unions as conspiracies in restraint of trade, and unions often suffered legal disabilities under the antitrust laws, the question arises whether, or to what extent, unions exercise monopolistic methods. It is true, of course, that the members do act in unison in bargaining and agree not to sell their services at all to those for whom they customarily work unless an agreement satisfactory to a majority of those concerned can be obtained. The right to do so is now recognized by federal statute; collective bargaining has been legally declared to be in the public interest. If an element of monopoly is economically involved in this practice, it is regarded as a legitimate means of obtaining equality of bargaining power with employers.

Most unions, however, are not monopolies in the sense that they are exclusive organizations which obtain benefits only for their existing members. Wages and hours specified in collective agreements cover all eligible employees in establishments where they are in force, nonunion workers as well as union members. Furthermore, except where closed shops are in force, the unions do not prevent the hiring of applicants who do not belong to the organization. On this account, unions as a rule do not place any long-run limitation on the supply of the services for which they exercise bargaining power. Control over supply is the usual touchstone of monopoly, for it is only through deliberate limitation of supply that prices above the competitive equilibrium level may be long maintained.

In the case of closed-shop unions, the employer is allowed to hire only union members. The union, however, may or may not exercise monopoly by limiting its membership. Such restriction is possible by highly skilled crafts, some of which limit the number of apprentices or learners, or charge such high initiation fees that only a small number of aspirants can pay them. "Closed unions" are few and usually exist only by collusion with employers who also maintain a monopolistic position— as in building trades, where a local combination is able to exclude outside contractors or material manufacturers, partly by control of licenses and partly by the refusal of unions to work for contractors not in the local association of employers. A monopoly of this kind is next to impossible on a broad scale and will soon succumb where the market is not strictly local. Even in local markets, substitute materials or methods sooner or later begin to undermine the monopolistic restrictions of those who price themselves out of the market.

Some employers may exercise monopsony (monopoly in buying) in dealing with labor. This is possible in a small town or a more or less isolated locality where there is only one employer or a few who have tacit understandings to keep wages down. Good roads, cars, and nation-wide unions have gone far to undermine such monopsonies. It might be supposed that the great industries in which oligopolies prevail could exercise monopsony on a national scale in dealing with labor. In such industries as the automobile, steel, and electrical equipment, however, the national unions often do not deal with the employers as a unit. Rather, they exploit the competition for position which flourishes among the big companies, by shrewdly picking one firm at a time in seeking con-cessions; they exploit the reluctance of a leader in the industry to lose sales during a strike while its rivals are busy. Having won advances in this way, the unions use them as a "pattern" for agreements with the other employers.

HAVE UNIONS INCREASED LABOR'S SHARE?

Economists disagree about whether it is possible for organized labor to increase the share of the total national product received by workers. There is no question that in any given instance a union can increase wages. Some evidence exists that in the same occupations unionized workers receive higher wages than those working in plants where unions do not prevail—though nonunion employers sometimes have paid high wages to keep the wage earners from organizing. So many variables, how-ever, influence the percentage of national income that goes to all those who are paid for their services, that collective bargaining alone may not be able to affect it. Bargaining by labor does not control the prices charged by employers, their investment policies, the interest charged for borrowed money, economic rent, the fullness of employment, and other important factors in the distribution of income. These other factors may respond in compensatory fashion to any changes in wages.

Excluding government employees, private employees have received for their work about 50 percent of the gross national product of private establishments in every year from 1919 to date. The variation up or down has never been as much as 4 percentage points and in most years has been much less. The extraordinary gains in real income made by earners of wages and salaries have in the main resulted not from an in-creased share in the total but from maintenance of the same share in a growing total. It should be remembered that the 50 percent of private gross national product not paid to workers includes not only the money spent for personal consumption by recipients of profits, interest, and rent, but also the large sums of money spent for renewal or replacement of plant and equipment, the amounts spent to enlarge productive capac-ity, and business transfer payments.

Even if collective bargaining does not increase the percentage of the national product which goes to labor as a whole, millions of workers have learned from experience that it has increased *their* wages. Furthermore, nobody questions that collective bargaining has markedly decreased standard hours, has improved conditions of work, and has performed numerous other services which lead workers to be loyal to their unions.

ECONOMICS OF THE MINIMUM WAGE

When a law establishing minimum wages was proposed, the arguments for the measure, aside from its humanitarian aspects, rested mainly on the proposition that many low-paid employees needed the protection of law because they were not members of unions and hence could not exercise collective bargaining. Opponents of the proposal contended that any minimum rate which was above that naturally resulting from market forces would merely diminish employment among those who received the lowest wages, since it would force employers to pay more than such labor was worth to them. No marked effect of this kind has been noticeable since the minimum wage laws have been passed. As a rule, however, the legal minima have been so low and have been increased so tardily, that they have barely, if at all, kept up with market wage rates. Meanwhile, union organization has spread rapidly.

ECONOMICS OF SOCIAL INSURANCE

Old-age pensions under social insurance (Old-Age and Survivor's Insurance) are, according to law, paid out of a fund to which equal contributions are made by employers and employees. The fund must, according to law, be invested in securities issued by the federal government. This fund is supposed to become so large that it will cover, from year to year, any difference between the pensions which the government is obligated to pay and the current contributions from the insured. All employees in occupations covered are obliged to contribute, whether they expect to retire on a pension or not. The contribution is a small percentage of earnings up to a maximum (at present $4,800). Those who receive more than this need not pay the tax on the remainder of their earnings. The employees' share of the contribution is withheld by employers from current pay and forwarded, together with their own share, to the federal government.

The annual pension to be expected is small—even at the maximum, barely enough to live on. Anyone in the system receives a minimum, whether or not he has paid in enough to finance it, but cannot receive more than a maximum, no matter how much he has paid in. Between the minimum and the maximum, what the pensioner receives depends on how much he has contributed. The amount paid to the wage earner is supplemented by additional payments for a dependent wife and dependent children; if the pensioner dies, his widow and dependent children receive benefit payments.

The federal pension is not supposed to offer to the retired a level of living anywhere near as high as that which he has earned by working. Retirement is permitted at or after age 65 for men and 62 for women, but is not compulsory under the law. The pension is designed to prevent absolute destitution and to lessen the load on philanthropic agencies for care of the aged, widows and their children.

A pensioner may receive additional income from his own savings, and from private insurance or pension plans. Even a millionaire who is not earning a salary but who has accumulated the necessary credits may "retire" at 65 and receive his pension in addition to his dividends.

In general, the social security pension plan helps to stabilize employment by contributing a steady (though small) amount of purchasing power to the retired, which continues through depressions as well as in prosperity, and almost all of which is spent as soon as it is received. The collection of contributions is largest in boom periods, and this may help to check inflation, by taking more money from the public at a time when less should be spent.

Unemployment insurance is intended to assure employees who are laid off or lose their jobs some income until they again find jobs. The payment is only a part of what the person would have earned if he had been working. There is a waiting period before the jobless worker becomes eligible, and the compensation is continued for only a limited number of weeks during any one year. Legislation specifying the amounts to be paid, the waiting period, and the duration of the compensation is within the powers of the several states, and state laws differ on these matters.

All the states and territories of the United States were induced to pass unemployment insurance laws by the federal Social Security Act of 1935, which imposed on all employers of eight or more persons in covered occupations throughout the country a tax of 3 percent of their payrolls. This tax is payable even if the state in which the employers operate has no unemployment insurance plan. If it has one, however, employers may pay to the state fund instead of to the federal government whatever the state requires, up to 2.7 percent of payrolls. The remaining 0.3 percent goes to the federal government for the expenses of administration. A state may enact as generous or as parsimonious a plan as it pleases, financing it by any tax it likes, so long as the 0.3 percent is paid to the federal government.

To become eligible for unemployment compensation, the jobless worker must register with a public employment exchange in his locality. These exchanges are operated by the federal government. If the employment office can find him a suitable job in his line of work, he must accept it or forfeit his insurance payments. According to federal law, compensation cannot be denied to a worker who refuses to take a job in an establishment where there is a strike or where pay and conditions of work are much less desirable than those which are locally prevalent. The system is thus in some measure a safeguard of collective bargaining and a deterrent to wage reductions, which might otherwise result from the competition among jobless workers during a slump.

The unemployment payments are intended to be sufficient to keep the workers out of want at least for brief periods of unemployment, without being high enough to tempt them to live on the compensation rather than look for work. At the beginning, unemployment payments averaged about 50 or 60 percent of the weekly wage, being a larger percentage of low pay than of high pay. The average percentage has fallen drastically since then because while wages have gone up, the laws governing compensation have lagged behind.

States almost universally charge lower rates to employers who have a good employment record than to those who have had within the past two or three years a high unemployment record. This advantage to the employer is supposed to be an incentive to regularize employment, although industries most subject to slumps or seasonal slacks often have little power to do so. The net result is smaller funds than would be accumulated during prosperity if the same percentage of payrolls were collected from all, and consequently less ability to pay adequate compensation, especially if a severe depression should arrive, or if it should last a long time.

Unemployment insurance is one of the leading measures in counteracting the swings of the business cycle. It operates automatically. During a boom, when employment is large and earnings are high, it takes more money from employers and employees (which otherwise they might spend) than is currently paid out in benefits. When unemployment rises, the flow of money is reversed. The government then pays out more than it receives, and so helps to check the decline of purchasing power. This effect is particularly valuable because it begins to operate almost as soon as unemployment rises, without any new legislation or other deliberate action. Measures used to check a slump before it becomes widespread are thought to be much more effective than those taken after it becomes serious.

The system as it stood in 1960 would be seriously defective in a long-continued unemployment crisis, since the duration of payments is too short and the funds with which to finance them are inadequate if they must be paid over extended periods. The plan has not been tested in a serious depression since its enactment, because it did not come into full effect until the war and postwar years of generally high employment. The recessions of 1949 and 1954 were mild and brief. In the recession of 1957–1958 and in that of 1960–1961, many workers were out of jobs for a longer period than their benefits continued, and the federal government assisted the states by paying subsequent benefits.

One omission of the law that might be of particular interest to college students is that the law makes no provision for payment of benefits to unemployed persons who have never had a job—mostly, of course, those leaving school. A considerable percentage of those out of work is in this category.

Relevant to this chapter are collective bargaining issues treated in the case studies of Chapters 27 and 31.

QUESTIONS

In 1960 it was frequently stated that although the average earnings of workers in industry in the United States could buy twice as much as before World War II, the purchasing power of the average college professor's salary had scarcely changed. Assuming this statement to be reasonably accurate, to what extent would you attribute the disparity to any of the following possible explanations?

(a) The fact that wage earners were organized and engaged in collective bargaining, whereas college teachers were not.

(b) A smaller increase in effective demand for college teachers than for wage earners.

(c) A more rapid rise in the number of those equipped to teach than of those seeking wagework.

(d) More rapid increase in productivity in private industry (output of goods or services per man-hour) than in higher education (educated students per teacher-year).

(e) A greater willingness of consumers to increase their expenditures for goods (for example, automobiles, TV sets, and other consumer goods) than for education.

(f) An assumption of parents and students that they could rely on legislative appropriations and philanthropic grants to pay a substantial part of educational costs, coupled with insufficient appropriations by legislators and insufficient grants by philanthropists.

(g) A reasoned judgment that the quality and worth of higher education are not high enough to compete with the advantages to be gained by acquisition of goods and services offered by private industry and vigorously promoted by modern advertising.

19 / AGRICULTURE IN THE

ECONOMY / The business of producing economic

goods by working the land is not a single industry in the sense that it is composed of establishments which turn out only one kind of output. There are hundreds of farm crops and animal products—each with its own market, its own characteristics of supply and demand. They include common foods and feeds like wheat and other grains, beef, pork, dairy products, eggs, poultry, vegetables, and fruit. They also include fibers like cotton and wool. Soybeans, used for numerous purposes including feed and industrial materials; tree crops such as pulp wood, turpentine, tar, nuts, and oil; and numerous other specialties add variety.

The organization of agricultural production differs from that of most other productive establishments, especially in the United States. Typically the farm is simultaneously a small business and a family home. It is not usually an incorporated company, in which outside investors may risk their money and delegate the work to hired employees. The number of farm operators is much greater than the number of farm employees. Of the operators, many more own their land than rent it, and most of those who rent farms aspire to own them.

Although farms differ widely in size and wealth, in almost no branch of agriculture is there a situation in which one or a few firms dominate the market for what they sell. Rather, there are thousands or even millions of competitive sellers.

Most farm families raise products for their own use as well as products for sale, though there are today few self-sustaining farms which raise almost everything they need, as there were when the country was first settled.

THE FARMERS' FINANCIAL CONDITION

A few figures from a report on the financial condition of agriculture issued by the United States Department of Agriculture point up the economic structure of agriculture as a whole. For the year 1959, the cash

230

TABLE 19/1

COMPARATIVE INCOME STATEMENT OF AGRICULTURE, UNITED STATES, 1940, 1958, AND 1959
(in millions of dollars)

Item	1940	1958	1959
How net income was obtained			
Gross farm income:			
Cash receipts from farm marketings.........	8,382	33,490	33,146
Government payments to farmers...........	723	1,089	681
Home consumption of farm products........	1,210	1,753	1,628
Rental value of farm dwellings.............	723	1,884	2,012
Net change in inventory	281	1,037	518
Total	11,319	39,253	37,985
Production costs, other than wages, rent, and interest on mortgages:			
Feed bought	998	4,496	4,623
Livestock bought, except horses and mules...	517	2,711	2,727
Fertilizer and lime bought.................	306	1,345	1,444
Repairs and operation of capital items......	1,006	3,832	4,087
Depreciation and other consumption of farm capital	796	3,961	4,125
Taxes on farm real estate and personal property	451	1,343	1,445
Seed bought	197	532	534
Miscellaneous	708	2,470	2,664
Total	4,979	20,690	21,649
Net income from agriculture..........	6,340	18,563	16,336
How net income was distributed			
Wages to hired labor (cash and perquisites).....	1,029	2,878	2,929
Net rent and Government payments to landlords not living on farms	448	1,141	1,001
Interest on farm mortgage debt..............	293	527	580
Net income of farm operators................	4,570	14,017	11,826
Net income from agriculture........	6,340	18,563	16,336
	1,770	5,446	14,500

From *Federal Reserve Bulletin,* August, 1960.

receipts of farmers for everything they sold were more than $33 billion. What they raised for their own consumption was worth about $1.6 billion, or less than one twentieth of what they sold. Their gross income (on an accounting basis) included also what farm owners would have had to pay for rent if they had not owned their homes—$2.0 billion. Minor items were governmental payments to farmers, $681 million, and net change in inventory, $518 million.

Out of the total of about $33 billion gross income, farmers paid to hired labor only about $2.9 billion; this figure includes not only cash but such things as board and lodging. Those farmers who did not own their farms paid slightly over $1 billion in rent. Those farmer-owners who owed mortgages paid $580 million interest. All the rest of farmers' expenses consisted of purchases of materials such as feed, livestock, seed, fertilizer and lime; of the costs of vehicle operation; of taxes; of miscellaneous items; and of a charge for depreciation and maintenance of their property. The total of these expenses was about $21.6 billion. Farm operators came out with a realized income from agriculture of about $11.8 billion.

It will be apparent that the net return to farm operators was more than four times as great as their payment to employees. It will also be apparent that the rental paid by nonowning farmers was a small fraction of total farm income. These figures reflect the fact that most farmers have few or no employees, and that most of them own their farms. The relatively small amount ($580 million) paid in mortgage interest indicates that, in the aggregate, mortgage debt of owners was not heavy.

The combined net income of farm operators and hired farm labor was, in 1959, approximately $14.7 billion. If this sum is divided by the approximately 8.5 million persons engaged in agriculture, the average income per person is in the neighborhood of $1,750. Such figures are often used to show that the return from agriculture per worker is less than that from any other major occupation. But this is a misleading type of average. In the first place, most of the hired farm labor works for only a few weeks in the year and is engaged in other occupations as well. Among farm operators themselves, there were many share croppers or renters in the South and owners of small, submarginal farms on poor, hilly soil, which raise little for the market. There is a grave problem of poverty in such regions, which warrants special study and remedy. Nevertheless, the same is not true of commercial farmers in the more prosperous agricultural regions, except in periods of general depression. Measures designed to raise the prices of major agricultural products do little to help those at the lower income levels because they have so little to sell.

The aggregate balance sheet of agriculture as of 1960 shows the total assets of farmers to be $203.6 billion. Of this amount, $129.1 billion represented the value of real estate, against which there was a real estate debt of but $2.6 billion. The farmers' assets also included $9.1 billion of bank deposits and currency, $5.2 billion United States Savings Bonds, and $3.8 billion investments in cooperative associations. Their cash and bonds, $14.3 billion, were large enough to have paid off their real estate mortgages five times over. Of course, this is an aggregate figure; it does not mean that the farmer who had a mortgage necessarily possessed enough liquid assets to pay it off. Some farmers had much cash and few or no debts; others had little cash and large debts; still others had little of either cash or debts.

Of the farmers' property other than real estate, the largest item was

TABLE 19/2

COMPARATIVE BALANCE SHEET OF AGRICULTURE,
UNITED STATES, JANUARY 1, 1940, 1959, AND 1960[1]

Item	Amount (in billions of dollars)			Net increase, or decrease (−)[2] (percent)	
	1940	1959	1960	1940–60	1959–60
Assets					
Physical assets:					
Real estate	33.6	125.1	129.1	283.8	3.2
Non-real-estate:					
Livestock	5.1	18.1	16.2	216.3	−10.3
Machinery and motor vehicles.	3.1	[3]17.7	18.4	502.1	4.0
Crops stored on and off farms[4]	2.7	[3]9.3	8.0	199.4	−14.5
Household furnishings and equipment[5]	4.3	13.1	13.5	214.8	2.6
Financial assets:					
Deposits and currency..........	3.2	10.0	9.1	182.6	−8.2
U. S. savings bonds.............	0.2	5.2	5.2	1,986.3	0.3
Investment in cooperatives......	0.8	3.8	4.1	390.8	6.8
Total[6]	53.0	[3]202.3	203.6	283.5	0.6
Claims					
Liabilities:					
Real estate debt..............	6.6	11.3	12.3	86.6	9.2
Non-real-estate debt to:					
Commodity Credit Corporation[7]	0.4	2.5	1.4	211.7	−44.3
Other reporting institutions[8]..	1.5	5.8	6.7	342.9	15.5
Nonreporting creditors[9]	1.5	3.7	3.9	160.0	5.4
Total liabilities[6]	10.0	23.3	24.3	141.5	4.4
Proprietors' equities	43.0	[3]179.0	179.3	316.6	0.2
Total[6]	53.0	[3]202.3	203.6	283.5	0.6

[1] Data for 48 states only.

[2] Computed from unrounded data.

[3] Revised.

[4] Includes all crops held on farms for whatever purpose and crops held off farms as security for Commodity Credit Corporation loans. On Jan. 1, 1960, the latter totaled $499 million.

[5] Estimated valuation for 1940, plus purchases minus depreciation since then.

[6] Total of rounded data.

[7] Although these are nonrecourse loans, they are included as liabilities because borrowers must either repay in cash or deliver the commodities on which the loans were based. The values of the underlying commodities are included among the assets; hence the loans must be included as liabilities to avoid overstating proprietors' equities.

[8] Loans of all operating banks, the production credit associations, and the Farmers Home Administration, and discounts of the Federal intermediate credit banks for agricultural credit corporations and livestock loan companies.

[9] Loans and credits extended by dealers, merchants, finance companies, individuals, and others. Estimates based on fragmentary data.

From *Federal Reserve Bulletin*, August, 1960.

machinery and motor vehicles, $18.4 billion; the next largest was live-stock, $16.2 billion. Crops stored were reckoned at $8 billion. This item corresponds to the inventory item in a corporate balance sheet; whether all the stored crops could be sold at the valuation assigned to them may be questionable.

The chief wealth of farmers obviously consists of their land, and American farmers have traditionally thought of their economic condition principally in terms of the value of land and of the rise or fall in this value.

GEOGRAPHICAL FARMING REGIONS

Although few farms are devoted to only one crop, specialization has gone far enough so that it is possible to pick out the dominant type of farming by regions. Climate and soil have much to do with the crops mainly raised in each region. Access to large, nearby markets also plays a role, especially in the case of quickly perishable products such as fluid milk. The present pattern was established only after many years of change; further changes may occur.

Beginning at the northeast part of the map (Fig. 19/1), we find a hay and dairy region covering most of New England; New York State; parts of New Jersey, Pennsylvania, and Ohio; Michigan; Wisconsin; and most of Minnesota. Because of hilly terrain or rocky soil in much of this country, open-field cultivation cannot compete with cultivation on broad plains or prairies in raising of marketable crops; as a rule, however, there is ample rainfall and plenty of good pasture. Nearby industrial regions furnish a large market for milk, butter, cream, and cheese.

Many other types of agriculture, though of smaller economic bulk, flourish in this region—potatoes in northeastern Maine and Long Island, tobacco for cigar wrappers in the lower Connecticut River valley, poultry in many locations, fruit orchards and vineyards in virtually every state but particularly near large bodies of water, and vegetable (truck) farms wherever the soil is favorable and nearby markets exist.

Just south of the western half of the hay and dairy region lies the corn belt, extending through western Ohio; most of Indiana, Illinois, Iowa; the northern half of Missouri; eastern Kansas; the southeastern corner of South Dakota; and the southwestern corner of Minnesota. Here rich and deep prairie soil, ample rainfall, and hot summers favor the growth of corn, used largely as feed for hogs. This region is the source of much of the nation's ham, pork, bacon, and lard; and its use for this purpose gave rise to great packing centers such as Cincinnati, Chicago, Kansas City, and St. Louis. Here also beef cattle—many from western ranges—are fed for market. The corn-belt farmers are among the most prosperous in the nation and have done particularly well in recent years.

Just below the corn belt lies the corn and winter-wheat belt, where corn growing is combined with wheat growing. The wheat raised here is

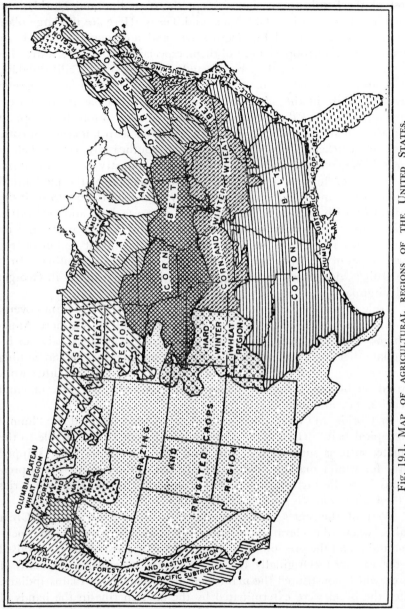

Fig. 19.1. Map of agricultural regions of the United States.

(Source: *Atlas of the Historical Geography of the United States*; reprinted by permission of the American Geographical Society and the Carnegie Institution of Washington.)

called "winter wheat" because it is sowed in the fall, lies dormant during the winter, and comes to life early in the spring; it is the first wheat crop to come to market. This belt begins at the East in southern New Jersey and southeastern Pennsylvania, extends down through Maryland and western Virginia, following the Shenandoah Valley, across western North Carolina, to Kentucky and Tennessee, southern Indiana, Illinois, Missouri, and eastern Arkansas. Here hogs and cattle are also raised.

South of the corn and winter-wheat belt lies the cotton belt, covering most of the Southeastern states except the coast line and Florida, and extending westward into Oklahoma and Texas. Here are the large plantations formerly worked by Negro slaves and now operated mainly by tenants and sharecroppers, most of them, especially in the eastern stretches of the region, with small acreages and worn-out soils. California has taken up mechanized cotton growing and now produces a large share of the crop, while in the Southeast, broiler production has in some areas supplanted much of the cotton. The cash return of cotton sharecroppers is small at best, and they eke out their existence with home-grown corn, pigs, and chickens. The character of the Southeastern cotton belt is slowly being changed by the growth of factory industry in a region formerly almost exclusively agricultural, the introduction of the mechanical cotton picker and other cotton machinery, and the attempt to diversify agriculture with grassland farming, which supports dairy and beef cattle. Other important cash crops of the region are broilers, peanuts, and tobacco grown mainly on small acreages in the Piedmont region on the lower slopes of the Appalachians in Virginia and North Carolina. Much tree fruit is also grown in the higher elevations—particularly in Georgia and Virginia.

Aside from the Southeastern cotton growers, most of the farm poverty is found among the descendants of white settlers in the southern Appalachians, who, with small farms on rocky, eroding hillsides, raise an inadequate diet for themselves and little of commercial value. Something has been done to improve their condition by educational and other work carried on by the Tennessee Valley Authority and other governmental agencies, state and federal.

In Florida and along the Gulf Coast lies what is called the "humid subtropical belt." Here is raised a large variety of crops suitable to the climate, such as sugar cane, citrus fruit, rice, vegetables to be shipped north for winter markets, and cattle adapted to the region. Many prosperous farms lie in this area; its only competitor within the boundaries of the United States is southern California.

West of the states bordering the Mississippi River lie the Great Plains, where the elevation of the land gradually rises to the Rocky Mountains and the precipitation is inadequate for most of the crops raised to the eastward. Originally the native grasses sustained great herds of bison, which constituted the main food of the dangerous Plains Indians. After the bison were exterminated by the modern rifle in the hands of both white hunters and Indians, the Plains became excellent and virtually costless grazing ranges for beef cattle. The land could not be farmed because there was neither wood nor stone to fence off fields from the widely ranging animals. In the 1870's, however, the invention and rapid manufacture of barbed-wire fencing enabled grain farmers to grow wheat in varieties adapted to the semiarid climate. In Arkansas, northern Oklahoma, the Texas Panhandle, and eastern parts of New Mexico and Colorado is grown winter wheat of a different variety from that planted to the eastward; it is known as "hard" winter wheat. In North and South

Dakota, Montana, and westward along the Canadian border is the great spring wheat region, where seed is sown in the spring as soon as the soil is in condition to be planted.

In the more arid western parts of the Great Plains, recurrent periods of drought destroy the crops, and dust storms blow away the topsoil on cultivated fields. Occasionally drought produces similar results even farther east. But periods of food shortage and high wheat prices—as in wars—lead farmers to try again, even though some soil conservationists warn that open cultivation may eventually turn the land into desert, and advise that grass should be restored.

In the Great Basin between the Coastal ranges and the Rockies, average precipitation is so light that grazing is the only profitable form of farming except where irrigation is practiced. Great deserts lie in the drier parts of this region. Cattle and sheep raising are the leading forms of agriculture. The arid region covers western Texas, most of New Mexico, Arizona, Utah western Colorado, Nevada, Wyoming, southwestern Calfifornia, southern Idaho, and eastern Washington. Heavy snowfall on the peaks of the mountains, however, and the few great rivers that traverse the region, make irrigation possible in many places. The development and apportionment of water supply, for irrigation, for hydroelectric power, and in some cases for city water supplies is a major concern of the inhabitants.

The Pacific Coast west of the Coastal ranges, a relatively narrow strip extending from the Canadian border to the Mexican, is roughly divided into two agricultural regions. In western Oregon, Washington, and northern California the rainfall is heavier than in most other parts of the United States and has nourished forests of great trees. On farmland, hay and pasture prevail. The central and southern California Coast has a subtropical climate similar in many respects to that of Florida, except that differences of elevation from the ocean to the mountain slopes present a greater variety of weather. Here are grown citrus and other fruits and numerous specialty crops.

FARM LABOR FORCE AND TECHNOLOGY

Farming was the occupation of an overwhelming majority of the workers in the United States when the nation was founded; even by 1820 it was the calling of more than 70 percent of those gainfully occupied. As cities grew and manufacturing and transportation flourished, the percentage engaged in agriculture gradually declined; it became just less than half in 1870 and 37.5 percent in 1900. After 1910 not only the percentage but also the absolute number of farmers and their employees began to decline. In the 1950's those engaged in agriculture constituted about one tenth of the labor force in the United States.

This decline is attributable partly to the fact that as the country became settled, there remained less good virgin soil to be occupied. With the prevailing system of family farms, young people whose work was not needed at home found jobs in other occupations. The rapid growth of urban pursuits offered them the possibility to do so.

During all this time the farmers of the nation grew all the agricultural products consumed by a rapidly expanding population, excepting only those unsuited to the highly varied climates of the country, such as coffee, tea, rubber, and tropical fruits. From the 1840's on, they also produced a surplus for export to industrializing Britain and western Europe. How could American farmers, a diminishing proportion of the population and eventually an actually diminishing number, on an acreage that was limited, supply the food and fibers to satisfy such an increasing demand?

The answer is that they did so because of a gradual and accelerating improvement in agricultural technology, which enabled them to produce more per person at work in the fields, pastures, and ranges, and recently to produce more per acre also.

Improved agricultural machinery is an important means of increased output per man-hour. The reaper, invented before the middle of the nineteenth century, was of use chiefly in harvesting broad acres of grain or hay. Improved plows, harrows, and cultivators were followed by machine planters and eventually by harvesters or pickers for crops other than grain, such as corn, potatoes, or cotton. The reaper itself was developed into the combine, which not only cut the grain but also threshed the wheat as it went along.

A great boost was given to mechanization of the smaller farms when gasoline-powered engines made possible the substitution of trucks and tractors for horses and mules as draft animals. This improvement saved farmers the time required for growing feed—except for animals raised for production of food—steers, pigs, cows, and chickens. It also released 75 million acres for marketable field crops. The trucks and tractors could do the work faster and better than equipment drawn by animals. By 1944 each tractor saved 850 man-hours per year; each truck or automobile 400 man-hours. Finally, the general use of motored vehicles stimulated the development of many new types of machinery to be used with them.

The general availability of electric power to farmers—which has occurred since the middle 1930's—has added not only conveniences but also the possibility of using more mechanical equipment around farm buildings and homes.

Equally important have been the achievements of scientific research, mainly carried on by governmental and educational agencies, in introducing better agricultural methods, such as the use of lime and fertilizers, soil conservation practices, improved varieties of seed adapted to special climate and soil conditions, improved control of plant or animal diseases and destructive insects, better feeds, and better breeds of farm livestock. One of the most recent and spectacular triumphs was the introduction of hybrid corn of numerous varieties, which during World War II enabled a reduced farm labor force to raise much more corn on a given acreage, because the new varieties were more highly productive and more disease-resistant.

The net results of such advances may be illustrated by a few rough figures. An index of output per farm worker (including farm operators, hired hands, and unpaid family workers) is based on the average of the years 1935–1939, which is taken as 100. By 1945 the index had risen to 145, an increase of 45 percent or nearly half in less than 10 years. The index number for 1910 was 71; thus there occurred an increase of about 55 percent in the quarter century preceding the base period. The rise in output per man-hour shows little sign of halting.

Meanwhile the output per acre of crops harvested increased also. In 1945 acres harvested had increased only 10 percent over 1910, but output of crops had grown 68 percent. It must be remembered that 1945 was the last year of World War II, when the intense demand for crops pressed into service every available man and acre.

ORGANIZATION OF FARMERS AND THEIR MARKETS

Between the farmer and the city consumer of his products is a highly varied and complex system of distribution, depending on the nature of the particular crop and the institutions which have grown up over many years for handling it. In almost all cases except that of the roadside stand along well-traveled automobile highways, the individual grower in selling his crop, and in buying his equipment or materials, has to deal with business organizations which are larger and have more financial resources than he. In some instances these dealers, manufacturers, shippers or transportation companies, are not highly competitive with one another.

For many decades this situation has led farmers to form associations which attempt to improve the economic status of their members. National associations like the Grange stimulated cooperatives both for selling and for buying. More recently the Farmers' Union and the Farm Bureau Federation have, among other endeavors, acted as pressure groups to support legislation favorable to farmers or to oppose legislation which seemed inimical to their interests. The economic effect of government on agriculture will be more fully discussed in Chapter 25, since theoretical considerations are essential to understanding it. Here, however, we may briefly consider the effort of some farmers to parallel the collective bargaining of organized labor by the use of marketing cooperatives to sell their products. Such cooperatives have received governmental sanction and, on occasion, governmental support, but they represent basically the effort of farmers themselves to seek a greater bargaining power in the markets where their products are sold than could any individual grower.

In spite of many attempts, some on a large scale and with wide support, marketing cooperatives have never succeeded in establishing themselves permanently in selling the great staple crops like wheat, cotton, livestock, corn, and tobacco. A few, however, have endured in specialties like California citrus fruit, and cooperatives handling dairy products are widely successful. Most farmers no longer cherish the hope that they can, without governmental assistance, maintain higher prices for their crops than those determined by demand and supply in the market.

Although growers of the staples are more widely scattered and see less of one another than the workers in a factory, it has been possible at times to enlist the membership of substantial majorities in marketing associations. Crops, however, unlike labor, are commodities. If a group of workers remain away from the factory, the labor hours they deny to the employer are gone forever; labor cannot be stored. Farmers, on the contrary, do not shut down production unless they intend to cease being farmers. Although on rare occasions growers of nonperishable crops have attempted voluntarily to limit their output or even to destroy crops, co-operative associations, without governmental police power, have not, with rare exceptions, succeeded in inducing all of them to do so for long. Someone can always make money producing more at any advance in price that the cooperative may obtain, and loyal members are the losers.

If those who buy a crop will not pay the price asked by the coopera-tive, the price cannot be enforced by limitation of the supply in exist-ence. The cooperative is forced to store any surplus in order to limit the supply offered for sale. Meanwhile, high or rising prices encourage the farmers to grow more. The result is that marketing cooperatives dealing in staples soon find themselves in this dilemma—either they must lose control of the supply so that the cooperative disintegrates, or they have to carry large and increasing stocks at a cost which their members cannot or will not pay. The unsold supply, overhanging the market, tends to depress prices, and when, as is almost inevitable, it must eventually be sold, prices may suffer a sharp break.

Aside from influencing legislation, the successful producer organiza-tions of farmers have achieved their gains (1) in establishing quality grad-ing, so that the grower of a superior size or quality may obtain the higher price to which market demand should entitle him; (2) in encouraging the growing of better qualities; (3) in establishing brand or trade names to apply to the product of the members (for example, Sunkist Oranges, Land-o-Lakes Creameries); (4) in advertising and publicity to increase public demand for the product. Such measures are more easily applicable to perishable products, and to those generally raised in a limited region, than to staples which may be indefinitely stored or to those which undergo extensive processing before reaching the ultimate consumer—for example, wheat, cotton, beef cattle, and pork.

In contrast with producing and marketing associations of farmers, their cooperative buying associations have been strikingly successful in many regions. They sell seeds, fertilizers, feeds, gasoline and other sup-plies, and insurance. They have played a large role in improving qual-ities, in testing, in choosing the best varieties for the needs of soil and climate, and in reducing costs. Many of them have reached back into production of commodities suitable for the needs of their members. The national association of these cooperatives is influential in affecting legislation. Cooperative credit associations are largely instrumental in distributing loans from funds provided by governmental agencies, and rural cooperatives distributing electricity generated by public power systems have played an important role in bringing electrical service to farmers.

See Chapter 28 for a case study of growth and technological change in an agricultural industry.

QUESTIONS

1. If the recent rapid technological advance and increase of output per worker in agriculture should come to an end, while the population of the United States grows by leaps and bounds, what would probably be the effect on the following?

  (a) Prices of food and fibers
  (b) Numbers of persons engaged in farming
  (c) The value of farm land
  (d) Exports and imports of farm products
  (e) Wages and material costs in industry
  (f) Competitive position of American manufacturers selling in foreign markets or competing in domestic markets with foreign manufacturers

2. If the output per acre of farm land in the United States should not increase while the encroachment of metropolitan regions, highways, and industrial development on good farm land continues, shall we, as Britain did in the nineteenth century,

  (a) Become dependent on imports of a large part of our food?
  (b) Find it more advantageous than at present to abolish or reduce protective tariffs and to encourage the development of a free world market unimpeded by trade restrictions?

20 / THEORIES OF AGRICULTURAL

BEHAVIOR / Since there are many competing pro-

ducers of agricultural goods, and no one of them can appreciably affect the market price either by restricting or by expanding output, farmers are usually regarded as examples of nearly perfect competition in selling. Under competition, each producer, regarding the market price as something which is incapable of being affected by anything he may do, will strive to produce as much as possible so that he will have more to sell at any given price. Supply will be limited by competitive producers only when the price does not cover the variable costs of production or when suppliers are forced out of business.

EFFECT OF FALLING PRICES ON SUPPLY OF CROPS

In one respect the typical American farmer is in a different situation even from the typical small competitive business in manufacturing or commerce. The family farm is not only a business; it is also a home. The farmer has either few employees or, more often, none. The work is done by him with the help of the family, who usually work without pay.

When the competitive manufacturer or merchant cannot sell all he can make or handle at a price which at least covers his variable costs, he will be impelled to cut production or his purchases of merchandise to the amount he *can* sell at that price. This involves part-time operation or actual layoff of employees and perhaps wage cuts as well. At most, the firm will lose the amount necessary to cover its fixed costs. If this loss continues for long, the owner must go out of the business in which he is engaged, and try to make his living in some other way.

The typical family farmer, on the other hand, cannot cut money costs by going on part time and laying off members of his family, since he has no cash expenses for labor in any event. In the short run, he is likely to respond to falling prices by producing as much as ever, and perhaps more, in order to earn the cash needed for current living expenses.

It takes a long time for low prices of agricultural products to reduce the supply by forcing farmers out of business. If the farmer owns his land and buildings and has no mortgage on them, and if he owns his equipment free and clear, those fixed charges payable in money will be relatively small. He will have to pay taxes, but little else in the way of overhead. He is, of course, much more reluctant to give up his home and his land than a city businessman is to close out his business and try another. The farmer can temporarily forego expenses desirable for upkeep and replacement of his machinery and buildings and hold on for a considerable period, hoping for better times.

Under accurate economic accounting the farm family producing at unusually low prices might be operating at a loss. This loss, however, might not appear on the farmer's books but rather in reduced levels of living, perhaps resulting eventually in undernourishment and loss of capacity to produce. It might also take effect in deterioration of the farmer's physical capital, such as buildings and equipment, or in the productivity of his land. But since the loss is not mainly an out-of-pocket expense, it does not force the farmer immediately to curb output, and consequently the reduction in supply of what he produces will not be marked until the loss has been suffered for many months.

EFFECT OF RISING PRICES ON SUPPLY OF CROPS

When demand for nearly all crops rises, as in a period of war, the farmers are likely to be producing all they can with existing methods and equipment before the price rise begins; they cannot readily increase their output, as can a manufacturer, by working the plant longer hours, hiring more labor, and buying more materials.

In the long run farmers can increase output if they have suitable land to be brought under cultivation or if they use more fertilizer, more modern machinery, and other technological methods to augment the output per acre. But at best such additions to output occur more slowly than those which can be made by an industry operating at less than existing capacity—as industry usually does.

RESPONSE OF PRICE TO CHANGES IN AGRICULTURAL DEMAND

Agricultural output, and consequently the supply of farm products, does not respond easily to changes in demand, whether upward or downward. When, as in a depression, the effective demand for crops at existing prices falls because of unemployment and reduced incomes of the urban population, what results typically is that the supply of farm products is not much diminished, and the reduction of demand is felt in prices low enough so that the crops can be sold. This is what occurred during the deep depression of the 1930's. When effective demand increases, as in periods of nearly full employment or in war, which results in increases in the purchases of food and fiber by warring nations, the effect on agricultural products is felt mainly in rising prices but not in increased output, at least for a year or two. During World War I total agricultural output in the United States, in spite of food shortages and high prices, did not increase until after the end of hostilities. During World War II it did increase through the adoption of new methods and more machinery, but not enough to check the rise in prices due to enlarged demand.

Statistical analysis of the behavior of prices and production during the business cycle has led to the generalization that, in agriculture, the increases and decreases of aggregate demand which go with booms and depressions are felt in price changes of crops more than in changed volume of output, whereas in most factory and other mechanical industries the reverse is true; volume of output varies widely between good and bad times, while prices of the product change much less. By and large, the farmer's economic experience thus differs from that of the city worker. In the short run changes in the income of the farmer arise more from changes in the price of what he sells than from changes in his employment (he is almost never without a job), whereas the city worker's income typically gains or suffers more in the short run by changes in employment than by changes up or down in the wage rates paid for his labor.

EFFECT OF NATURAL FORCES ON SUPPLY OF CROPS

Weather affects the output of crops much more than short-term variations in their selling price. A drought will reduce output in the regions suffering from lack of rainfall, as will disastrous floods or untimely freezes in the regions affected. Good growing weather, on the contrary, will, within the year when it occurs, bring bumper crops to market. If not readily controlled, insect pests or diseases of plants and animals may quickly reduce output. New invasions of such pests frequently assume epidemic proportions. Changes in supply arising from such sources will quickly bring rise or fall of the prices of the crops affected.

EFFECT ON SUPPLY OF SHIFTS IN DEMAND

In the aggregate, changes in demand for farm products will be registered in changes of price much more than in output. This principle, however, does not hold when applied to shifts in demand for particular crops.

Over a long series of years, the diet of the average American consumer has shifted. He eats less bread and fewer potatoes, but more dairy products and fresh fruit and vegetables. Insofar as market forces have been allowed to take effect without governmental control, these shifts in demand have worked, through varying prices, to diminish the relative output of wheat and potatoes and to increase the relative output of dairy products and fresh fruits and vegetables. Changes in industrial demand for agricultural raw materials or in demand by farmers themselves for feed raised by other farmers have had much the same effect on relative supplies of crops. In recent years many farmers have shifted some of their resources to the output of soybeans, because of the rapidly increasing demand for this product in animal feed and industrial products, or to production of broilers in the years when beef was relatively scarce and high.

In many areas where general farming is practiced, individual growers can make such shifts rather quickly by devoting more of their land and other resources to one crop rather than to another. In other cases the conditions of climate or soil are such that an individual farmer would have difficulty in altering the type of product yielded from his land. It would seem impossible, for example, for a wheat grower in the semiarid Great Plains to use his land for dairy products or fresh vegetables. In the Southeast, the system of sharecropping and tenancy tends to perpetuate cotton growing, although in many cases better uses of the soil and agricultural labor supply may be found in other types of output.

The excess of supply over demand, which sometimes occurs in such crops as wheat and cotton, would force the prices of these commodities down to a point where the marginal farmers would be compelled to try some other type of farming or to abandon agriculture altogether, if competition and market forces prevailed.

ECONOMIC CYCLES IN SPECIFIC CROPS

Well-defined cycles of successive increases and decreases in production of certain agricultural commodities have been observed by agricultural economists. One is the corn-hog cycle. The chief use of corn, though not the only one, is the feeding of hogs. When corn is abundant and is cheap relative to the price of pork products, there is ample profit in hog raising. This stimulates hog production. Rising production of hogs soon increases the demand for corn and consequently raises its price. At the same time it depresses the price of hogs. The reduced margin between the price of hogs and the price of corn before long leads to the farrowing of fewer pigs. This again reduces the price of corn and raises the price of hogs, and so starts the upward phase of hog production again.

Many hog raisers grow their own corn and consequently do not have to pay market prices for their feed. If this practice were universal and if there were no demand for corn other than for hog feeding, the corn-hog cycle might disappear. But as things are, when the price of hogs is relatively low and the price of corn relatively high, the grower of both is induced to sell more corn and raise fewer hogs, and vice versa. The length of one complete corn-hog cycle averages about three years, though variations are introduced by other circumstances, such as war demand or weather conditions.

A longer cycle is observed in the raising of beef cattle. When prices of beef are high, cattlemen are likely to raise more calves and feeders to "finish" more young steers. Increasing the number of marketable cattle, however, is a relatively slow process, and so the stimulus to enlarge the supply continues beyond the point where it will be sufficient, several years hence, to meet the demand without reduction of prices. Eventually the number of steers ready for sale becomes so large as to depress the price of beef, and the cattle herds begin to decrease again (or to grow more slowly).

ELASTICITY OF DEMAND FOR AGRICULTURAL PRODUCTS

What about the influence of crop prices on demand? Does demand for agricultural products rise sharply when prices fall, or diminish rapidly when prices rise?

A large part of agricultural output consists of food. Food is, of course, a basic necessity and will be bought even by consumers who can buy little else. Moreover, most food products will be consumed daily, soon after they reach the markets. However, the capacity of the body to ingest food is limited, and a population of a given size will not eat much more than a given number of pounds or calories at the maximum.

The result is that the demand for food products as a whole does not vary much in response to price changes. Relatively high prices will not much decrease the demand for food as long as consumers can buy anything, and relatively low prices will not much increase it beyond the point where consumers can satisfy their hunger. By and large, the domestic demand for food in the United States grows only with the growth of population. Demand for a particular food product, however, like fluid milk or butter, may be elastic.

Most agricultural products that are not used for food consist of fibers, needed for the manufacture of textiles. The largest market for textiles is in the manufacture of clothing, though they have many other uses. Clothing is a necessity second only to food, and a minimum is likely to be bought by a given population, no matter what the price. Yet the purchase of textiles can be affected by changes in price more than the purchase of food. Clothing is not, by and large, so perishable as food and can more easily be stored by the individual consumer. When prices are high in relation to incomes, old clothes can be made to serve a while longer. When prices are low, there is an incentive to enlarge wardrobes. Style changes, however, stimulate the purchase of clothing whether prices are low or high. The aggregate demand for clothing, year in and year out, is little affected by price changes.

Over the long run, more clothing, and hence more fiber raised on farms, may be bought as incomes rise; an upper limit is not fixed by the size of the population, as in the case of food. Nevertheless, budget studies indicate that expenditures for clothing do not rise proportionally with the growth of income.

The demand for specific textile products often does, however, vary with their relative prices. And the production of fibers, unlike the production of food, is affected in the long run by the introduction of numerous products of the chemical industry, such as rayon, nylon, and other synthetics.

PRICES RECEIVED BY FARMERS AND PRICES PAID BY CONSUMERS

Only a tiny part of agricultural products is sold by farmers direct to consumers, as in roadside markets or by mail. Staple crops like grains must be stored in elevators, transported to millers, processed, sold to distributors, transported again to centers of population, and eventually sold, usually in prepared and packaged form, by retail stores to ultimate consumers. Beef cattle, sheep, and hogs pass through stockyards to packers, who process them and sell the products through various channels for retail distribution. Cotton is ginned, warehoused, and sold to textile mills, which spin and weave the fabrics, apply finishing or dyeing processes, and sell them in turn to garment manufacturers, who prepare them for consumption and market the products for ultimate sale in retail stores. With each type of crop the course of processing and distributing differs, but in almost all cases the flow from grower to ultimate consumer is long and intricate.

The result is that the price paid by the ultimate consumer is often many times as great as the price received by the farmer for the raw material. At each stage of the flow there are necessary productive labor costs and capital costs. To these are added costs of selling, which are often swollen by costs of advertising packaged and branded products. Each stage in the chain of distribution also, of course, takes its toll of profit whenever it can do so. It is a mistake to believe, however, that the farmer would receive much more, or the consumer pay much less, if all processing and distributing profits were eliminated. It should be remembered, too, that much of what business accounting calls profit or net income is not true economic profit but rather payment for services of managing owners and for use of the owners' capital.

Since the great bulk of what is added to the prices of raw products by processing, transportation, and distribution consists of payments for labor and the capital equipment used in the various operations, much more is to be gained in any attempt to cut distribution costs by improvement of distributive efficiency than by any other method. That such improvement can in some instances be achieved has been demonstrated by chain stores and supermarkets, which have made money while reducing retail prices. In certain instances the incentive for profit by monopolistic competition or oligopoly has appeared to raise costs through decreased efficiency, as in the high cost of advertising branded-food products or in the frequent insistence of those who control milk distribution that as much shall be charged per quart by retail stores as for milk delivered by wagon to the consumer's door, although the latter method is more expensive.

In the past, farmers have often objected to monopolistic buying (monopsony) by large business concerns which purchase their products, and from time to time have supported and obtained legislation designed to force the buyers to compete. The Stockyards Act, the Interstate Commerce Act, the Sherman Antitrust Act, and much other legislation directed at monopoly in either selling or buying arose largely from the discontent of farmers who believed that, as competitors, they were being unfairly treated by large corporate interests.

The extent to which such legislation has achieved its avowed purpose is much debated. In the nature of things, however, the big processor or distributor is in a much better position to safeguard his economic position than the small farmer, since the middleman is almost always in a position to sell at margins which will at least cover his costs, while the farmer bears the chief brunt of fluctuations in the prices and yields of the raw product. The processor or distributor usually passes on to the consumer any increase in the price of his raw material.

One often-noticed effect of the long process of distribution is that a marked change in prices received by farmers is usually accompanied by only minor changes in prices paid by consumers. The retail prices of food never change so rapidly or so much as the wholesale prices of food staples, and prices received by farmers fluctuate more quickly and violently than wholesale prices. This difference results partly from the fact that only part of what the consumer pays covers the cost of the raw material. The rest goes for labor and capital costs, which, as a rule, do not fluctuate so much or so rapidly. For example, if the consumer pays 15 cents for a loaf of bread, only 2 cents of which, let us suppose, represents the cost of the wheat of which it is composed, a fall of 50 percent in the price of wheat per bushel, which would represent a disastrous blow to the wheat farmer, could be passed on to the consumer by a reduction of only 1 cent a loaf of bread, or one fifteenth (6.7 percent) of what he pays. The same principle works also when prices are rising. Prices of fresh meat and vegetables, which are not so fully processed, however, often do respond rather quickly to changes in prices at the farm.

PRODUCTIVITY, PRICES, AND FARM INCOMES

Since the disappearance of the frontier, the total supply of agricultural products could not be much increased by bringing additional acres into production. Between 1900 and 1910 the acreage in all farms in the United States increased by only 5 percent. In the same years there was an increase of less than 4 percent of persons working on farms, or about 400,000. During these same years the nonrural population of the United States, which had to be fed and clothed by what the farmers raised, grew by 40 percent, or about 12 million persons. Since before 1910 such technological improvements as gasoline tractors and machinery for small and medium-sized farms had not come into use, neither output per farm worker nor output per acre was much increased. The result was a marked rise in prices of food and other crops. The prices received by farmers rose more rapidly than the prices they had to pay for what they bought. There was enough farm output for the rapidly growing population mainly because the rising prices discouraged foreign buying of American farm products; exports were drastically cut. The income of farmers rose markedly.

Between 1910 and 1920 a growing population again increased the demand for food, and to this domestic demand was added the purchases by foreign nations during World War I, which were abnormally large because of war shortages. Meanwhile, total output of American farm products was scarcely increased, in spite of the utmost efforts of the farmers. Bad weather had something to do with this situation. The result was that prices of farm products soared to unprecedented heights. There were scarcities of many foods, and rationing had to be introduced. Farmers' incomes were correspondingly increased. The gain in prosperity of the farmers between 1900 and 1920 is indicated by the fact that the average value of farm land per acre increased from $19.81 in 1900 to $69.38 in 1920, and the total value of farm land, buildings, machinery, equipment, crops held for sale, livestock, and poultry grew from $20 billion to $80 billion. Prices of manufactured products had risen too, but not nearly so much as the items mentioned. The number of farmers actually decreased after 1910, and so the increased wealth was shared by fewer persons. There had been no governmental intervention with free markets for farm products, except for a short period during the war.

Beginning in 1920, crop prices fell rapidly; many were more than halved within a few months. This reduction stemmed from a drop in the demand from former European belligerents and also from the domestic urban consumers, who began to suffer from depression and unemployment. The industrial depression was sharp but short-lived. A spirited revival occurred in 1923, and business prosperity continued, with minor interruption, until 1929. Farmers, however, received a heavy blow. Many had incurred their mortgage and other debts during the war boom and could not now repay. Crop prices fell much more than other prices and did not recover so rapidly or so far. For example, in 1922 the farmers could buy only three fourths as many shoes, suits of clothing, or other necessities with the proceeds of 100 bushels of wheat as they could in the years before 1914, when the war started. Though prices of crops slowly recovered, never during the decade did they attain the same percentage above the prewar level as did the prices of goods the farmers bought.

Many farmers lost their farms through mortgage foreclosures. The

number of farms declined between 1920 and 1930 by nearly 250,000, the
number of owning farmers by 400,000. The number of persons engaged in
farming decreased 239,000. Nevertheless, the total crop output increased.
The index of output per worker on farms rose from 88 in 1920 to 96 in
1930 (the base, or 100 percent, of this index being the average output
per worker in the years 1935–1939).

This increase in output per worker resulted from the rapid introduction of gasoline-powered tractors and farm machinery, more use of
lime and fertilizer, and other advances in agricultural technology. It had
two major economic results: (1) to restrict rise of prices of crops by
increasing their supply and (2) to increase average farm income by
enlarging the quantity produced and sold per man-hour. The total net
income to persons on farms, which had been $3,795 million in 1921,
averaged $6,600 million in the latter years of the 1920's, and this larger
total income was distributed to fewer people. Meanwhile, the surplus
farm population drifted to the cities, where most found jobs. It is clear
that farmers as well as urban consumers were benefited from higher
productivity. The price at which they sold their crops was not the only
factor affecting their economic welfare; at least as important was sale of
the increased output per farm worker.

GOVERNMENTAL PRICE SUPPORTS IN DEPRESSION

In the depression beginning with the stock-market crash of 1929, the
farmers suffered misfortune even worse than that in the early 1920's.
The effective demand of the domestic population was greatly reduced by
unemployment, which at its peak reached about 25 percent of the labor
force. Foreign purchasers of American crops also had fewer dollars with
which to buy them. Farm output was but little reduced, and the result
was a drastic fall in crop prices, which again dropped much more than
the prices of industrial products, interest, taxes, and other charges which
the farmers had to pay. Farm mortgages were being foreclosed; farms
were subject to forced sale for nonpayment of taxes.

It was during this period that the federal government first intervened with attempts to sustain the prices of farm products. The aim was
to bring them as nearly as possible to the same relationship to the prices
of industrial products as in the years immediately preceding 1914, when
World War I broke out. This historical relationship was called "parity."
If a given amount of farm products would now buy the same amount of
the things farmers consumed as before 1914, the parity index would be
100. If the same amount of crops would buy only three quarters as
much of what the farmers had to purchase as in the base period, the
parity index would be 75. The 1932 parity index was in fact only 55.

The effort to bring the parity index up was pursued by a number of
intricate devices, most of which consisted of efforts to restrict the output
or sale of farm products—that is, to raise the price by limiting the supply.

Most of these devices were based on restricting the acreage devoted to the growth of various marketable crops. For several years the supply was in fact restricted; it fell about 6 percent between 1932 and 1936, but these were years of drought, which would have reduced output in any case. Output per worker was lower in 1936 than in 1932. Farmers whose acreage in crops was restricted strove, however, to produce as much as possible by using the best of their land, applying more fertilizer, and making use of other technological improvements. Though 33 million fewer acres of fifty-two marketable crops were harvested in 1939 than in 1932, the index of aggregate farm output (in physical terms) rose from 96 to 106. Prices of crops increased, not so much because of restriction of the supply as because industrial recovery had augmented incomes of urban consumers.

In the meantime, chief reliance for maintaining crop prices had come to depend on limiting the amount offered for sale to a total which, it was estimated, would not be so large as to depress the price below that which it was desired to maintain, called the "support price." This result was accomplished mainly through a governmentally owned Commodity Credit Corporation. In the case of crops capable of being held for long periods in storage, like wheat and cotton, farmers could borrow from the CCC, at the support price for each bushel or bale they produced, enough money to cover their output. If the market price should turn out to be higher than the support price, the farmers could sell their crops and repay the loan. If, however, the market price fell below the support price, the CCC would take over the crops, which constituted collateral for the loans, and hold them in storage. The farmers were then not required to repay the loans; in effect, they had sold their crops at the price representing the percentage of parity which, under the provisions of the law, the government had decided to maintain. "Surpluses" of perishable crops necessary to hold off the market in order to maintain prices were simply bought by the government at the support price and either used for unemployment relief, disposed of abroad, or destroyed.

One result was that in the years before World War II, the CCC built up large holdings of nonperishable crops, which it could not sell without causing a break in prices. The chief economic effects were as follows:

1. The consumers paid higher prices for farm products than if a free market had existed. (Of course, most farmers themselves were consumers of products of other farmers, either food, fibers, or feed for their livestock.)

2. The consumers, through taxes, paid the expenses of the CCC in buying crops that they were not allowed to consume as individuals. In effect, this was a governmental subsidy to the growers.

3. The government stimulated more production of the price-supported crops than could be sold at the prices maintained, thus wasting resources and labor. The same resources and labor might have been diverted to production of other things which consumers would have bought, if crop prices had been allowed to seek the market level. Thus the market was not allowed to play its full role in allocation of resources.

Spokesmen for agriculture justified these measures by the argument that, if market forces remained unchecked, the farmers suffered an unfair disadvantage in comparison with industry, where ability to restrict output, monopolistic practices, the protective tariff, minimum wages, collective bargaining, unemployment insurance, and other measures private or public dulled the keen edge of competition.

PRICE REGULATION IN WAR

When, in 1940, the abnormal demands of World War II began to take effect, the shoe was on the other foot. The parity index soon rose above 100—that is, farmers now could buy more industrial products with each bushel or pound of crops produced than they could before World War I. Price and wage control restricted increases in price of industrial products, while market forces were allowed to boost agricultural prices, now that demand exceeded supply. Emphasis was laid not on reducing farm output but on increasing it. The surpluses held by the CCC were sold at higher prices than they cost. Not until 1949 did the price of any staple crop fall below parity.

Commercial farmers, selling large quantities of output at high prices, became more prosperous than ever before. Per capita net income in agriculture more than doubled from 1940 to 1949—in terms of 1935–1939 dollars. With the proceeds, farmers not only improved their farms and bought the latest equipment but also paid off mortgage and other debts, built up cash balances in the banks, and bought government bonds and other investments. Mindful of the previous postwar experience, few bought land with borrowed money.

Government guarantees of farm prices were set during the war by a "forward price" system to encourage growth of the most needed crops. These support prices were, of course, above parity. It was in no case necessary to hold stored supplies off the market in order to maintain the forward price. Ceilings were placed on the prices of major food crops, but these ceilings, too, were far above parity, and rarely had to be applied.

POSTWAR DILEMMA

Though the parity index fell to 100 in 1949, the outbreak of war in Korea in June, 1950, raised it again. Commercial farmers were even more prosperous in 1951 than during World War II. A law passed during the War had sought to encourage increased output by guaranteeing the farmers 90 percent of parity for two years after the end of hostilities was formally declared. This guarantee was extended, before its expiration, for two more years. The parity index, however, did not fall to 100 between 1949 and 1952.

New legislation, passed in anticipation of the end of the guarantee of 90 percent of parity, sought to prevent the building up of unsalable surpluses by a more flexible policy. It reintroduced a prewar system of permitting the variation of support prices between 75 and 90 percent of parity. In addition, it redefined parity to account for changes in relative demand for the several crops, and based the calculation on the relationship between crop prices and other prices not in the long-past years before World War I but in a moving average of recent years.

When the new law was first applied, early in 1955, farm prices had already fallen so far below parity that huge surpluses had been held and stored by CCC. Farm output per man-hour was about 30 percent above 1949 and was still increasing more rapidly than the nonfarm population; the abnormal demand for exports of food had fallen off. The parity ratio sank to 84 in 1955. Real per capita income of persons on farms was well below the 1949 peak and continued to fall, though even in 1955 it remained farther above the 1940 level than nonfarm per capita income. The question whether to support farm prices in a period of general prosperity, and, if so, how to do it without ultimate damage to the economy, remained unanswered, either politically or economically.

See Chapter 28 for a case study and Chapter 33 for a suggested program.

PROBLEM

It has been proposed that the federal government cease buying perishable commodities to support their prices, but allow these commodities to sell at the prices determined in a free market. To safeguard the grower from unduly low income which might result, the government would, on such crops, pay to each grower a subsidy sufficient to bring his revenue from the sale of the crops up to what he would have received at parity prices.

1. Would the consumer pay less under this plan, including both prices and taxes?

2. Would the farmer receive less, the same, or more?

3. Would resources be better allocated than under the price-support system?

21 / FOREIGN TRADE AND

FINANCE / Division of labor, Adam Smith pointed out, leads to the most efficient economic performance; it benefits both producer and consumer. Specialization of production enables each businessman, farmer, or worker to be occupied with the task for which his talents and the resources available are best fitted. And, as Smith also emphasized, essential to such specialization is the existence of broad markets, so that there shall be the greatest possible demand for a variety of products. To put the matter in another way, the best allocation of resources to satisfy human wants is aided by unobstructed trade and good transportation over wide areas.

The framers of the United States Constitution were aware of this fact when they specifically reserved for the federal government jurisdiction over interstate commerce. Their motive was political as well as economic—to create a nation out of a loose confederation of sovereign states—but their foresight had the important economic outcome of preventing states from erecting barriers to trade on their borders. The states might never have done so in any case, but the constitution forestalled any possibility of such action. The "founding fathers," also recognizing the importance of exports from the new country, wrote into the Constitution a prohibition against any tax on exports by the federal government itself.

The tremendous and rapid economic growth of the United States has been attributed to many sources, but among them is almost always mentioned the fact that this country is perhaps the largest area in the world throughout which there are no political barriers to trade, transfers of money, or movement of people. This object lesson has in recent years been influential in leading great nations of western Europe to join in the endeavor to create a common market throughout their domains by gradual abandonment of trade barriers and monetary restrictions.

The same principles that hold in trade within a nation may be applied to international trade. In spite of such barriers as exist—and

254

there have been many—exports and imports of the United States have been important to this country and virtually indispensable to many others. The importance of the United States to the international economy is indicated by the fact that even by the 1920's this country was producing about one fourth of the output of the whole world and about 40 percent of the world's manufactured products. Our percentage of world trade was not so large as this—it was about 10 percent of the total. In the years 1956–1958 the exports of the whole world were running at the annual rate of $91,349 million; of this amount, the United States provided $12,375 million, or about 13.5 percent.

Yet the large variety of food products, raw materials, and manufactured products which other nations obtained from the United States was of vital importance to them. The United States would have been seriously inconvenienced, to say the least, without the coffee and other tropical food products which its people obtained from foreign sources, the metals relatively scarce in this country but essential to industry—such as nickel, tin and copper—and a large variety of manufactured products. Other countries are dependent, too, on our orders for manufactured goods, food products, and raw materials.

THE INTERNATIONAL ACCOUNT OF THE UNITED STATES

We learned in previous chapters that, for an understanding of the economic transactions of a business firm, a government, or a whole nation, it is helpful to look first at the accounts that summarize such affairs. The same is true of foreign trade and investment. Let us therefore begin with an examination of an account covering the international payments of the United States for a recent year. (For purposes of illustration, any year will do. Tables 21/1 and 21/2 show figures for 1954; Table 21/3 shows figures for a series of years.)

First of all, to understand the design of this sort of account we may look at a highly simplified summary of what is called the "United States Balance of Payments" (Table 21/1). This, like many other accounts, is drawn up similar to a balance sheet, in which the accuracy of the statement is tested by balancing one set of figures against another. The table shows the payments made by the United States to the rest of the world and the payments received by the United States from the rest of the world. It includes, of course, payments of individuals and business concerns as well as governmental transactions.

Item 1 shows that we exported more than we imported; that is, foreigners bought from us more goods and services than we bought from them. If exports had exactly equaled imports, the trade would have amounted to an even swap. In fact, the trade of the year resulted in a balance due the United States (on trade only) of $1,850 million.

During 1954, however, there were also large financial transactions

TABLE 21/1

UNITED STATES BALANCE OF PAYMENTS, 1954[1]
(in millions of dollars)

	Receipts by Americans	Payments by Americans	Differences
(1) Sales of goods and services.......	17,938	16,088	+1,850
(2) Unilateral transfers	----	2,262	−2,262
(3) Increase of American capital abroad	----	1,526	−1,526
(4) Increase of foreign capital in U.S.	1,462	----	+1,462
(5) Gold sales to U.S................	298	----	+ 298
(6) Totals	$19,698	$19,876	− 178
(7) Errors and ommissions...			+ 178

[1] Table adapted from "United States Balance of Payments," *Economic Report of the President,* January, 1957, p. 194. (Military transfers omitted.)

between the United States and the rest of the world, the net result of which was to supply foreigners with money or credit enough to buy the goods and services for which they could not pay out of the proceeds of their sales to us. These are listed in the table as items 2–5.

Items 2 (gifts and government grants) and 3 supplied more than enough to enable foreigners to pay for the American export surplus. At the same time, however, foreigners paid us a large amount (item 4), in purchase of American securities or other property and in loans in this country. They also shipped over gold (item 5), which they sold for dollars to spend in this country.

If we add up the total receipts by Americans and the payments by Americans, we see that they are approximately equal. The receipts appear to have been $178 million more than the payments—a difference of slightly less than 1 percent of the total transactions (item 6). But, since the receipts should theoretically equal the payments, this difference is regarded as the sum of errors in the many records of transactions which are totalled, to obtain the items in the table, and of omissions unavoidable in such large aggregates of figures (item 7).

It may seem puzzling that the sum of the millions of miscellaneous payments to foreigners during the course of a year should anywhere near equal the payments made to us by them. Why should inward and outward payments be even? This equality is not, however, a coincidence; the balance is a necessary consequence of the way the accounts are drawn up. No nation can buy abroad without paying in goods and services, in cash, in debt charges (which from the creditors' point of view are loans or investments), or with the proceeds of gifts. All these are included in the international account.

If the aggregate transactions among all the nations in the world are considered, it is obvious that total outgoing payments must equal total incoming payments, since what is an outgoing payment for one nation must be an incoming payment for some other. Then if the transactions of a single nation with all the rest of the world are considered, it is true that for this nation also incoming payments must equal outgoing payments. Perhaps, like a profit-making merchant, the citizens of this country sell abroad goods of a greater value than they buy from other nations. But how do the countries that buy more than they sell get the money with which to pay the balance? They must borrow the money from the country which has an export surplus, or must get it from that country in some other way, as through investments or gifts from the country or sale of gold to it.

It should be remembered that no purchaser, by directly using his own money, can buy in a region which has a different currency. The purchasers of one nation cannot buy goods or services in another without first buying the currency of that nation. If, for example, a South American nation could not get, in some way or other, enough dollars to buy in the United States as much as its citizens wanted to buy, it could not remedy the situation by printing more of its own currency, even though it printed by the billion. What the United States can sell to other countries is absolutely limited by the total of outgoing payments of United States dollars. These payments, of course, include loans and investments to cover debts not paid in cash.

BALANCE OF PAYMENTS BETWEEN
SINGLE COUNTRIES

It is not true, however, that incoming and outgoing payments between one country and any other or between one country and any particular region, must come out even. The United States may, for example, in any year pay into Canada more than Canada pays into the United States, or vice versa. This is because trade is not just a two-way street. Each nation deals with many others. Trade and payments usually are, as the economists say, "triangular," or follow an even more roundabout route. The United States may buy tin from Malaya, which may buy machinery from Britain, which may buy wheat from Canada, which may buy machinery from the United States. In the aggregate, a deficit in the balance of payments between country A and country B will be canceled out by a surplus in the balance of payments between country A and countries C, D, E, and so on.

ITEMS OF EXPORTS AND IMPORTS

A slightly more detailed list (than that shown in Table 21/1) of United States exports and imports for 1954 is given in Table 21/2. In this table, one may find items that had not occurred to him.

The meaning of exports or imports of merchandise is clear enough.

TABLE 21/2

UNITED STATES EXPORTS AND IMPORTS, 1954
(in millions of dollars)

Exports of goods and services		
Merchandise	12,814	
Transportation	1,171	
Travel	584	
Miscellaneous services	963	
Military transactions	179	
Income on investments		
Direct investments	1,725	
Other private	230	
Government	272	
Total		17,938
Imports of goods and services		
Merchandise	10,354	
Transportation	1,026	
Travel	1,000	
Miscellaneous services	677	
Military expenditures	2,603	
Income on investments		
Private	360	
Government	59	
Total		16,088

Transportation, as an *export,* accounts for freight charges foreigners pay on American ships or other transport charges. As an import, it covers charges paid by American shippers to foreigners. Foreign travel in the United States is an export from this country, since it involves sales to foreigners; travel of Americans abroad is, for similar reasons, an import. Miscellaneous services cover matters like insurance payments, earnings of individuals abroad, legal fees, and other such items. Military expenditures, when paid to foreigners, are an import to the United States; as, for example, when our troops are quartered abroad in friendly nations. Foreign military purchases in the United States are exports. (This table does not cover *grants* of money from the United States for military purposes or the expenditure of these funds.)

Income from American investments abroad is, naturally, an export. It is regarded as payment for services—that is, the use of our capital. Direct investments cover earnings from American ownership of factories, oil wells, commercial establishments, and other businesses. Other private, sometimes called "portfolio," investments yield income from ownership of securities in foreign concerns. And income from investments under the head "Government" is interest received from foreign government bonds.

Frequently, merchandise in foreign trade is called "visible" exports or imports; all the other items for which payments are made are called "invisible" exports or imports. For example, if a student travels abroad, he becomes an invisible import of the United States, strange as that may sound. Everything he buys from foreigners, from passenger fares to food and lodging, is of course a service paid for in United States dollars—dollars which then become available for foreigners' use in buying exports from the United States.

It will be interesting to note a few relative magnitudes in this Table 21/2. Important though merchandise trade is, it makes up only about two thirds of foreign payments; the "invisibles" are also of importance. Next, in every item except two, exports from the United States are larger than imports to it. These two exceptions are travel and military expenditures. If it were not for these two, the export surplus of the United States in 1954 would have been some $2.5 billion greater than it was.

A more detailed table would show the nature of merchandise exported from the United States and imported to it. United States exports include manufactured goods of many kinds, food products, petroleum, cotton, tobacco, and a few other raw or semimanufactured materials. We import manufactured goods, too, but the bulk of imports into the United States consists of materials for industry and of tropical food products—merchandise that cannot be produced within our boundaries or cannot be obtained in sufficient quantity. Since World War II, the largest single item (by value) on our import list has been coffee.

Of the "unilateral transfers" from the United States, which made it possible for foreign nations to buy as much as they did from this country in 1954, $452 million consisted of private gifts and $1,706 million consisted of governmental grants for such things as reconstruction, development, and technical aid. This is exclusive of military aid. The new capital flowing abroad from the United States in 1954, which also supplied foreigners with dollars, consisted of a net total of $1,621 million in private investment and $93 million from the United States Government. In private investment, the biggest item was direct investment—that is, investment in enterprises owned by Americans—and the next largest was short-term credit. At least until 1957 the bulk of private foreign investment from the United States was devoted to development of raw materials such as petroleum or iron.

The following table from the *Economic Report of the President* (January, 1959) shows the balance of payments for a series of recent years.

AIMS OF FOREIGN-TRADE POLICY

There are two traditional views of foreign-trade policy, opposite to each other both in economic theory and in popular opinion. One, which originated in the early days of modern capitalism, was that the aim of a nation in foreign trade, like the aim of a merchant, should be to accumulate as much wealth as possible by selling goods and services of a value

TABLE 21/3

UNITED STATES BALANCE OF PAYMENTS, 1953–1959[1]
(in millions of dollars)

Type of transaction	1953–55 (annual average)	1956	1957	1958	1959 First quarter	1959 Second quarter	1959 Third quarter
United States payments: Total	20,502	25,846	27,374	27,079	6,513	8,962	7,343
Imports of goods and services: Total	16,890	19,829	20,923	20,951	5,422	5,992	6,162
Merchandise, adjusted, excluding military	10,957	12,804	13,291	12,946	3,604	3,885	3,852
Transportation	1,104	1,408	1,569	1,599	381	470	455
Travel	1,030	1,275	1,372	1,460	257	415	612
Miscellaneous services, excluding military	688	807	873	854	199	208	263
Military expenditures	2,654	2,955	3,165	3,416	801	821	765
Income on investments:							
Private	377	426	452	537	128	134	141
Government	80	154	201	139	52	59	74
Unilateral transfers, net, excluding military: Total	2,401	2,398	2,318	2,318	619	575	529
Government grants	1,795	1,733	1,616	1,611	433	390	331
Remittances and other transfers	606	665	702	707	186	185	198
United States capital, net: Total	1,211	3,619	4,133	3,810	472	2,395	652
Private, net: Total	1,066	2,990	3,175	2,844	383	752	431
Direct investments, net	721	1,859	2,058	1,094	267	450	291
New issues	236	453	597	955	163	115	170
Redemptions	−151	−174	−179	−85	−22	−36	−12
Other long-term, net	41	324	441	574	147	154	42
Short-term, net	219	528	258	306	−172	69	−60
Government, net: Total	145	629	958	966	89	1,643	221
Long-term capital, outflow	468	545	993	1,272	287	[3] 1,654	205
Repayments	−470	−479	−659	−647	[3] −263	−116	−134
Short-term, net	147	563	624	341	65	105	150
United States receipts: Total	18,610	24,235	27,094	23,223	5,456	5,988	6,017
Exports of goods and services: Total	18,345	23,705	26,733	23,199	5,381	5,798	5,883
Merchandise, adjusted, excluding military	13,120	17,379	19,390	16,227	3,798	4,061	4,032
Transportation	1,263	1,642	1,999	1,650	386	434	457
Travel	608	705	785	825	170	224	286
Miscellaneous services	968	1,210	1,306	1,279	318	322	330
Military transactions	192	158	372	296	74	88	57
Income on investments:							
Direct investments	1,693	2,120	2,313	2,198	468	488	536
Other private	235	297	363	417	108	121	113
Government	266	194	205	307	59	60	72
Foreign long-term investments in the United States, net [4]	265	530	361	24	75	190	134
Net United States payments (−)	−1,892	−1,611	−280	−3,856	−1,057	[2] −2,974	−1,326
Increase in liquid dollar holdings by foreign countries and international institutions	1,089	1,274	330	1,140	744	1,876	1,031
United States gold sales or purchases (−)	500	−306	−798	2,275	96	741	167
Errors and omissions	303	643	748	441	217	357	128

[1] Excludes transfers of goods and services under military grant programs.

[2] Includes $1,375 million for increase in United States subscription to the International Monetary Fund, of which $344 million was in gold and $1,031 million in non-interest-bearing notes.

[3] Includes $150 million advance repayment by Germany on postwar debt to the United States.

[4] Excludes investment in U.S. Government securities.

Source: Department of Commerce.

higher than the cost of the goods and services it buys. In consequence, this policy encourages measures which restrict imports, such as protective tariffs, and measures which expand exports, such as subsidies to exporters.

What this policy achieves, if successful, is either to pile up a larger and larger hoard of precious metals or steadily to increase the indebtedness of foreigners to the citizens of the nation which maintains an excess of exports over imports.

The other view of foreign-trade policy is that outlined by Adam Smith in *The Wealth of Nations* and endorsed in principle by most economists in the classical tradition since his day. This is that the aim of a nation's international trade should be not to accumulate treasure but to benefit the citizens as consumers by allowing them to seek the least costly and best goods wherever they may be bought, whether abroad or at home. Everyone admits that the people of any nation benefit by absence of obstruction to trade within its boundaries; free competition leads to the survival of the more efficient producers and the specialization of individuals and regions in whatever they can do to the best advantage. Would it not be absurd, for example, if the Northern States should raise a tariff wall against citrus fruit from Florida and California, while Florida and California obstructed the importation of motor vehicles from Detroit? The same principles, according to the classical theory, apply to international trade.

Britain adopted the policy of lowering or abolishing import duties early in the nineteenth century, thus putting into practice Adam Smith's doctrine. As a result, she was able to buy staple foodstuffs more cheaply abroad than British farmers could produce them, and to import as cheaply as possible industrial raw materials, many of which she lacked. At the same time, her factory industries, developed earlier than those of most other countries, prospered by selling to a world-wide market and needed no protection. The profits so earned not only financed enlargement of British industry but also made London a leading center of international finance, which supplied capital for new developments throughout the world. British capital, for example, was heavily invested in expanding United States railroads and industries. Return on these investments eventually became an important factor in enabling British subjects to buy foreign products.

The United States and modern Germany, on the contrary, adopted a policy of erecting high tariff walls on imports of manufactured products in order to shelter the home market for their own industries against British competition, believing that newly established manufacturing concerns could not survive the competition of the more experienced British producers.

Protective tariffs endured long after the domestic industries had become rich and powerful. In essence, the tariff was a subsidy of manufacture at the expense of consumers, including the majority whose products could not benefit from import duties—farmers who sold a large part of their products to other countries outside the tariff wall and persons in occupations which foreign competition could not threaten in any case, such as retail and wholesale trade, construction, internal transportation, and all those who provided services, like public utilities and the professions. It should be noted that everyone who has to pay a duty on an imported product not only pays a higher price for it than he otherwise would, but also pays a correspondingly higher price for any competing article of domestic manufacture.

Although the tariff was frequently reduced when one party came into power and raised again when the other party came back in, no lasting policy aimed at lowering trade barriers was effective until the 1930's, when the United States adopted the Reciprocal Trade Agreements Act during the great, world-wide depression, in an effort to stimulate international revival and, in particular, to enlarge American exports by getting rid of foreign obstructions to them. By this statute, Congress delegated to the President the power to make bargains with foreign nations for mutual reduction of tariffs, within certain limits and for a limited period. The Act has periodically been renewed since that time, recently with more loopholes for preservation of high duties. After a quarter century of operation, it still leaves the United States with a considerable degree of protection. As a rule, large and powerful industries, which are now interested in foreign markets and are efficient enough so that under most conditions they do not fear foreign competition in the United States, have ceased to support high protective duties, whereas more vulnerable industries—some large and some small—continue to demand them.

POSSIBLE EXCEPTIONS TO THE FREE-TRADE DOCTRINE

Infant Industries. One exception to the free-trade doctrine frequently supported is, as we have seen in the experience of the United States, the belief that in a country just beginning to build up modern industry, it is necessary to provide subsidies for "infant industries," especially in manufacture. A tariff is one way of providing such a subsidy; direct financial assistance by government is another. Alexander Hamilton, who as Secretary of the Treasury under George Washington advocated governmental aid to new industries in his noted *Report on Manufactures,* favored direct subsidy over import duties, on the ground that it could be more easily removed when no longer needed, and did not raise prices for consumers.

In underdeveloped countries at present, restrictions on imports are frequently thought necessary in order to stimulate domestic growth of industry. The theory of protection for infant industry, first systematically outlined by a German-born economist, Friedrich List, holds that *after* all nations suited to modern industry have developed a well-integrated industrial economy, it will be to the advantage of all gradually to reduce, and finally to abolish, protective duties. This course, however, is easier to advocate than to accomplish, because protected industries are often politically powerful and often unwilling to surrender government aid.

National Defense.   Another commonly sanctioned exception is the need to protect an industry essential for national defense, which might otherwise suffer from foreign competition. Adam Smith himself applied this to merchant shipping, which of course is essential to the survival of an island nation like Britain. The United States has, for similar reasons, subsidized the American Merchant Marine ever since World War I, although in this case the necessity is not quite so obvious. Minor manufacturing industries have gained increased tariff protection on this ground under a clause of the Reciprocal Trade Agreements Act, although their connection with defense needs is not always beyond question, as in the case of protection of United States watch manufacturers against Swiss competition.

Retaliation.   It is sometimes argued that if nation B has or erects high duties against imports from nation A, the latter may justifiably retaliate by raising its duties against nation B, in order to furnish a motive for reduction of the duty. Such retaliation may work, but experience with tariff "wars" indicates that they are injurious to both parties and sometimes difficult to end. A better system is that of reversing the process with systematic reciprocal trade agreements by which existing duties are reduced by both parties.

Equalizing Protection (Dumping).   Growers of major agricultural staples in the United States which have an export market—for example, wheat—have often complained because they buy manufactured goods which are protected, but cannot themselves benefit from import duties on the crops which they grow. Having a surplus beyond the needs of American consumers, they experience little competition from abroad in any case, and the domestic price of their product cannot be affected by any device, like the tariff, to raise the price of imports. This argument has been used to support "agricultural adjustment" measures by which a government agency buys and stores enough of the crop in question to maintain whatever may be regarded as a reasonable domestic price. If, as has sometimes been done, governmentally held grain is sold abroad (in addition to the normal amount of exports which arrive in ordinary trade), the consequent increase of supply on world markets tends to decrease the price for foreign growers. This is called "dumping" and is strenuously opposed by foreign producers and their governments, except in special cases where the exported American grain is used for famine relief.

Supporting High Labor Costs.   Some agricultural products, especially those requiring a high proportion of hand labor, must be sold in the United States at a higher price than they could be bought abroad if American producers are not to go out of business or at least are not to suffer severely. The same situation exists in some manufacturing industries. Among products thought to be in this category are sugar, wool, some textile products, and gloves. The relatively high wage level in the United States is believed to threaten such industries if they are not in some way safeguarded from foreign competition, whereas United States industries with a maximum degree of mechanization and technological advantage can pay high wages and still have low enough labor costs to compete successfully in a world market. In the case of sugar (and more recently, petroleum and cheese) the United States Government has restricted imports by import quotas so determined as to let in just enough of the foreign product to satisfy American demand (at predetermined prices) and still allow the American producers to make a profit. In other cases, such as wool, protective duties are used, although the general principle of United States tariffs is to let in free the raw materials of which this country does not produce enough to supply the domestic demand. To analyze the problem of whether relatively high American wages must be protected, it is necessary to look further into theory—the theory of "comparative advantage."

COMPARATIVE ADVANTAGE

Briefly stated, the theory of comparative advantage holds that in a really free market each region in a country, and each region or nation in the world, will tend to concentrate its resources on those types of production which it is best fitted to carry on; and that this will be to the advantage of the people of every region—both as producers and as consumers and both as sellers and as buyers. The advantage may be one of location, natural resources, climate, skill, amount and quality of labor, or a combination of two or more of these factors. Any region or country is wasting its resources if it continues to support any occupation which would not survive in a market with no artificial barriers. The inhabitants of the country, including the workers employed in the less advantageous industries, are worse off in the long run if these industries are sustained by quotas, tariffs, or other subsidies. A country is even wasting its resources to use them in less efficient industries, even if these industries could cope with foreign competitors.

For example, the workers engaged in growing sugar in the United States are among those who receive the very lowest wage levels in the country and who work under some of the worst conditions. Because of the import quotas on sugar, inhabitants of the United States must buy their sugar at higher prices than would otherwise prevail. If people could buy their sugar more cheaply, they would have more money to spend for other things and there would be a correspondingly higher demand for labor in other industries. Unless sugar growing in this country could be brought to a point of efficiency where it could compete on even terms with foreign-grown sugar, it would be better even for labor, in the long run, to find less employment in sugar growing and more employment in more efficient industries where pay is higher.

This principle does not mean that sudden abandonment of governmental aid to submarginal industries would create no immediate hardship or that special measures might not be necessary to avoid human suffering. But even if removal of import duties or quotas made it necessary to pension a small minority of the workers of the country for the rest of their lives, the ultimate cost would probably be less to the nation as a whole than to keep inefficient industries alive.

FOREIGN EXCHANGE

If there were a single international currency (which of course would have to be accompanied by an international banking system), it would be as easy for an inhabitant of one American state to buy in England, Germany, or India as it is for him to make and receive payments in any part of the United States. But since each nation or region has its own currency, the money of one cannot ordinarily be used to buy in another, without being exchanged for the currency of the nation where the seller does his business.

For many years before the depression of the 1930's, the exchange of one currency for another was a relatively simple matter. Each government issuing money established by law the weight in gold (or silver) of its basic unit—the dollar, pound, franc, mark, ruble, or other monetary unit. Since most important nations were on the gold standard, it was easy to calculate the value of any nation's basic unit in terms of any of the others.

In the financial capital of each nation there exists an exchange market (not a literal market place but a group of dealers and banks who make a business of buying and selling foreign exchange). If a buyer in the United States, for example, needs funds to pay a bill in London, he buys pounds with his dollars. (What he actually buys is a "bill of exchange," ordering the pounds to be delivered in London.) At the same time, people with British pounds come to the market to buy dollars with which to pay charges in the United States. Demand and supply affect prices in this market, as in others. If the demand for dollars is greater than the demand for pounds, the price of dollars in pounds rises (which is equivalent to saying the price of pounds in dollars falls.)

The great banks to which the actual bills of exchange come for collection in any market match the total demand for one currency against that for the other, and, at the prevailing rates, payments both ways are nearly even. Excess of either demand or supply takes effect almost immediately in changed prices for the currencies in relation to each other, so that the *values* to be exchanged balance.

When the gold standard was in effect—that is, when the possessor of any nation's money could at any time redeem it in gold at the legal parity—fluctuations in exchange rates themselves could not be wide. If, for example, a London businessman found that he could not buy so many dollars with his pounds as would equal their gold value, he would usually buy gold instead and pay his dollar obligations with that. He certainly would do so if the cost of shipping gold were less than the depreciation of the pound. The banks which settled international balances would therefore notice that gold began to flow out of a country after the exchange value of its currency had fallen below what was called the "gold export point," and would sooner or later flow in when the exchange rate rose above the "gold import point." These points were close together. And these points, of course, narrowly limited the fluctuation of exchange above or below the parities resulting from the legally set gold values of the currencies.

This system worked as long as a nation with an adverse balance of payments had plenty of gold. But when its gold was nearly exhausted, such a nation had to stop redeeming its currency freely in gold, and thereafter there was no limit to the depreciation of its exchange. That is what occurred in many important nations in the 1930's. The United States did not lose gold by this route, but stopped gold redemption of currency because lack of confidence in the banks had caused depositors to withdraw so much gold—and other cash—that the basic money supply was disappearing into private hoards. Even after gold returned to the American banks, however, the nation stayed off the gold standard for other reasons.

During the 1930's, exchange rates often fluctuated widely, since they were no longer tied to gold. Such fluctuation was bad for international trade, since no one could do business abroad or invest there with any confidence that the money he expected to pay or to receive would be worth the same amount when he paid or received it as when the sale or other contract was made. The situation also provided a great gambling game for speculators in exchange. When World War II came, the governmental controls, not only of exchange rates but also of all international and many internal transactions, replaced ordinary market forces. At the end of the war, something had to be done to restore the solvency of war-torn nations and to encourage world-wide trade and investment. This action resulted in a series of new international institutions and new policies toward international payments. The more important of these new developments are described briefly here.

NEW INTERNATIONAL AGENCIES

The International Monetary Fund. This Fund was set up by international agreement as a substitute for the gold standard in stabilizing exchange rates. (International balances are still settled in gold, but gold redemption of currency is not permitted except by the banks auth-orized to make these settlements.) Under its charter, each nation was permitted to fix the gold value of its currency only at a figure to be approved by the Directors of the Fund, and thereafter could not change the value up or down by more than 10 percent without the approval of the Directors. If any nation has to buy its own currency in exchange markets in order to keep the exchange rate up to the agreed level, it can borrow from the Fund gold or the currency of any other country to do so, up to a certain quota. Thus, if the pound sterling sinks, vis-à-vis the dollar, the British government can borrow dollars with which to buy pounds, provided its quota is not exhausted. Each participating nation contributed to the Fund an amount of gold and of its own cur-rency, according to its capacity to do so.

This device is sufficient to prevent much fluctuation of exchange rates from day to day or month to month. It is not, however, capable of stemming a persistent fall in the rate of any currency, if the country in question is suffering a continued and heavy excess of outgoing payments. When and if such a situation arises, the only recourse of the Fund is to permit the deficit nation to devalue its currency.

The International Bank for Reconstruction and Development.
This Bank was founded to make long-term loans to participating nations which needed them not for temporary postwar relief but for making permanent improvements in their capacity to produce and thus to enhance their ability to buy and sell both abroad and at home. The Bank was, in a sense, intended to provide a substitute for the foreign investments which had contributed so largely to economic growth before the depression but had virtually disappeared during the 1930's and the subsequent war.

All participating nations contributed to the capital of the Inter-national Bank, in proportion to their resources. The Bank can lend either its own money or money raised by bond issues backed by its own resources. It cannot lend, however, when any need which it recognizes can be met by private loans on reasonable terms.

Before authorizing loans, the International Bank makes a thorough investigation of the project for which financing is requested, and often gives valuable advice to the borrowing country or institution, which must be accepted as a condition of the loan. It has lent both to nations which suffered from the war and to underdeveloped countries. At the begin-ning, its funds were far from sufficient to meet all needs. Its lending policy has been conservative; its investments have proved so sound that it has earned substantial amounts to add to its reserves, and it has little difficulty in floating bond issues in the leading money markets. The Bank could not, however, lend enough to cope with postwar emergencies, which turned out to be much more serious than had been anticipated. Its pioneer work might prepare the ground for a much larger volume of private foreign investment than otherwise would be forthcoming.

The European Recovery Program (Marshall Plan). Soon after World War II, it became evident that the nations of Europe would need prompt and substantial help to restore their economies and, in some cases, to save themselves from international bankruptcy. They needed to buy a great deal from the United States to feed their populations, to restore war damage, and to build up their industries both for domestic consumption and for exports which would enable them to stand on their own feet in the future. This aid had to be prompt and generous in order to avoid calamity.

The United States therefore offered help to any European nation that would accept it on the conditions specified. The aid was to consist of both grants and loans to be used for expanding production and trade, and it was to cease at the end of five years. The offer was accepted by most western European nations but rejected by the Soviet Union and, under pressure from Russia, by her satellites. Greece and Turkey were already receiving help as nations threatened by Communist aggression; Germany, still under military occupation, was in a separate category. The dollars flowing abroad under this offer permitted the Marshall Plan nations to buy what they needed on this side of the Atlantic. With this stimulus, plus the advice of Americans mobilized by ECA (European Cooperation Administration), they made a quick recovery. One of the lasting benefits was OEEC (Organization for European Economic Cooperation), composed of the countries receiving Marshall Plan help, which aided removal of trade barriers among nations, straightened out tangles in their exchanges, and coordinated their economic planning. European economic unity was subsequently aided by such agencies as the Steel and Coal Community. Little by little, governmental controls of foreign exchange and trade were dropped and reserves of gold and dollars restored. Production and exports shot up; the chief difficulty in recent years has been to avoid inflation rather than to prevent unemployment.

Economic Aid to Allies. Before the Marshall Plan was scheduled to come to an end, the Korean War broke out, and the United States adopted a new program for aid to allied nations threatened by Communist aggression, such aid to consist of both military grants and economic aid to compensate the nations in question for concentrating on defense. This aid provides dollars not only to members of the North Atlantic Treaty Alliance (NATO) but to Korea, Nationalist China (on Taiwan), and other nations.

Aid to Underdeveloped Nations. This program, inaugurated by President Harry S. Truman, for helping nations which had made too little use of modern technology and had suffered from low living levels was, at the beginning, generally called "Point Four." The program has concentrated on technical assistance, with a minimum of financial aid. A similar agency was established by the United Nations. This endeavor, though it has performed a useful service, has been dwarfed in recent years by the programs having chiefly a military purpose and has frequently been confused with them both at home and abroad. Yet in the long run technical-aid programs might easily be more important, even for the security of the United States, than any direct military assistance.

World-wide Reduction of Trade Barriers. Restoration of world trade was recognized by all as a major postwar objective. To further it, numerous nations met periodically and negotiated multilateral agreements to reduce tariffs, import quotas, and similar barriers. These collective agreements are known as GATT (General Agreement on Tariffs and Trade). The United States has participated in this activity, and by agreements limited to short periods, much headway has been made. An effort to establish a permanent international organization, the World Trade Organization, devoted to this purpose and parallel with the Monetary Fund and the International Bank, though originally backed by the United States Government, has not, at this writing, been adopted because of the refusal of the United States Congress to authorize American participation.

The cost of all these activities to the American people has been relatively small. It has never exceeded more than 1 or 2 percent of the gross national product.

It is perhaps paradoxical that among the most striking economic recoveries achieved since World War II are those which have occurred in Germany and Japan, the two leading enemies (now allies) which suffered defeat. In their revival, American military occupation played an important role.

The history of the postwar years supplies striking evidence that, under some conditions, governmental action may be necessary to stimulate world production and trade, though political intervention has traditionally been regarded as injurious to a world-wide private enterprise economy. However, the influence of pressure groups in various nations has led to some governmental actions in support of special interests, contrary to the general policy. In this regard the United States is not an exception; it still subsidizes some exports of agricultural products, imposes import quotas on others, and has recently increased tariff duties on some imports.

THEORIES OF INTERNATIONAL EQUILIBRIUM

Brief mention may be made, in conclusion, of equilibrium theory as applied to international trade. Until the 1930's, traditional theory depended on the classical analysis of money and prices. If any nation suffered from an adverse balance of payments, the necessary result would be a tendency for its currency to fall in exchange markets. This would immediately lead to an outflow of gold. What was to prevent this outflow from continuing until the nation had to stop paying gold and so suffer a severe economic crisis?

A widely accepted theory was that as the gold reserve of the deficit nation decreased, the effect on the banking system would be to restrict credit, diminish the money supply, and so bring about a fall in its price level. Meanwhile the countries to which the gold was flowing would, by the reverse process, experience a rising price level. In a free world market, the consequence would be that the country losing gold would find it more expensive to buy abroad and so would restrict imports, while the countries gaining gold would find it cheaper to buy in the country losing gold and expand their imports from it. Thus the imbalance in trade and payments would be corrected, the exchange rates would come back to parity, and the gold flow would cease or be reversed.

Clearly, the classical theory did not work out after the economic collapse of 1929. Most nations either were forced off the gold standard or thought it wise to abandon it. The emphasis changed from a purely monetary theory to one based on the flow of income and payments. We have seen how this theory was applied to analysis of a nation's internal economy by John Maynard Keynes and others. Similar applications occurred in foreign transactions. The new school of theorists regards an increase of receipts from foreign transactions as identical in its effect with an increase in domestic investment, and a decrease in earnings from abroad as identical with a decrease in investment at home. Saving and investment, under the Keynes theory, may reach an equilibrium not only at a high level but also at a low level, which is accompanied by depression and unemployment. For this reason governmental intervention is thought desirable to prevent either depression or inflation on a world-wide scale.

In this connection, as in the theory of domestic stabilization, it should be pointed out that many support the policy conclusions of the new theory without accepting the theory itself, in all its implications. Stabilization and economic growth are desirable guides to policy, even if one accepts no theory of automatic equilibrium.

Chapter 35 involves some of the material discussed in this chapter, in reference to loss of gold by the United States in the late 1950's.

QUESTIONS

Use as a starting point the 1958 figures in the table of United States Balance of Payments on page 260. Assume that in a future year payment for imports to this country were reduced by $1 billion, and that no changes occurred other than any which might offset this drop in outgoing payments. Draw up the account for the year in question. (Note that there may be a number of different correct answers.)

Describe in words what your figures imply about changes in our foreign transactions and about governmental policies or other influences that might have caused them.

22 / CONSUMER BEHAVIOR / Now that we have

examined markets and prices, and the manner in which a "free" market is affected by such influences as marketing controls; the practices of business, labor, and agriculture; and foreign transactions, let us turn to the person in whose interest all these activities are supposed to be carried on—the consumer.

Every person is a consumer. When we speak of consumers, therefore, we are not speaking of a separate class of persons. We are referring, rather, to that part of everybody's activity or attitudes having to do with purchase for individual use.

Consumption, said Adam Smith, is the end and aim of all economic activity; production is secondary. Whether or not that is wholly true, consumers certainly occupy a strategic place in the circular flow of spending and income. If consumers bought no goods and services, nobody would be paid for providing them. And in buying goods and services intended for individual use, consumers indirectly stimulate businessmen to purchase capital goods—the buildings and machinery required to make what consumers will buy. Even as citizens, people can be thought of as consumers of goods and services provided by government. So consumer spending directly activates the production of consumer goods and services and indirectly activates the production of capital goods, while political representatives of consumers determine spending by governments for the many kinds of goods and services that governments provide. These are three of the four main sources of national income. The fourth, and for the United States the smallest, source—foreign trade—is dependent on American consumers as far as imports are concerned and on foreign consumers as far as exports are concerned.

Consumers not only initiate the demand for everything in the aggregate; their decisions concerning what to buy determine what particular things or services can be sold (though in our modern order it is often the sellers who influence the consumers' decisions). This consumer preference in turn furnishes a guide to business and professional men concerning what kinds of production, and how much of each kind, it will pay them to offer for sale. Ultimately, consumer choices thus determine roughly the allocation of available supplies of the three main factors of production—land, labor, and capital. It is sometimes said that in a free, competitive market system, every dollar in consumers' hands constitutes an economic vote. Thus, it is contended, by a democratic process consumers decide what shall be produced, how much of it, and, in the end, the allocation of the nation's resources to the best possible satisfaction of the people's wants in the relative order of their urgency.

If no qualifications of the foregoing statements were necessary, we should obviously be living in an economic utopia. As will later appear, this is far from the whole story. No doubt consumers' purchases do, in a market system, determine what shall be produced by private enterprise. It would be well, however, to ask a few questions. One of the more important with which economists have been concerned is, what determines consumers' purchases?

CULTURAL THEORIES OF CONSUMPTION

Somewhat at variance with the classical theory are contemporary views that consumption is largely determined by the culture in which one lives, that it is fully as much a matter of social habit as it is of individual choice. Everybody in the same cultural group or subgroup lives—and buys—in much the same way as everybody else in it; the culture, superimposed on basic physical requirements, provides a pattern of needs and desires and of ways of satisfying them. Often this culture is more influenced by the desires of powerful sellers to sell their products than by any autonomous wants of consumers. Ideas of how much many individual articles are worth in money depend largely on what one is used to paying for them, or on what others are paying for them, rather than on what each individual thinks each article or service he might want is worth to him. In many cases the prestige associated with high-priced articles leads a person to buy at higher prices what he might not buy at lower ones.

In some old or primitive cultures, the pattern of wants is likely to change little and relative prices themselves are likely to be determined by custom. In our rapidly changing culture, with its continual innovation and hundreds of new products, the producer or seller actively creates and maintains consumer wants and preferences by psychologically devised appeals to basic drives; preferences do not often originate spontaneously with the consumer. Competition among producers is focused not just on supplying what the consumer wants at as low a price as possible, but even more on advertising and merchandising intended to stimulate wants for today's new products or to reinforce wants for yesterday's familiar ones. Much of the advertising is devoted to establishing demands for particular brands. Once a brand name is widely known and the consumer forms a habit of buying a certain kind of cigarettes, cosmetics, cars, or what have you, he no longer is likely to shop around to see whether better qualities can be obtained at the same price or whether a virtually identical article can be had at a lower price; he is likely to shift, however—*if* he does so—because of some competitor's advertising appeal. Indeed, when so many products are for sale which embody the results of technical or scientific knowledge about which most consumers know little, they are often ill equipped to judge relative values, at least without expert assistance.

Attempts to discover consumer habits and preferences now depend not only on intuitive theories but also on objective research. Psychologists and economists make surveys, often by a sampling process, to learn how, when, and, if possible, why consumers at various income levels and in various places spend their money. Business organizations employ marketing research to learn what the prospects of a product are or how consumers could be induced to want more of it. Economists accumulate and interpret statistical information about consumers' habits in the past and their intentions to buy or not to buy various classifications of goods in the future.

Nobody denies the importance of consumers in the economy or ignores the momentous results that may flow from their decisions. But instead of supposing that the economic order must operate to the best advantage of all because it depends on a rational choice of "utilities" by the individual consumer, modern students of the subject concentrate on discovering what consumers really do. Only on the basis of such knowledge is it possible to judge whether what they do serves their welfare as consumers or the health of the economy as a whole. Education of the consumer regarding the real values of articles offered for sale is often thought desirable.

DIFFERENCES OF INCOME AND FAMILY BUDGETS

One frequently verified discovery is not surprising. The proportion of the family income spent on the various groups of commodities in any one year varies with the size of the income. Low-income groups of city families spend a larger proportion of their incomes on food than those with higher incomes. As income rises, the percentage spent on clothing seems to vary very little, but housing expenses—rent or "imputed rent"—rise considerably. There appears to be no great variation with respect to size of family income in the percentage spent on the "miscellaneous" item—which includes everything except food, clothing, and shelter. The most striking variation is perhaps in what is left, or saved, after all expenditures have been made. As has been previously noted, low-income families, on the average, save less than nothing in any one year; families of average income, on the whole, just about break even; high-income families account for most of the saving.

These variations in average family expenditures are about what is to be expected. Necessity dictates some purchases, but the consumption pattern set by any particular culture becomes more important as incomes rise. Hunger is the most pressing of urges, and no matter how small the income, hunger will be satisfied first of all, even if little is left for other things. Families with incomes above the lowest level do indeed spend more in absolute dollars for food than those at the bottom; they can buy more expensive cuts of meat, for example, and have it more often. Nevertheless, the capacity of the human stomach is limited, and a family with an income of $25,000 will not normally spend ten times as much on food as one with $2,500. The result is that high-income families have a larger percentage of income left for other things. Clothing, another pressing want but also a mark of prestige and style, can be bought in larger quantities with satisfaction as incomes rise, yet few have the closet room for, or want to take care of, an indefinitely large wardrobe. The result is that the *percentage* of the budget spent on clothing remains about the same as income goes up. Much greater variation, however, is possible and customary in expenditures for housing; rent varies all the way from payment for an overcrowded tenement in a district of low land values to ownership of a luxurious city house in a fashionable neighborhood plus an estate in the country—perhaps two or three of them.

CHANGES IN SPENDING OVER THE YEARS

The average rise of real income and the increase in variety of products over many decades is clearly reflected by the shifts in allocation of average wage-earners' incomes. The National Industrial Conference Board, a research organization of employers, estimates that in the 1870's wage-earners' families spent a little over half their money on food, about 23 percent for housing, and about 15 percent for clothing. This left approximately 11 percent for everything else (called in the budget "miscellaneous"). By the late 1930's the percentage of the budget spent for food had shrunk to about 34 percent, the housing percentage had risen slightly, to 24.5 percent, the clothing percentage had fallen to about 11 percent, while about 30 percent of the income was spent on "miscellaneous." In the 1950's, the food and clothing percentages had changed little from the level obtaining before World War II, but there was a marked decrease in the percentage spent on housing (largely because of public-housing programs and rent control). Most striking of all was the rise in the percentage spent on "miscellaneous" to nearly 39 percent of the budget, or more than was spent on food in the 1950's and more than was spent on rent and clothing combined.

It should be remembered that the incomes to which these percentages apply were far higher in the 1950's than in the 1870's, so that even the reduced percentage spent on food covers a larger intake per family of relatively expensive and nourishing foods like fresh meat, milk, fresh vegetables, and fresh fruits.

Perhaps the most revealing aspect of this historical shift is the great growth in the "miscellaneous" item, which covers everything except such

TABLE 22/1

1953 PERSONAL CONSUMPTION EXPENDITURES

	Billion $	Percent*
Total	230.1	100.0
Durable Goods	29.7	12.9
Automobiles and parts	13.1	5.7
Furniture and household equipment	12.8	5.5
Other durable goods	3.9	1.7
Nondurable Goods	118.9	51.7
Clothing and shoes	19.8	8.6
Food and alcoholic beverages	71.8	31.1
Gasoline and oil	6.6	2.8
Semidurable housefurnishings	2.5	1.5
Tobacco	5.3	2.3
Other nondurables	12.9	5.6
Services	81.4	35.4
Household operation	12.0	5.2
Housing	27.7	12.0
Personal services	4.4	1.9
Recreation	4.4	1.9
Transportation	7.1	3.1
Other services	25.8	11.2

* Percents do not add to 100 because of rounding.

basic physical necessities as food, clothing, and shelter. It includes such things as automobiles, radio and television, motion pictures (all of which first came upon the market in recent decades), medical care, travel, books and magazines, theatre and music, sporting goods, gardening implements and materials, cosmetics and perfumes, and thousands of other commonly purchased goods and services. Combining the effect of (1) rising incomes and (2) larger percentage of the budget spent on "miscellaneous," it may be estimated that wage-earners' families in the 1950's spent per person ten or twelve times as much for goods and services other than food, clothing, and shelter as wage-earners' families did in the 1870's. This increase could not have occurred without the marked increase in productivity which has taken place, and especially without the marked decrease in working hours, which has given people time to use and enjoy things not needed for mere physical subsistence.

National income figures show how all consumers together, including those of low and middle incomes and the well-to-do, apportion their spending. In 1953, a year fairly typical of others since World War II, consumers in the United States spent $230 billion altogether. Of this amount, about 31 percent went for food and alcoholic beverages, 12 percent for housing (rent or "imputed rent"), and 7 percent for clothing and shoes. Food, clothing, and shelter—which used to be called the "basic necessities"—thus consumed about half the American consumers' budget. Durable goods—of which expenditures for automobiles and parts, and for furniture and household equipment each made up nearly half—

took 13 percent. Nondurable goods, other than food and clothing, made up for another 13 percent of the total spendings, the most important items being gasoline and oil, tobacco, and semidurable housefurnishings. The rest of the budget—about 24 percent—went for a wide variety of services. Table 22/1 indicates in more detail the personal consumer expenditure for 1953.

The following table shows consumers' expenditures from 1929 to 1959 for the main types of purchases. In interpreting these figures, it should be remembered that what could be bought for a dollar increased

TABLE 22/2

PERSONAL CONSUMPTION EXPENDITURES, 1929–1959
(in billions of dollars)

Period	Total personal consumption expenditures	Durable goods			Nondurable goods					Services				
		Total	Automobiles and parts	Furniture and household equipment	Other	Total	Food excluding alcoholic beverages[1]	Clothing and shoes[2]	Gasoline and oil	Other	Total	Housing[3]	Household operation	Transportation	Other
1929	79.0	9.2	3.2	4.8	1.2	37.7	19.5	9.4	1.8	7.0	32.1	11.4	4.0	2.6	14.0
1930	71.0	7.2	2.2	3.9	1.1	34.0	18.0	8.0	1.7	6.3	29.8	11.0	3.9	2.2	12.7
1931	61.3	5.5	1.6	3.1	.9	28.9	14.7	6.9	1.5	5.7	26.9	10.3	3.5	1.9	11.2
1932	49.3	3.6	.9	2.1	.6	22.8	11.4	5.1	1.5	4.8	22.9	9.0	3.0	1.6	9.3
1933	46.4	3.5	1.1	1.9	.5	22.3	10.9	4.6	1.5	5.3	20.7	7.9	2.8	1.5	8.5
1934	51.9	4.2	1.4	2.2	.6	26.7	12.2	5.7	1.6	7.2	21.0	7.6	3.0	1.6	8.8
1935	56.3	5.1	1.9	2.6	.7	29.3	13.6	6.0	1.7	7.9	21.9	7.6	3.2	1.7	9.4
1936	62.6	6.3	2.3	3.2	.8	32.8	15.2	6.6	1.9	9.1	23.5	7.9	3.4	1.9	10.3
1937	67.3	6.9	2.4	3.6	1.0	35.2	16.4	6.8	2.1	9.8	25.1	8.4	3.7	2.0	11.1
1938	64.6	5.7	1.6	3.1	.9	34.0	15.6	6.8	2.1	9.5	25.0	8.8	3.6	1.9	10.7
1939	67.6	6.7	2.2	3.5	1.0	35.1	15.7	7.1	2.2	10.1	25.8	9.0	3.8	2.0	11.0
1940	71.9	7.8	2.7	3.9	1.1	37.2	16.7	7.4	2.3	10.8	26.9	9.3	4.0	2.1	11.4
1941	81.9	9.7	3.4	4.9	1.4	43.2	19.4	8.8	2.6	12.3	29.0	10.0	4.3	2.4	12.3
1942	89.7	7.0	.7	4.7	1.6	51.3	23.7	11.0	2.1	14.5	31.5	10.8	4.8	2.7	13.1
1943	100.5	6.6	.8	3.9	1.9	59.3	27.8	13.4	1.3	16.7	34.7	11.3	5.2	3.4	14.7
1944	109.8	6.8	.8	3.8	2.2	65.4	30.6	14.6	1.4	18.7	37.7	11.9	5.9	3.7	16.3
1945	121.7	8.1	1.0	4.6	2.5	73.2	34.1	16.5	1.8	20.8	40.4	12.4	6.4	4.0	17.5
1946	147.1	15.9	3.9	8.7	3.3	84.8	40.7	18.2	3.0	22.9	46.4	13.8	6.7	5.1	20.8
1947	165.4	20.6	6.3	11.0	3.4	93.4	45.8	18.8	3.6	25.2	51.4	15.6	7.4	5.5	23.0
1948	178.3	22.7	7.4	11.9	3.4	98.7	48.2	20.1	4.4	26.0	56.9	17.6	7.9	6.0	25.4
1949	181.2	24.6	9.8	11.5	3.3	96.6	46.4	19.3	5.0	25.9	60.0	19.3	8.4	6.1	26.2
1950	195.0	30.4	13.0	14.0	3.4	99.8	47.4	19.6	5.4	27.4	64.9	21.2	9.3	6.3	28.1
1951	209.8	29.5	11.6	14.2	3.7	110.1	53.4	21.1	6.0	29.5	70.2	23.2	10.1	6.9	29.9
1952	219.8	29.1	11.0	14.1	3.9	115.1	55.8	21.9	6.7	30.7	75.6	25.4	10.8	7.4	32.0
1953	232.6	32.9	14.0	14.7	4.1	118.0	56.6	21.9	7.5	31.8	81.8	27.5	11.7	8.0	34.6
1954	238.0	32.4	13.4	14.8	4.3	119.3	57.7	21.9	8.0	31.7	86.3	29.1	12.1	7.9	37.1
1955	256.9	39.6	18.3	16.6	4.8	124.8	59.2	23.4	8.8	33.4	92.5	30.7	13.5	8.3	39.9
1956	269.9	38.5	15.8	17.4	5.3	131.4	62.2	24.5	9.6	35.2	100.0	32.7	14.8	8.6	43.8
1957	284.8	40.3	17.0	17.4	5.8	137.7	65.2	25.4	10.4	36.8	106.7	35.2	15.8	8.9	46.8
1958	293.0	37.6	14.0	17.4	6.2	141.9	67.4	26.1	10.5	37.9	113.4	38.0	16.9	9.1	49.4
1959[4]	311.4	43.0	17.9	18.6	6.5	147.8	69.3	27.7	11.2	39.6	120.6	40.7	17.7	9.4	52.8

[1] Quarterly data are estimates by Council of Economic Advisers.
[2] Includes standard clothing issued to military personnel.
[3] Includes imputed rental value of owner-occupied dwellings.
[4] Preliminary estimates by Council of Economic Advisers.
Note: Detail will not necessarily add to totals because of rounding.
Source: Department of Commerce (except as noted).

markedly in the 1930's, and then fell again with rising prices. What is significant are the changes in allocation from year to year.

CONSUMERS' CHOICE AND SAVING

As incomes rise, consumers may exercise a much wider range of choice among things and services offered for sale. Shall the family buy a new TV set or take a vacation trip? Do hobbies and recreations of the individual lie in the direction of winter sports, sailing, golf, reading, gardening, or tinkering in a cellar workshop? Such widening of choice increases competition among producers in different industries making the goods consumers use in their spare time, stimulates the growth of some new industries, and causes the decline of some old ones. Many producers now compete not only for the consumers' dollars but also for the time when consumers are not on the job and are not eating or sleeping. Advertising and merchandising are correspondingly emphasized.

It has often been said that the most steady and reliable part of the income flow was that represented by purchases of consumer goods, as contrasted, for example, with capital investment. This is still true, in a comparative sense; it becomes less true as a larger proportion of consumer income becomes available for purchases of things that are not physical necessities, especially of those known as "durable goods," because these may last for a number of years instead of being used up daily, like food, or worn out, like many items of clothing. Consumers' durables are, in a sense, capital investments just as are factories and machinery.

As a consequence, a much larger number of consumers than formerly have an opportunity to decide whether to buy the new automobile or other kinds of durable goods this year or later. If they decide to buy this year, their decisions will greatly stimulate sales, production, and income this year. If they decide not to buy this year, a corresponding drop in sales will occur.

The other side of this picture is that when consumers are buying avidly, those who pay cash do not save the money and the much larger number who pay on the installment plan borrow the money. This combination of less positive and more negative saving reduces the percentage of income saved. Exactly the opposite results occur when large numbers of consumers decide not to buy the things they can do without. Thus, in effect, consumers' enlarged opportunity to decide whether to save or spend can result in a far less steady aggregate consumer demand than has previously been expected, and in a far less steady rate of saving than some theorists have supposed.

COOPERATIVE BUYING

Cooperative societies of consumers formed to handle their own retail distribution on a nonprofit basis originated more than a century ago in

England; since then the consumers' cooperative movement has spread in many countries and has become a powerful economic force. Associations of retail cooperatives have established wholesale cooperatives to purchase from the producer, and these in turn have in many cases combined in the ownership of actual factories or processing plants. From the beginning the cooperative movement has been motivated not merely by a desire to obtain better goods more cheaply but also by the ambition to introduce gradually a less competitive and less commercial type of economic order.

The original cooperative in Rochdale, England, established a procedure which has in the main served as a model for other successful cooperative societies. The necessary initial capital is contributed by members who expect to do their purchasing through the society. No dividends are paid on the capital. Officers are elected by the members, not on the basis of one vote for each share, as in the case of a profit-seeking corporation, but on the basis of one vote per member, no matter how many shares he may own. The members' monetary gains, if any, come as a result of paying less for their purchases.

It has become customary for most retail cooperatives to charge the regular market price, established in commercial markets, for what they sell. A record is kept of the purchases of each member. At the end of the year any profit that is not applied to the expansion of the enterprise is distributed to the members as dividends on their purchases—so much per dollar's worth bought.

Any consumer who expects to save huge amounts by eliminating retailers' profit is likely to be disappointed in most cases, since the profit, however large it may be in the aggregate, does not amount to much per dollar of sales. Most of the margin between what the retailer pays for his merchandise and what he charges for it is eaten up by such costs as rent, wages to his staff, advertising, and other expenses. Consumers may, however, benefit from the fact that it is not so necessary for their societies to pay high executive salaries as it is for profit-making organizations, or to lay out much for advertising and salesmanship. Moreover, cooperatives may save by not carrying in stock such a large variety of goods as a store appealing to the general public, thus concentrating on a smaller number of standard commodities that their members principally buy.

In the United States the consumers' cooperative movement has not made so much headway with retail establishments handling food or general merchandise as it has in Europe. One reason is that it is difficult for any small retailing establishment to succeed, and cooperatives usually cannot be inaugurated on a large scale, since they need to build up the loyalty of their members and the skill of their managers (and cannot pay executives well). In addition, the vigorous enterprise of American chain stores and department stores has made it difficult for the cooperative movement to enlist members, except under special circumstances. Nevertheless, there are probably between one and two million members of cooperative retail stores and buying clubs in the United States, and their organizations do a business approaching $1 billion annually. Moreover, there are a large number of cooperative-buying associations which provide their members with gasoline and other petroleum products, in the sale of which price competition among private sellers is exceptional.

The cooperative principle has been successfully extended to other fields such as distribution of electric light and power in rural regions (there are some 900 associations with approximately 3 million members) under the aegis of the federal Rural Electrification Administration. A still larger number of individuals are members of approximately 10,000 credit unions, which extend personal loans at interest rates lower than those obtainable commercially. Cooperative insurance associations have the largest membership of all—some 11.5 million—and their great resources are available for financing of cooperative housing projects as well as for investments of a more usual sort.

These various societies are affiliated in a number of federations regionally, nationally, and in some cases internationally. Thus the cooperatives are in a position to narrow as much as possible the costs of distribution between production and consumption. These costs are inevitably heavy, however, in markets where there are a great variety of products to choose from, frequent style changes, or many services rendered to the consumer, such as individual delivery, privilege of return, charge accounts, obligations for repair and servicing, and similar services.

THE COST OF ADVERTISING

Much controversy has been aroused by the expense of advertising, which of course is added to the retail price of the product. According to a publication of the United States Treasury Department, *Statistics of Income, 1947,* advertising costs compose only one-half cent of each dollar of gross sales by food stores and range upward from that low figure to three cents of each dollar of receipts by motion picture theaters. Manufacturers as a rule pay a larger percentage of their sales dollar for advertising than retailers; these costs, though relatively moderate in products where brand names are less important, may range as high as 10 percent for cereal preparations, 12 percent for soaps and soap products, and 20 percent for cosmetics. Cooperatives can, of course, avoid such costs by manufacturing—or having manufactured to specification—products of their own. Sometimes they can improve quality as well, at least from the point of view of practical usefulness. Aside from what advertising adds to the price, fraudulent advertising may be immensely costly to the consumer.

Defenders of advertising argue that while it is expensive, it also makes possible mass distribution, which in turn reduces the cost of production by making possible mass production. In many cases there is undoubted force in this argument, but it would be extremely difficult to measure how much of the added cost due to advertising is canceled by a diminished cost of mass production attributable to the advertising. Some advertising offers valuable information and has economic value for that reason. But some advertising is a means of building up a virtual monopoly.

PROTECTION AND EDUCATION OF CONSUMERS

An old principle of law, *caveat emptor*—"let the buyer beware"— holds that if the purchaser is dissatisfied or cheated, it is his own fault and he cannot recover damages from the seller. In the absence of specific regulation, this principle still is recognized by the courts—except, of course, in cases where a statute is involved or a contract is fraudulently made or is violated. Both by government enactment and by private practice, however, many protections for the purchaser have been installed.

The Federal Trade Commission can act to stop false or misleading advertising—though it has neither a large enough staff nor big enough appropriations to scrutinize all advertising for dubious statements. About 75 percent of its "cease and desist" orders are directed at fraudulent advertising. This power applies only to trade across state lines, but many states have enacted similar laws. The federal Food and Drug Administration compels manufacturers to put their names on labels, to state the weight of the contents and the minimum standards of quality, as well as to warn against misuse. The Post Office can exclude fraudulent advertising from the mails. The National Bureau of Standards establishes standard weights and measures and performs tests for quality both for private and for governmental agencies. State and local governments carry out sanitary inspection of food, water, milk, and other locally distributed products.

Many private organizations, stimulated by concerns which find it to their advantage to maintain a reputation for fairness and honesty, also adopt codes and standards. Better Business Bureaus, to which consumers can carry their complaints, police advertising and shady practices.

Consumers themselves can do much to improve their satisfaction in the goods and services which they buy, and consequently the allocation of the nation's resources, if they avail themselves of expert information concerning what is offered for sale. Cooperative consumer services such as Consumers' Research and Consumers' Union have a sizable and growing membership; their publications can be had for a low subscription price. The more active consumers become in making intelligent choices and in seeking remedial action against questionable business practices, the more support they give to both private and public agencies established to serve their interests.

Finally, consumers should not overlook the fact that a large and growing segment of their needs is served by governmental agencies. If, as citizens, they take an active interest in the organization and practice of these agencies, the adequacy and quality of public services can be greatly strengthened. Parent-teachers' associations are needed to support and improve the schools; civic organizations of many other kinds can influence both legislators and public employees.

UNEASINESS IN THE CONSUMER'S ECONOMY

No one would deny that a major necessity is the satisfaction of hunger and of the need for clothing and shelter. Yet for more than a century leading thinkers have expressed disenchantment with a commercial economy which absorbs a major part of human energies in providing goods and services to be sold for indefinitely "higher" levels of consumption. No philosopher has regarded the satisfaction of appetites as the chief end of man.

In the early stages of the industrial revolution, criticism was often centered on the "cheap and nasty" factory products made for sale, as contrasted with the honest worth of the handiwork by craftsmen who put heart and conscience into their work because it satisfied a creative need. William Morris, among others, thought that tastes were being debased, and strove to produce (and sell) articles of high esthetic quality and sound worth.

Another, though similar, attitude was expressed in mid-nineteenth century America by Henry David Thoreau in his *Walden*. He advocated simplicity in living, frugal tastes, and plenty of time for enjoyment of nature and things of the mind. He thought the struggle to "get on" in the world was not worth the time.

In the 1890's Thorstein Veblen, in his *Theory of the Leisure Class*, aimed still another broadside at the prevailing consumption culture. What people bought, he argued, was determined not primarily by their real needs but by the effort to ape the wealthy, nonworking class, who spent their money mainly for things which proclaimed their status as persons who never had to descend to manual labor. "Conspicuous consumption" was the goal. Though social habits have changed since the turn of the century, there have recently been traces of much the same status seeking in buying the most expensive or biggest cars, living in the most exclusive suburbs, and similar behavior. Advertising and promotion have repeatedly played on this motive, as pointed out by numerous recent sociological studies.

We have had complaints about the "organization man," who abandons individuality and personal integrity in order to earn promotion in large corporate industry—all for the purpose not of creating or building anything, as leading "captains of industry" did in the balmy days of private enterprise, but of seeking large and steady income, security, and a life exactly like that of other "successful" men. And yet, the implication is, such a success, marked by ample consumption of all the approved symbols of status in both goods and services, turns out to be hollow indeed. All such goals are busily and ingeniously promoted by specialists, paid for helping business to establish sales for anything conceivable that they think people may possibly want to buy.

These and other dangers of inner corruption are persuasively described by John Kenneth Galbraith in *The Affluent Society*. Of course, still far too many people live in stultifying poverty. But as our output of goods and services continues to increase faster than the numbers of persons who consume them, there is a growing danger of having *too much*—at least, too much of the wrong things and not enough of others more necessary for a good life, such as liberal education, mental and physical health, and goals worthy of the best capacities of human beings.

It is not necessarily true that the things easiest to sell to the most people are the things that add most to the dignity and stature of a man or a woman. There is danger that, in an economy highly successful in purveying commercial products and services, more valuable goals will be smothered by its very affluence.

Chapters 31 and 32 involve consumer behavior in actual situations.

QUESTIONS

1. Assume that a college student annually receives $2,500 from all sources—relatives, earnings, borrowing, scholarships, and so on. On the basis of your experience and observation, how much would he be likely to pay for the following?
   (a) Taxes
   (b) Tuition, textbooks, and other educational expenses
   (c) Ordinary living expenses
      (1) Food, drink, and tobacco
      (2) Housing (room rent)
      (3) Clothing
      (4) Miscellaneous, such as travel, transportation, entertainment, charity, doctors' bills or health insurance, toilet articles, and anything else not included above

2. How much income do you think the student would need in order to save anything?

3. On the basis of your figures in the answer to the first question, what percentage of the student's receipts might logically be called "disposable income"? What percentage of his income would be spent for the following?
   (a) Nondurable goods
   (b) Durable goods
   (c) Services

4. In view of the above answers, to what extent, and how, does the consumer behavior of college students bear on the theory that consumer choices in a free, competitive market determine the allocation of productive resources?

23 / TECHNOLOGY AND

PRODUCTION /

The people cannot eat any more food than the farmers can grow, buy any more clothing than the clothing workers can make, or ride in any more cars than the automobile industry can produce. If every worker is employed, if his hours of work are not increased, and if the labor force does not become larger, the total output of a nation cannot be augmented except by turning out more per man-hour of work.

Ability to produce more things in the same time makes it possible for real income (that is, income in purchasing power) to grow faster than population. Without increase in aggregate productivity, no one could add to his real income except at the expense of someone else. Without productivity increase, an increase in money spent could result only in higher prices for the same quantity of goods and services.

The discoveries of scientists and inventors and application of these discoveries in the technology of production are therefore the chief sources of growth in economic well-being. How are such discoveries and applications made?

Each discoverer or inventor stands on the shoulders of all his predecessors. The various branches of science bulwark one another. For this reason technical progress is attributable, not merely to the ingenuity of a few great inventors but also to the gradual accumulation of knowledge and skills, to thousands of small changes that eventually may be put together in one big change. An important discovery or invention cannot be made until the time is ripe, and then it is likely to be made by a number of individuals at about the same time.

For example, in America mechanical harvesters were patented by Obed Hussey in 1833 and by Cyrus McCormick in 1834; harvesters were invented also in England. The high-pressure steam boiler, which made railroad locomotives possible, was invented in the early 1800's by Oliver Evans, an American, and by Richard Trevithick, an Englishman.

There are many names associated with the development of the internal-combustion engine, which made possible the motor car—Markus, Lenoir, Otto, Daimler, Benz, Levassor, all in Europe; Selden in the United States.

Though centuries ago alchemists and other possessors of special knowledge used to work in secret, the code of modern science demands that verified results be published for the use of all. In this way the community of knowledge grows. Even when one government strives to keep secret the applications of science which have a direct military use, other nations are likely to duplicate its achievements before long, even though none of the essential information leaks out or is transmitted by spies. Meanwhile, the more a government limits communication among scientists, the more it risks retardation of its own progress.

DISCOVERY AND RESEARCH

At the beginning, discovery of improved methods was scattered and accidental. Nobody knows who first found out that fire could be of use to man; who first hit upon the idea that fire could be made at will. But both were great discoveries, almost certain to have been made by many and in many places. Once made, the knowledge that fire could be productive as well as destructive was sure to spread by imitation. Gradually, the use of fire was extended from providing for warmth and heating of food to smelting of metals, fashioning of weapons and tools, and eventually to providing of mechanical power.

Hidden in the mists of prehistory are other great productive discoveries, such as those concerning cultivating of the earth, raising of food crops, and domestication and breeding of animals. Mystery also surrounds the development of elementary crafts such as preservation of skins, tanning of leather, spinning and weaving of fibers to make fabrics, making of pottery, and such supreme intellectual skills as communication by words, counting and use of figures, and recording of knowledge in writing and elementary mathematical symbols. Apparently man has a propensity to putter and tinker, to try new things, to observe, and to make systematic use of his observations.

Sometimes, when a number of discoveries seem to fit together successfully, they become arranged in a social behavior pattern which resists further changes. This is true especially when, as often occurs, productive practices are tinged with ideas of magic or invocation of spirits or deities and thus become absorbed in some sort of religious cult. In early cultures there were likely to be long periods when technical progress occurred only slowly or was even actively resisted. Thus, primitive farming methods still survive in many societies, in spite of the immense advances in agricultural technology that have already been made elsewhere. On the other hand, there appear to be periods when technical progress is extraordinarily rapid. Something occurs which breaks the traditional cultural pattern—perhaps an important new discovery, perhaps a change introduced from outside the group. Thus, the dike is broken, and a flood of new changes pours forth. Stagnation, followed by an outburst of activity, is typical of growth in individuals, ideas, and societies.

Modern Western culture is distinguished from most of those which preceded it not only by the fact that its accumulated knowledge is much deeper and wider, but also by the fact that scientific discovery and technological change are no longer left solely to sporadic discoveries or to chance. Most of the fertile ideas, however, occur in the minds of individuals and are later developed by systematic research. Much of the research is carried on by governmental agencies or is subsidized by government (about 60 percent in 1952); much is done by business organizations; and much by institutions of higher learning.

Governmental research in the United States covers a wide area. The most spectacular—and most expensive—recent research activity of government is that devoted to atomic energy, which of course has immense civilian, as well as military, importance. But other and less well-publicized governmental research has achieved results of great economic value, such as the work of agricultural scientists in helping to improve and enlarge the output of farms, the operations of the U. S. Bureau of Standards in the physical sciences, and the gathering and analysis of information by the Census Bureau, the Department of Labor, and many other governmental statistical services. Much of government-financed research is carried on by private industry, and a good deal of it by universities.

Industrial research is largely, though not entirely, devoted to technological application of basic scientific knowledge for business purposes. A large amount of money is regularly spent on the development of new products, new machinery and methods of production, and other such aids to business. The independent inventor still exists, but much of the developmental work today is carried on in industrial laboratories with equipment and trained staffs such as few individuals, and indeed few small business concerns, could afford.

Educational institutions carry on systematic research in virtually every field of knowledge from astronomy to medicine. Much of this research is applied to the solution of pressing problems, such as the widely publicized search for the virus that causes poliomyelitis and the discovery of an effective vaccine with which to combat it. Some study, however, seeks the expansion of systematic knowledge irrespective of the possibility that any practical use can be made of it. Long experience has indicated that without advance in this "pure" or basic scientific research, many practical achievements of great usefulness would have been impossible.

As far as one can tell, the organized and persistent attention now devoted to research should render technological progress in the future more rapid than it has been in the past. Several dangers, however, may tend somewhat to offset the efficacy of the effort. One is that both government and industry, with their eyes on practical objectives, are inclined to

underemphasize the disinterested scientific curiosity which in the end
makes practical results possible; pure research may be starved of support.
Another is that control, organization, and teamwork, necessary though
they are for many purposes, may lead to ignoring or stifling of fertility
of the individual creative mind. Even the scientist himself may fall prey
to the attractions of expensive equipment and laboratory gadgetry, over-
looking the fact that the chief requirement for major scientific advance
is ability to think, including that combination of imagination and intui-
tion which often flourishes only in the absence of bustle and pressure.
(A recent study of the most eminent American scientists showed that a
majority received their undergraduate education in small liberal arts
colleges rather than in professional technical schools.) Occasionally, business concerns holding patents may "hoard" them—that is, may not put
them on the market—to safeguard existing investments. Finally, of
course, freedom of inquiry and communication, which is the *sine qua
non* of good thinking, may be hampered by political authority or pressure
from those who harbor a hostile suspicion of candid intellectual activity.

MEANS OF MORE EFFICIENT PRODUCTION

In the growth of output for use, certain major lines of achievement
stand out. One line is the discovery of hitherto unused materials and of
means of preparing and fashioning them for whatever purpose may be
in hand. Historians of culture have roughly classified the great ages of
mankind's advance as the stone age, the bronze age, and the iron age.
Civilization is still largely based on use of iron and its products, but so
many metals, chemicals, and even synthetic materials that do not occur
in a natural state have become important that our culture can scarcely
be identified any longer by the name of any specific substance. There
is a hint of this in the expression the "atomic age." The ultimate building blocks of all substances, which science is learning to rearrange for
many purposes, are now at man's disposal.

Of even greater significance in production is the gradual harnessing
of energy derived from inanimate nature to do the work hitherto performed by the physical force of human or animal muscle. Man himself
may be regarded as a mechanism for the conversion of the energy which
he takes in from food, light, and air, but he has potentialities much
higher than those of beasts of burden. Man has discovered that it is
better economy for him to devise means of using wind, water power,
heat, oil, electricity, and ultimately atomic energy to help him in transportation and in fashioning materials. The increase of productivity in
the past eighty years is almost exactly paralleled by the increase in use
of mechanical power from nonliving sources.

The third line of achievement in the enlarging of production is, of
course, the substitution of power-activated machinery for the hands or
the manipulated tools and instruments of manual labor. This develop-

ment" as we all know, is what marked the great shift of production from handcraftsmanship to machine industry, commonly known as the "industrial revolution." Machines multiply the output of human labor many times.

Machines are of many different kinds; they have evolved and developed as the industrial revolution has matured. At an early stage machines were substituted for skilled trades such as those of hand spinner or hand weaver. These machines were tended by operatives who could learn their jobs in a brief training period; such operatives are therefore often called "semiskilled labor." Not until much later, as a rule, were machines substituted for heavy muscular work such as road building, farm labor, and the like, often called "unskilled labor."

Now machines are rapidly being introduced as a substitute for the machine tender or operative and the assembly-line worker, as well as for the routine clerical worker in the office. As a result the fully automatic factory is in immediate prospect in numerous industries. The automatic process is a novelty in plants engaged in producing the more complex products made of materials difficult to fashion, such as metals, but something very like it has existed for years in the relatively simple processing industry of flour milling. The automatic loom is more than a century old.

"Automation," the name popularly given to use of the new automatic control and calculating devices, is simply another step in the continuing march of technology. It has aroused somewhat exaggerated fears of unemployment, though such fears may be justified only in particular occupations, just as they were at every previous step of the industrial revolution. In the long run, however, automation is but another extension of the capacity to turn out more output per man-hour, which has been the mainstay of economic growth. The development of electronic calculators is a great boon to those who have to solve complex problems in mathematics or logic, since it saves an immense amount of time and drudgery. We should not forget, however, that every advance in the technological revolution poses with greater insistence the questions: For what purposes is it best to use our immense powers of production? Are we wisely allocating our resources for the service of what has been called the "good life" in a healthy and valid society?

INANIMATE RESOURCES AND THEIR CONSERVATION

When men first turned to natural substances for the resources of production, they laid their hands eagerly on available land or minerals, without much concern whether these necessities for production, all limited in quantity, might some day be exhausted. This was especially true in countries newly populated by immigrants from Europe, like the United States. A pioneer would clear the trees off new land; burn what lumber he did not need for his own uses; reap the vigorous crops obtainable from virgin soil; and later, when the fertility of his land became exhausted or the soil itself was washed or blown away by erosion, he would move on to another fresh location. Lumber companies slashed through great forests of virgin timber, taking no precautions against forest fires and leaving no young trees standing for future harvesting. Owners of competitive oil wells got as much as they could out of their own wells without caring or perhaps even knowing that overdrilling would leave much oil unrecoverable in the pool beneath. Miners of coal, iron, and other metals used up the best deposits as fast as there was any demand for their products. All this does not mean that the farmers, lumberers, and miners were any more selfish, greedy, or imprudent than the general run of citizens. There seemed to be an abundance of everything, and if any one of the producers had undertaken the expense necessary to practice conservation, others who did not would have been able to undersell him, and he might not have been able to remain in business.

An expenditure of money or labor desirable in the interests of the whole people and the national economy is often not remunerative to the individual businessman or farmer within a period which is not longer than he is willing to wait. For example, a factory may pollute the air with smoke and noxious gases; or a mill may empty chemicals into a flowing stream, thus making the water unfit for use by man or beast. The social costs of such practices are heavy, but these costs do not appear in the accounting of the firms which resort to them. Therefore there is no financial incentive to the private enterprise to go to the trouble and expense required to stop the pollution. Good forestry practices on the farm wood lot, desirable to preserve the nation's supply of usable wood, may not pay off quickly enough to benefit the individual farmer. In such cases governmental intervention is often required, either by regulations or by planning and sharing of costs.

During the past fifty years, when short supplies of basic resources began to appear imminent, much has been done to conserve them. Government has played a leading role in aiding the conservation of renewable resources like farm land and forests. Producers' cooperative agreements, backed by state legislation, have diminished wasteful exploitation of exhaustible resources like oil deposits. Scientists have discovered methods of conserving land and forests, which can sometimes be practiced with profit to the individuals concerned, especially when they act as a group or when a large company, concerned about its own future, controls great tracts of forest land. There is, however, room for much improvement in the adoption of conservation practices.

It should also be noted that the market accomplishes some conservation in its own way, if it is left free to do so. This it does through prices. As any resource becomes scarcer relative to the demand for it, its price will rise. Two results will follow. On the one hand, its buyers will, more carefully than ever, have to ration the resource to its most important uses, present and future. (The order of importance of alternative uses is determined ultimately by consumers and expressed through their "dollar votes.") On the other hand, the higher price will bring to market a greater supply of the resource, if any is available at all. Thus, when top-grade ore has been exhausted, an increase in the price of iron may stimulate a search for new mines or may make it profitable to use lower grade ores. In addition, substitutes for the scarce resource will be encouraged.

In spite of every possible safeguard, however, experts point out the danger that, if the world's population continues to grow and if production grows even faster, we shall sooner or later reach the limits of renewable natural resources, and shall use up at least some of the more important minerals—iron, coal, or copper—that cannot be renewed. Such an eventuality would put an end to the growth of production, as Malthus predicted in the case of agriculture and food.

Science and technology, nevertheless, have done much, and can do still more, to postpone that evil day. Output of crops has never grown faster per person engaged in agriculture—and, what is more important in the long run, per acre—than in recent years. Exhaustible sources of power like coal and oil have not only been extracted with less waste but are used more efficiently in the production of energy. New and abundant sources like nuclear fission and solar energy have yet to be tapped for industrial use. Supplies of metal ores have been extended by the use of scrap; improvements in the quality of metals themselves and of equipment made from them permit greater output for a given quantity. New metals, in many cases obtainable from abundant natural resources, are coming into wider use. Some materials have already become obsolete because of the substitution of new ones for the same purpose—for example, wood in office furniture. Lower grade ores, hitherto thought commercially too expensive, can now be processed by new methods. Eventually, it may be possible to obtain every raw material needed by man from such abundant sources as sea water, ordinary rocks, air, and sunlight.

There is a visible limit to the growth of output, but it will keep retreating for a long time to come unless men and their institutions cease to make good use of science and technology.

Chapter 28 deals with the effect of technology on production in a specific industry. Chapters 31 and 35 are also relevant.

QUESTIONS

Suppose that the advance of technology should so increase the hourly output of goods and services that enough could be produced by a fully employed labor force working an average of three seven-hour days a week to provide everybody with everything required for a reasonably high standard of living. The manner of allocating the expenditure of

free time would then have become far more important than it is even
now. The allocation of dollars spent would have become secondary,
important though it is.

1. Do you think your education is helping to equip you for the
most rewarding and socially valuable use of free time?

2. How would you apportion your time among the many possible
uses for it, such as:

(a) Watching spectator sports or other forms of passive entertainment—movies, TV, radio, theater, concerts, and the like?

(b) Engaging in sports or other games?

(c) Travel?

(d) Reading (the kind of reading)?

(e) Developing special talents which you have not had time to
cultivate?

(f) Production of some sort for your own use and enjoyment—furniture making, gardening, cooking, photography, music, painting?

(g) Engaging in work not normally paid for—volunteer social work
or politics?

24 / POPULATION AND

WELFARE / If we are concerned with the welfare

of the people in a nation—and not simply with its military strength or manpower—we must look not only at its efficiency of production but also at the number of people who must share what it produces. Aggregate figures of national income or production are meaningless unless they are compared with the size of the national population. If population grows as fast as real income, or faster, the average income per person or per family cannot increase. Therefore, ideas and data about population growth are among the most important considerations studied by economists.

In the early years of the nineteenth century poverty and often even starvation were prevalent among the workers of Western Europe. At the same time many thinkers both in England and in France were suggesting utopian plans for the improvement of society. A young English clergyman, Thomas Malthus, was much concerned about the widespread misery, but he could not bring himself to believe that the ideas of the utopians would work in practice. Searching for a fundamental cause of the existing evils, to find an effective remedy, Malthus hit upon the theory which still bears his name.

THE MALTHUSIAN THEORY OF POPULATION

Reduced to its simplest terms, the Malthusian theory holds that the population tends to increase faster than the food supply. There is only a limited amount of good agricultural land. Though the food supply may be increased by extending the land devoted to farming, poorer and poorer land is thus brought into use. On a given acreage of farm land, improved methods may increase crop yields, but not indefinitely. Population, however, grows in a geometrical ratio, since every couple can have

291

a large number of children, each couple of the second generation can also have a large number, and so on indefinitely.

If people employ to the full their procreative capacity, as Malthus thought they usually did, there would soon be too many to feed. In these circumstances the population would be held in check only by famine, pestilence, and war.

The only remedy for the miseries which Malthus, through a study of history, thought had periodically engulfed humanity because of overpopulation, was, he declared, "moral restraint." People should be educated to marry late and to have no more children than they could support. If through ignorance or recklessness they violated this moral regimen, Malthus believed that charity could not provide a remedy, for such charity would only serve to aggravate the general evil which it strove to alleviate in particular cases.

THE THEORY OF DIMINISHING AVERAGE RETURNS

Closely related to the Malthusian population theory is an idea often applied in economic analysis even today, called the "law (or principle) of diminishing returns." Take, for example, any given farm. Its output can probably be increased by the use of more fertilizer, more labor, or more and better machinery. If this land had not, in the past, been farmed to the best advantage, such improvements would add to bushels or pounds of crops produced. If the units of output were divided by the units of input, the result would be an increasing ratio of total output to total input. During this period, the farm would yield *increasing* returns. But there would come a time, as the process continued, when the units of added input would begin to mount up faster than the added yields. After this point was reached, extra fertilizer would not bring correspondingly higher yield or might even injure the soil, additional workers would get in one another's way, and extra machinery would be superfluous. The point at which the farmer would no longer be able to increase the size of his crops from a given acreage without increasing his input by a larger percentage than his output is called the "point of *diminishing* average returns." This theory bulwarks the premise of Malthus that the food supply cannot be increased indefinitely; for, after diminishing returns set in, a point is in sight where output from land of a given acreage and quality cannot be further increased without technological improvement.

The "law" of diminishing returns has been extended to apply to single business concerns or even to whole industries.

THE "IRON LAW" OF WAGES

An early theory of wages—the subsistence theory—was merely a variation of the Malthusian theory of population. The earnings of labor, according to the "iron law," could not indefinitely exceed the amount essential for the worker to subsist, since in that case he would have more children; the number of workers would thus be increased more than the demand for their labor, and wages would fall. On the other hand, wages could not long remain below the minimum level necessary for subsistence, since in that case workers would die off and have fewer children, the working class would decrease in number, and the demand for their services would boost their wages.

Theories such as the iron law of wages and the Malthusian theory of population led Thomas Carlyle to call economics the "dismal science."

Malthus observed, at the time when he wrote, as Adam Smith had observed before him, that wages in North America were much higher than in Europe. He attributed this phenomenon to the fact that the population was still small in comparison with the available land, and predicted that the time would come when American wages would fall to the European level.

MALTHUS AND HISTORY

It is about a century and a half since Malthus enunciated his theories. During this time the population of Western Europe has greatly increased (although Malthus thought that the old world was overpopulated). During the same period, levels of living and wages in Western Europe have also greatly increased. In the United States the population during the nineteenth century expanded by leaps and bounds. Yet American levels of living and wages have increased even more markedly than European. By about 1890 there were no longer in the United States many tracts of unsettled land suitable for farming. Yet incomes in the United States apparently have increased more rapidly since the good farm land was filled up than before.

In many other areas of the world, however, particularly in Asia, the same kind of poverty still exists for a large part of the population as at the time Malthus wrote; famine and pestilence still hold the population in check.

Apparently Malthus did not anticipate the great outburst of technological progress which occurred in the Western world in the nineteenth and twentieth centuries. Production kept increasing faster than population, even when population was growing rapidly. Scientific and technological progress was marked not only in industry but also in agriculture. In more recent years, when Malthus might have expected the point of diminishing returns to be passed in agriculture, birth rates in the Western world fell off, and in some countries, such as France and England, population became for a time virtually stationary.

Whatever part the "moral restraint" advocated by Malthus may have played in the falling birth rate, the decline certainly was not stimulated by any general scarcity of food. Researches reveal that the birth rate has usually been smaller in higher income groups than in lower ones, and until recently has dropped, by and large, as income has risen. In the Western world, the birth rate is almost universally lower in cities than in rural regions, so that the larger the part of a population engaged in city occupations, the lower the birth rate. Birth rates therefore have in many cases declined with the advance of industrialism.

Population experts have inferred from such statistically established facts that higher standards of living, not lack of food, induce parents to limit their families. (A standard of living is a prevalent idea of what is appropriate to one's status.) Bearing, rearing, and educating children become more expensive as standards of living rise. Children, instead of going to work at an early age and helping to support the family, must be supported until their education is completed. More goods and services—aside from food—become necessary to retain or improve a family's relative social status.

Technological advance, in turn, not only provides additional production necessary to maintain rising standards but also stimulates the incentive to achieve improved status. Thus it not only increases the output of goods rapidly but makes possible the limiting of population as well.

IRREGULARITIES IN DECLINE OF BIRTH RATE

The observed decline of the birth rate in technologically advanced countries is not steady. There is some evidence that it swings in cycles of about twenty years. During war the birth rate often rises; apparently the imminence of military service stimulates early marriage and the desire to start a family. This was the case at least in the United States during World War II and the defense economy of the 1950's. In deeply depressed years, as in the 1930's, the birth rate falls. Hard times and unemployment discourage marrying and incurring the responsibility of a family.

VARYING COMPOSITION OF POPULATION

In underdeveloped societies which have high birth rates, high death rates usually prevail also. There is in such societies a high rate of infant mortality, and many of those children who survive infancy die before reaching maturity partly because of malnutrition and partly because of diseases that modern medicine and sanitation prevent or cure in more highly developed nations.

The result is that in nations where science and technology have not been widely applied, the age composition of the population differs greatly from that in nations which practice more modern hygiene. In the more

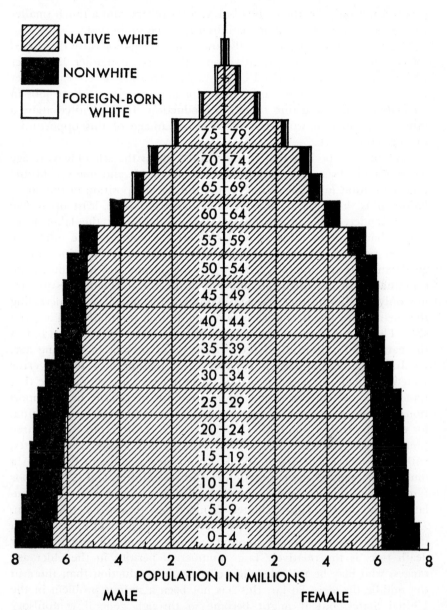

Fig. 24.1. ESTIMATED AGE DISTRIBUTION OF POPULATION IN THE UNITED STATES—ASSUMING HIGH FERTILITY AND MEDIUM MORTALITY. (Source: W. S. Thompson and P. K. Whelpton, *Estimates of Future Population of the United States*, Washington: National Resources Planning Board, 1943, p. 26.)

primitive society, a much larger part of the population consists of young children, a much smaller part of young people or adults who are capable of productive work. In a technologically developed nation, a larger part of the population at any one time is of an age at which people can produce not only for themselves but also for others, and a much smaller part is below the age at which children must be supported.

Since the birth rate is usually lower in a technologically developed society than in a more primitive one, the average mother has fewer children to care for and child care as a rule occupies fewer years of her life. Therefore the opportunity exists for more women to have jobs in factories or offices and thus to add to production. In the United States a growing number of women have taken advantage of this opportunity during recent years.

In spite of the fact that in the United States the school-leaving age has gradually been increased from 10 to 14 or 16, and many continue their education into college or beyond, the age composition of the population, plus the entry of women into industry, has—at least up to the 1950's—rendered the proportion of the population in the labor force larger than in most other countries. This has increased the total production per capita of the population, over and above the increase of goods and services obtained from a growing output per man-hour. The combination of low birth rate and low death rate thus enhances welfare not only by diminishing wastage of human life but also by increasing the quantity of goods and services available to a population of a given size. The recent upsurge in the birth rate, however, following its fall in the early 1930's, diminished the percentage of persons of working age.

Incidentally, population experts call attention also to the error sometimes made by popular writers on military affairs who assume that underdeveloped nations with large populations necessarily have proportionally large manpower for fighting or for war industries. Could China, for example, with a population of perhaps 650 million, put two to three times as many well-equipped soldiers into the field as the United States, with a population of 180 million? By no means, since in China (1) a much larger part of the population consists of children and (2) the labor force, in addition to being a much smaller fraction of the total population than in the United States, is much less productive per person.

An offset, however, to the relatively small number of children in a slowly growing or stationary population with a low birth rate and a low death rate, is the relatively large number of persons in the older age ranges, who may be retired or less effective in production than those in the middle decades. So far, this has not been a serious problem in the United States, but it might become so through general compulsory retirement at 65, especially if life were further prolonged by medical advances. Aside from the fact that a good deal of valuable productive power is lost if jobs are denied to those older people who may be quite capable of filling them and who frequently wish to remain at useful work, the support of a large number of older persons at anything like a decent standard—whether through old-age pensions or otherwise—would be far more costly than the support of an equal number of children and might place a heavy burden on the rest of the population. This possibility is being enhanced by two important developments in the United

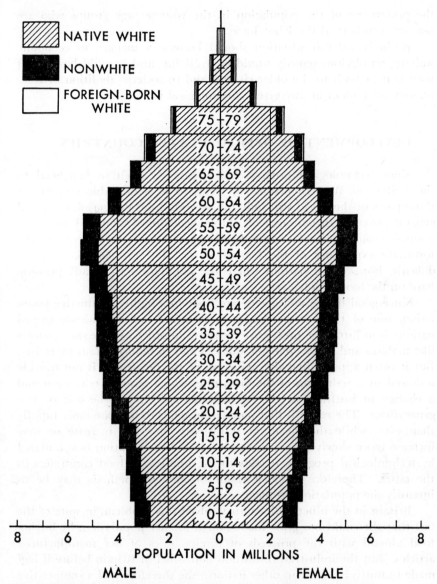

NATIVE WHITE

NONWHITE

FOREIGN-BORN WHITE

75-79
70-74
65-69
60-64
55-59
50-54
45-49
40-44
35-39
30-34
25-29
20-24
15-19
10-14
5-9
0-4

8   6   4   2   0   2   4   6   8
POPULATION IN MILLIONS
MALE   FEMALE

Fig. 24.2. ESTIMATED AGE DISTRIBUTION OF POPULATION IN THE UNITED
STATES—ASSUMING LOW FERTILITY AND MEDIUM MORTALITY.
(Source: W. S. Thompson and P. K. Whelpton, *Estimates
of Future Population of the United States,* Washington:
National Resources Planning Board, 1943, p. 26.)

States as we approach the fourth quarter of the twentieth century. One
is the effect of modern medicine and public health measures in increasing the numbers who survive beyond middle life—it is estimated that, by
the 1970's, there may be 20 million over 65, or about 10 percent of the
population. The other is that the "baby boom" of the 1940's and 1950's,
coupled with lengthening of the educational period, has greatly increased

the percentage of the population in the younger age groups who are not yet members of the labor force.

If, however, this situation should become a menace to economic welfare, an obvious remedy would be available, and it could be applied with benefit both to the older citizens and to society—abolition of compulsory retirement at any given chronological age.

DEVELOPMENT OF OVERPOPULATED COUNTRIES

Since technological progress has apparently been so beneficial to the welfare of Western peoples, it seems to be a desirable remedy for those parts of the world still suffering severely from hunger, disease, and general poverty. In nations with ample agricultural land and untapped natural resources, there is certainly an opportunity to repeat roughly the fortunate experience of the United States. The problem is far more difficult, however, in nations where the population is already pressing hard on the food supply.

Since good health and energy are basic to a highly productive population, one of the first necessities of technical aid to underdeveloped nations is to introduce preventive measures in order to wipe out scourges like malaria and other epidemic diseases and to reduce infant mortality. But it often appears that the reduction of the death rate is not quickly followed by a reduction of the birth rate, which requires education and a change in institutions; the lag is sometimes said to be one or two generations. The result is that population tends to increase more rapidly than ever, while the means of subsistence may not increase or may increase more slowly than population. If industrialization is stimulated by technological progress, it adds to the number of food consumers in the cities. Therefore the first result of modern methods may be to intensify the population problem.

Britain in the nineteenth century solved this problem, in spite of the fact that she could not grow food enough for her population, by buying food abroad with the proceeds of foreign sales of her manufactured articles. But the industrial revolution flourished in Britain before it had made so much headway in other nations; she therefore had a competitive advantage in selling her exported textiles, iron goods, and other manufactures. Now it is much more difficult for a nation which is a newcomer on the industrial scene to sell exported manufactures in competition with highly developed nations.

For this reason, experts concerned with the improvement of welfare in thickly populated underdeveloped countries have stressed the need for augmenting agricultural output, if possible, as a basis for any of the more ambitious plans for industrialization. In any case, the effort to promote economic growth in underdeveloped regions involves many problems, not to be easily or quickly solved.

OPTIMUM POPULATION

Too small a population in a given region may be just as deleterious to real output per head as too many people. The number of people should be sufficent to make possible a wide variety of skills and the economies achieved by division of labor. It should also be large enough to provide a market for the goods that can be produced most economically only when large numbers of substantially identical articles are sold. It is often said, for example, that an important reason why the United States has the most efficient automobile industry in the world—an industry which has made good use of mass production—is that there exists in the United States by far the largest market for cars.

No matter how rich the soil of a country or how many mineral treasures lie beneath it, these boons are worthless to man unless there is the labor power to use them in production and to consume the product, and sufficient technical knowledge to make this possible. Only when natural resources begin to give out and population centers become too overcrowded does overpopulation threaten a region.

For this reason some theorists have developed the idea of an "optimum" population for any given region—one neither too small nor too large. Though this is a useful concept in theory, it is a difficult one to apply. What may be an optimum population in one generation might be either too large or too small in another. One region which is too overcrowded to live on its own resources may do very well by trading with others. How else could Britain or Switzerland—or, for that matter, New York City or Chicago—survive?

Technical progress often finds ways to use resources which were undreamed of by earlier stages of civilization—as by the successive development of steam power, electricity, and atomic energy, or by the fabrication of new materials like plastics. A culture which, like that of the American Indians, subsisted on hunting and primitive agriculture could have overpopulated the United States with a few million persons; the culture in which we live has scarcely overpopulated it with 180 million.

On the other hand, climatic changes which have occurred in the past seem at one time or another to have converted vast regions into deserts and have covered others with glaciers, thus making once populous areas next to uninhabitable. Great changes of this sort will of course change the size of an optimum population for the regions concerned.

QUESTIONS

1. Was the United States once an "underdeveloped" region? If so, in what sense?

2. Can underdeveloped regions in the world today make good use of the methods by which the United States was developed?

3. Do you fear that the United States is becoming overpopulated? Why?

4. Assuming that increases in productivity will permit further reduction of working hours, would you choose to use this gain in:

(a) Supporting more (and more adequately) retired old people? or

(b) Giving everyone (including old people competent to work) a fair share in both jobs and leisure?

25 / GROWTH OF THE UNITED STATES

ECONOMY / In recent years economists—and a large

part of the general public as well—have been concerned about the
rapidity and nature of economic growth. One stimulus to this interest
is the rivalry between the Soviet Union and the Western Powers—especially the United States. Since the eighteenth century, Western Europe,
Japan, members of the British Commonwealth like Canada and Aus-
tralia, and the United States have experienced a rapid growth of population, modern industry, and mechanical production of many kinds.
Russia, a backward country before the Revolution in 1918, has guided
its policy largely by an intense effort to catch up with the leading industrial country, the United States. This contest has stimulated widespread
interest in the relative speed of growth, its nature, and its origins.

At the same time many "underdeveloped" nations have begun to
seek improvement of the material conditions of their populations by a
more rapid increase of production and growth of efficiency. China, for
centuries a stagnant power, has, under its new Communist regime,
accented rapid growth of industrial and agricultural production. India,
with a democratic government, also seeks more production and higher
productivity. Nations in many stages of development throughout the
world are seeking the same goals. It therefore becomes more important
than ever to know at least some of the major facts about economic
growth in the United States, and also, if possible, in the Soviet Union.

ESTIMATES OF GROWTH

Raymond W. Goldsmith, in a recent (1960) study, submitted to the
Joint Economic Committee of Congress, estimates that during the 120
years 1839–1959 the aggregate real gross national product in the United
States (in 1929 prices) increased at an average yearly rate of 3½ percent.
Per head of population, it grew 1⅝ percent annually. Real personal

301

consumption per head of population (which occupies about four fifths of the real GNP), when adjusted for changes in the age and sex composition of the population, had an average growth for the 120 years of 1½ percent annually.

When short-term variations are eliminated by means of a five-year moving average, the curve of real GNP per head went outside a band between 10 percent above and 10 percent below the straight-line trend (on a ratio scale) only on three occasions: it sank below during the Civil War and the depression of the 1930's and rose slightly above during World War II.

The course of prices made little or no difference in this relatively steady rate of growth. For example, although prices were extremely irregular between 1839 and 1899, rising markedly in the Civil War inflation and then resuming their former downward trend so that by 1899 they were slightly lower than sixty years previously, the average annual increase in real GNP per head was almost exactly the same as in the sixty years between 1899 and 1959, when prices had a strong upward tendency.

The remarkable historical regularity in growth, Goldsmith emphasized, may change in the future. Specifically, he suggested, there is reason to believe that the trend in productivity "may now be undergoing acceleration."

Goldsmith estimated that the growth of real GNP in the Soviet Union, 1913–1958, was at the average rate of "between 2 and 2½ percent" a year. However, it has been more rapid between 1951 and 1958. When divided by population to obtain the real growth per head, the recent rate is 4½ or 5½ percent annually. Mainly responsible for gain of output and income per head was, of course, an increase in productivity.

GAINS IN PRODUCTIVITY

Solomon Fabricant, in *Basic Facts on Productivity Change,* a study made for the National Bureau of Economic Research, shows that in the United States the average annual gain of productivity in 1889–1919 was 1.3 percent and that it became 2.1 percent in 1919–1957. Productivity is here defined as the combined physical output per unit of labor (manhours) and tangible capital in the domestic private economy. During the business cycle, productivity rises most rapidly, on the average, just before and after the trough. It continues rising fairly rapidly on the way up until the peak is reached, and then flattens out.

Real hourly earnings of wage earners have risen more rapidly than productivity, Fabricant finds, not merely recently but since 1889—as far back as the study goes. The average annual increase in real hourly earnings, 1889–1919, was 1.7 percent, as compared with a rise in productivity of labor and capital combined of 1.3 percent. Manufacturing wage earners had an annual gain of 1.9 percent. Between 1919 and 1957 the average annual gain in real hourly earnings of all workers in the private domestic economy was 3 percent, and of manufacturing wage-earners 2.6 percent, against the annual gain in productivity for the private economy of 2.1 percent.

Moses Abramovitz presents the results of a study of "long swings"—cycles of growth averaging about twenty years. He not only estimates the aggregate figures but also presents an analytic description of what happens during the swings. The cycles consist of up and down movements, not of total output but of its long-term *rate of growth*. When the rate of growth reaches its troughs, Abramowitz observes, we have our most destructive depressions. In 1960 we appeared to be nearing the end of a retardation. He observes that a substantial increase in the average rate of growth could be achieved if we could prevent the severe slumps. The long cycle in construction is a prominent component of these swings.

DISPOSABLE INCOME

Perhaps more to the point as far as individuals are concerned is the disposable personal income per capita, modified to take account of price changes. Disposable income is what individuals have left to spend or save after paying taxes. These figures are available since 1929. In 1958 dollars, per capita disposable income shows an increase from $1,148 in 1929 (a prosperous year) to $1,830 in 1958—a rise of more than 50 per-

TABLE 25/1

DISPOSABLE PERSONAL INCOME, TOTAL AND PER CAPITA, IN CURRENT AND 1959 PRICES, 1946-1959[1]

Year	Total (billions of dollars)		Per capita (dollars)	
	In current prices	In 1959 prices [2]	In current prices	In 1959 prices [3]
1946	160.6	226.8	1,136	1,605
1947	170.1	217.5	1,180	1,509
1948	189.3	228.6	1,291	1,559
1949	189.7	231.3	1,272	1,551
1950	207.7	249.6	1,369	1,645
1951	227.5	256.5	1,474	1,662
1952	238.7	263.5	1,520	1,678
1953	252.5	276.0	1,582	1,729
1954	256.9	278.0	1,582	1,712
1955	274.4	296.0	1,660	1,791
1956	292.9	310.3	1,742	1,845
1957	307.9	316.8	1,799	1,851
1958	316.5	319.7	1,818	1,836
1959 [3]	334.6	334.6	1,891	1,891

[1] Disposable personal income is personal income less personal taxes.

[2] Dollar estimates in current prices divided by the implicit price deflator for personal consumption expenditure component of gross national product on a 1959 base.

[3] Preliminary; includes fourth-quarter estimate by Council of Economic Advisers.

Sources: Department of Commerce and Council of Economic Advisers.

cent. The dip due to the depression of the 1930's is clearly shown in Table 25/1; almost all the increase over the 1929 level has occurred since 1940.

DISTRIBUTION OF INCOME

The effort to abolish want and poverty has been a leading social aim, expressed or implied, in all enlightened economic orders. Relevant to this aim is the distribution of income according to income classes. If a relatively small number of persons at the top receive a large share of the income, while a relatively large number at the bottom receive little, great inequalities exist not only in material welfare but also, as a rule, in political and economic power and in social status. Such a situation is repugnant to the ideals of democracy, personal freedom, and dignity.

To say this is not to say that absolute equality is possible, or, even if possible, is desirable. When total income is small per head, it would not be possible to raise appreciably the income of the many poor by distributing among them the income of the relatively few who are rich. A basic essential for abolishment of poverty is a large total income per head. We are therefore primarily concerned with the growth of income. But we are also concerned that, as income grows, a closer approach to equality be achieved by raising the income at the bottom of the scale more than income at the top.

What would be an ideal distribution of income is difficult to say. Variations should exist to reward outstanding effort or skill; it is also desirable to attract recruits to the kind of work which society most needs. Perhaps we should pay higher wages for jobs which are disagreeable or involve drudgery than for those which offer more intangible rewards. One aim of distribution long ago enunciated by the socially minded was, "From each according to his ability, to each according to his need."

Differences in pay should not, of course, exert an influence contrary to the major needs of a society as often they seem to do. If we depend largely on a price and market system for the most desirable allocation of resources, the relative pay for different skills and professions should be in accord with our major requirements. Some of the most essential needs are not, as a rule, supplied through the ordinary market system. Among these are the needs for teachers, scientists, and creators in the arts.

At any rate, historically our distribution has been so unequal that an approach toward equality, especially by raising the lower incomes, seems desirable.

INEQUALITY OF DISTRIBUTION HAS DIMINISHED

Inequality of income distribution is much less marked today than it was in 1929. The change has taken place not by reduction of the incomes at the top but by great increases of incomes at the bottom. In other words, the gains in real national income which have occurred have made possible larger real income for the many without taking it away from the few. Raising the lower incomes is generally held to be a desirable social objective.

The following figures are from Simon Kuznets' summary of income distribution by families. Note that the figures are of income *before direct taxes (income taxes)* and do not include governmental payments for relief and assistance. Therefore, tax or social legislation was not responsible

TABLE 25/2

Percent of families (excluding single individuals)	Percent of national income	
	1929	After World War II
Upper 5	31.0	20
Upper 20 (including upper 5)	55.0	44
Next 40	31.5	38
Lower 40	13.5	18

for the change. This legislation merely narrowed the inequality still further than the figures show.

If change toward equality should continue at the same rate for a few generations more, complete equality would be approximated. The chances are, however, that complete equality will never exist. It is not found today in any society. Even in the Soviet Union, which calls itself socialist and in which little productive property is owned by individuals, a considerable degree of income inequality prevails. Probably any society will reward exceptional ability and effort (or power) more than the average.

Even at the present level of distribution in the United States, however, a quintupling of average real family income—from $5,000 to $25,000— could wipe out poverty as it is known today. What has already occurred since 1929, in approach to equality, has been called by Arthur F. Burns, President of the National Bureau of Economic Research and one-time Chairman of the President's Council of Economic Advisers, a "social revolution"—occurring quietly, almost unnoticed, and without violent upheaval.

GROWING AND DECLINING INDUSTRIES

The fact that the whole economy is growing rapidly does not mean that all industries grow at the same rate, or indeed that there are not at any one time some industries that actually decline. From decade to decade the kinds of products most in demand change. When automobiles came in, carriages went out. Not all shifts of demand are so dramatic as this, however. At present, for example, although the steel industry is growing, industries producing lighter metals, such as aluminum, magnesium, and titanium, are growing more rapidly. Consumption of daily necessities—food and clothing—does not grow much more rapidly than the population, but industries providing things that people use in their spare time (many of which, like automobiles and radio, are classified as durable goods) have a tendency to grow more rapidly than the population. Among these, sales of recently developed articles, like TV sets, grow more rapidly than articles introduced earlier, like radios. Services grow more rapidly than goods of any kind.

Output per labor-capital unit grows faster in some industries than in others, too. It does grow, however, in virtually all industries, even in those in which total output is stationary or declining. For the nation as a whole, productivity grows more rapidly at some times than at others. Apparently it does not increase so much in war as in peace or so much in periods of depression as in periods of prosperity.

WHAT IS PROGRESS?

Producing more and more things for a larger and larger population has traditionally been regarded in the United States—indeed in the whole Western world—as progress. There is no doubt that more things are needed if the needy segments of the population are to be lifted out of want and poverty. But questions have often been raised about the values that determine consumers' wants above a moderate standard of life.

Are we persuaded by shrewd advertisers to desire many things that do not add real and permanent satisfaction to living? The long-term trend toward shorter hours of work gives evidence that many have felt they could make better use of much of their time than to spend it earning money with which to buy goods and services offered for sale.

The immensely enlarged free time of the population raises a new economic problem. Are people allocating their free time to the best advantage? In choosing how to use hours of leisure, they must make choices not measurable by dollars and cents. In this realm a wholly different scale of values from that of the market place is needed. Do we have a valid system of values for apportioning our free time? What is most worth while?

Are we making and elaborating so many goods so rapidly that we are exhausting the natural resources of the earth on which all life depends? What about our iron and other metals, our forests, our petroleum and coal? What about our water supply? Do growing cities occupy fertile soil only to build on it slums and crowded streets? Is speeding along superhighways a good substitute for a walk in unspoiled woods?

Rapidly advancing technology has brought possibilities of destruction along with its gains. Much of our recent advance has been devoted to instruments of war capable of wiping out whole populations. While we are engaged in stripping the earth of the resources on which life depends, are we in danger of wiping out life itself?

No sensible person would wish to forego the advance of knowledge and skills which has brought us so long a distance from primitive man. But we cannot take "progress" for granted. In justice to ourselves and our children, we should increasingly ask to what ends we are using the great powers of modern civilization.

THE FUTURE OF ECONOMIC GROWTH

The average annual increase of per capita real income, mentioned earlier, accumulates like compound interest on money in a savings bank. If the increase in income continues, it will mount up incredibly as time goes on. A graph picturing such growth looks something like this:

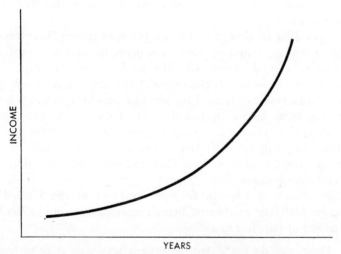

Fig. 25.1. AVERAGE ANNUAL INCREASE OF PER CAPITA REAL INCOME.

The curve rises slowly at first, but the fact that the starting quantity to which the percentage is added is each year larger than that of the year before leads to a continually increasing annual growth in absolute terms. Such a line is sometimes called an "exploding curve," since the farther it is continued from its starting point the more closely it approximates the vertical. It goes off into vertical space indefinitely without ever turning back. If taken to illustrate the growth of per capita real income, it signifies that everyone will come closer and closer to receiving an *infinite* amount of goods and services yearly as time passes, without ever quite reaching that goal.

Will the growth of income continue at the same rate as in the past? In fact, it has been somewhat more rapid since 1919 than before. There is no sign that the technological advance on which it mainly rests is slowing down; the contrary seems to be true. Nevertheless, few would really believe that in the course of time the average American can be richer than Croesus. One reason is that an end of the climb must appear sooner or later, at least on the planet Earth, because its resources of power and materials are not inexhaustible.

Before an overwhelming abundance of available goods and services is limited by approaching exhaustion of natural resources, however, another limiting factor is likely to take effect—the choices by human beings concerning how they wish to use their own limited amounts of time and energy. Already workers in the Western world have chosen to take a large part of the gains of higher productivity in shorter hours on the job, longer vacations, more time in school and college. Producers of goods offered for sale have to compete ever more sharply with the desire of individuals for more time of their own—more time to spend as they please—rather than to work for pay in order to be able to buy more of the goods and services which must be bought, if at all, with money. As incomes rise and possessions become easier to acquire, this trend is likely to be emphasized.

The spending of time, like the spending of money, involves a basic economic problem—how can scarce resources be best allocated for the satisfaction of wants? Time, like the land, labor, and capital which economists have classified as the essential elements of economic production, is a scarce resource indeed for any one person, no matter how long his life may seem before he has lived it. How people may choose to allocate their time among the many opportunities for spending it determines how they will fill their lives. The answers they make will affect not only the quality of their individual existences but also that of their society and their culture.

Before Abraham Lincoln became President of the United States, John Stuart Mill, the celebrated British economist, wrote in Book IV of his *Principles of Political Economy:*

> Those who do not accept the present very early stage of human improvement as the ultimate type may be excused for being comparatively indifferent to the kind of economical progress which excites the congratulations of ordinary politicians, the mere increase of production and accumulation.

Mill looked forward to a state where there could be a more nearly equal distribution of income and

> . . . a much larger body of persons than at present, not only exempt from the common toils, but with sufficient leisure, both physical and mental, from mechanical details, to cultivate freely the graces of life.

In such a "stationary state," Mill thought,

> There would be as much scope as ever for all kinds of mental culture, and more and more social progress; as much for improving the Art of Living, and much more likelihood of its being improved, when minds ceased to be engrossed by the art of getting on. Even the industrial arts might be as earnestly and as successfully cultivated, with the sole difference,

that instead of serving no purpose but the increase of wealth, industrial improvements would produce their legitimate effect, that of abridging labor.

See Chapters 28, 35, and 37.

QUESTIONS

Economic growth is commonly measured by percentage increase of real gross national product per capita of the population. As you have learned, GNP is an estimated sum of the value of all goods and services for which money is exchanged.

1. Does this aggregate throw much light on the question whether the population is increasing too rapidly for the welfare and comfort of the people or not rapidly enough to make the best possible use of a nation's resources or to provide military manpower for a possible war?

2. Can the percentage growth of the GNP of a highly developed industrial nation be usefully compared with the percentage growth of a less well-developed nation, in view of the fact that a small percentage of a large base may be absolutely much greater than a larger percentage of a small base?

3. Although a large percentage growth of GNP per capita may make it easier to approach equality in the distribution of income, does comparative growth of two nations actually throw much light on their progress toward this social goal?

4. Does the size of the GNP throw much light on the quality of the goods and services produced, as well as on the quantity? Is not quality fully as important to a civilization as quantity?

5. What light, if any, does the size of the GNP throw on the length of working hours in a nation and on the intelligence with which its citizens use their free time?

6. One cannot measure by GNP the amount or usefulness of work carried on by the worker or family for use rather than for sale. This includes work in the home by both women and men. Are comparisons of such activity among nations irrelevant to the success of their cultures?

7. How can one measure attainment of nonquantitative goals of the democratic tradition, like liberty and justice?

8. In view of considerations like the above, are we wise to emphasize a race for growth in GNP without giving equal prominence to other social goals?

26 / WHAT KIND OF ECONOMIC

SYSTEM? | What kind of economic system exists in

the United States? What kind is most desirable? The almost continual succession of crises in world affairs since the two world wars of the first half of the twentieth century and the rapidly growing power of the Communist bloc have stimulated the historic debate about these questions.

Much of the argument states the issues in grossly oversimplified terms, used by extremists on both sides. The doctrines of Russian Communism occupy one extreme. They picture the United States as a capitalist society, meaning by this term a regime in which the "means of production"—buildings, factories, machinery, and the like—are owned by rich men who exploit the workers to augment their own fortunes. This regime, it is argued, maintains wide and unjust inequality in distribution of income, is subject to frequent and increasingly severe industrial depressions and unemployment, and promotes war by imperialist expansion and exploitation of subject peoples. Such a regime is historically doomed to eventual collapse. The Communist system, on the contrary, is pictured as one which substitutes for the control of capitalists a "dictatorship of the proletariat" (temporarily exercised by a well-indoctrinated minority party in the interest of the workers), which is capable of stimulating more rapid economic growth than that of the decadent capitalist states, and will eventually produce material abundance and social justice for all.

The extremists on the other side accept the definition of their economy as a capitalist society—though they prefer to call it "free, competitive private enterprise." They argue that this economy, if left unhampered by "socialistic" measures or governmental interference, is more highly productive than any regime subject to central direction, and is certain to produce material abundance for all, plus the priceless good of individual freedom. The chief danger, these extremists argue, is "big government" with its interference with the operation of the market and price system, its bureaucratic inefficiency, and its invasion of the "natural rights" of the owners of private property. Governmental measures taken in the supposed interests of social welfare, these conservatives contend, are merely steps in the direction of Communist dictatorship.

In the meantime, the contest between the Communist bloc and the Western nations for the allegiance of uncommitted, underdeveloped peoples plays up the question whether one system or the other is better capable of stimulating rapid economic growth and the abolition of poverty and disease.

Both extremes of opinion present a crude caricature of the actual economy of the United States, not to speak of those of other modern industrial societies such as Great Britain and the highly developed nations of Western Europe. Chapter 16 has presented the facts of the growth of "big government" in this country and the important role it plays in the operation of the economy and the lives of the citizens. Government does, to be sure, leave important roles to be played by private enterprise, but as a result of the democratic process it has assumed many functions which private enterprise cannot exercise or cannot perform so well as public agencies. These functions have been delegated to government not because of any rigid social philosophy, such as Communism or Socialism, but as a result of pragmatic judgments of need in each case.

Through the years, the United States has become a regime not well described by the term "capitalism" in either the Communist or the conservative sense, but better termed a "mixed economy," or a "welfare state." The outcome has been, at least so far, a dramatic increase in real incomes, in leisure, in approach toward equality of income distribution, and in material security. Many problems remain to be solved, but in the end they are capable of solution by use of selective methods, depending both on private and on public enterprise, which have been used in the past.

REASONS FOR GROWTH OF GOVERNMENTAL FUNCTIONS

If expansion of governmental activities in the United States has not been the result of a general belief in socialism or any other political or economic dogma, what reasons may be assigned for it? One historical reason, often ignored in theoretical discussions of the subject, is that ever since the foundation of the nation, government has been regarded as an indispensable aid in promoting the development of the country.

When the Union was first formed, it fell heir to all the land not already privately owned or within the boundaries of the thirteen original states along the Atlantic seaboard. Methods by which this huge area should be disposed of in the public interest constituted the subject of long and bitter political controversy. Much of it was sold to private owners. By grants of land the federal government helped to support education and subsidized essential development of transportation, first by turnpike and canal, then by railroad.

Government explorers and surveyors (for example, the noted Lewis and Clark expedition) assessed the possibilities of new regions and laid out possible routes for roads and railroads. The Constitution vests control over interstate commerce in the federal government. Navigable waterways have always been subject to federal development and regulation. During Thomas Jefferson's administration, the Secretary of the Treasury, Albert Gallatin, suggested a nationwide plan for roads and canals to be federally built and owned—a plan which, more than a century ago, suggested the intracoastal waterway along the Atlantic and a St. Lawrence waterway. Routes for turnpikes projected in this plan now are traced by a number of the leading United States automobile highways. States built and operated many canals within their borders—for instance, the Erie Canal in New York.

The Constitution also gives control of the value and issuance of money to the federal government. This is the authority behind the Federal Reserve System. A prototype of that system was the Bank of the United States, proposed by Alexander Hamilton, Secretary of the Treasury in George Washington's cabinet. This bank was in part owned by the government, and the Secretary of the Treasury supervised it. Its notes circulated throughout the nation as paper currency.

Hamilton also, in a report to Congress, discussed the question of how manufacture could be encouraged, and suggested subsidies or protective tariffs for young industries. Later, when it became necessary to raise large sums of capital for railroads, the federal and state governments chartered private corporations for the purpose, granting them the right of eminent domain to acquire necessary land, and limited liability so that they could attract investors. The privilege of incorporation was later widely extended. The special government interest in chartered corporations eventually became a basis of regulation.

Financial crises and depressions from time to time stimulated more extensive use of governmental powers to aid the economy of the nation and protect those who suffered from distress. This was particularly true of the unusually severe depression of the 1930's.

Meanwhile another deep-seated influence began to be felt. As industry and transportation grew, cities grew. The populations of cities required services that had been needed less by farm dwellers—in many cases services that only the municipal governments could adequately provide. And as the industrial system grew, the number of wage earners increased, and their welfare gradually became a matter of public importance.

Statistics of employment and income reveal that as production per capita increases, a larger and larger percentage of productive effort and of consumption is allotted to services rather than to goods. Governments can provide many sorts of services that private enterprise cannot offer or cannot perform so well. A relative growth of governmental activity must be expected as the demand for services increases. It is in this area, rather than in the production of goods, that the main expansion of government in the United States has taken place.

War or the threat of war has, of course, necessitated immense and rapid extension of governmental control from time to time, but the increase in governmental services would undoubtedly have occurred even if there had been no wars.

INTERVENTION TO PRESERVE LAISSEZ FAIRE

One curious development of governmental intervention is caused by adherence to the doctrine of laissez faire (absence of governmental intervention) itself—the whole body of antimonopoly legislation described in Chapter 10. In this historic and varied activity, government has been exercising its police power to prevent monopolistic practices or to break up monopolies, on the theory that only competition can protect the consumer and serve the public welfare in areas where private enterprise prevails.

Still more paradoxical is the occasional effort of government to help small competitors to survive by allowing them to use monopolistically controlled prices as a defense against big concerns. The "fair-trade laws" passed by some states, with approval by Congress, are measures of this kind. To aid agriculture, government itself employs a favorite monopolistic device—holding goods off the market and attempting to restrict output in the interest of higher prices—in order to support prices of certain crops and so to aid competitive farmers.

Government regulation of prices charged by electrical and other public utilities has often proved to be clumsy, slow, and ineffectual. Moreover, the great political power of regulated industries has been revealed by investigations of their lobbying and public-relations campaigns. Such considerations have led many local governments to adopt public ownership of utility services.

In the case of the federal government, great public hydroelectric generating and transmission systems, like that of the Tennessee Valley Authority, have been advocated partly on the ground that they would provide a "yardstick" by which the reasonableness of rates charged by private utilities could be measured. The yardstick has actually been difficult to apply, because of controversy about the comparability of TVA costs with those in private systems.

In another way, however, TVA has had a large share in educating privately owned electrical utilities to an important economic truth that many of them apparently did not understand before. This is that the agencies which distribute electric power to consumers can make more money by selling enlarged quantities at lower rates than smaller quantities at high rates. The TVA limited the rates that could be charged by the private distributing companies which bought power from it, and thus enforced rate reductions to consumers. Since this practice went into effect, the private companies have been more prosperous than ever because of their greatly increased revenue from sales. Stated in terms of economic theory, this experience demonstrated (1) that the demand was highly elastic and (2) that the industry had never arrived at the point of increasing costs, or, in the common phrase, that it is a "decreasing-cost industry."

REGIONAL AND CITY PLANNING

There is nothing new about the idea that planning should be applied to the layout of towns or cities and to the land-use in and around them. The early settlers in New England designed their towns with a common or green in the center, around which the public buildings and churches were built, and apportioned the surrounding farm land to families of the community. Washington, D. C., was originally designed by Pierre L'Enfant, a French engineer and architect.

As towns and cities grew, however, it became apparent that in many cases the original plan was insufficient. Laissez faire could not be depended on for desirable results as the city expanded. Overcrowding, slums, transit difficulties, traffic congestion, and all the other plagues of urban life could not be held in check, not to say abolished, without more far-seeing planning and rigorous control. Zoning ordinances; regulation of the size and general design of buildings; construction of additional parks, playgrounds, and arterial highways; and finally public slum-clearing and housing projects were utilized. As a guide to development, many municipalities and states set up planning commissions to forecast future growth and to coordinate the numerous factors in a long-term program. Planning has had to be undertaken not merely for individual cities but for whole metropolitan regions as well. All these activities necessitated a mixture of public with private enterprise.

In a much larger region—the states of the Tennessee Valley—a coordinated and planned development was undertaken by the federally created Tennessee Valley Authority. It combines, as only a governmental agency could combine, flood control, reforestation, soil conservation, hydroelectric power, aids to better farming, and encouragement of industrial development. Its policy has been to cooperate in all respects with local communities and to rely chiefly on education rather than regulation. The income of the region has risen rapidly, and TVA has achieved an international reputation.

In this instance, as in many others, government has called into being an independent agency set up like a business corporation (though not for profit) and operating under broad directives, to seek objectives which would be difficult to achieve under an old-fashioned governmental bureau with its limited field of authority and its centralized control.

The problems which city and regional planning were devised to meet have not been banished; on the contrary these problems are becoming more grave. Expansion of means of dealing with them in a coordinated fashion has been slow. There is every indication that if large metropolitan regions are not to strangle themselves, effective planning must play a stronger role than in the past.

OVER-ALL FISCAL PLANNING

We have seen how the Federal Reserve System can exercise influence over the quantity of money so that there may be neither too much money nor too little. The law directs the Federal Reserve authorities to exercise this power in the public interest—that is, without regard to the volume of profits made by the Federal Reserve banks or the member banks. Thus, as a result of long and bitter experience, the nation has deliberately limited laissez faire. Only within conditions controlled by Federal Reserve monetary policy can private enterprise play its role of competitive profit seeking in the nation's money markets. The principle of central control in monetary policy is almost universally approved not only by contemporary economic theorists but also by bankers, businessmen, political leaders, and the informed public, though there are controversies over the application of the principle in specific cases.

As we have also seen, however, the banking authorities cannot do the job alone. When there is a serious depression and extensive unemployment, the Federal Reserve authorities may create ample reserves in the member banks, but they cannot force the money into circulation if business is reluctant to borrow or banks or reluctant to lend. In that case the spending power of the public—and so its income—can be replenished only if government borrows and spends money available from the banks.

The same principles apply to control of the money supply and its use in periods threatened by inflation. A government surplus means that government is restricting public purchasing power. It is important, therefore, that governmental fiscal policy operate to reinforce rather than to undermine Federal Reserve monetary policy.

For control of governmental spending the President bears the initial responsibility, for he must submit to Congress near the beginning of every year a budget, estimating expenditures and revenue and consequently planning for either a surplus or a deficit. The Secretary of the Treasury has an important role in recommending taxation policy.

Congress, according to the Constitution, has the sole right to appropriate money for federal governmental agencies, and the sole right to vote taxation measures for paying the bills. The question whether the federal government has a deficit or a surplus is therefore ultimately decided by Congress. The budget message is only a means of making sure that the legislators have the best possible information and know the wishes of the President, as a basis for decision.

Congress may—and frequently does—fail to carry out the President's recommendations. The process of appropriating money and legislating tax measures, moreover, is slow, cumbersome, and subject to influence by special interests. Although Congress gets the budget message in January, it frequently does not pass all the necessary appropriation before the new fiscal year starts on July 1. Deliberate governmental fiscal policy is therefore not a sensitive or reliable method of bringing governmental influence to bear on short-run instability in the national economy.

The existence of a large national debt as a result of governmental borrowing for war complicates the fiscal task of the government. The Secretary of the Treasury is not responsible for the existence of the public debt, since that arises from the decisions of Congress; but he is responsible for the form which the debt takes, since he has power to make decisions about the nature of the securities issued. This involves highly technical problems, wise solution of which is important in the public interest.

For example, short-term securities as a rule bear lower rates than those of longer term. This means that if a large part of the debt is financed by short-term issues, the interest burden on the Treasury is lighter than it otherwise would be—an advantage to the taxpayers.

There are, however, countervailing disadvantages. Short-term issues need continual refinancing because they mature frequently. This is the type of government security in which commercial banks mainly invest and which business concerns often use for temporarily idle cash balances. Banks may, by selling government securities or cashing the securities when they mature, add to their reserves without seeking aid from the federal reserve banks. Business concerns can replenish their cash at frequent intervals by the same process. Thus short-term government securities are almost the same as money, and the public debt may be "monetized" almost at the will of the holders insofar as it consists in those securities.

Monetary and fiscal policies have long been recognized as a paramount public concern. In recent years they have become regarded almost universally as a necessary avenue of governmental influence on the total economy. They do, in fact, exert an influence, for better or for worse, whether they are deliberately planned to do so or not.

OVER-ALL PLANNING OF ECONOMIC POLICY

There remains the nongovernmental or private sector of the economy, which as a whole is much greater than the public sector. What consumers spend and what they save, how much business enterprises invest, and the timing of changes in these streams of investment and saving, are even more influential on the condition of the economy in times of peace than governmental monetary and fiscal policy. The activities of organized labor, of farmers, and of other aggregations of producers are important. International trade is greatly influenced by the activities of importers and exporters, of foreign investors. The interplay of prices and costs in many types of markets affects the economic condition of the country.

Virtually every activity of government has a bearing of some sort on economic decisions made by consumers, business concerns, labor, and agriculture. This influence is clearest in such matters as governmental purchases from private contractors, types of taxation, regulations over and taxes on foreign trade, aids to agriculture, and regulation of public utilities. Each of these government activities has been undertaken for some specific purpose or other, but they all add up to an effect of some kind on economic growth, allocation of resources, regional problems, and cyclical variations of production and employment. Yet until recent years, governmental responsibility for coordinating its policies in pursuit of general objectives and for stating those objectives has never been recognized. The government was still supposed to be carrying on its affairs in an isolated compartment, while it remained "neutral" about most private activities, assuming no economic responsibility in regard to them.

After World War II Congress, by passing what is usually called the "Employment Act of 1946," enacted a basic statute which for the first time dispelled this fiction. This law contains the following statement of policy:

> The Congress hereby declares that it is the continuing policy and responsibility of the Federal Government . . . with the assistance and co-operation of industry, agriculture, labor, and state and local governments, to coordinate and utilize all its plans, functions, and resources for the purpose of creating and maintaining . . . conditions under which there will be afforded useful employment opportunities, including self-employment, to those able, willing and seeking to work, and to promote maximum employment, production and purchasing power.

The omitted passages (designated by the three dots) are qualifications which do not negate the broad statement. The means used by government must be "practicable," as well as "consistent with its needs and obligations and other essential considerations of national policy." The purpose must be carried out "in a manner calculated to promote and foster free competitive enterprise and the general welfare."

Such a declaration, though a landmark in American thinking about the functions of government, would lack practical consequence without arrangements for carrying it into effect. These are provided in the law, as far as is possible under a democratic, constitutional government.

The act creates a Council of Economic Advisers, responsible to the President. The council consists of three persons, one of whom acts as chairman. The members are supposed to be competent economists, not political appointees. They form part of the Executive Office of the President. The Council is provided with its own staff and has available the immense informational resources of the various federal departments and bureaus which collect statistics.

The President is directed by the Act to submit to Congress every January an Economic Report, assessing the existing state of the national economy in respect to the declared aims of the law, and stating what measures are required to achieve these aims. In preparing this Report, he is aided by the Council of Economic Advisers. It is one of the three chief annual Presidential messages—the first being the traditional Message on the State of the Nation; the second, the Budget Message; and the third, the Economic Report.

The Employment Act also creates a Congressional Joint Committee (of the House of Representatives and the Senate) on the Economic Report. This committee studies the report, holds hearings to which expert witnesses may be called, informs the two Houses of Congress of its attitude on the proposals by the President, and sponsors legislation to put into effect any that it favors. The Committee has its own expert staff, keeps tab on the national economy throughout the year, and issues its own comments on economic developments. This activity of Congress not only assures close attention to the President's report but also greatly aids the education of the national legislators on economic matters.

The President's Report is available as a public document at a moderate price to anyone who wants it, and has a wide circulation. It frequently makes recommendations not only for governmental policy but also for private action. In the few years of its existence the Report has contributed greatly to understanding of national economic problems. It is not to be expected that everyone will agree with it on all points, but in any case it constitutes a coherent view of the national economy, about which specific measures may be coordinated, and helps discussion of such measures not as separate projects which may be mutually inconsistent, but as parts of a larger whole.

Fifteen years after the adoption of this new approach, no serious upsets had threatened the economy, and growth of its capacity and its output had been rapid. Whether such good fortune will continue nobody can predict with certainty, but it looks as if we should be able to foresee and avoid better than in the 1920's a climb to speculative inflation or a major crash following such a boom. The best-informed experts, however, know that there is much still to be learned about the behavior of the modern economy.

WHO CONTROLS GOVERNMENT?

The Marxist doctrine, followed by Communist party theorists, holds that in a society characterized by capitalism, the owners of capital—that is, of the means of production—control the government and use it for their own purposes. Therefore, they contend, it is beside the point to speak of governmental intervention in a private enterprise system as if it were motivated by a desire to serve the welfare of "the masses." There can be no doubt that in the United States business and financial interests have been powerful, but even the most superficial knowledge of the history of this nation shows clearly that these interests have frequently been divided among themselves and have not always had their way.

This is not the place for an analysis of the complexities included under the convenient phrase "democratic process," but any responsible study of modern political science indicates that the government of the nation represents a shifting balance of power which no ruling class wholly dominates, at least for very long.

Our political order is characterized by numerous "pressure groups" seeking particular ends, such as wage earners, farmers, small-business men, large corporations, underprivileged races, retired persons, and so on indefinitely. Any political candidate, to be elected, has to put together a constituency of enough of such interests in his district to attract a majority. If he does not also convince a considerable number of voters that what he advocates is in the general interest of all, his position may be vulnerable. In such a situation, impartial researchers who can discover the facts and put them in order often furnish the materials for popular discussion. Ideas and programs are sometimes at a premium. Leaders of thought may influence the policies of political leaders and often have done so. Similar observations hold true of highly developed "capitalist" nations in Western Europe. It is forces such as these which have transformed the primitive capitalism existing when Marx wrote into the modern welfare state or mixed economy. This, of course, is not the final stage of our society; because of its teeming vitality it is certain to undergo further development.

Those in our society who fondly look backward and strive to restore a primitive type of private enterprise often fear not only what they regard as a drift toward a governmentally dictated economy which curbs individual freedom and enterprise, but also bureaucratic inefficiency, clumsiness, and occasional corruption which they believe must characterize "big government." The dangers of overcentralization and inflexibility are no mirage, but they occur in big business, big labor, and big private organizations of other kinds, such as those in medicine and education, as well as in government. The remedy does not lie in a futile effort to return to earlier centuries and tear our economic and social structures to pieces, but rather in a combination of eternal vigilance and a technique of management which develops both centralization and decentralization as complements of each other. Central direction should be used only for those important functions which must be centrally exercised if they are to be exercised at all, and it should allow plenty of room for individual variation and local initiative in making judgments according to circumstances.

BASIC POLICY QUESTIONS

As this book is written, two basic policy questions of concern to the nation as a whole have assumed such prominence that they have become leading issues in a presidential campaign. This development is logical,

since both involve invoking central action in which government must
play a leading role if effective action is to be taken.

The first question concerns the rate of economic growth. Many contend that the rise of national product or income should be more rapid
than it has been lately, for the following reasons:

The Soviet Union has recently had a more rapid economic growth
than the United States. If this continues, the time may come when
Russia succeeds in its long-proclaimed resolution to "catch up with and
surpass" the United States, now and for many previous years the leading
and most productive economy in the world. Such a development might
embarrass the United States in the struggle for power between Communism and Democracy. Already some underdeveloped nations are
swinging to the Communist bloc because they believe its methods offer a
swifter advance to abundance.

It is also argued that for purely internal reasons more national income is necessary to provide employment and a decent life for our
rapidly growing population. There are dozens of unfinished tasks to be
done at home, such as urban renewal, more and better education, better
social services, conservation of natural resources, encouragement of the
fine arts, a better solution of the transportation problem—all this without
skimping an immensely expensive defense and foreign-aid program.

The second issue is closely related to the first—the question whether
we are making the best possible allocation of our resources by creating
an affluence in consumer goods, many of them of dubious basic value,
while we let more important needs be starved.

It is argued by some that such goals, desirable as they are, should be
sought mainly through private enterprise and voluntary action rather
than through more governmental intervention. But a national will to
solve them cannot find adequate expression without governmental action
of some sort or other, even though the main reliance for action were
placed on private enterprise.

Take, for example, the basic aim of rapid growth. Stimulation of
growth depends in large degree on raising the ratio of savings and
investment to spending and consumption. A change in this ratio does
not seem likely to occur spontaneously in a system dominated by private
enterprise and free markets. Either government must achieve it through
more activity of its own (financed by taxing at the expense of consumption), or it must stimulate private investment by revision of income and
profits taxes, use of its influence on interest rates, or other measures affecting the private economy. These two approaches are not mutually exclusive; both might be used in combination.

The same logic applies to allocation of resources. In every market
system using money, the way money is spent largely determines allocation. Consumers cannot buy in supermarkets many of the goods and
services to which, it is argued, a larger proportion of resources should be
devoted. They cannot buy in this way intercontinental ballistic missiles,
universities and colleges, scientific laboratories, aid to underdeveloped

nations, even efficient health services (without the aid of some nonprofit cooperative). To gain such ends, consumers must rely largely on their influence on government, insofar as private philanthropy does not suffice.

Such dogmas as that everything must be done by central direction or that everything must be done by private or voluntary activities are, and long have been, useless as guides to intelligent action. The relevant questions are: What is most needed? What sort of organization can best supply it? There are, and probably long will continue to be, important roles both for private enterprise and for public activity.

The chief danger of a system dominated by private enterprise is that it will fail to visualize clearly or to attain the most important goals; the chief danger of a system dominated by central direction is that it will deny to individuals freedoms of choice that they should have the right to exercise. The great task of democracy is to maintain an ever-changing and viable adjustment among the available instrumentalities for seeking common ends.

QUESTIONS

1. In a mixed economy, what criteria would you use as a basis for the decision whether any given industry or service should be owned and managed by one of the following:
   (a) Private persons
   (b) A government agency
   (c) A cooperative society of consumers or producers

2. In numerous foreign nations, none of them under Communist domination and all containing many important industries privately owned and operated, one or more of the following are publicly or cooperatively owned. Would you favor the transfer of ownership to public or cooperative agencies in the United States of any of these?
   (a) Railroads
   (b) Telephone and telegraph systems
   (c) Subsoil resources such as coal, oil, and minerals
   (d) Airlines
   (e) Long-distance road transport
   (f) Electric-power generation and distribution
   (g) The central bank
   (h) Radio and television broadcasting

3. A number of nations, which are not regarded as Socialist or Communist, have far more comprehensive systems of social insurance than that in the United States, often subsidized out of general tax revenues. These usually include complete coverage of all medical expenses, hospitalization, physicians and surgeons, medications, optical and dental services, and necessary apparatus such as eyeglasses and artificial limbs. Would you favor such a system in this country?

PART III / CASE STUDIES

Analysis of contemporary documents which discuss problems and policies can with great benefit occupy part of a beginning course in economics. In such study much that is learned earlier can be applied; use of knowledge is an excellent method of bringing it to life and fixing it in memory. The teacher will find plenty of good new material suitable for reading and class discussion, such as the annual Economic Report of the President, the Economic Survey of the United Kingdom, the annual reports of international or governmental financial and commercial institutions, leading articles in the *Federal Reserve Bulletin* or the *Monthly Labor Review,* publications by private research or publicity organizations. In many cases the simpler of such documents may be utilized as the basis of oral reports by students while the more systematic parts of a text are still being studied.

The following case studies constitute a few illustrations of how such material may be treated and, as such, may be of use to both teacher and student.

27 / ISSUES IN COLLECTIVE BARGAINING AND LABOR'S USE OF FINANCIAL STATEMENTS /

In Chapter 1 we took a brief look at a balance sheet and income statement of a business firm. The main purpose was to understand one of the methods of measurement which are basic in recording the performance of the nation's economic activity, as in national income accounting. But analysis of business financial statements may also be put to various other uzes, which are enlightening to students of the national economy. For example, the operating records of companies are frequently cited in collective bargaining between union and management.

THE UNIONS' CONCERN WITH PROFITS

The AFL-CIO publishes a monthly *Collective Bargaining Report,* prepared by its Department of Research. In March of 1958 the subject of this report was "Financial Information in Collective Bargaining." Following are some of the main points emphasized in this document:

"In most negotiations," writes the author of the report, "profits end up as a comparatively minor factor." The main considerations are such subjects as "the amount of wage increase needed to make up for an increase in the cost of living, productivity advances, the need for improvement of living standards, the need for correction of wage inequities." Yet it may be easier to obtain an increase demanded on these grounds if the company is doing well financially than if it is in difficulties. In preparing for wage negotiations, most unions check as carefully as possible the financial statements of the employers.

Neither management nor labor will admit that there is any close relationship between the proper rate of wages and the rate of profits. Yet one side or the other is likely to introduce the subject into bargain-

325

ing discussions—labor when profits are ample and the employer seems well able to afford what is requested, and management when profits are low or absent and the company representatives argue that it cannot afford to pay what is asked. In the first instance, according to the AFL-CIO report, "Management usually replies that it is not arguing inability to pay and that its profits are irrelevant." In the latter case, management may argue "that general business conditions and a slackening in its profit rate require restriction of wage increases" or "that the costs of a wage increase might threaten its solvency."

When management contends that large profits are irrelevant to the wage issue, unions may reply, in the words of this report, that "workers should share in their employers' well-being" on purely social grounds. Also, "the economy needs balanced growth . . . . If profits are built up while wages—the main source of consumer buying power—are allowed to lag behind, an imbalance is developed, with the lag in consumer buying power having a depressing effect on the economy."

When the management refers to its poor financial condition as a reason for "inability to pay," several replies may be made by union negotiators.

If the decline in profitable operations seems to be due to a temporary business recession, the union may argue that:

1. "Widely spread and substantial union-negotiated wage increases can, by bolstering buying power, help generate a marked upturn in business activity."

2. If the employer's continued existence is not actually threatened by temporarily reduced earnings, a wage raise may "be taken in stride over the long run."

3. If a business upturn appears likely, "a downturn in past months does not, of course, limit a company's ability to pay higher wages in future months of improved business."

If the employer can prove that his business is in such bad condition that the wage raise demanded would endanger his solvency, the union may take one of the following positions:

1. It may accept a smaller increase than it thinks due, on the ground "that there is no practical alternative and that such action is required to keep the company going and maintain jobs for their members."

2. The union may decide that it is not "a responsibility of workers to subsidize a company by accepting wages which lag far behind those being paid elsewhere." This might be the case if the company's problem cannot be solved by restricting wages, but requires an improvement in efficiency or business practices such as "new machinery, a change in management, a revised product line, new marketing methods, or some other specific change."

If the union takes the last of these positions and the management cannot improve its position, "that may mean the loss of some poorly paying jobs. But even though any job loss is serious, this may be only a temporary blow, for the bulk of the workers involved very likely will then gradually improve their position as they gain better paying jobs elsewhere." But, "considering the number of claims of inability to pay, amazingly few companies actually end up going broke merely because of a wage raise. For the fact is that, when actually forced to adjust to reasonably higher wages, management has normally managed to do it."

Managements often make adjustments, moreover, with the help of the unions. "While unions basically have not sought to assume managerial responsibility they often have offered aid to accomplish needed changes in production and/or distribution practices." Unions frequently help "in seeking and eliminating waste" and in developing "more efficient methods."

Three Debatable Questions.   Three important questions, on which considerable disagreement may arise, are suggested by the preceding advice to union bargainers.

1. Is it necessarily true that if profits rise faster than wages, an "economic unbalance" must follow because of a lag in consumer buying?

Let us illuminate some aspects of this question by an imaginary conversation between the management negotiator, whom we shall call M, and the union negotiator, whom we shall call U. Occasionally the argument is interrupted by E, an economist.

M. Don't profits belong to the stockholders? And aren't stockholders consumers?

U. Yes, but the big stockholders don't use as much of their incomes to buy consumers' goods and services as do wage earners. The stockholders invest more money, or the company does it for them out of undistributed profits, and so finance new productive facilities. Then you will be increasing output of what consumers are supposed to buy faster than you are increasing the amount of money they can spend to buy them. That will bring a slump, with unemployment.

M. What happens to the invested money? Isn't it spent for buildings and machinery made by wage earners? And doesn't that increase employment and wage payments?

U. Let's test your argument by carrying it to a logical extreme. Suppose management kept on indefinitely increasing profits without increasing wages, and suppose this occurred also in the construction and machinery-making industries. You would eventually arrive at a point when the whole labor force would be employed full time. You could not further enlarge the total of wage payments by hiring more workers. And you would not be increasing that total by wage boosts. Consumer buying power would be limited, while you were making more and more things for consumers to buy. No matter how high dividends might be, there are not enough stockholders to make up the difference. You would find yourselves with excess capacity; you would have to stop investing in new production; and there would be a slump. There must be a point where there is a correct balance between growing consumption and growing output, and hence between wages and profits.

E. Let me, as a neutral observer, make one point here for the record. Over the long run, in the United States at least, wage-earners' purchasing power *has* increased at least as fast as the production of consumer goods. Our market system seems to attend to that in a rough sort of way, whether money wages rise or not. There have been relatively long periods when an increase in consumer buying power has occurred mainly because of a falling level of the prices consumers have to pay. Lately it has occurred because wages have risen faster than prices. What we have to worry about is not so much this balance as the shorter cycles of boom and depression, with which *uneven growth* of investment has much to do.

M. Do you mean to imply that every increase in profits should be accompanied by an equal increase in wages? In that case wouldn't it be necessary to decrease wages by an equal amount when profits fall?

E. No, I don't. We all know that from year to year profits rise or fall much more rapidly than wages, and that labor could not get along with any such uncertainty about its income as most business concerns must expect.

U. Don't you think that we should have more stability in the economy if the amount of new investment jumped up and down less rapidly than it does, and grew more regularly?

E. I do, indeed. But I don't think the short-term fluctuations of new investment can be corrected by wage policy. Let me propose a general policy to which all three of us might agree, at least in principle. The real incomes or purchasing power of wage earners should be increased over the long term as fast as the real output of consumer goods and services. In addition, it is up to business, with the aid of government and the financial and the monetary authorities, to try to minimize "imbalances" by a more regular growth of investment. As long as growth is reasonably regular, it can occur as fast as you like without becoming "unbalanced," provided business is willing to let prices fall when more can be produced for consumers than consumers can buy with the money they earn.

2. The AFL-CIO report states that during an economic recession, when the employer is in difficulty, "widely spread . . . wage increases can, by bolstering buying power, help generate a marked upturn in economic activity." What might our trio of debaters say about that?

M. During a slump, the business has had to lay off workers and go on short time because it cannot sell enough to keep up production. If, in addition, it had to raise wages, it would just get deeper into the red. No business can afford to increase its costs when it cannot even sell enough goods at the prevailing prices to come out even. To increase wages at such a time would mean that it would have to lay off more people or perhaps close down altogether. Decreased employment would cut wage earnings more than higher wage rates could increase them.

U. You know as well as I do that the great majority of American business firms make profits during relatively mild depressions. They just make *smaller* profits. If wages were raised for all competitors at once, it wouldn't alter their competitive position. They would still go on producing as much as they could sell.

M. What about those which were operating at such a narrow margin that they would have to sell at a loss if wage rates were increased? You can't go on losing money, just to keep people at work.

U. They might lose less by selling all they could than by cutting output or closing up. They'd soon benefit by the demand created by wage-earners' increased incomes. Anything that increases demand in a recession helps to bring a recovery.

M. What does the Economist have to say about this proposition?

E. Well, it is true that firms sometimes *lose less* by continuing operations than by shutting down, even if they can't make a profit. That is because they have to pay their fixed costs—often called "overhead"— even if they don't produce anything. As long as they can cover their direct costs for such things as labor and materials, any margin above that figure helps to meet fixed costs. But the union would certainly be gambling if its own action put many firms in such a position. The longer a firm operates at a loss, the more it uses up its liquid assets and the shakier it becomes.

U. Well, what would you recommend?

E. As far as the union is concerned, I'd say that, as labor has learned by experience, it's a lot harder to get an increase when there are many unemployed workers than when job seekers are scarce. The employer would suffer less from a strike at such a time than normally. Perhaps the best way to improve the position of the workers in the long run would be to help the employer improve his efficiency when business is bad. Everybody would benefit from that. A study by the National Bureau of Economic Research shows that, on the average, productivity advances most rapidly near the bottom of a recession. It's a good time to cut costs without cutting wages.

3. In the case of an employer who is in special difficulty, not shared by competitors, the report suggests that it is not the "responsibility of workers to subsidize a company by accepting wages which lag far behind those being paid elsewhere." Even if such a company goes out of business, with consequent loss of jobs, labor may benefit in the long run. Is this true, and if it is true, will the total economy as well as labor benefit from the failure of this firm?

As the report points out, the inability of some employers to pay a generally accepted rate of wages stems from inefficiency, poor production practices, bad management, or need to change the nature of its product. The union may try to help the company to become more efficient. But, unless such defects can be remedied, the business is not doing well by its customers and its owners, and it is not likely to be saved very long merely by paying substandard wages. If the company went out of business, the employees could probably find better jobs, and society would not suffer the waste of resources in an inefficient operation.

One economic theory holds that, in a purely competitive market, the price paid all the producers of an identical product will tend to equal, at a given level of demand, the price which must be charged by the producer with the highest cost who can just manage to stay in business. In so far as this theory applies, the elimination of higher cost producers as a result of their being required to pay standard wages would benefit the workers immediately concerned; and consumers would not have to pay higher prices, provided the remaining firms increased output.

INTERPRETING FINANCIAL STATEMENTS

The AFL-CIO report points out that financial statements often do not contain the data that would be most useful for collective bargaining. Especially in the case of closely owned companies which are not obliged by law to make a "full disclosure" of their affairs, financial statements sometimes distort the situation by revealing only the figures that seem likely to support the employers' case. Furthermore, a record of the past is not always a good indication of what a company can do in the future. It is necessary to examine financial statements with great caution.

Suppose, for example, a company wishes to make its profits appear as small as possible. The federal tax authorities are on guard against some devices which do so, but there is no requirement that a business concern show to anyone else a statement which would be acceptable to the tax authorities.

Any item which can be entered on the income statement as an expense is deducted from gross income before net income can be shown. Here are some of the ways by which such subtractions decrease the profit figure.

Depreciation. If the company habitually buys a good deal of new plant and equipment, it can increase its annual charge for depreciation by assuming that the new equipment will rapidly become worn out or obsolete. If, for example, the company assumes that new machinery must be replaced in three years, it will probably deduct one third of the cost of each new purchase every year for three years. This will reduce profits more than if it assumes the machines are good for five years, and so deducts one fifth of the cost every year.

Reserves. The company may set up reserves against various possible contingencies. Deductions for such funds result in a smaller total of stated profits, though the company has received the money and is holding it.

A large expense for development of a new product or special advertising campaign may be charged up in one year, although the benefits will be felt in the future. This will decrease profits in the year in question but help to increase them in the future.

Close Corporation. A company owned by a family or a small number of partners may pay its owners high salaries and bonuses, allow them large expense accounts, or put on the payroll family members who do little or no work. All such devices will reduce recorded profits, although they are, in essence, a substitute for paying larger dividends.

Subsidiary Companies. A business may have a fully owned subsidiary company which is not expected to make profits, since its function is to serve the parent company. Employees of this subsidiary company might be shown a statement which indicated little or no profits, although the profits were actually being drawn into the parent company, whose statement they do not see.

Measurement of Profits. There are various ways of measuring profits. Union negotiators may have to show that one way is more relevant to a wage-increase demand than the others.

For example, a management representative may use a figure of profits *after* the payment of income taxes is deducted. The remaining figure is, of course, what is available for distribution in dividends or for "plowing back into the business." But, asserts the AFL-CIO report, a wage increase unaccompanied by offsetting economies would affect not this figure but profits *before* income taxes were deducted. If profits before taxes had been reduced by a wage increase, income taxes would have been lower also. Much of a wage increase might be absorbed by lower tax payments. For example, if profits before taxes were reduced by a wage increase to the extent of $10,000, profits *after* taxes would be reduced by only about $4,500.

The significance of profits of a certain number of dollars will naturally depend on the number of dollars the owners have invested in the business. The proper figure with which to compare profits in order to find the *percentage* of return is the "net worth," or "stockholders equity." This figure, the report states, "allows comparison of profitability from one company or industry to another, or from one year to another." Net worth consists of the figure on the balance sheet showing the value assigned to all the shares of stock outstanding, plus the surplus accumulated out of past profits (and "capital surplus," if any) which has been invested.

Sometimes management representatives point out that the percentage of the sales dollar which goes to profits seems relatively small. But this is not a good measure of profitability, since with a large volume of sales a small percentage of each dollar's worth of sales may add up to a big return on the investment. Industries and companies vary widely in this respect according to the nature of the business. The highly profitable food industries, for example, get along with a low profit per dollar of sales, because of the rapid turnover of the goods they buy and sell. A company engaged in building bridges, on the contrary, would require a much larger percentage of the price paid for a bridge in order to obtain a reasonable return on its net worth, because bridges take a long time to build.

FINANCIAL DATA USED BY UNIONS—TWO EXAMPLES

1. General Motors. Table 27/1 is reproduced from data prepared by the United Auto Workers for use by its representatives. The data in the table were compiled from the published annual reports issued by

TABLE 27/1

GENERAL MOTORS CORPORATION
SALES, PROFITS, EMPLOYMENT AND PAYROLL

	1947	1948	1949	
Sales (million)	$3,815	$4,702	$5,701	$
Profit Before Taxes (million)	$ 554	$ 802	$1,125	$
Profit After Taxes (million)	$ 288	$ 441	$ 657	$
Company's Net Worth at Beginning of Year (million)	$1,428	$1,571	$1,800	$
Profit Before Taxes as Percent of Sales	14.5%	17.1%	19.7%	24
Profit After Taxes as Percent of Sales	7.5%	9.4%	11.5%	1
Profit Before Taxes as Percent of Net Worth	38.8%	51.1%	62.5%	86
Profit After Taxes as Percent of Net Worth	20.2%	28.1%	36.5%	39
Average Number of Hourly Rated and Salaried Employees	375,689	380,329	401,326	465
Average Number of Hourly Rated Employees in U.S.	268,479	269,056	286,525	336
Average Hourly Earnings of Hourly-Rated Employees in U.S.	$ 1.51	$ 1.65	$ 1.73	$
Average Weekly Hours Worked by U.S. Employees	38.3	38.9	39.5	
Payroll for All Employees (million)	$1,155	$1,284	$1,441	$1
Payroll for Hourly-Rated Employees in U.S. (million)	$ 808	$ 897	$1,019	$1
Payroll for All Employees as Percent of Sales	30.3%	27.3%	25.3%	24
Number of Vehicles Sold, World-wide (thousands)	1,992	2,221	2,896	3
Number of Vehicles Sold from U.S. Plants (thousands)	1,846	2,052	2,673	3

Note: Beginning with 1954 the company's financial statements include the operations of all U.S. and foreign subsidiaries engaged in manufacturing operations. Prior to 1954 the operations of the English and German manufacturing subsidiaries were not included.

General Motors to its stockholders. Since General Motors stock is publicly offered for sale, its financial statements must abide by the accounting standards set up by the U. S. Securities and Exchange Commission.

Among the interesting facts revealed by these figures are the following, which might be of use to union negotiators:

TABLE 27/1—Continued

51	1952	1953	1954	1955	1956	1957	1958
465	$7,549	$10,028	$9,824	$12,443	$10,796	$10,990	$9,522
189	$1,502	$ 1,653	$1,645	$ 2,543	$ 1,741	$ 1,649	$1,115
506	$ 559	$ 598	$ 806	$ 1,189	$ 847	$ 844	$ 634
387	$2,530	$ 2,727	$2,983	$ 3,339	$ 4,255	$ 4,582	$4,905
9%	19.9%	16.5%	16.7%	20.4%	16.1%	15.0%	11.7%
3%	7.4%	6.0%	8.2%	9.6%	7.8%	7.7%	6.7%
4%	59.4%	60.6%	55.1%	76.2%	40.9%	36.0%	22.7%
2%	22.1%	21.9%	27.0%	35.6%	19.9%	18.4%	12.9%
197	458,680	585,602	576,667	624,011	599,234	588,160	520,925
418	308,455	385,929	367,462	410,022	371,296	350,398	281,732
.96	$ 2.11	$ 2.20	$ 2.26	$ 2.41	$ 2.48	$ 2.64	$ 2.82
8.9	40.4	41.9	40.4	42.5	39.0	38.6	38.1
368	$2,021	$ 2,676	$2,610	$ 3,127	$ 2,896	$ 2,955	$2,688
293	$1,367	$ 1,852	$1,747	$ 2,183	$ 1,866	$ 1,855	$1,573
0%	26.8%	26.7%	26.6%	25.1%	26.8%	26.9%	28.2%
197	2,629	3,760	3,800	5,031	4,091	3,885	3,310
329	2,234	3,277	3,296	4,477	3,508	3,237	2,526

Source: Corporation's Annual Reports to Stockholders. Prepared by U. A. W.

The largest dollar volume of sales (before 1959, which is not contained in the table) was in 1955, when the industry experienced a temporary boom. The slump of 1957–1958 is clearly revealed. Yet the net worth of the corporation kept right on growing (largely by reinvestment of profits). At the beginning of 1955 the company's net worth was $3,339 million; at the beginning of 1958 it had become $4,905 million. Profits in the depressed year of 1958 amounted to the not inconsiderable sum of $634 million, which yielded, before income taxes, 22.7 percent on the net worth, and after income taxes, 12.9 percent.

The company could argue that this return was smaller than that to which it had become accustomed since World War II; profits on net worth (before taxes) had been as high as 86.6 percent in 1950 and 76.2 percent in 1955. Yet the corporation could hardly contend that it was being impoverished, even in a year of recession (felt with special severity in the automobile industry).

To make 22.7 percent on net worth when sales had dropped from the 1955 peak output of 5,031,000 vehicles to 3,310,000, was an indication of great strength, especially since the corporation has large fixed costs, which have to be paid even at a low level of output. Fixed costs are high because of its heavy investment in plant and equipment and its large administrative staff. It should be noted in this connection that the total of wages paid in 1958 to all its employees was 28.2 percent of its sales revenue, only a slightly larger percentage than in previous years.

The average hourly earnings of General Motors' hourly rated employees in the United States—constituting most of the production labor force—rose from $1.51 in 1947 to $2.82 in 1958, or nearly 80 percent. During this period the consumer price index rose by about 30 percent.

A rise of 30 percent in hourly wages would therefore have been necessary to keep the same purchasing power of an hour's wages as existed a decade before. This would have brought the hourly wage to about $1.96 in 1958. The additional 86 cents constitutes an increase of about 44 percent in real wages per hour.

Did the rise in wages necessitate the rise in prices of automobiles to the consumer?

This question is almost impossible to answer, because the 1958 cars were very different products from the 1947 cars. They were larger, heavier, and contained many features not found in the cars of the previous decade. Much of the extra cost was due to more materials, and the materials cost more per ton as the general price level rose. Yet it is possible to infer that, because of increased productivity, even the big 1958 cars could have been sold *at lower prices* than the 1947 cars, as far as labor costs were concerned, if wages had not increased. A rough calculation indicates that the output of vehicles produced per man-hour increased about 30 percent from 1947 to 1958.

Since this must, in any case, be a rough calculation, it may be carried out in round numbers. Average weekly hours were not very different in the two years; therefore it may be assumed that output per employee is as good a measure as output per man-hour. Here is the calculation:

TABLE 27/2

	1947	1958
Number of Vehicles Sold........................	1,846,000	2,526,000
Average Number of Hourly Employees (Approx.)......	268,500	281,500
Vehicles Sold per Employee........................	6.88	8.97
Increase in Vehicle Output per Employee.............	30%	

If some correction could be applied to take account of the differences between the 1958 vehicle and that of 1947, the increase in productivity would undoubtedly be larger than 30 percent and might well equal or exceed the 44 percent increase in real wages per hour which was received.

2. Southern Indiana Gas and Electric Company. It is relatively easy for union representatives to obtain relevant financial information about a gas and electric company, because such companies are public utilities regulated by governmental agencies, and their operating figures have to be made available to the public.

The material here presented was put together by the International Brotherhood of Electrical Workers from *Moody's Public Utility Manual.*

The first point made by the union is that the company grew considerably from 1951 to 1958. The increases cited are in the following areas:

TABLE 27/3

	Percent increase 1951–1958
Customers for Electricity............................	29
Customers for Gas.................................	25
Revenue from Electricity...........................	74
Revenue from Gas.................................	84
Net Profit	71

According to the union, the most significant evidence of the company's ability to pay is the fact that net profit per employee has steadily risen and was in 1958, nearly 50 percent higher than in 1951. This rise, argues its memorandum, indicates "a whopping increase in productivity" in which the employees are entitled to a share. Have wages risen in line with the increase in productivity? The union suggests that each group of employees figure this out and compare the results with the table.

TABLE 27/4

PROFIT PER EMPLOYEE

Year	Net Profit	Number of employees as of December 31	Profit per employee	Profit per employee as percent of 1951
1958...........	$2,885,587	738[1]	$3,910	147
1957...........	2,744,639	724	3,791	142
1956...........	2,312,301	706	3,275	123
1955...........	2,455,037	699	3,512	132
1954...........	2,468,094	668	3,695	139
1953...........	2,119,592	648	3,271	123
1952...........	1,879,969	630	2,984	112
1951...........	1,688,306	635	2,659	100

[1] Estimated by adding 2 percent, shown to be the approximate company trend over the past eight years.

The union also contends that the company is benefiting because the total of salaries and wages (including pay of executives) has become a smaller percentage of total revenue, having shrunk from 20.6 percent in 1956 to 18.9 percent in 1957.

What might management reply to these contentions? It could scarcely deny that the company is in good condition—and probably would not wish to do so, since it might wish to raise capital for new facilities by selling securities to the public. It might, however, raise the question whether the contention that an increase in profit per employee is as significant as the union argues. Presumably, in order to increase output per man, the company has installed more highly productive equipment and has thus enlarged its plant and investment in these years, so that the dollar figure of profits would have had to increase in order to make possible a fair *percentage* return on the stockholders' equity, or net worth.

The union does not submit figures to show whether or not this is the case. It does, however, supply recent income statements and balance sheets which indicate that the return on stockholders' equity slightly exceeded 9 percent in 1957 and in 1958. (See following tables.) This return is figured *after payment of income taxes.*

The company might also argue that if its rate of return proved to be higher than the regulating commission thought was proper, the consequence would be a reduction of rates (or a curb on their rise) and that a sharing of productivity gains with consumers was preferable to any wage increases greater than those which had occurred.

Material relevant to this case study may be found in Chapter 1, Business Financial Statement; Chapter 10, Business Organization; Chapter 17, Labor and its Organization; and Chapter 18, Theories Concerning Labor and Wages.

TABLE 27/5

SOUTHERN INDIANA GAS AND ELECTRIC COMPANY
(Most Recent 12-Month Income Statement to June 30)

	1959	1958
Gross Revenue	$20,453,536	$19,801,644
Operating Expense	9,640,982	9,331,771
Depreciation	2,111,979	1,972,233
Plant Acquisition Adjustment..................	67,443	109,026
General Taxes	1,829,555	1,692,450
Federal Income Tax.........................	2,055,090	2,131,165
Deferred Income Tax........................	903,336	821,910
Net Operating Income.......................	3,845,153	3,743,090
Bond Interest	896,250	896,250
Interest to Construction......................	(cr) 24,152	(cr) 36,580
Dept. Discontin. and Expends.................	(cr) 2,634	(cr) 2,653
Other Deductions	25,907	26,054
NET INCOME	$ 2,949,782	$ 2,860,020
Preferred Dividends	531,046	418,563
Balance	2,418,736	2,441,456
Earned per Preferred Share....................	$26.58	$25.79
Earned per Common Share....................	$ 2.43	$ 2.45
Number of Preferred Shares...................	110,895	110,895
Number of Common Shares...................	996,363	996,363

Dividends: Currently paying $.40 per quarter (3 months) per common share.

Source: Moody's Public Utilities, Vol. 31, No. 5, page 1950.

QUESTIONS

1. In the preceding discussion, between union, management, and economist, the union representative made the point that if wages were not increased as fast as the amount invested, there would be a shortage of consumer purchasing power to buy the goods from the new productive facilities resulting from the investment. The national income (or product) must be divided between investment and consumption, so that a larger percentage invested must mean a smaller percentage consumed.

Since World War II, Soviet Russia has invested a much larger percentage of its national income than the United States, and so has had more rapid economic growth. How do you suppose Russia has managed this without producing more than the citizens could buy and so without suffering unemployment?

2. On the balance sheet of the Southern Indiana Gas and Electric Company (Table 27/6, page 338), the items making up the current assets and the current liabilities are indented. By adding up the items under each head, you can compare the current assets with the current liabilities

TABLE 27/6

SOUTHERN INDIANA GAS AND ELECTRIC COMPANY
Balance Sheet, as of December 31:

Assets	1958	1957
Utility Plant	$79,804,715	$74,552,539
Plant Acquisition Adjustment..................	212,706	314,225
Investment	190,530	178,530
Current Assets:		
Cash	862,455	1,256,949
Receivables, Net	1,665,311	1,791,822
U.S. Government Securities..................	1,753,690	
Special Deposits	58,110	58,110
Materials and Supplies......................	1,878,080	2,017,970
Gas Stored	97,293	85,070
Prepayments	25,279	35,765
Capital Stock Expenditures..................		236,999
Deferred Charges	243,345	208,699
Total Assets	$86,791,514	$80,736,678
Liabilities		
4.8% Preferred Stock, $100 par..................	$11,089,500	$ 8,589,500
Common Stock, no par......................	14,076,138	14,076,138
Deferred Federal Income Tax..................	2,855,536	1,984,150
Earned Surplus	6,687,429	5,884,183
First-Mortgage Bonds	27,500,000	27,500,000
Current and Accrued Liabilities:		
Accounts Payable	1,032,567	1,013,852
Dividends Payable	112,970	103,074
Taxes Accrued	2,754,927	3,341,182
Accrued Interest, etc.......................	653,198	636,702
Depreciation Reserve	15,842,118	14,157,025
Advances for Construction.....................	3,650,316	2,923,259
Debt Premium	130,922	136,872
Other Reserves	405,893	390,741
Total Liabilities	$86,791,514	$80,736,678
Stockholders' Equity	$31,853,067	$28,549,821
Rates of Return	9.05%	9.61%

Source: Moody's Public Utility Manual, Vol. 30, No. 69, page 1604.

in two ways. (1) The ratio of the first to the second will give you the "current ratio." (2) You can find the "net working capital" by subtracting the second total from the first.

On the basis of these figures, does the current position of the company seem good to you? That is, does it seem to you to be well able to pay its bills from month to month? In considering this question, identify the items under Current Assets which either are in cash or can most readily be turned into cash, and the items under Current and Accrued Liabilities which it is most necessary to pay promptly.

What items constitute the company's inventory? For which of these is it most likely to receive full value if they were sold?

Under Current Assets you will notice two items which signify that the company is now receiving benefits from something previously paid for, Prepayments and Deferred Charges. If, for example, "Prepayments" means that the company has paid rent in advance, it will benefit by not having to pay this rent. Such items obviously cannot be directly turned into cash or used to pay bills. If so, why are they included as current assets?

Would the current ratio of a public utility company be expected to be larger, smaller, or about the same as the current ratio of concerns engaged in each of the following businesses; why?

(1) A chain store company selling food
(2) An automobile manufacturer
(3) A building construction company
(4) A firm making women's dresses

3. On the same balance sheet (Southern Indiana) you will find under Liabilities an item entitled "Depreciation Reserve." Many balance sheets would show this listed in the Assets section, but in that case it would be *subtracted* from the investment in plant, and the result would be carried as the *net* value of the plant (that is, plant less depreciation). But in either case the depreciation is subtracted from the amount invested, in the process of obtaining the stockholder's equity, or net worth.

You will see that the Depreciation Reserve increased from 1957 to 1958. You will also see that the value of the utility plant (before depreciation) also increased from 1957 to 1958. By comparing these two increases, can you gain a rough idea about how fast the company expects additions to its plant and equipment to wear out or become obsolete?

If this depreciation rate were higher than the facts warranted, how would it affect stockholders, government, customers, and wage earners?

Bear in mind that, if the income statement figures for this company covered years ending December 31 (instead of June 30 as they do), the depreciation deducted from gross revenue on the income statement, in the process of arriving at net income, would be exactly the same as the figure added to the Depreciation Reserve on the balance sheet of one year to form the Depreciation Reserve of the next year.

Another link exists between an income statement and a balance sheet dated the same day as that ending the year covered by the income statement. The difference between the balance sheet figure of earned surplus (or reinvested earnings) of one year and that of the next is the same as the net income of the intervening year, less all dividends paid in that year. So the stake of the stockholders grows from year to year by the reinvestment of the undistributed earnings.

4. You will note that on the Southern Indiana balance sheet (Table 27/6) the last item of the liabilities is entitled "Other Reserves." Why is a reserve a liability of the company?

Is it not a fund laid aside for some special purpose or contingency? Does the company not actually have the money? The answer to both questions is "yes, it is a special-purpose fund and the company does have the money—or whatever securities the reserve may be invested in." The ownership of this money by the company *is* recorded on the balance sheet on the assets side—it is part of Cash, United States Government Securities, or perhaps Special deposits there listed. The "Reserves" entry among the liabilities means only that this money is earmarked for the purposes in mind when the reserves were set up.

What if the reserves were spent for purposes in mind when they were set aside? The entry for reserves would, of course, disappear from the liabilities. At the same time the money so spent would disappear from the assets. The balance sheet would still balance.

If there were no advance reserves set up for the purposes in mind, there would, of course, be no such entry among the liabilities. How would the assets balance the liabilities in this case? The amount of assets would be the same as if the reserves *had* been set up. The sum now under "Reserves" would instead be part of the earned surplus, which, of course, would thus be correspondingly larger than it is on the printed balance sheet.

Whenever a reserve is set up, the appropriation to the reserve is deducted from earnings. This makes profits smaller than they would have been without the reserve. If no reserve were set up, and in a future year the money had to be spent for whatever contingency the company had in mind when the reserve was in fact established, the money would have to be deducted from the earnings of the year when it was spent; thus profits would be smaller in the year the money was spent.

Now we can see why the tax authorities are wary of allowing companies to set up reserves for this, that, or the other contingency which may never occur. Such a habit on the part of a company would lead to repeated reduction of recorded profits, without any subsequent need for so doing. Meanwhile its assets would correspondingly increase, without ever having been recorded as profits when the money was received.

Do you think it would be fair for a company to set up large reserves to combat possible future strikes? What would you say about such a practice if you were a union representative? What would you say if you were an income tax official? a labor mediator?

28 / PRODUCTION AND PRICES IN AN
   AGRICULTURAL INDUSTRY / The effect of

rapid technological change on farming has recently attracted much attention. A case in point is the production of chicken for broiling and
frying, which within little more than a generation has changed from a
by-product of the family farmyard to a big industry in which the independent farmer no longer plays a significant part. The history of this
agricultural industry illustrates not only the industrialization of agriculture but also the changing fortunes and structure of an industry subject to rapid growth and subsequent approach to saturation of its
market.[1]

TECHNOLOGICAL SPECIALIZATION

For untold generations farmers kept flocks of poultry partly as a
source of their own food and partly as a source of income from the sale
of eggs and surplus birds. Chickens were fed mainly from grain grown
on the farm and from kitchen wastes, and by their own scratching for
worms and by catching grasshoppers. Mother hens hatched out their own
chicks; surplus males, at maturity, were eaten or sold. No specialized
techniques were required. There was no distinction between chickens
destined to lay eggs for the table and chickens destined to be eaten.
Such breeding as was carried on was mainly for color and appearance or
for purposes other than food consumption, such as the production of
fighting cocks.

Within a few decades, this traditional manner of poultry raising has
been supplanted by specialized techniques, most of them applied by
separate types of business inappropriate for the farm family. In the case

---

[1] This chapter is based on Herman Bluestone, *Broiler Statistics and Related
Data, Maryland, Delaware, and Delmarva,* College Park, Md., 1958; as well as on
George Soule, Martha V. Taber, and others, *Vertical Integration in the Broiler Indus-
try on the Delmarva Peninsula and its Effect on Small Business.* Chestertown, Md.,
Washington College, 1961.

of chickens destined for the frying plan or the broiler oven, there have sprung into existence no less than seven stages in the productive process, each carried on in a specially designed and equipped establishment. In this development it was the chicken, not the egg, which came first. The stages are as follows:

Breeding of "meat-type females" capable of laying eggs which, when hatched, will become birds with light and attractive skin and much tender and tasty white meat, and will take the shortest possible time in growing. (The life span of the average broiler from egg to execution is now about nine weeks.)

Management of *laying flocks* composed of "meat-type females" and a few well-bred cockerels also born for their destined purpose, to engage in mass production of fertilized eggs which will become marketable broilers.

Hatcheries which incubate broiler-type eggs by the hundred thousand. These have banks of great steel incubators, each with dials indicating such conditions as temperature and humidity, and a door leading to a center aisle on each side of which a series of rows of egg trays extends from the floor to above a man's head. The eggs are automatically turned from side to side at regular intervals, as a hen turns eggs on which she is sitting. Newly laid eggs are put in the top trays, which are moved down from shelf to shelf until the eggs about to hatch are at the floor level, so that chicks can tumble out without harm. Chicks taken from the incubator are debeaked by machine, sprayed with antibiotic in another machine, and packed in cartons, each containing 102 chicks, for prompt delivery to nearby growers.

Feed is prepared by broiler *feed mills* near the growers, which mix to order the numerous ingredients which, research has found, promote rapid growth, fine flesh, and resistance to diseases which attack poultry. In a modern feed mill the mixing is controlled at instrument panels which can be set by an attendant for any desired combination and quantity; no other human hand is required for the process. The order (usually not packed in bags as formerly) falls into a bulk delivery truck, which deposits it in a bulk bin at the growing house. No small hand-mixing operation, whether on the farm or in the more primitive mill, can compete with the automated mill.

The mixing mills usually grind the chief ingredient—corn—but obtain soybean meal from specialized mills and numerous ingredients such as fish meal, antibiotics, and other medications from the specialized producers. Mills usually handle the sale of chicks and other supplies needed by growers.

Broilers are fed in *growing sheds,* each containing, as a rule, 10,000 birds at a time. A flock is ready for sale about nine weeks from the time the baby chicks are delivered. One square foot or less of floor space is allowed for each bird. One man and his wife can attend to the chickens under modern growing practices. Growing houses are expertly designed with concern for feeding and watering equipment, litter on the floor, disposition of the litter (which is an important by-product), ventilation, sanitation, and continual inspection for disease. Injection of vaccines and other medications is customarily employed.

On the Delmarva Peninsula and some other regions the "finished" live birds are sold at a *Poultry Exchange* to buyers who have previously inspected the flocks and who bid against one another. Birds are sometimes sold "off the auction" at private sale, but in such cases auction prices usually govern the transaction.

The purchasers are *processors,* who dress the birds. They employ skilled "catchers," who take the birds from the growing sheds and crate them for shipment to the processing plant. There the birds are killed and hung from a conveyor which moves steadily past a line of workers, each of whom performs one operation in the course of evisceration, inspection, cutting, and packing. Automatic machinery defeathers, chills, transports, and sorts the poultry by weight. By-products made from the waste include ingredients of poultry feed. Many processors market fresh, ice-packed chicken; some freeze it; some cook and freeze it.

Some large wholesaling meat packers own processing plants and distribute their product.

GROWTH OF THE MARKET

The change from broiler growing on the family farm as a by-product of the egg business to a highly specialized industry began in the 1920's with the development of broiler-type stock by breeders and the sale of chicks by commercial hatcheries. In the 1930's, when unemployment was widespread and incomes were low, the cheaper meats were in demand. Technological advance, reducing the cost of poultry, enabled broiler producers to compete successfully with sellers of other meats. Between 1934 and 1940, sales of broilers in the United States increased from 90 million pounds a year, or 4.4 percent of all chicken marketed, to 413 million pounds, or 16 percent of the chicken sold. In a time of difficulty for businessmen, investors, and workers in city and country, it was natural that resources should be attracted to a new industry in which profit resulted from a growing market stimulated by reductions of cost and improvement in quality of the product.

During the subsequent war years, growth of output continued, though at a somewhat moderated pace. Producers suffered from a shortage of labor and facilities to meet the demand, yet profits were made by broiler producers in spite of rationing and price ceilings. By 1945, during which year the war ended, broiler output in the nation was more than one billion pounds, or 26 percent of total poultry sales.

After the postwar readjustment years 1946 and 1947, this boom industry took wing and soared, aided by postwar prosperity and the rapid growth of population which increased the number of consumers. Broiler output jumped from slightly less than a billion pounds in 1947 to 4.7 billion in 1957—78 percent of total chicken output in the nation.

These figures for the nation as a whole do not take account of the fact that markets for the product were largely regional. One of the largest markets—the Northeastern states along or near the Atlantic seaboard from Maine to Virginia, with their great metropolitan regions, was served to a large extent by producers in three farming regions: rural New England (primarily Maine), the Delmarva Peninsula (consisting of Delaware and parts of Maryland and Virginia east of Chesapeake Bay) and, more recently, Georgia and other South Central states. In each of these farming areas there developed the complex of feed mills, hatchers, growers, and processors required for efficient broiler production; competition exists not only within each of the areas but also among them. This study is concerned mainly with the Delmarva region, which pioneered in the industry.

PRICES, OUTPUT, AND REVENUE

Every advance in technology reduced the production cost of broilers per pound; at prevailing market prices each such reduction temporarily increased profit margins and stimulated output; and increase in output tended to reduce selling prices.

In 1921 the average price of live broilers at farm markets was $1.15 a pound. Prices of dressed broilers at retail stores were, of course, considerably higher. Even in 1929, a year following Herbert Hoover's campaign slogan of "A chicken in every pot and two cars in every garage," chicken was still a luxury, though the live-weight price had fallen to 55 cents a pound.

The economic crash which began in 1929 and reached its bottom in 1933 was marked by a catastrophic fall of all farm prices, including that for broilers. The live-weight price in Delmarva had fallen to 20.3 cents a pound by 1934. Thereafter it drifted down during the 1930's, reaching a low of 16.1 cents in 1939.

During the ensuing war shortage and general increase in prices, live-weight broiler prices in Delmarva rose to a high of 25.1 cents a pound in 1945—less than half the 1929 price. In the postwar period the price fell irregularly but persistently, although most prices rose sharply in the inflation which began in 1946. By 1960 broiler prices in Delmarva were no higher than those reached at the lowest point in the great depression—16 to 17 cents a pound.

For many years during which prices fell either absolutely or relative to other prices, broiler sales had increased sufficiently to yield increased revenue to Delmarva producers. But there proved to be a limit beyond which not enough additional sales were made at falling prices to bring larger revenue. There is a limit to the number of pounds of broiler any consumer will eat, and as that limit is approached, increased sales can result only from growth in population. In economic terms, we may say that although the elasticity of demand was positive during a large part

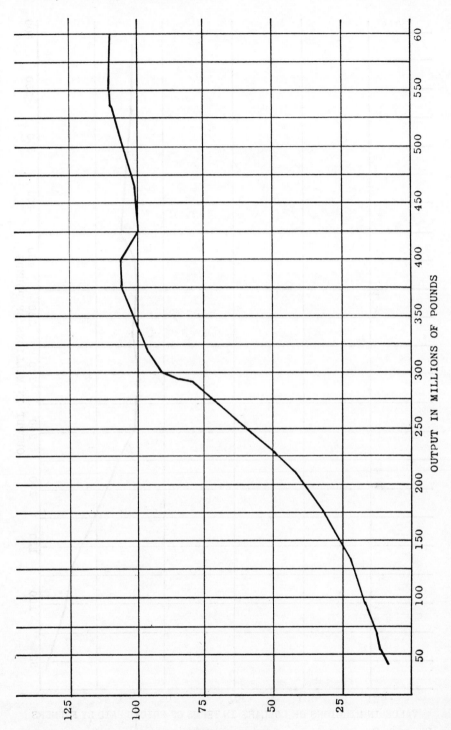

VALUE IN MILLIONS OF CURRENT DOLLARS

Fig. 28.1. DELMARVA BROILER PRODUCTION AND VALUE (FOUR-YEAR MOVING AVERAGE).

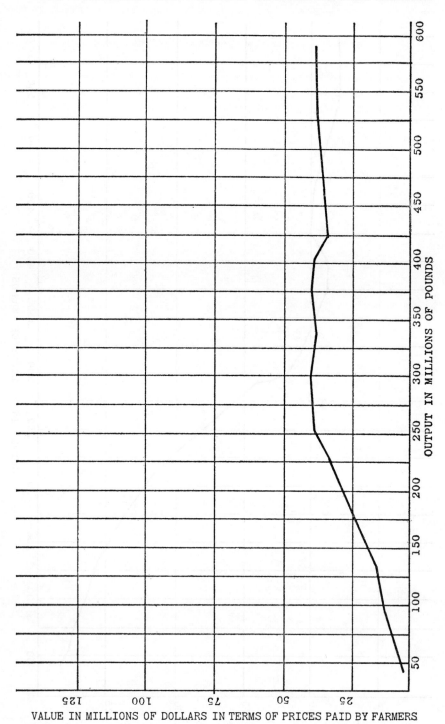

Fig. 28.2. DELMARVA BROILER PRODUCTION AND VALUE IN CONSTANT DOL-
LARS (FOUR-YEAR MOVING AVERAGE). Current dollars deflated
by index of prices paid by farmers, base 1910-1914.

of the broiler boom, it eventually became zero, and threatened to be negative, as saturation of the market was approached.

Sales revenue from broilers produced in Delmarva rose rapidly until annual output reached 300 million pounds; it grew more slowly up to an annual output of about 375 million pounds and thereafter gained little, though output continued to increase to 600 million pounds. Figure 28/1 shows roughly what occurred. Because of minor annual variations, a four-year moving average was used to compute the figures on the graph.

The above figures for revenue are in terms of current dollars. But after the 1930's the value of the dollar in terms of what it can buy has had a falling tendency because of rising prices. To compensate for this change, the annual revenue figures may be modified by the index which shows changes in prices paid by farmers. Measured roughly in such "constant dollars," sales revenue to Delmarva producers did not increase above an output of 250 million pounds. The year when the revenue stated in current dollars ceased to increase was 1953, and the year when it ceased to increase in constant dollars was 1945.

VERTICAL INTEGRATION AND THE PRICE-COST SQUEEZE

As specialization in the various stages of broiler production became prevalent, firms at each stage competed among themselves in buying from firms at the preceding stage and selling to firms at the succeeding stage. Yet, in many cases, processes at two or more successive stages came to be combined under a single ownership. Such vertically integrated firms eliminate buying and selling between the stages which they include, together with the costs and uncertainties of the buying and selling involved. But they still may compete in buying at the stage below the lowest under their control, and in selling at the stage above the highest in their chain.

Many feed mills bought or built hatcheries, since they often sold chicks, as well as feed, to growers. Many mills and many hatcheries acquired growing flocks; some acquired laying flocks. One firm integrated all stages exclusive of breeding, all the way from laying flocks to and including a processing plant.

During the boom period when such combinations were put together, the incentives to do so were numerous. One was to participate in the profits at more than one stage in a rapidly growing industry. Another was to make sure of a source of supply and to avoid high buying prices which might result from a shortage at any stage. Another was to exercise quality control as a means of market advantage. Still another was to reduce costs by increased efficiency.

Aside from ownership of successive stages, vertical integration could be achieved by a contract system. This system became prevalent between feed dealers or mills and growers who used their supplies. Under such contracts the feed, chicks, and other supplies are not sold by the producer but are charged against the grower, to be paid for from the proceeds of sale of the fully grown birds. Chicks remain the property of the contracting dealer or mill and are sold by him, when they are ready for the processor. Any margin between the sales proceeds and the charges for supplies is divided according to terms, specified in the contract, between grower and supplier. From this sum the grower has to meet expenses for property taxes, rent, depreciation, labor, and the like. When prices for broilers are low, the grower may not even cover these expenses, to say nothing of making a true profit. He is, however, guaranteed against out-of-pocket loss if the proceeds of the sale of broilers does not cover the charges for supplies; this loss is borne by the contracting mill or dealer.

Such contracts provide for supervision of the growing process by the supplier or his agents. Important management decisions, such as how many chicks to grow, when they are to be started, and when they are to be sold, are made by the supplier or with his consent.

Vertical integration of one sort or another became dominant in the Delmarva industry when lower prices no longer brought increased revenue from expanded production. Except in one case, common ownership did not link the processor with the seller of live birds. The breeder, who had a strong market position through his control of the widely favored variety of bird used, remained independent. But about 90 percent of sales of finished live broilers were made by ten feed mills and three hatcheries, which either owned the growers outright or had them under contract. Almost all the buying of these birds was in the hands of twelve processors. Several of the feed mills were owned by national milling companies, and some of the large processors were owned by national meat-packing companies. It would be contrary to the antitrust laws for either of these groups to agree to control either selling or buying prices; however, in a market composed of only a few buyers or a few sellers, individual competitors have more power over price setting than in a market composed of many buyers and sellers. In this case direct negotiation between the principal sellers and the principal buyers was limited by the existence of an auction market separating them, but the sellers at least were in a strong market position relative to the stages of the industry engaged in producing live birds.

Low broiler prices which did not yield increased revenue through sufficiently increased sales brought a price-cost squeeze to the producers. The breeder who furnished the laying birds was in a position to maintain his selling prices, and did so. The prices of corn and soybeans—the principal ingredients of broiler feed—were supported by governmental action under farm legislation. Wages had a rising tendency. Taxes were increasing. Under these circumstances there arose redoubled pressure for cost reduction through greater efficiency in broiler production, and a likelihood that those firms in the industry having the highest costs or occupying the weakest market positions—the marginal firms—would suffer losses and might be forced to discontinue.

The growers, of whom there were many and most of whom were

relatively small and without easy access to capital or credit, occupied the weakest position in the industry. Most of the "independent" farmer-growers who were not already under the contract system took advantage of its benefits. The feed mills now began to use the contract system to reduce costs and protect their profits. They virtually eliminated from the industry the local feed dealers who formerly had bought from the mills and sold to the growers, and made direct contracts with the growers. Two large concerns retained their better dealers but took control of the contracts. Some dealers got jobs in mills as servicemen to supervise the growing process. The mills selected the better growers among those anxious for contracts, and redoubled their efforts to increase efficiency among these. Any grower refused a contract still had the legal right to buy chicks and feed, but few had the resources to do so. Since independent growers became as scarce as hens' teeth, independent hatcheries could find few customers except the feed mills who furnished the chicks to growers under contract. This situation strengthened vertical integration of hatchery and mill.

Feed mills customarily set their prices for feed at a markup over costs; firms at other stages in the industry (excepting the breeder) are forced to accept prices determined by the interplay of supply and demand. During recent years of the price-cost squeeze (1953–1957) the price of live broilers varied each year much more widely and more frequently than the price of feed. Chick prices varied more widely than the price of feed.

The percentage of price fall, 1953–1957, figured separately between the highest prices, and the lowest prices, of the two years, was as follows:

TABLE 28/1

PRICE DECLINE, 1953–1957

	Between annual highs	Between annual lows
Broilers	24.0%	15%
Feed Mash	8.7%	5%
Chicks	21.0%	13%

The feed mills, of course, owned and sold the live broilers and apparently incurred losses in sales, figured on the basis of the charges for feed and other supplies. But it is probable that the charges for feed were high enough so that in most years they more than made up, in profit from the feed, for losses on sale of broilers. The grower, however, whether under contract or not, received no net return under these conditions, since he was entitled only to what might be earned from the margin between the cost of his supplies and the revenue from the live birds.

This was the situation in the industry when the study on which this chapter is based was made. One can only guess what the possible future of the industry will be. There can be little doubt, however, that so far the consumer has gained from technological advances under competition, and that in the future the industry will be largely in fewer and stronger hands. The independent farmer-grower of broilers has virtually disappeared. Broiler growing is no longer "agriculture" in the traditional sense, but a highly organized business, in which machinery and technological advances have greatly diminished the role of labor both on the farms and in the factories.

Material relevant to this case study will be found in Chapter 9, The Theory of Supply and Demand; Chapter 10, Business Organization; Chapter 11, Theories of Business Behavior; Chapter 19, Agriculture in the Economy; Chapter 20, Theories of Agricultural Behavior; Chapter 25, Growth of the United States Economy.

QUESTIONS

1. The costs of producing broiler feed consist mainly of (a) costs of corn, soybean meal, and other ingredients, (b) depreciation on plant and machinery, (c) direct labor cost, (d) administrative salaries and bonuses, and (e) property taxes.

Which of these expenses would you roughly classify as fixed costs; which as variable costs?

Feed mills, being highly mechanized, have relatively large investment in plant and machinery and relatively small direct labor costs. All mills in a given region pay about the same prices for materials and labor, and charge about the same prices for feed. If two mills sold about the same number of pounds of feed, which one would make the most profit—one operating near full capacity or one operating at half capacity?

2. In what respects are farmer-growers under contract to feed mills like employees? In which respects are they unlike? Do you think they should organize a union and bargain collectively with the feed mills?

3. The United States Government, in the interest of farmers, supports the prices of corn and soybeans above those which might exist in a free market. Though these are the principal ingredients of broiler feed, the government does not support the price of broilers. Do you think it ought to do so? Or, on the contrary, do you think it ought to abandon price support of corn and soybeans?

4. If price supports are retained for feed grains but are not applied to broilers, do you think the government should allow the firms engaged in broiler production to act together in setting prices and controling output?

If it did this, what protection would the consumer have against high prices for broilers?

Should the government regulate these prices as it now regulates prices for electricity and other monopolistic businesses which it permits?

29 / ARE STEEL PRICES TOO

HIGH? / *(The Bethlehem-Youngstown Merger Case)*

The two major federal antitrust laws are the Sherman Act, passed by Congress in 1890, and the Clayton Act, passed during the administration of Woodrow Wilson in 1914. The latter was intended mainly to stop loopholes in the Sherman Act. Either or both acts have occasionally been employed to break up large combinations or to curb monopolistic practices, but the legal processes required to enforce them are slow, costly, and sometimes unsuccessful. Neither has prevented the growth of big business in many industries or has assured the prevalence of competition of a kind which, according to economic theory, is necessary if prices are to result from the free play of economic forces in the market rather than from decisions of powerful sellers.

In order to provide the federal government with a more effective means of preventing monopoly, Congress passed in 1950 an amendment to the Clayton Act (Section 7), which prohibits any company from acquiring the shares or assets of another company when the effect of the merger "may be substantially to lessen competition or to tend to create a monopoly." The purpose of this relatively new section is to give the government power to *prevent* a step toward monopoly before it is taken—a much less expensive and complicated procedure than to break up monopoly after it has been created or to curb the activities of an existing big business.

After the passage of this amendment the Bethlehem Steel Corporation, the second largest company in the steel industry, formally announced (in 1956) its intention to merge with the Youngstown Sheet and Tube Company, the sixth largest. The U. S. Department of Justice, through its Antitrust Division, took legal action to prevent the merger under Section 7 of the Clayton Act. In January, 1959, Judge Edward Weinfeld, of the Federal District Court of New York, after hearing the arguments of both sides, decided that the proposed merger would be illegal. This decision, though it might later be upset or modified by the

Supreme Court, sets an important precedent in the annals of big business and the law.

THE LEGAL ISSUE

The case is of particular interest because of the main arguments of Bethlehem Steel. The largest firm in the industry is the U. S. Steel Corporation. Bethlehem contended that by uniting with Youngstown Sheet and Tube, it would be enabled to provide better competition with U. S. Steel than at present, and therefore the proposed merger would increase competition, not diminish it. The merged concern would be, it was argued, in an improved position to compete, especially in the Chicago district, and planned to enlarge productive facilities by new and more efficient plants in that area. (Bethlehem's main plants are now near the Eastern seaboard, while Youngstown's are in Ohio. U. S. Steel's numerous plants include those located near Pittsburgh, in south Chicago, and in Gary, Indiana—only a few miles from Chicago.)

The government's evidence supported the argument that, in those states, sales by Bethlehem and Youngstown to the same customers were already larger in volume than those of most other steel companies, and therefore competition of sellers would be lessened in important areas by the combination of these two present competitors.

Judge Weinfeld's opinion accompanying his decision states,

> The government is not required to establish with certitude that competition in fact will be substantially lessened. Its burden is met if it establishes a reasonable probability that the proposed merger will substantially lessen competition or tend to create a monopoly.

If this merger were allowed, Judge Weinfeld commented, would not the decision encourage other mergers in the industry, with the result that the existing number of companies would be further reduced and concentration of economic power thereby enhanced?

If the merger offends the statute in any relevant market

> [Judge Weinfeld wrote] . . . then good motives and even demonstrable benefits are irrelevant and afford no defense. Congress in seeking to halt the growing tendency to increased concentration of power in various industries was fully aware of the arguments in support of the supposed advantages of size and the claims of greater efficiency and lower cost to the ultimate consumer.
>
> It made no distinction between good and bad mergers. It condemned all which came within the reach of Section 7.

THE ECONOMIC BACKGROUND

Without questioning Judge Weinfeld's interpretation of the law, one may ask what the chances are that effective competition in the steel industry would have been increased, or decreased, if the merger had been permitted. One may also ask whether any further measures are desirable in order to obtain the public benefits supposed to arise from competition, and if so, what these measures might be. To discuss such questions, it is necessary to know something about the nature and practices of the industry.

Ever since the beginning of the industrial revolution, steel has been a basic necessity of civilization. Its importance has increased with the years. Recently a few substitute metals or other substances—for example, aluminum or concrete—have begun to compete with steel for specific purposes, but they have not greatly limited its main markets. Steel is needed for such important products as industrial and farm machinery, factories, commercial and public buildings of all types, railroad rails, locomotives and rolling stock, automobiles, trucks and tractors, ships, bridges, military equipment of many types, and a thousand and one other articles of daily use. Our whole economic structure literally rests on the abundance, quality, and availability of steel products at reasonable prices. All great industrial nations depend on steel; most of them have their own important steel industries using largely domestic deposits of coal and iron.

The steel industry as it exists today is vertically integrated as far as the manufacture and sale of "basic" steel is concerned. The larger companies, of which U. S. Steel is the prime example, own or control raw materials, such as coking coal and iron mines; transportation facilities for them; blast furnaces, which refine the iron ore; steel furnaces, by which iron is converted into steel and steel alloys of many qualities for specific uses; rolling mills, which turn out sheets, plates, bars, rails, and other primary steel products such as beams and girders for buildings and bridges. Only at this stage is steel usually disposed of to other industries or firms under separate ownership, for fabrication into the many steel products for final use.

Such vertical integration is said to be desirable for the most efficient operation, since it minimizes transportation and handling costs in the production of basic steel. It requires very large investment in plant and equipment, so that nobody now can enter the steel industry "on a shoestring." Indeed, only a large corporation with ample capital resources can hope to be successful in the industry. There have been very few newcomers during the past half-century. Since many of the older companies have merged, the number of steel producers is narrowly limited.

CONCENTRATION IN THE STEEL INDUSTRY

The U. S. Steel Corporation, formed by merger in 1901, has, ever since then, been the leading factor in the industry. At the beginning, it controlled about half the basic steel output in the United States, though in certain products it provided 90 percent or more of the total supply. Since then, its share of the market has somewhat declined, through the relative growth of some of the other companies and the geographical expansion of the market for steel. The cost of transporting such a heavy and bulky product, added to the cost of production, gives an advantage to mills located near the market for their products (though a mill must also be located where iron ore and coal are available without too high a cost of transportation).

In 1936 the largest ten companies in the industry had 88 percent of its invested capital. The order of the first five was as follows:[1]

TABLE 29/1

Company	Percent of invested capital
U. S. Steel..............................	40
Bethlehem	15
Republic	8
Jones and Laughlin.......................	5
Youngstown	5

Measured by value of shipments, the following figures show the degree of concentration of the industry in more recent years:[2]

TABLE 29/2

PERCENTAGE OF TOTAL VALUE OF SHIPMENTS
(111 steel works and rolling mills)

	1947	1958
4 largest companies.................	48%	54%
8 largest companies.................	63%	70%
20 largest companies.................	81%	85%

These figures indicate that, in proportion of sales, the degree of concentration in the larger companies has increased since World War II— though not necessarily the predominance of the single largest, U. S. Steel. (U. S. Steel did, however, achieve regional dominance in the west by purchasing from the United States Government a large plant in Utah after World War II.)

STEEL PRICES AND COMPETITION

If competition is to have any effect favorable to the consumer, the manner in which it affects prices, if at all, is certainly one of the most important. Competition may also affect the quality of the goods offered

---

[1] Temporary National Economic Committee, *Hearings,* Part 18, p. 10408.
[2] *Statistical Abstract of the United States,* 1959.

by competing producers, but in basic steel this factor is largely eliminated by the fact that qualities of steel are almost universally measured by engineering standards. The purchaser usually specifies exactly what he wants; he is able to test the product for adherence to the specifications, and he is therefore able to compare products strictly on the basis of relative price.

According to a recent study,[3] "The quoted basic price for basic steel tends to be uniform among firms following the lead of United States Steel." The "price leadership" of U. S. Steel has long been generally acknowledged. An agreement by competitors to maintain a price would be a violation of the antitrust laws. Nevertheless, there is no law forbidding competitors to charge the same price, providing there is no agreement to do so. Customarily, U. S. Steel has announced the base mill price (so much per ton) it intended to charge. Other steel companies would thereafter charge that price. The announced price would, as a rule, remain unchanged for months at a time. One can only guess why this practice prevails. An occasional price-cutter has been

> . . . "disciplined" by other sellers who met his price, so that he obtained no advantage from his move. Presumably the firms following U. S. Steel's lead do so because of their knowledge that if they should start a price war, they would soon be undercut by the dominant concern, and their resources are considerably less than its. A price war might be temporarily embarrassing for U. S. Steel, but could be disastrous for smaller concerns. Furthermore, it has been alleged that U. S. Steel is one of the least efficient producers in the industry, and its prices afford smaller concerns a handsome profit.[4]

In these circumstances, it appears easy to understand why other steel companies normally regard major price competition with the leading company as "out of bounds."

According to the Brookings Institution study quoted above,

> . . . extra charges, which are imposed for variations in alloy and other specifications, are important to the final delivered price. Up to the Second World War, the industry apparently agreed on uniform extras to tie in differences in specifications with a uniform base price; but in recent years, this practice seems to have become less prevalent.

A footnote explains that "special prices are made for large contracts" and "charges for extras are less uniform than they once were." But there is no real prevalence of price competition either publicly or secretly. "Everyone knows everyone else's costs." There are differences in price because of different freight delivery charges, but delivered price in a given locality is generally the same regardless of the location of the seller.

Variations from the U. S. Steel basic price do sometimes occur with swings of the business cycle. When the industry is operating at virtually

---

[3] Kaplan, Dirlam, and Lanzillotti: *Pricing in Big Business*. Washington, D. C.: The Brookings Institution, 1958.

[4] Adams and Gray, *Monopoly in America*. New York: Macmillan, 1955, pp. 123–125.

full capacity, smaller competitors may raise their prices though U. S. Steel does not—at least for a time. When business is expected to be slack, smaller companies may reduce prices somewhat, though they are probably restrained in doing so by a policy expressed in a public announcement by U. S. Steel in October, 1953, that when necessary to get the business, it would meet the lower delivered price of a competitor.

Yet pricing in steel is done deliberately and according to plan, not under the type of compulsion felt by small competitors in a fully competitive market. As the Brookings study points out,

> Competitors, . . . even when they believe that U. S. Steel's prices are not high enough, will not ordinarily go above them. The period following the Second World War was an exception. When U. S. Steel has suffered a decline in volume, as in 1954, its pricing philosophy has predisposed it to resist significant cuts. The relative regularity of steel prices through marked changes in operating levels occurring since 1947 seems to bear out the traditional tendency to resist price revisions in steel until action is unavoidable.[5]

PRICING POLICY OF U. S. STEEL

Since other steel companies closely follow prices set by the largest company, it is interesting to note how U. S. Steel decides what price to charge.

According to the Brookings study, U. S. Steel attempts to maintain a "stable margin" between prices and costs, "despite variations in sales volume." If the reader will consult Chapter 11, he will see that unit costs of a single firm vary, largely according to the amount of output. This variation occurs in the main because total "fixed costs"—sometimes loosely called "overhead"—must be met, no matter how large or small output may be; if output is small, each unit of output must bear a larger fraction of the fixed costs than if output is large. The variation is particularly marked in an industry like steel, where the investment in plant and equipment is heavy, and a high degree of mechanization is the rule.

In following this policy, the company determines unit "costs," not by discovering what they actually are, but by using "standard costs." Standard costs are defined as follows by an accounting expert: ". . . predetermined cost for each operation, or each unit of finished product . . . intended to represent the value of direct material, direct labor, and manufacturing burden normally required under efficient conditions at normal capacity to process a unit of product."[6]

It will be seen that "standard" costs do not vary with volume of output or sales, since they are calculated by an estimate of what costs *would* be with "efficient conditions at normal capacity." The level of

---

[5] *Op. cit.*

[6] Green, *National Association of Cost Accountants Bulletin,* Vol. 16, cited in *Accountants' Handbook* (1944), p. 225.

output so regarded by U. S. Steel, according to the Brookings study, is 80 percent of total capacity.

Standard costs of U. S. Steel are revised annually to account for changes in the factors which compose them.

The upshot of this process is that if U. S. Steel averaged 80 percent of capacity over good times and bad, the margin charged above standard costs would yield a stable return over good times and bad. The dollar total of profit would, of course, increase with any enlargement of investment and capacity. When volume of output exceeds 80 percent of capacity, U. S. Steel profits are greater than expected over the whole period for which prices are set; when output is less than 80 percent, profits are smaller. But they do not necessarily disappear at low levels of output; in 1931 U. S. Steel reported a profit of $13,000,000 after taxes, at 37.5 percent of capacity. The company did lose money in 1932 at 17.7 percent of capacity.

Doubtless a plan of this sort is particularly appealing to steel executives because the industry experiences wide swings in sales between depression and prosperity.[7]

How does U. S. Steel determine what margin to add to standard costs when deciding on its price? This question is answered, in the Brookings study, by the U. S. Steel revision of prices following the upward wage adjustment of 1956. To quote from the study,

> According to a tradition in the steel industry, each cents-per-hour increase in direct labor costs adds another cent to steelmakers' nonwage costs per ton of steel. This working figure has been derived from experience in earlier wage settlements. With this labor-total-cost ratio, the anticipated wage settlement is roughly doubled and multiplied by a traditional figure of twenty man-hours (more recently, a figure of fifteen has been used to reflect higher efficiency) to yield the expected cost of a new wage package per ton of steel. Since the new contract (July 1956) was estimated to add 24 cents to the company's hour labor cost per ton, an increase of $9.60 per ton was indicated.

The process is actually somewhat more complex than this, since each product department submits estimates of cost and recommendations for price changes. The product executives are required to make recommendations on forms which call for "a detailed justification of the recommendation in terms of the pricing history and competitive information on the product and the expected impact of the proposed revision on specific company accounts or industries." The price authorities consider these recommendations in terms of profit return on sales. The "top-level management," however, "views price policy primarily in terms of return on investment," which it hopes to keep from falling below a given percentage over a term of years. As it turned out, composite average price

---

[7] A letter from the Secretary of Agriculture to the Senate in 1935 stated that prices of iron and steel had declined only 20 percent in the depression, though output had fallen 83 percent. In agriculture, prices declined 63 percent but production fell only 6 percent. (Senate Document No. 13, 74th Congress, 1st session.)

was increased $8.50 per ton. This was much more than was required to cover the wage increase in cents per hour, but probably not quite twice as much.

DIFFERENCE FROM A COMPETITIVE MARKET

What would happen in a fully competitive market when a wage increase was granted? In such a market, theoretically, the individual seller would have no power whatever over the price at which he would sell, provided he wanted to sell at all. He would have to pay the increase by narrowing his profit margin per unit, unless he could make other economies to compensate for the wage rise. He might even continue for a while to sell at a loss, so long as his variable costs were covered, since that would be less costly than shutting down entirely.

Eventually, if prices did not rise, the less efficient firms subject to the wage increase would either reduce output or go out of business; ultimately, only those would remain who could make something over and above their total costs—fixed and variable. This might give the survivors enough greater volume to maintain their profits. Eventually, so long as consumers' demand for the product did not decline, the price would cover the wage costs of the least efficient firm remaining in business. But costs other than those attributable to wage rises in direct labor of the firm itself would not be reflected in the price unless or until such costs actually occurred.

By what logic does U. S. Steel assume that any increase in steel wage cost will automatically give rise to an equal increase in other costs? Surely this cannot be the result of anything like an exact calculation. Apparently the reasoning process is something like the following. If steel wages go up, so will wages in other industries. If steel prices go up, so will prices of other products. Steel makers will have to pay more for the steel they use for their own equipment, more for coal and other supplies, more for transportation and other services, more for all the goods and services they buy which reflect increased prices to steel users.

Against all such possibilities, U. S. Steel and all other steel companies who follow its lead expect to insure themselves by at once making an increase in price which will assure their margin of profit if wage and price increases spread, just as their policy of charging a margin over standard costs insures them a steady return on capital averaged over good times and bad. They are enabled to do this only because price competition in the industry is, at most, a minor factor. They attempt to protect their investors against the hazards of economic fluctuations by passing on the costs, and at the same time to provide against any return of higher costs to their own operations.

Such a policy does not necessarily forestall public gain from gains in output per unit of labor and capital which occur in steel making. However, so far as productivity may differ from one steel company to another,

it tends to channel that difference into larger profits for the more efficient, without lower prices. In an industry subject to prevailing price
competition, the more efficient would also make greater profits than the
less efficient; but increases in efficiency would more readily be reflected in
lower prices, and the *average* output per unit of labor and capital in the
industry as a whole might increase more rapidly than if the less efficient
could find shelter under an industry-wide price umbrella.

Material relevant to this case study will be found in Chapter 8,
Markets and Prices; Chapter 9, The Theory of Supply and Demand;
and Chapter 10, The Theory of Business Organization.

QUESTIONS

1. If Bethlehem and Youngstown were permitted to merge, would
the presence of a competitor closer to the size of U. S. Steel affect the
price policies of the steel industry?
In discussing this question, one should consider:
(a) The prevailing practice of "standard costs"
(b) The policy of maintaining a margin over such costs
(c) The possibility of merger of smaller companies
(d) The danger of price wars to large corporations with heavy capital
investment
(e) The price policies of another industry where the top companies
are more nearly equal in size—for example, General Motors and Ford in
the automobile industry. Do they engage in price competition with each
other?

2. If the consuming public cannot be protected by installation of
effective price competition in steel, are there any alternatives? Under this
head, one might discuss:
(a) Public regulation, dependent on supervision and publicity for
cost determination and price policies
(b) Public ownership of part or all of the industry
(c) Voluntary change of practices by the companies themselves,
adopted in the public interest

3. In the interest of price competition, do you favor further antitrust
action in the steel industry? Under this head, one might consider:
(a) In view of the economies of scale in steel, would dissolution of
the big combines create enough companies to lead to real price competition?
(b) Is there a possibility that through antitrust action the existing
companies might be compelled to change their existing price policies?

4. Do you approve of the present practices in steel? Do you believe
that the problem would disappear if similar practices could be extended
to more competitive industries?

30 / THE KOREAN WAR

INFLATION[1] / The United States experienced post-war inflation beginning in 1946. Between 1945, the last year of World War II, and 1948 the consumers price index (1947–1949 = 100) had risen from 76.9 to 102.8. In 1949, however, a moderate business recession occurred, during which wholesale prices fell slightly and retail prices stopped rising. Recovery during the first half of 1950 brought wholesale prices up again to about the 1948 level. Authorities hoped, and indeed most of them expected, that no further general price increase would take place.

In June, 1950, the Korean War broke out. The United States as a member of the U. N. sent armed forces to aid the South Koreans and at the same time began an accelerated defense program. There arose intensified fears of a new world war. During the second half of 1950 the wholesale price index rose 10.9 percent, and the consumers price index went up 3.2 percent.

The problem before us is to analyze the origins of this price increase.

PRODUCTION (SUPPLY)

A general increase in prices may be expected when the effective demand rises faster than the supply of goods and services at existing prices. It will be well to begin, then, with an inquiry of what happened to supply in 1950.

There are no figures covering total production, in physical terms, of goods in the United States. There are, however, a somewhat incomplete

---

[1] Data on the subjects summarized in this chapter may be found in *The Economic Report of the President*, January, 1951, U.S. Government Printing Office, 1952; *Monetary Management and Fiscal Policy*, Congressional Joint Committee on the Economic Report; and 1950 and 1951 issues of *Federal Reserve Bulletin*, Board of Governors of the Federal Reserve System.

index of industrial production, figures on the output of farms, and figures on building construction. These are the three main components of the national output of physical goods. Output of services is more difficult to estimate (in physical terms) than output of goods, but production in at least one type of services is recorded—electrical-power output. Much can also be inferred from the course of employment; it is almost certain to increase over the short run if production is growing. Let us see what these figures indicate about the trend of supply from 1949 to 1950.

The index of *industrial production* rose throughout the year. For the year as a whole it was about twice the 1935–1939 average; it stood at 14 percent above 1949, and more than 4 percent above 1948, the most highly productive preceding year of peacetime. The greatest rise was in durable manufactures, but nondurable goods and minerals also increased.

Output of farms was the fourth largest on record and was only 4 percent below 1949. Livestock output increased 2 percent over 1949.

Building construction reached an all-time peak during the second half of 1950, and for the year as a whole was 17 percent above 1949.

Electrical-power output expanded steadily during the last half of 1950, and for the year as a whole was 13 per cent above 1949.

All the above figures are in terms of physical units of output; they therefore indicate that the price rise *did not result from any diminution in the supply of goods*. On the contrary, production of goods was rising rapidly and, for the year, was higher than ever before, except possibly in the war years 1943 and 1944.

Between the middle of 1949 and the end of 1950 the average work week in manufacturing rose from about 38.5 to 41 hours. Figures on employment indicate that during the year many unemployed persons found jobs. At the end of 1950 only 3.6 percent of the labor force was unemployed—a low figure. There were probably more shortages in the labor supply than in the supply of goods.

INCOME (DEMAND)

The gross national expenditure was $255.6 billion in 1949; its annual rate was $266.8 billion in the first half of 1950 and $290.6 billion in the second half. Total expenditure in the last six months of 1950 was therefore running about 12 percent more than in 1949 and about 8 percent more than in the first half of 1950.

The total money spent in 1950 was therefore larger than in 1949, and it was larger in the second half of 1950 than in the first half. Since we have no complete figures of the growth of physical production in this period, we cannot make any precise calculation to see whether spending increased faster than physical output. We do know, however, that between June and December of 1950 wholesale prices rose 10.9 percent and retail (consumers') prices rose 3.2 percent. We may reasonably infer from this fact that spending increased faster than output. The price increase must be accounted for by a rise in effective demand exceeding the apparent rise in supply.

WHOSE SPENDING INCREASED THE DEMAND?

In order to analyze the sources of the Korean War inflation, it would be helpful to know from what kinds of spending the increase in demand arose. What groups of spenders contributed to the expansion of demand, and how much did they contribute?

Consumers spent, in the last six months of 1950, at the annual rate of $13.9 billion more than in the first six months. This increase, of course, added to total demand.

Business spent (as gross investment) at the annual rate of $18.4 billion more in the last six months of 1950 than in the first six months. Business, therefore, added more to total demand than did consumers.

International transactions did not contribute to demand at all. In fact, during the last six months of the year, they *subtracted* from demand at the annual rate of $3.4 billion, or $1.6 billion more than they had subtracted in the first six months.

Government spent less in the second six months of the year than in the first six months. The reduction was at the annual rate of $3.2 billion. In the last six months government was taking more cash from the public than it was paying out, and therefore subtracted from demand.

These figures are taken from "The Nation's Economic Budget" as tabulated on page 165 of the *Economic Report of the President* for January, 1951. They are rough figures, but they unquestionably indicate that the whole increase in demand came from consumers and business, and that neither foreign aid nor government spending played a part in the inflationary spurt. On the contrary, these two sources of spending were declining.

Now let us look more closely at the behavior of the main groups of spenders.

CONSUMER SPENDING

The first point to note is that consumers had much larger incomes at their disposal in 1950 than in 1949. In 1949 their disposable income was $187.4 billion; in the first half of 1950, it rose to an annual rate of $196.6 billion, and in the second half of the year to $207.6 billion. Consumers' incomes for the year (1950) as a whole rose mainly on account of increases in wages, salaries, and other payments for work. The rise in property income (profits, rent, interest) was barely more than one fourth as large as the increase in labor payments. (See Table A–5, p. 175, *Economic Report of the President,* January, 1951.)

The increase in income from wages and salaries was largely the result of fuller employment. Even if ceilings on wages had been in force in

June, 1950—and they were not—some increases in wage rates could not have been avoided. But if no wage advances had been permitted during the year, the major part of the increase in consumer income would still have occurred because more people worked more hours to supply the increased demand.

Consumers would not have spent so much of this disposable income as they did if they had saved more. According to Keynes, the consumption percentage ordinarily falls as total income rises; that is, consumers will spend a smaller proportion of their incomes and save more, when their incomes are increased. In this case exactly the contrary occurred. In the second quarter of 1950 personal saving was $10.4 billion, or 6.5 percent of disposable income—a fairly high rate for a peacetime year. In the third quarter personal saving dropped to $6.4 billion, or about 3.1 percent of income. People borrowed more for installment payments, drew from their savings accounts, and cashed in government savings bonds (Series E).

The jump in consumer demand was largely for automobiles, other consumer durable goods, and semidurable goods such as tires and clothing. Over one half of the increase in consumer purchases between the second and third quarters of 1950 was accounted for by these types of goods. The spurt in demand for durable goods between the second and third quarters was 7 percent—the largest on record. In the fourth quarter this part of the demand slackened away, but an increase in demand for nondurables partly made up for the drop.

One major result of increased consumer demand was somewhat higher prices for what the consumers bought. Did prices rise enough so that in the aggregate consumers could acquire no more goods than before? Between the first and second half of 1950, there was a gain of about 2 percent in the purchasing power of consumers' disposable income as a whole. Since consumers spent a larger percentage of their income in the second half than in the first, they were able to make a substantial addition of goods to their possessions.

BUSINESS SPENDING

Business, of course, spends a great deal of money for current production by buying materials and paying wages; rent, interest, and other expenses. But in national income accounting the amount spent in the production and marketing of goods sold is not counted under business spending, since it becomes part of the amount paid by consumers, government, and other purchasers; and it is their spendings that *are* counted.

What we do add to total national spending is the business outlay for goods which are retained at least for the time being; that is, additions to investment, or capital goods. There are three main categories of business investment—producers' durable equipment, construction, and net change in business inventories.

The investment in producers' durable equipment—machinery, fac-

TABLE 30/1

THE NATION'S ECONOMIC BUDGET, CALENDAR YEARS 1949 AND 1950
(in billions of dollars, annual rates, seasonally adjusted)

Economic group	1949 Receipts	1949 Expenditures	1949 Excess of receipts (+) or expenditures (−)	1950, First half Receipts	1950, First half Expenditures	1950, First half Excess of receipts (+) or expenditures (−)	1950, Second half[1] Receipts	1950, Second half Expenditures	1950, Second half Excess of receipts (+) or expenditures (−)
Consumers									
Disposable income	187.4	—	—	196.6	—	—	207.6	—	—
Consumption expenditures	—	178.8	—	—	183.8	—	—	197.7	—
Personal net saving (+)	—	—	+8.6	—	—	+12.7	—	—	+10.0
Business									
Retained receipts	30.2	—	—	30.1	—	—	28.4	—	—
Gross private domestic investment	—	33.0	—	—	44.3	—	—	52.7	—
Excess of receipts (+), or investment (−)	—	—	−2.8	—	—	−14.2	—	—	−24.3
International									
Cash loans abroad	1.1	—	—	−.2	—	—	.1	—	—
Net foreign investment	—	.4	—	—	−1.8	—	—	−3.4	—
Excess of receipts (+), or investment (−)	—	—	+.7	—	—	+1.6	—	—	+3.5

Government				
Cash receipts from the public....	57.6	58.8	62.7	59.8
Cash payments to the public....	60.2	63.0	63.0	—
Cash surplus (+), or deficit (−)	−2.5	−4.2	—	+2.9
Adjustments				
(To arrive at gross national product)				
For receipts²	−20.7	−18.5	−8.2	−16.2
For expenditures³	−16.8	−22.5	—	—
Difference between adjustments	−4.0	+4.1	—	+7.9
Total gross national product	255.6	266.8	290.6	290.6

¹ Estimates based on incomplete data.

² Includes receipts which do not arise from current production and hence are not a part of the national income: Transfers to individuals, government interest, cash loans abroad, and the difference between tax liabilities and cash receipts; also includes statistical discrepancy.

³ Includes all cash payments which are not payments for goods and services and hence are not included in the gross national product.

Note: Detail will not necessarily add to totals because of rounding.

tories and the like—had been at a high level in 1948 and was slowly rising until near the end of the year. Then, during the mild recession, it began to fall slowly, but did not fall below the point at which it started at the beginning of 1948. In the 1950 recovery, the purchase of equipment turned sharply upward and was already rising when the Korean War started. Thereafter it rose even more rapidly. Purchase of machinery and other equipment (at the seasonally adjusted annual rate) rose from $19.9 billion in the first quarter of 1950 to $22.3 billion in the second quarter and ended the year at $28.7 billion in the fourth quarter. After June, 1950, business was responding (1) to government orders to be executed in the future, for which government had not yet paid but which demanded preliminary expenditures by business and (2) to enlarged consumer demand.

Residential construction (not on farms) had been rising ever since the middle of 1949 and continued the rise until the third quarter of 1950, when it began to recede. This rise was more moderate than that of business equipment.

Business inventories consist of stocks of raw materials, goods in process, and finished goods not yet sold. Inventories were accumulated all through the spring of 1950. This is usual in a period of recovery, since, in the preceding slump, businesses usually curtailed their orders for supplies and tried to sell off as much as possible of what they had on hand. In the third quarter of 1950 consumer demand was so insistent that business sold goods faster than it could replenish its stocks, and inventories declined again sharply. This demand stimulated production, so that, after the first rush, inventories shot up again in the fourth quarter, largely because of greatly increased production. Thus, an appreciable share of the enlarged physical output of 1950 did not get into the hands of final purchasers before the end of the year, but remained in the stock rooms and warehouses of business establishments and was later to cause them some concern.

INTERNATIONAL SPENDING

If United States exports of goods and services equaled imports, its people would be receiving from abroad the same value of goods that they sent there, and the aggregate supply of goods in the United States would not be affected. Any influence on American prices would result from international transactions which might affect demand in the United States. Transactions other than those which arise from current trade in goods and services are chiefly loans, investments, or grants. If, at a time when trade was balanced, foreign nations transferred to the United States loans, investments, or gifts which were to be spent for factories, public improvements, or other products in this country, demand in the United States would be increased. If the United States transferred such funds to other nations, demand in this country would be decreased.

In 1950 the United States had a small and diminishing export surplus. Other nations were selling more here than formerly and buying less. The United States, needing strategic materials for its defense program, bought many of them abroad, and so great was its demand that the prices of rubber, tin, and other materials rose drastically. The net result was that the United States export surplus decreased to about $1.8 billion for the year and to about $0.6 billion (annual rate) in the second half of the year. In view of the fact that our gross national output was approaching $290 billion, this was a negligible net drain on domestic supplies, as well as a diminishing one.

At the same time United States Government aid to other countries, plus private investments, loans, and gifts, greatly exceeded the export surplus. The 1950 total of these transfers of money from the United States to foreign nations was in the neighborhood of $5.5 billion. The government and the people of the United States, in their foreign transactions, were transferring abroad much more demand (money and credit) than they were losing in supply (goods and services constituting the export surplus). International transactions in 1950, and especially in the last half of the year, thus constituted a *counter*inflationary force.

Incidentally, the foreign nations receiving this surplus of money and credit used it largely in building up their reserves of dollars and gold—a highly necessary purpose, since in past years they had drawn down these reserves dangerously, to pay for necessary imports from the dollar area.

GOVERNMENT SPENDING

The 1950 budget of the federal government as conventionally set up showed a deficit of $422 million. This budget, however, contained numerous items of expense which do not increase the current income of private persons, since they are payments into government trust funds for social security and the like. The only governmental transactions that can directly add to or subtract from aggregate demand are cash payments. The federal government in 1953 received about $500 million more from the public than it paid out in *cash*. It was not, therefore, making any net addition to demand, but on the contrary its fiscal policy was checking inflation. This may surprise persons who remember the large appropriations for defense, but the sums appropriated in 1950 were not for the most part actually spent in that year, because time was required to prepare orders, sign contracts, and manufacture the goods.

Adding receipts and expenditures of state and local governments to those of the federal government, in the first half of 1950 all governmental cash expenditures exceeded receipts by $4.2 billion but in the second half governmental receipts exceeded cash expenditures by $2.9 billion. Government was therefore stimulating demand during the recovery of January–June, but was restricting it after inflation took hold with the outbreak of the Korean War. This is, of course, exactly the course recommended by those who advocate a compensatory fiscal policy.

SUMMARY OF DEMAND

The figures prove that the jump in demand which made possible the price increases after June, 1950, came solely from consumers and business investment. Foreign aid and government fiscal policy were acting in the contrary direction.

What activated this demand? Apparently the outbreak of hostilities led both consumers and businessmen, who vividly remembered the shortages of World War II, to expect higher prices and scarce supplies. Both hastened to stock up with goods that were not perishable—consumers, in order to get the goods before prices rose and to have them on hand; businessmen, in order to get the goods before prices rose and to sell them to consumers. Both together caused the price rises that they anticipated, but no important shortages developed. After the price increases had appeared, consumer demand slackened and businesses engaged in manufacturing for consumers or selling to them were left for several months with greatly enlarged stocks of goods.

At the same time much of the business demand arose from well-founded anticipation that the government would require large quantities of supplies and munitions. The new defense program was responsible for this type of investment, even though the spending it involved did not come directly from government.

What did government do to curb the price rise? It did not at once impose price and wage ceilings or rationing of consumer goods, but merely announced that it would do so when and if necessary. This announcement probably stimulated buying rather than the reverse, since it held before consumers' eyes the prospect that there might come a time when it would be difficult to find wanted goods at present prices. It also stimulated business to raise prices before any price freeze went into effect. Practically, however, it would have been difficult to enforce controls at once, since the administrative machinery for doing so had been disbanded.

The government also announced that supplies were so ample and production so high there was no danger of shortages. Hoarding of goods could only drive prices up unnecessarily and was contrary to the public interest. As usual, such appeals to public morality had little influence on the hoarders, who were seeking their own interest.

The government did act to keep down prices of a few imported strategic materials of which it was the chief buyer, by temporarily ceasing to buy them.

WHERE DID THE MONEY COME FROM?

In addition to checking-account balances, savings accounts, and the like, consumer liquid funds included the National Service Life Insurance dividend distributed to veterans in the first part of 1950. Consumers also borrowed large sums on installment credit and increased the charge accounts which they owed. This new borrowing involved an enlargement of credit by the banking system.

Corporations which invested money derived about $12.5 billion of it from net earnings not distributed as dividends—several billion more than in 1949. From depreciation reserves they derived slightly more than in 1949. The remainder—and the largest part, $19 billion—they derived from sale of new stocks and bonds, an increase of bank loans amounting to $2.5 billion, and an expansion of trade debt amounting to $3.5 billion. The latter two items contrasted sharply with 1949, when corporations were paying off both bank loans and trade debt.

Undistributed corporate profits represent corporate saving. Sales of new stocks and bonds also depended partly on current saving by the public. Nevertheless, an important fraction of the expansion of business spending, like that of consumer spending, rested on expansion of bank credit—the ultimate source of money added to the income-spending flow.

Loans and investments of all banks increased by about $7.5 billion in 1950. This was not a remarkably large increase, but more significant than the change in the total was the shift of loans and investments within it. Bank loans increased nearly $11 billion—by far the largest increase in one year on record. Total investments fell by about $3.5 billion, but this decline of investments occurred entirely in United States Government obligations. Indeed, a large enough total of federal securities was sold by the banks not only to finance much of the expansion of loans but to enable the banks to buy new securities issued by business and local governments as well. What the banks were doing was to dispose of federal securities in the open market in order to obtain additional cash which they could use to supply the urgent demand for loans to consumers and business concerns.

FEDERAL RESERVE POLICY

During World War II and afterward the federal reserve banks had been buying federal government securities in the open market whenever necessary to keep up their prices. This made it easy for banks (as well as others) to sell such securities without loss and thus to obtain money to lend. Any purchase of securities by reserve banks increased the reserves of the member banks by an amount equal to the purchase price; every dollar added to reserves permitted an expansion of money in the hands of the public (including bank deposits) five to six times as great as the increase in member bank reserves. As long as this policy prevailed, credit expansion could be curbed only by increasing the reserve ratio required of the member banks or by curbs on specific types of credit such as installment or mortgage loans. (See Chapter 13.)

Between the beginning of 1950 and June 30, the federal reserve banks had slightly decreased their holdings of government securities. But between June 30 and December 31, 1950, they bought more than $2.4 billion of these securities, thus supporting their prices as the member banks sold them and increasing member bank reserves by a like amount. The Reserve authorities took this action not because they wanted to expand credit; on the contrary they wished to restrict it. But they had been unable to reach an agreement with the Treasury which would release them from the obligation to support the price of government securities, and had to acquire some in the maneuvering which finally brought the disagreement to a head. On the other hand, they did take restrictive measures, such as raising the discount rate in August. They also imposed selective controls on borrowing for real-estate developments and on installment buying by consumers. These restrictions somewhat restrained the credit expansion. They were aided by a small outflow of gold to foreign nations.

In 1949 the people of the United States obtained a real increase in goods and services. But the increase in effective demand and the preparation by business concerns to fulfill it brought about a substantial rise in prices. It would be interesting to consider how the nation might have enjoyed a real gain without rising prices. The following problem may help to do so.

Material relevant to this case study may be found in Chapter 13, Federal Reserve and Government; Chapter 14, Theories of Money and Income; Chapter 15, Business Cycles; and Chapter 16, Government Spending, Lending, and Taxing.

PROBLEM

Assume that, taking the gross national product as a whole, 7 percent more goods and services were produced in 1950 than in 1949.

Assume also (contrary to historical fact) that there was *no* average price increase for the gross national product as a whole.

Draw up a tabulation of the nation's economic budget for the second half of 1950 which might reflect this situation. This table should be carried out in the same detail as Table 30/1 on page 364. Assume that the adjustments required to arrive at gross national product at the end of the table remain unchanged by the above assumptions.

Explain what your tabulation implies, under each main heading. Suggest what policies, if any, might have achieved the increase of production which did actually occur, without the price increase which historically accompanied it.

Note that there may be numerous correct answers to this problem. Answers should be tested (1) by their consistency with the assumptions, (2) by their internal consistency, and (3) by their probability in view of known and relevant facts.

The chief purpose of this exercise is to illuminate the issues involved in restraining inflation. Discussion may well center about answers presented by members of the class. These points might be considered:

Business incentive to produce more without anticipation of rising prices.

Consider this situation in the light of Fisher's "equation of exchange." If, as is assumed, T (transactions) increased without a change in P (price level), what possible changes in M (volume of money) or V (velocity) might have been necessary?

What would have been the implications for federal reserve policy?

31 / INFLATION, 1948-1958, AND THE AUTOMOBILE INDUSTRY /

The Subcommittee on Antitrust and Monopoly of the Committee on the Judiciary, a body of the United States Senate, became interested in the rising prices which characterized the economy between 1948 and 1958. They regarded "creeping inflation" as a great menace. Some members of the Committee attributed this inflation in large measure to the raising of prices by oligopolistic industries like steel and automobiles, in which a few big concerns dominate the market and have the power to decide at what prices they will sell their products. The question whether action of this kind held prices unnecessarily high became even more crucial in the latter part of 1957, because a business recession had set in, with growing unemployment and reduced sales, particularly in the automobile industry. This recession, however, was not accompanied by any drop in the index of consumer prices or by any reduction in automobile prices. On the contrary, the price trend continued upward.

A representative of the Ford Motor Company—Theodore O. Yntema, Vice President—Finance, a well-known economist with a creditable record in university teaching, governmental work, and research—testified before the Committee on this subject. The following is a brief summary of some points in the printed record of his testimony.[1]

Dr. Yntema begins by saying that inflation may be of two types: (1) that in which prices are pulled up by an excess of demand for products on the part of purchasers or (2) that in which prices are pushed up by rising costs of labor and materials, the prices of which may be arbitrarily raised by the sellers, even though there is no shortage of supply. "In actual experience we do not get pure cases of demand-pull inflation or cost-push inflation, but . . . some inflations are predominantly of one

---

[1] Theodore O. Yntema, *Statement,* before the Subcommittee on Antitrust and Monopoly of the Committee on the Judiciary, U. S. Senate. Detroit: Ford Motor Company.

type, some are of the other type." The existing inflation, Dr. Yntema believed, was of the cost-push variety. Therefore he proceeded to ask whether the upward push was caused mainly by labor or by business.

WAGE PAYMENTS UP; PROFITS DOWN

His first exhibit, based on U. S. Department of Commerce figures, covers business corporations in the United States as a whole. It shows that from 1948 through 1957, total compensation of corporate employees rose by 75 percent, or $68 billion. In the same period total taxes on profits rose $9 billion. And also in the same period, profits after taxes—that is, the proceeds of corporate business which belonged to the stockholders—shrank slightly, from $17.3 billion to $17.0 billion, or by $300 million.

Expressed in constant dollars (with the same value as in 1956), the return on invested corporate capital shrank from 11.9 percent to 8.6 percent, and the return on sales shrank from 4.4 percent to 2.8 percent. Dr. Yntema concludes that wage payments, which expanded, pushed prices up, while profits, which shrank, did not.

WHEN, SUPPOSEDLY, DID COST-PUSH
BECOME DECISIVE?

Another exhibit in the testimony (Exhibit 3) is introduced as evidence that, although rising demand was the chief influence in boosting prices between 1939 and 1951, rising costs became the chief factor between 1951 and 1957. The argument is an interesting one. Between 1939 and 1951, corporate profits, *as a percentage of the national product,* rose when wholesale prices were rising, and fell when wholesale prices were falling. A rise in wholesale prices usually indicates an upward shift in the demand schedule and accompanies a period of business prosperity. But when demand falls off, wholesale prices usually fall, and profits fall with them, partly because less can be sold at the lower level of demand and partly because prices charged may be lower. But, after 1951, argues the witness, although wholesale prices had a generally rising tendency, the share of profits in the national income had a falling tendency. This is taken to indicate that profits were being squeezed by higher costs. As support for this contention, the Exhibit states that in the years 1955–1957 output per man-hour in manufacturing rose only 1.1 percent, while in the same period average hourly earnings of manufacturing labor rose 10 percent. The inference seems to be that in face of rising material prices and labor costs, manufacturers wished to protect profit margins by raising the prices of their products, but demand was not strong enough so that aggregate profits could maintain their customary share of the national income even at higher prices.

COSTS AND PROFITS IN AUTOMOBILES

In the automobile industry, the witness states, demand did decline after 1955, but costs went up at the expense of profit margins, and total profits fell. Automobile companies did increase their prices, but not enough to maintain profit margins at the former level, in spite of all advances in productivity the automobile industry could achieve.

Exhibit 5 of the testimony compares the average hourly labor rates with Ford car prices, showing that, whereas prices were 13.1 percent higher in 1958 than in 1954, hourly labor rates were 19.8 percent higher. "The Company's hourly labor rates," Dr. Yntema writes, "represent the largest single factor in our product costs." Note that he does not say that they are more than half, or even half, of costs, but are "the largest single factor." What other factors are important? Steel-mill products obviously are, and these went up 27.4 percent 1954–1958—far more than automobile hourly labor rates. So did metal-working machinery and equipment, which went up 28.6 percent in the same period. So did durable goods in general.

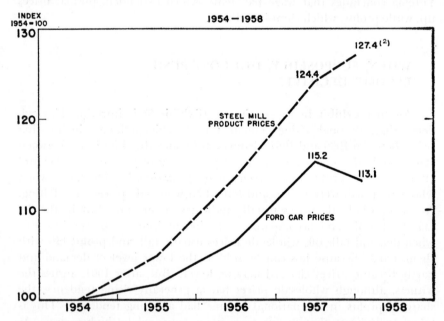

Fig. 31.1. FORD CAR PRICE INDEX[1] COMPARED WITH BLS WHOLESALE
PRICE INDEX FOR STEEL-MILL PRODUCTS, 1954-1958.

---

[1] Based on 1957 custom 300 8-cylinder 4-door sedan and most comparable models in other years.

The witness did not discuss what prompted the rise in steel prices, but it might be difficult for the steel industry to prove that rising labor costs compelled it to raise its prices as much as it did. During the recession, early in 1958, U. S. Steel reported sufficient profit—in spite of operation at about half capacity—to pay its usual dividends and add a substantial amount to earned surplus. The burden of fixed costs in steel is heavy, because of the huge investment required in steel mills. If not only variable costs but also fixed costs were handsomely covered when plants were running at only half capacity at the bottom of a recession, it would appear that the more prosperous steel companies, at least, might have absorbed some of the rise in labor costs without raising prices as much as they did.

Further exhibits indicate how much more material went into Ford cars in 1958 than in 1954—a fact which would be generally acknowledged.

The cars became larger and more powerful and contained more equipment and special features. The price index previously cited "contains adjustments for certain equipment changes" but "does not reflect all of the increased cost. . . ." No doubt a good deal of the rise in cost, one must infer, arose because each car represented *more* labor and *more* materials in 1958 than in 1954, not merely because prices of labor and materials rose.

ADMINISTERED PRICES AND COMPETITION

Dr. Yntema freely admits that each automobile concern sets the prices at which it will sell its products, and he defends this practice as the only practicable method. A price set by the producer is an "administered" price, as distinguished from a price which arises solely from the interplay of demand and supply in a market, as it does in the case of many agricultural products. A wheat grower does not decide how much he will charge per bushel of wheat when he plants his seed; he knows he will have to sell it for what he can get. What he can get may be influenced by governmental price support, but it is not set by the individual producer.

Many things that we buy are, in the above sense, sold at administered prices. This is particularly true of manufactured goods produced by large corporations. Automobile companies do compete in seeking favor of the purchasers, but they set prices at what they hope will bring a planned profit. If, at these prices, they cannot sell all they can produce, they curtail operations and lay off employees. Thus, the supply is trimmed as close as possible to the demand *at the prices set*.

Now let us examine the points made by Dr. Yntema, to see what might be said on the other side of the controversy.

CAN WE HAVE COST-PUSH INFLATION?

There is disagreement among economists as to whether increase of prices in any one sector of the economy *can* cause a general price rise, in the absence of a general increase in demand. On this question there are a number of positions, the more prominent of which may be summarized as follows:

1. If aggregate demand does not rise, a pushing up of prices in any one or more parts of the economy must have one (and perhaps both) of the following consequences: (a) diminished purchases of the goods and services, the prices of which have risen, or (b) diminished purchases of other goods and services. In either case the result is slackened production and unemployment. This slump will lead to reduction of prices and possibly of wages at least in the more highly competitive sectors of the economy, with consequent fall of average prices, so that the average price rise is not maintained. Consequently, if prices in general actually do continue upward, the rise must be due, at least in large measure, to an increase in aggregate demand greater than the increase in supply.

2. A similar theory also begins with the conception that price increases, in the absence of increased general demand, will bring about unemployment. It proceeds from this conclusion, however, to the proposition that when recession occurs, government and central banking authorities will try to increase aggregate demand by deficit spending and easy credit, so that, in the end, recovery follows, but only at higher price levels than before the slump. In this sense, long-term "creeping inflation" cannot take place without a demand which rises faster than the supply, but this increase in demand may nevertheless be triggered by the upward push of prices and/or wages in key industries.

3. Some economists point out that, whatever the theoretical explanation, prices have, until the recent past, fallen in contractions and risen in recoveries. If, therefore, prices do not fall in recession, we are virtually certain to have a long-term upward tendency in prices, because they will usually rise when business is good and employment is high.

The witness did not discuss such theoretical questions in detail. We shall therefore consider his main arguments, as summarized above.

WAGES AND PROFITS

Discussing his first exhibit, Dr. Yntema asks, "Can there be any possible question as to which is the dominant force in inflation—the profits that declined $300 million or the wages and salaries that went up $68 billion?" At first sight, it may look as if higher wages and salaries must be responsible for the rise of prices. But, in the spirit of scientific inquiry, let us see whether there *can* be any question.

First, let us note that these figures of profits represent what remained *after federal taxes on them had been paid.* Do such figures tell us anything as to whether corporations have tried to increase their profits by raising prices? Certainly not much, since corporations might have raised prices and still have come out, in the end, with smaller profits after taxes. One important reason is that the government increased tax rates. If we add together the profits and the taxes paid on them, we find that corporate profits *before* payment of taxes rose from $29.8 billion in 1948 to $38.4 billion in 1957—an increase of $8.6 billion, or about 22 percent. This is a sizable percentage increase, though a smaller one than that in aggregate earnings of employees (which, of course, are taxed also).

Next we have to consider whether the corporations might have made more money than they did if they had charged lower prices. We do not know. It is theoretically possible that the elasticity of demand was great enough so that lower prices would have increased corporate sales and revenue. The aggregate figures simply do not tell us whether profits were limited, on the one hand, by restraint in raising prices or, on the other hand, by price increase.

POSSIBLE REASONS FOR INCREASE
IN WAGE PAYMENTS

Next, let us think a little more carefully about the possible reasons for the 75 percent jump in wage and salary payments between 1948 and 1957. Does this mean that wage rates per hour or per piece were raised 75 percent? Not at all, since there were many more corporate employees in 1957 than in 1948. Wage rates did rise, but not by anything like 75 percent. And it is the wage per hour or per piece that bears on *costs*. Does an increase in wage rates cause an equal increase in the unit cost of labor? Not unless the output per man-hour does not rise as much as the pay. Suppose ten men working 40 hours can produce the equivalent of two automobiles. If they get $2 an hour, the weekly wages paid to the ten (in a 40-hour week) will be $800, and the labor cost in each car will be $400. Now suppose their wages are raised to $3 an hour, and at the same time they are enabled, by more efficient machinery and methods, to turn out three cars a week. Their total weekly wages will be $1,200, but the labor cost in each car will remain $400. Higher pay will not have raised the cost of a car, because labor productivity has risen 50 percent while hourly wages increased by the same percentage.

Although no figures exist for productivity in *all corporations*, the Department of Labor has estimated that output per man-hour for employees in *manufacturing* probably rose about 30 percent between 1948 and 1957. Between the same years hourly wage earnings in manufacturing (hours actually paid for, whether or not worked) rose by about 58 percent, or more than the rise in manufacturing labor productivity.[2] These figures (not cited in the document we are discussing) do indicate that unit labor costs in manufacturing may have risen. There is some doubt about this conclusion, however, since, as the Economic Report points out, these productivity statistics are far from perfect as a measure of labor input.

---

[2] *Economic Report of the President*, 1958, pp. 108 and 145.

Even more dubious is the conclusion that if labor costs have risen through a rise in money wage rates greater than the simultaneous increase in productivity, the rise in wages is a cause rather than an effect, at least in part, of the general price rise. Suppose the cost of living has already risen when a wage demand is made. The worker's dollars will buy less than when his existing wage rate was fixed. He has to get more dollars just to stay even. Can the part of his wage increase granted to cover a prior rise in prices be held responsible for a future price rise? If so, then one must conclude that, in order to stop rising prices, it is necessary to reduce the purchasing power and the levels of living of wage earners. That scarcely seems either logical or fair.

An increase in hourly wage rates larger than an increase in output per man-hour does indeed raise labor cost, however just the wage boost may be. But this does not necessarily lead to higher prices in a market not fully competitive, unless the employer raises his selling price, thus contributing his bit to the upward wage-price spiral. Unions frequently argue that the employer can more easily absorb a reduction in profit margin than wage earners can absorb a decline in level of living, especially if profits seem ample.

The consumer price index for city wage earners and clerical workers' families (1947–1949 = 100) stood at 121.6 in November, 1957. Thus, the cost of living rose about 20 percent during the same period when hourly earnings in manufacturing rose 58 percent. *Real* hourly earnings, therefore, rose only about 30 percent. (See Chaper 6 for method of calculation.) Is not this the proper figure to compare with the rise of 30 percent in output per man-hour?

A careful estimate of productivity in the private sector of the economy, made for the National Bureau of Economic Research[3] finds that physical output per weighted man-hour increased between 1945–1948 and 1953–1957 by an average 2.9 percent a year, while at the same time real hourly earnings in manufacturing increased by an annual average of 2.7 percent, or slightly less.[4]

Dr. Yntema states that, in the automobile industry, demand for cars fell after 1955, and in spite of increased prices, profit margins were narrowed.

This statement about the automobile industry raises some interesting questions, which remain unanswered.

1. Is it possible that the decline in demand for automobiles was due not to a fall of demand in general but to the rise in prices for cars or to

---

[3] Solomon Fabricant, *Basic Facts on Productivity Change.* New York, National Bureau of Economic Research, Inc., 1959.
[4] In this study the figures for output per man-hour are weighted by giving greater weight to high-pay industries than to low-pay industries, in order to account for "change in the composition or quality of labor." If the unweighted figures are taken, the growth in output per man-hour for the period in question is 3.3 percent—even further above the gain in real hourly earnings.

other factors peculiar to the automobile industry, such as changes in consumers' tastes?

2. Is it not possible that rising costs of the materials of which automobiles are made contributed as much—or even more—to the squeeze on automobile profits as did a rise in the unit cost of automobile labor?

Competition among a few big concerns, however keen it may be, does not affect prices as does competition among many small ones, which can exert no control over the prices at which their products are sold. As long as this is the case, can rising labor costs alone be regarded as the cause of higher prices for industrial products? Must we not include also the manufacturer's effort to support profits by maintaining prices above costs, even though this effort is unsuccessful in achieving its object of preventing a shrinkage of profits?

Material relevant to this case study may be found in Chapter 10, Business Organization; Chapter 18, Theories Regarding Labor and Wages; and Chapter 23, Technology and Production.

QUESTIONS

We are now in a position to consider a few basic questions.

1. What would have happened to manufactured goods in 1958 if all manufacturers, like the many small competitors which are assumed by the textbook price theory, had been compelled to accept whatever prices the market would bring, and had kept right on producing as long as their variable costs were covered, profit or no profit? Would their prices not have fallen until all the automobiles (and other factory products) that could be made with existing equipment were sold at a price that would at least repay variable costs?

2. If it is true that rising costs pushed up prices, did not *both* labor and business play a role in the process? Would not a rise of costs anywhere in the flow of goods be followed by a rise of prices which, in turn, would be reflected by a rise in costs to those who bought the product, as long as business concerns try to maintain profit margins by raising prices enough to compensate for rising costs?

On this point, we may consider a passage on the economy of the United States from the 1958 annual report of the Bank for International Settlements, a highly respected and influential institution. The Bank points out that in this recession there was

> . . . one economic indicator that did not behave according to the usual pattern. Prices—both consumer and wholesale—were still rising in March, 1958.
>
> This continuous upward movement took place, although the prices of

important internationally traded raw materials and foodstuffs had been falling since the end of the Suez crisis. The reason must be sought at least partly in the continued increase in wage costs in 1957. Gross hourly earnings, excluding overtime in manufacturing industries, were on an average 3.5 percent higher at the end of 1957 than at the end of 1956. . . . The available evidence suggests that productivity per man hour increased less than wages. . . . But this wage movement cannot be the whole explanation. One would have expected that competition in a weakening market would have brought down prices at the expense of profits. Total profits after taxes were, however, just as high in the first three quarters of 1957 as they had been in the corresponding period in 1956 (at an annual rate of $20.8 billion against $20.6 billion) . . . . In the last quarter profits fell to about $18 billion, but this fall was probably attributable more to the decline in output than to a reduction in unit profit margin. It seems, then, that business preferred to keep prices unchanged, or even to raise them together with wage costs, rather than to stimulate demand by letting prices fall, thus maintaining output as far as possible. . . .

3. So far in this chapter we have been speaking of productivity in terms of *output per man-hour* in specific industries or sections of the economy. There is also a broader and somewhat different concept of productivity—output per person in the population. Clearly, it is the relation between the total of goods and services produced and the number of persons who exist to share in this total output, that determines whether or how much real incomes may rise on the average.

For a long recent period, according to national income statistics, the real net national product per capita of population rose at an average rate of about 1.9 percent annually. The increase was greater in some years than others—this was the *average* yearly increase. It was this long upward trend in output per capita of population that made possible the marked rise in real incomes which took place—including, of course, the rise in wages.

Now, suppose that we use some such figure as a measure of how much the real incomes of workers can rise without adversely affecting any other type of income. Let us assume that real national output per capita of population has, in any given year, increased 2 percent. Then it is obvious that total real-wage incomes could in that year be increased by 2 percent, and at the same time total profits, interest, rent, or any other form of income could also increase, in real terms, 2 percent.

If real-wage incomes are to be increased 2 percent, how is the result to be achieved? There are three ways in which this might roughly take place, depending on what has happened to prices.

(a) If the prices which consumers have to pay are the same when the wage adjustment is made as a year earlier, then real hourly wages could be increased 2 percent by adding 2 cents to every dollar of wages paid.

(b) If consumer prices have risen during the year, then real hourly wages would first have to be restored to the level at which they stood a year earlier by granting a percentage increase in money wages equal to the percentage rise in consumer prices which has occurred. Real wages could then be increased 2 percent by adding 2 cents for every dollar paid.

(c) If consumer prices had fallen during the year, real wages would go up proportionally without any change in the dollars paid. If, for example, the consumer price index had been 100 a year earlier, and now was 98, every wage dollar would buy 2 cents worth more than a year before, and therefore a 2 percent rise in real wages would occur purely in consequence of the fall in prices. If the fall in prices were less than enough to increase real wages 2 percent, some increase in money wages would be necessary.

Up to this point, we have been thinking of the *total* of wages paid in the nation, as well as the total of all other forms of income. Actually, wages are not paid out in a single lump and then divided pro rata among all the millions of wage earners, any more than profits, interests, or rents are paid in single lumps and then apportioned to the recipients of these forms of income. Wages are paid by single employers, whose circumstances differ.

The ability of any business concern to pay higher wages without suffering reduction of profit or raising prices depends, as we have seen, on the increase of output per unit of input in that concern. But productivity (defined in this way) varies widely among different firms and among different industries and other types of employer. For example, a college usually does not strive to increase the number of graduates per teacher, since education is not a mere matter of quantity of output. And usually a college makes no profit at all. On the other hand, productivity may, and usually does, increase far more rapidly than the national average in a mechanical and mass-production industry like automobiles. Yet a gain of real income as national productivity rises is no less desirable for employees of a college than for employees of an automobile company.

Against this background, here are some interesting questions to think about and discuss. For each of the following questions let us assume, in the interest of simplicity, that no change in the price level has occurred during the previous year.

(a) Suppose that each group of employees obtained an increase of money wages or salaries fully equivalent to the gain in output per man-hour in the establishment of their own employer—no less and no more—and suppose no prices were increased in consequence. Would the national average of real wages (and salaries) rise by the same amount as the national average of output per man-hour? What would be the effect on the sharing of the national gain among various groups of employees?

(b) Suppose no group of employees obtained any gain in money rates of pay, but that each employer reduced his selling prices by the same amount that his unit costs were reduced by greater productivity. Would the national average of real wages (and salaries) rise by the same amount as the national increase in output per capita of the population? Would the gain in productivity be shared by everybody?

(c) Suppose that each firm or employer increased real wages (and salaries) by the same percentage as the *national* gain in output per man-hour, regardless of the amount that productivity gained in his own establishments. And suppose that the firms whose productivity gain was greater than the amount of wage increase paid did not reduce their selling prices accordingly, while those whose gain in productivity was less than the wage increase paid raised their prices enough to compensate for the resulting addition to their costs. What would be the effect on average prices? And could the productivity gain be distributed fairly in this way?

32 / THE SLUMP IN AUTOMOBILE SALES,

1957-1958 / Sales of new passenger automobiles in the United States were at a high point in 1955, during which year 6,720,000 were bought—an increase of 1,730,000, or 35 percent over 1954. Not so many were purchased in 1956 or 1957. Motor car manufacturers, however, expected that 1958 would be another big year, since by then the models bought in 1955 would be three years old—a period in which many new-car buyers customarily turn in their old cars for new ones. At the end of three years also, most installment buyers will have met in full the monthly payments which are due on a car, and presumably will be ready to undertake new obligations of the same kind.

In July, 1957, the index number of new cars produced in the United States (based on 100 in 1947–1949) was 147. It fell in September to 84 and in October to 88. These are months in which demand for new automobiles normally declines, partly because of the approach of winter and partly because new annual models are in prospect. Manufacturers begin to change over for the new-model year, while many buyers wait in order to obtain the latest style. Production normally picks up again in November, as manufacturers prepare for the new demand, and, if demand is active, it continues generally upward through the spring and perhaps the early summer.

The index of United States car production for the model year 1958, however, ran as shown in Table 32/1, according to the Survey of Current Business, published by the U. S. Department of Commerce:

This was a disappointing record indeed. No sooner had the new models got into the hands of the dealer than production began to decline, and by April it was even below the level of ten years before. June, usually a good month, was below even January, February, or March, and from then on the decline was rapid. Is it possible to guess why this slump occurred?

TABLE 32/1

INDEX OF MOTOR CAR PRODUCTION FOR MODEL YEAR 1958
(1947–1949 = 100)

1957—Nov.	171
Dec.	151
1958—Jan.	132
Feb.	122
Mar.	106
Apr.	89
May	99
June	100
July	87
Aug.	53
Sept.	37

WAS THE RECESSION RESPONSIBLE?

In July, 1957, there began a downswing in the business cycle, which reached its bottom early in 1958. As measured by the usual indicators, this contraction was more severe than the two which had preceded it after World War II (in 1949 and 1954), though not so severe as the marked downswings reaching their bottoms in 1921, 1933, and 1938. The history of business cycles indicates that one type of activity which shows comparatively great variation between boom and depression is output of consumers' durable goods, of which automobiles are a major component. Was the recession, then, the cause of the drop in automobile sales?

If this were so, one might expect that sales fell off because the income of consumers was reduced by unemployment, part time, wage and salary cuts, and other factors. But this recession was unusual in that total personal income was little affected. The personal income in the United States (that is, all the money paid out to persons in wages, salaries, interest, dividends, rent, pensions, and the like) fell very little, and quickly recovered. Aggregate income of individuals, corrected for the usual seasonal variations, was running at the annual rate of $352.1 billion in August, 1957, before the recession had begun to be much felt. From there the figure fell to a low point of $346.4 billion in February, 1958, and thereafter recovered to $352.0 billion in June, 1958, and to $357.5 billion in September, 1958. In other words, the recession cut aggregate personal income, from the top of the former expansion to the bottom of the 1957-1958 contraction, only by about 1.6 percent. By September, 1958, personal income had recovered to a figure higher than that of a year before.[1] Would such a slight drop in personal income, followed by a recovery which left it above the level from which it began, account for

---

[1] U. S. Department of Commerce, *Survey of Current Business* monthly issues September, 1957, to December, 1958.

a marked drop in the output of passenger motor cars? At first glance, it hardly seems likely.

DISPOSABLE INCOME, CONSUMER PURCHASES, AND AUTOMOBILE SALES

Aggregate personal income is not the best measure of the amount consumers can spend, for out of this consumers are obliged to pay taxes. If obligatory expenses of this nature are deducted, there is left the amount available for consumer spending, known as "personal *disposable* income." Figures of disposable income, corrected for seasonal variations, published quarterly, indicate that in the second quarter of 1957, the disposable income received was running at an annual rate of $305.7 billion. In the *third* quarter of 1957, after the general contraction had begun, it was $308.7 billion (annual rate). From there it shrank to $306.8 billion in the fourth quarter of 1957, and $305.4 in the first quarter of 1958. Then it rose again to $307.5 in the second quarter of 1958—almost as high as in the preceding September.[2] The drop from the highest point (September, 1957) to the lowest (March, 1958) was slightly more than 1 percent— even a smaller percentage fall than in aggregate personal income.

How much of their disposable incomes did consumers spend? (They had the alternative of spending or saving.) In the second quarter of 1957, they spent at the annual rate of $282.5 billion; in the third quarter, $288.3 billion; in the fourth quarter, $287.2 billion; in the first quarter of 1958, $286.6 billion; in the second quarter of 1958, $288.3 billion. Thus, consumer spending was running at a *higher* annual rate all through the general economic contraction than before it began! This was apparently made possible because individuals saved less of their disposable income during the recession than before. Here is a table showing the figures.[3]

TABLE 32/2

(annual rate; in billions of dollars)

Quarter ending	Disposable income	Consumer expenditures	Personal savings
1957 June	$305.7	$282.5	$23.2
Sept.	308.7	288.3	20.4
Dec.	306.8	287.2	19.6
1958 Mar.	305.4	286.6	18.8
June	307.5	288.3	19.2

If the figures for disposable income and consumer purchases (which include both goods and services) are accurate, the slight slump in per-

---

[2] *Economic Report of the President,* January, 1959, p. 154.
[3] *Ibid.*

sonal income was more than offset by a decline in personal savings. According to the best figures we have, consumers in the United States, taken as a whole, spent *more* for all that they bought, at the same time that they were buying fewer new automobiles. This observation seems to strengthen the probability that the slump in automobiles was not due to any decline in the income of consumers.

Consumers apparently bought fewer American automobiles than in previous years; this is general knowledge and is confirmed by the official figures of production. But the prices of automobiles were somewhat higher. There remains, therefore, a possibility that consumers actually *spent* more for new cars than before, even though they bought fewer. We may check this possibility by taking a look at the figures for passenger automobile sales at retail outlets. They were reported by the U. S. Department of Commerce[4] as follows:

TABLE 32/3

AUTOMOBILE SALES (RETAIL)
(in millions of dollars)

1957—July	....	$3,085
Aug.	....	3,037
Sept.	....	2,995
Oct.	....	3,002
Nov.	....	2,975
Dec.	....	2,899
1958—Jan.	....	2,906
Feb.	....	2,506
Mar.	....	2,485
Apr.	....	2,583
May	....	2,616
June	....	2,551

We would have to know more about these figures in order to make any precise calculation based on them. Do they represent, for instance, total sales as carried on the books or the amount of cash payments actually received? How do they treat installment sales? Do they include used cars? imported cars? Whatever the details, however, the record certainly indicates a marked slump in dollar value of retail sales of motor cars, amounting to a total of over a half billion dollars within six or seven months. This may be contrasted with the actual increase in total spending of consumers during the same period.

CONSUMER SPENDING HABITS AND THE COST OF LIVING

Before concluding that the severe automobile slump was due to some extraordinary factor unrelated to the general economic situation, how-

---

[4] U. S. Department of Commerce, *Survey of Current Business,* December, 1948.

ever, we shall have to consider a few other generalizations based on observation of business cycles of the past.

Some types of activity customarily fluctuate far more widely between
the top of the cycle and its trough than do others. Prominent among
those which show the widest amplitude, as we noted earlier, are consumer
purchases of durable goods. Automobiles constitute by far the largest
category of consumer durable goods (about one half). On the other
hand, industries which provide goods or services bought from day to day
or month to month, and consumers' purchases of such goods and services,
vary relatively little between prosperity and depression. Such goods include food, many articles of clothing, rent, transportation fares, household
fuel and electricity, telephone service, and the like.

One reason seems fairly obvious. The goods and services to which
one has become accustomed are regarded as "necessities," even though a
family may be eating more expensively than is required for an adequate
minimum of nutrition, or may be buying more clothing than is necessary
for warmth and decency. It is difficult to retrench much on such things
without changing cherished habits or surrendering a tenacious standard
of living. Such a sacrifice is felt almost immediately if nondurable goods
are not regularly bought. An automobile, on the other hand, though it
may be an equally necessary part of the household equipment, does not
have to be replaced in any given year, unless it is near the point of collapse. The purchase of a new car may be postponed for a while, as a
rule, without suffering even a loss of prestige, unless one belongs to a
social set in which possession of the very latest model is a sign of status.
In consequence, those who wish to economize will be likely to put off the
purchase of a new car before skimping on less durable goods or services,
even though a trade-in may involve nothing more than the assumption of
a new monthly installment obligation to replace a recently expired one
of about equal size.

The fact that during 1957–1958 consumers in the aggregate spent
more than previously does not, on the surface, look as if they were trying
to economize. But this inference overlooks two important facts. One is
that because of a growing population and of expectation of rising standards of living, there is a continual tendency in the United States for
aggregate consumer spending to rise. The other is that this recession,
unlike most others, was not accompanied by any general fall of prices.
Prices charged consumers, on the contrary, showed a slightly rising tendency, especially in food, rent, and other important services.

The national consumer price index, calculated for city wage earner
and clerical-worker families, showed the following increases from July,
1957, when the recession began, to March, 1958, when the general upturn
became evident. (The figures are index numbers based on 100 for 1947–
1949.)[5]

It may be noted that durable goods were even higher before March,

---

[5] *Economic Report of the President*, January, 1959, p. 185.

TABLE 32/4

	July, 1957	March, 1958
All items	120.8	123.3
Food	117.4	120.8
Durable goods	108.2	109.6
Nondurables (other than food).......	116.3	116.9
Rent	135.2	137.1
Other services	138.9	143.1

1958. They reached their top in November, 1957, at 110.9. Automobiles constituted no exception to this upward price tendency. Consumers, in general, continued to buy most of the nondurable goods and services they wanted, even at some sacrifice to their savings; but, in doing so, they failed to spend as much as before on new cars. Thus, indirectly, even the small drop in consumer disposable income may have led to a major drop in automobile purchases.

In order to include the effect of population growth on income, let us look at a table which shows disposable income per capita (aggregate disposable income divided by population). These figures are adjusted for seasonal variation and are expressed at the annual rate. The effect of rising prices on the purchasing power of per capita disposable income is shown in the second column, which gives the figures in 1958 dollars. Finally, the third column indicates expenditure per capita in 1958 dollars (also at annual rates, seasonally adjusted).[6]

TABLE 32/5

	Per capita disposable personal income	Per capita disposable personal income (1958 dollars)	Per capita consumption expenditures (1958 dollars)
1957			
2nd quarter	$1,789	$1,844	$1,705
3rd quarter	1,799	1,834	1,713
4th quarter	1,780	1,800	1,693
1958			
1st quarter	1,762	1,773	1,664
2nd quarter	1,770	1,766	1,657
3rd quarter	1,800	1,795	1,666

These figures reveal the pressure on consumers for cutting their spending and the fact that less was actually bought *per person* during the recession. Though *total* disposable income fell only a little, as we have seen, and the lack of any marked decline checked any fall in total

---

[6] *Ibid.*, p. 155.

consumer spending, there was not so much income to go around because it had to be distributed among a larger number of persons. *Per capita* disposable income fell steadily from the third quarter of 1957 to the second quarter of 1958. When rising prices are taken into account, the purchasing power of this income fell further and continued longer. *Real* purchases per person—which indicate the physical quantity of demand— fell still more markedly and had not recovered to the early 1957 level even by the third quarter of 1958.

That consumers did actually economize in declining to buy new cars is shown by the total figures of outstanding installment credit extended for the purchase of automobiles. It has been usual for installment credit to grow except in recessions; it does so because new obligations undertaken grow at a more rapid pace than old ones paid off. Automobile installment debt reached a cyclical peak in October, 1957, at $15,542 million. From this point it fell steadily month by month, until in August, 1958, it reached $14,625 million.[7] During these months American consumers liquidated nearly a billion dollars of installment debt, *net,* thus reducing their average monthly payments on automobiles by a considerable amount.

OTHER EVIDENCE—BUYING PLANS; INCREASED CAR SALES

Motives of immediate economy, whatever their role in the situation, may have been supplemented by motives of a different type. Decisions about economic action are not always so clearly motivated by rational logic as economists like to assume, for purposes of simplicity. Indeed, human beings are not often capable of analyzing objectively their own motivation; everyone knows that motives are likely to be mixed.

One important piece of evidence that should not be overlooked is a survey by Consumers' Union, a cooperative organization which supplies to its subscribers regularly information to aid them in buying intelligently; for many years Consumers' Union has been particularly thorough in its testing and reporting on automobiles. Most of its subscribers are automobile buyers; indeed, they constitute a large sample of the American automobile market, especially in the income ranges at or above the median. Consumers' Union has regularly sent a questionnaire to some 100,000 families, including questions about buying plans. In April, 1958, a special survey, answered by 34,000 members, indicated, according to *Consumer Reports,* January, 1959, that "Buying plans for April–October, 1958, were less than those previously reported for October, 1957–April, 1958. Decline in planned spending was *not* due primarily to adverse changes in income or even income prospects, but appeared to be associated with pessimistic views about general business conditions."

---

[7] U. S. Department of Commerce, *Survey of Current Business,* December, 1958.

April, 1958, was near the bottom of the general economic contraction. If these consumers had not suffered then and were not expecting any decline in their own incomes, as the report seems to indicate, how could a gloomy economic outlook have affected their buying plans? It might have exerted a sort of pessimistic contagion which leads people to hesitate to assume new obligations. Or, more concretely, it may have led them to expect lower prices in the future, so that they could get a better bargain by waiting. At any rate, *consumer expectations* thus enter the picture as an important economic influence, just as business expectations have long been recognized as a major influence in business plans for investment.

Still another bit of evidence is the rapidly growing sale of foreign-made cars, which never grew more rapidly than during the slump in sales of American cars; foreign sales were estimated to have been 9 percent of total United States sales in 1958. Most of these foreign cars were smaller, cheaper, and more economical to operate than the typical American car. Since manufacturers of foreign cars do not, like those of American cars, make drastic annual changes in styling, the annual depreciation is usually less, especially if, as is often the case, the workmanship is good, and the cars stand up well under use. The small size, which may be of some relative discomfort to driver or passengers, is a convenience in parking, and difficulty of parking in congested areas is perhaps the greatest deterrent to the use of automobiles in our rapidly growing metropolitan regions. It is not only a practical inconvenience but also a disagreeable emotional hazard.

In years past, social prestige has been associated with ownership of big, expensive, powerful cars. But recently there seems to have been a change in this respect. Ownership of foreign sports models became a sign of distinction some years ago. This mark of discrimination and individuality appears to have spread over ownership of foreign cars of other types. Some think that there has been a subtle change in popular standards of preference, according to which the showy, nonfunctional car, house, or other possession comes to be thought vulgar as compared with the simpler, more economical, and more tasteful product well designed to serve its purpose.

Finally, the most dramatic evidence either of a need for economy or a change in taste or both lies in the fact that while sales of other American makes fell drastically, one American manufacturer who featured lower price, a smaller car, some economy of operation, and sound construction experienced a striking growth in sales—American Motors, with its Rambler. Perhaps some of the hesitation in buying was due to the expectation of consumers that new cars of some such type would be more generally offered in future years by other companies, and that while such a marked change was in prospect—with possible lower prices—they might as well wait another year or two to see what might appear to be the best buy for them, whether foreign or domestic. The recession marked the beginning of a minor revolution in the automobile industry.

Material relevant to this chapter may be found in Chapter 15, Business Cycles; and Chapter 22, Consumer Behavior.

QUESTIONS

1. Changes in automobile design, especially basic changes, must be prepared at least two or three years in advance of the time when they are introduced to the buying public, because of the time required to develop prototypes, carry on tests and make necessary changes, order and install new equipment, plan advertising. If, say in 1955, you were head of one of the "big three" automobile manufacturers and had been able to foresee the possibility of the slump of 1957–58, would you have:

(a) Planned to introduce smaller and more economical models?

(b) Reduced the prices of existing models even though that involved smaller profit margin per car? (See Chapter 35 on inflation and automobile costs and prices.)

Among the problems you would have to consider are the elasticity of demand for automobiles (how could this be tested?) and the price policies of your chief competitors (oligopolies usually avoid price wars—why?).

2. Do you think more automobiles would have been made and sold in 1957–1958 if the automobile industry had consisted not of three major concerns and a couple of smaller ones, but of numerous manufacturers of more nearly equal size—say, fifteen or twenty?

3. Do you believe that the competition of foreign cars in the American market is good for (a) the American consumer, (b) the American automobile manufacturers, (c) labor? Would you raise the present protective tariff on automobiles or lower it? How does your answer bear on the national interest as a whole, both in the long run and in the short run?

4. What is the relationship between automobile design and economy of natural resources? growth of population? city and regional planning?

5. Why do people buy automobiles?

33 / WHAT SORT OF FARM

PROGRAM? /

The "farm problem" in the United States has been a matter of public interest ever since 1920, and the debate about it has been particularly sharp ever since the federal government began to support the prices of major crops during the depression of the 1930's. Urban consumers, a substantial part of whose living expenses consists of payment for food, ask why government should try to help farmers by raising food prices, when it does not help other producers in the same way. Some farmers themselves, like growers of meat animals and poultry, whose products are not subject to price support, ask why they have to pay supported prices for grains which they use for feed.

A number of the important price-support programs of the government are intended to hold up prices by restricting production or marketing of the crops in question. But usually the devices used do not work well enough to limit the supply sufficiently, and in such cases the government has to attain its price objective by buying and holding off the market (in storage) "surpluses" of the crops in question. This is costly. People ask whether it is fair and wise to make taxpayers carry the burden of holding crops off the market in order that these same taxpayers may be required to pay higher prices for food and fibers.

Spokesmen for the farmers who grow the price-supported crops argue that such measures are necessary to equalize the economic opportunity of the farmer with that of other producers. Farmers sell in a highly competitive market at prices determined (if there is no government intervention) solely by demand and supply. Most of them cannot, as can wage earners, successfully combine to engage in collective bargaining and so increase their incomes. They cannot, as can big business concerns, individually curb their output to hold to any predetermined price line. They cannot, as manufacturers can, be benefited by protective tariffs so long as they produce a surplus in excess of the wants of domestic consumers. The average incomes of farmers are lower than average incomes of any other major group in the nation. If the economy is to be fair to the farmers and is to maintain a healthy agriculture, say the farm spokesmen, government must intervene to counteract such handicaps.

In 1958 the CED (Committee for Economic Development) published a pamphlet, *Toward a Realistic Farm Program*. CED describes itself as follows: [It] "is composed of leading businessmen and scholars who, working together, conduct research and formulate policy recommendations on major economic issues. . . . CED's objectives are to contribute to full employment, higher living standards and increasing opportunities for all Americans, to promote economic growth and stability, and to strengthen the concepts and institutions essential to progress in a free society."

The pamphlet itself comes from the Program Committee of the Research and Policy Committee of CED and does not necessarily represent the opinions of any other individuals associated with CED.

ARE THE EXISTING PROGRAMS SUCCESSFUL?

In 1933 the United States Government, in establishing the Commodity Credit Corporation, announced its purpose of "stabilizing, supporting, and protecting farm income and prices." (Sec. 2 of Charter)

"Farm income," states the pamphlet on its first page, "is declining. It has declined about 30 percent from 1951 through 1956. This decline has occurred in the face of a general, high level of prosperity and growth of population that have increased total domestic consumption of U. S. agricultural products by 11 percent over the past decade."

The CED report also states, at the beginning of its argument, "In the last quarter century we have spent well over $22 billion on programs to help the American farmer. About half was spent to stabilize farm prices and income. We have spent another $22 billion on other programs, not specifically designed for agricultural aid, but of direct or indirect benefit to the farmer. In mid-1957 the government was holding $7½ billion of surplus farm products." ("We" here refers to the United States Government.)

"There is only one reasonable conclusion," continues the pamphlet. "Our farm programs have not accomplished their announced purpose."

Let us stop for a moment and examine this reasoning. The figures need not be questioned—they are approximately accurate. The conclusion, too, may perhaps be justified. But so far, the evidence presented for it would seem to be somewhat incomplete. We may legitimately ask the following questions:

1. The farm program was inaugurated in 1933. If we are to judge the effectiveness of the expenditures made, the totals of which encompass the whole period from 1933 to 1958, should we not also examine the fortunes of the farmers for the whole period since 1933? So far, the pamphlet states only that farm income declined after 1951.

2. Does the fact that farm income has been declining—for whatever period—prove that the program has had no beneficial results? How do we know that farm income would not have declined even more than it did if the program had not existed?

To test the conclusion announced, obviously more facts are needed than these so far presented. A number of these facts are summarized later in the argument. But first let us see what other conclusions are stated in the Introduction.

One is the following: "The basic difficulty with present public agricultural policy is simple: in trying to underwrite farm prices and income it perpetuates an unreal price structure that encourages overproduction of farm products and keeps too many people in farming, resulting in ever-growing surpluses of foods and fibers in government storehouses, surpluses that weigh down the very price structure public policy tries to underpin."

On first reading, this statement seems not to be compatible with the declaration that farm programs have failed to accomplish their purpose. Apparently, government support *has* kept up farm prices and incomes at least to some extent. Otherwise, how could it "perpetuate an unreal price structure," or "encourage overproduction of farm products," or keep "too many people in farming"? The logical implication is that the Committee thinks prices for crops and farm incomes ought to have been lower than they were so that surpluses would not have been accumulated and more people would be compelled to abandon farming.

Is there any possibility, theoretically at least, that both conclusions might be correct? Let us suppose that:

1. Lower prices than those that existed might have led to sufficiently larger sale of farm products on the commercial markets so that aggregate farm revenue would have been as large as it was, or larger, even though the government paid no subsidies and bought and stored no "surpluses."

2. The lower prices might have forced out of commercial farming the less efficient, less profitable farms, thus concentrating the demand on the more efficient (that is, those with lower average costs per unit of output). The aggregate revenue from crops would thus have been distributed among a smaller number of farm operators. Since we have assumed in 1 above that the revenue was as large as it actually was, or larger, average revenue per farmer would have been greater than it was.

Is this outcome conceivable? Is it probable? What is the bearing on these questions of the elasticity of demand for the various farm products? Do we need to know more than we do at this stage of the inquiry to guess whether the statements of the Committee are credible?

Still another aspect of the subject is emphasized by the Committee. The bill for subsidies to the farmers (through price support or otherwise) must be met by the taxpayers. This money might better be devoted to other purposes—as well as the money spent by consumers of farm products to pay the prices in excess of those which would exist in a free market. "Basic to every other defect is the economic waste involved in public policy that keeps people, and material resources, at work *producing surpluses* of farm products while the nation is straining to fulfill simultaneously its desires for economic growth and national security."

This is a persuasive statement. Certainly it is a waste of resources to spend capital, labor, and land piling up in warehouses crops for which no good use can be found. The critical reader, however, may have questions even about this statement. If we stopped wasting labor power in agriculture, does it necessarily follow that we should find some good use for the farmers who would be forced off the land by an end to price supports? Certainly the chance of doing so would not be bright if employment in nonagricultural pursuits were not growing rapidly, and if unemployment were widespread. It might be cheaper to support surplus-growing farmers by letting them stay in their homes and buying their produce (even if there is no market for it at present prices) than to pay them unemployment compensation or throw them on the relief rolls. Any abandonment of governmental price and income supports for agriculture must, on this ground alone, carry with it a successful high-employment policy, if the present waste of human resources is to be avoided. And would it not be necessary, too, to make sure that some other desirable use be found for the land now in surplus crops?

Clearly we need to know much more than is stated in the Introduction before being sure that all the statements made in it are correct.

We now turn to sections of the CED pamphlet which offer us a more detailed and factual picture of the farm situation.

FARM PRODUCTIVITY

Although the farm program was designed to limit the output of crops in order to keep prices up, by limiting the acreage devoted to these crops, farmers learned how to produce more on the acres they were permitted to plant. They used their best land, took better care of it with modern machinery, applied more and better fertilizer, and planted better seeds. Agricultural scientists and technologists, many of them employed by the government, helped them to do this.

During a recent thirteen-year period, the CED points out, the yield per acre planted in corn increased by about one third, cotton acreage yielded about three eighths more, rice one fourth more, and wheat one tenth more. Similar increases in yield per acre occurred in tobacco and peanuts. These are the six "basic" crops in which acreage limitation has been compulsory.

This increased productivity is a major reason why the market prices of crops, since the immediate postwar period, have not been as high as were regarded "fair" under the provisions of the law, so that the government had to buy and hold the "surplus" to keep prices up.

Not only have farmers learned how to produce more per acre; they have also learned how to produce more per man, just as industry has.

TABLE 33/1

YIELDS PER ACRE

	Corn (bu.)	Wheat (bu.)	Rice (lbs.)	Cotton (lbs.)	Tobacco (lbs.)	Peanuts (lbs.)
Average 1939–1943...	31.2	16.4	2101	249.7	985	703.8
Average 1952–1956...	41.1	18.7	2693	404.9	1333	952.3

More than one fourth (28 percent) of those engaged in agriculture left the farms between 1940 and 1956. The total number of persons who earned their living in agriculture (or tried to do so) decreased from 10,987,000 to 7,869,000. And yet the farms have continued to grow "surpluses."

THERE ARE DIFFERENT KINDS OF FARMERS

There are "small" farmers and "large" farmers, and some in-between. There are farmers who make their livings—or try to do so—by farming, and farmers who devote only part time to growing and derive income from other pursuits. We make a mistake if we think of "the farmer" as a statistical average.

More than half the money paid for farm products (58 percent) goes to only 12 percent of the farms. These are the farms which receive $10,000 or more each for their yearly output. Together, they comprise 43 percent of the acreage used for agriculture. Maybe these "large" farms need price supports, but they certainly are not in such dire straits as some of the smaller farmers.

Commercial farmers with annual sales of $2,500 each or upward receive nine tenths of the money paid farmers for their output. Yet they comprise less than half (44 percent) of all farms. They have 76.3 percent of the acres in use.

The farmers in worst trouble are the full-time commercial farmers with annual sales of less than $2,500 (out of which, of course, they have to pay their expenses of production before clearing any profit). They need help more than any of the larger farmers. They produce only enough to receive 12.7 percent of the money paid to farmers, though their farms comprise 25.7 percent of the total number. No conceivable increase in the prices of what they sell could help them much, because they sell so little. Is there not some better way to help them?

Finally, we come to the part-time, residential, and other farms, such as those run by institutions or for experimental purposes. These have 30 percent of the farms, 2 percent of the sales, and 11 percent of the farm acreage. Most of them surely do not constitute an important part of the "farm problem."

TABLE 33/2

FARM CLASSIFICATIONS

	Number of farms	Percent of total farms	Percent of total dollar output	Percent of acres used
I. Commercial farms having market sales of:				
$25,000 or over...........	134,000	2.8	31.3	22.4
$10,000 to $24,999........	448,945	9.4	26.9	20.8
$ 5,000 to $ 9,999........	706,929	14.8	20.5	19.0
$ 2,500 to $ 4,999........	811,965	17.0	12.1	14.1
Total, over $2,500........	2,101,839	44.0	90.8	76.3
II. Small full-time commercial farms having market sales of:				
$1,200 to $2,499	763,348	16.0	5.7	8.8
Less than $1,200...........	462,427	9.7	1.4	3.9
Total, less than $2,500.....	1,225,775	25.7	7.1	12.7
III. Part-time, residential and other[1] farms	1,455,404	30.4	2.0	11.0

[1] This classification includes 2,693 institutional and experimental farms.

HOW ARE THE FARMERS DOING?

The assumption back of price-support legislation is that without it farmers would suffer more than other businessmen, who sell at prices that do not receive government support.

During and immediately after World War II, the demand for farm products was so great that price supports were not needed to keep up farm income. Farmers, in general, paid off many of their debts and put money in the bank. The problem was to keep retail prices within reach of the consumer.

Since then, farm income has decreased while other incomes have been rising. Between the top figure of 1948 and 1957, the farmers' total net income from farming dropped 34 percent.

But during this period, because of increased efficiency, the *number* of farmers decreased, so that there were fewer to share the income. Also, some farmers had income from other sources. The income per capita of the farm population declined only 6 percent from its 1948 top through 1956. During this same period the per capita income of all persons in the United States *increased* 37 percent. There is no doubt that, in terms of current income, farmers did not share in the general postwar prosperity.

Yet there is another way to look at the situation. The value of property that farmers own *free and clear of debt* has risen rapidly, both during and since the War. Though their average incomes have recently fallen, they do not have to pay out as much as before in interest and repayment of debt. According to the Annual Balance Sheet of Agriculture, issued by the U.S. Department of Agriculture, the *equity* of owning farmers in their property increased from $43 billion on January 1, 1940, to $118.2 billion on January 1, 1950, and to $157.6 billion on January 1, 1957. Real-estate debt (such as mortgages) was 20 percent of the value of their land in 1940 and only 9 percent in 1957. Farmers' liquid assets in 1957 more than covered their nonreal-estate debt.

PRICE SUPPORTS DO NOT PROTECT ALL FARMERS

More than half the dollars spent for farm products in the United States *are not* paid for crops supported by the farm program. For example, prices for the following are not supported by the government: beef, lamb, veal, pork and other hog products, chickens and other poultry, eggs, fruits, and vegetables. The farmers who grow such products do have to pay for price-supported farm products like corn, soybeans, cottonseed, oats, barley, and dairy products. If price supports really are effective in keeping up the prices of the crops which they cover, then growers of 55 percent (by value) of our farm products would benefit, not only as individual consumers but also as producers, from the lower cost which would follow abolition of the program.

THE TROUBLE WITH PRICE SUPPORTS

The CED study finds the following faults with price supports.

First, they discourage the movement out of agriculture of some farm families who are not needed there.

Second, since the price maintained is higher than the market price, it stimulates more production than people will buy at the price maintained. Government agencies have to buy and store the "surplus." This creates an increasing burden on taxpayers and so endangers the future security of farmers.

Third, by raising prices of staple crops above prices in the world market, price supports diminish our exports of these crops.

THE TROUBLE WITH THE SOIL BANK

The Soil Bank program (put into effect in 1956) was designed to reduce output (and so increase prices) of farm products by keeping land out of production. With a few exceptions, it has not succeeded in its aim. The reason, the CED report states, is that the program has not concentrated on the effort to take whole farms out of production. When only

TABLE 33/3

TOTAL MARKET SALES OF AGRICULTURAL PRODUCTS—1955

Crops	Market sales[1] (in millions of dollars)	Percent of total market sales
TOTAL	$29,264	100.0
I. Under Price Supports	$13,324	45.5
A. Under Mandatory Support	$11,296	38.6
1. Basic Commodities	$ 6,968	23.8
Cotton	2,320	7.9
Wheat	1,687	5.8
Corn	1,307	4.5
Tobacco	1,225	4.2
Rice	246	.8
Peanuts	183	.6
2. Non-basic Commodities	$ 4,328	14.8
Dairy products	4,212	14.4
Wool	101	.3
Mohair	14	—
Tungnuts	1	—
Honey	(not separately reported)	—
B. Under non-Mandatory Support	$ 2,028	6.9
Soybeans	819	2.9
Cottonseed	243	.8
Oats	247	.8
Barley	234	.8
Dry beans	129	.4
Flaxseed	133	.5
Sorghum grain	202	.7
Rye	21	.1
II. Not Under Price Support	$15,940	54.5

[1] Detail may not add to totals exactly due to rounding.

Source: Department of Agriculture.

part of a farm is taken out of any crop, farmers are likely to raise more on what they have left.

THE SUGGESTED PROGRAM

The CED committee recommends:
"1. A three-part program to bring agricultural production and supply into balance with demand."

The student of economics will at once comment that neither "demand" nor "supply" has specific meaning unless one couples them with the price. In a perfectly free market, demand *will* approximately equal supply at what is called the "equilibrium price." Does the committee propose, then, that all intervention with the markets for farm products be abandoned forthwith, so that prices will be determined by competition in the market? Under present circumstances, such prices would undoubtedly be lower than those resulting from price supports and subsidies. What, then, are the "three parts" of the program? They are as follows:

"(a) Gradual removal, within definite time limits, of farm price and income supports except for temporary emergency situations."

The committee apparently does, then, aim at prices determined by the market, but only "gradually." And there may be exceptions for "emergency situations." Evidently something else is to be done before supports are removed.

"(b) A Land Retirement program dedicated—unlike the present Soil Bank—specifically and singly to reducing the resources devoted to agriculture, including both people and land, so that farmers may share equitably in the national prosperity and economic growth, at free market prices."

"(c) Disposal of surplus now held by the government." Clearly this is desirable on general grounds. But how are the surpluses to be disposed of? The government may have difficulty in doing so without selling a substantial part of these surpluses in the United States. That certainly would tend to depress domestic crop prices. Occasionally, large amounts have been given or sold to foreign countries in need.

All these measures lead to the next recommendation:

"2. Removal, at the end of a limited transition period, of acreage allotments and marketing controls, and restoration of the farmer's freedom to manage his own enterprise."

This final removal of controls is intended to occur when enough resources were taken out of agriculture so that the remaining farmers would not produce more than consumers would buy at prices considered fair to the farmers.

"3. [Retain] "stand-by authority for the temporary use of price support loans . . . to shield the farmer from severe and sudden depletion of his income by forces, such as unexpectedly favorable growing conditions or general economic reversals, that he cannot influence." The loans are to be based "on expected, normal market prices." The assumption is evidently that the farmers will be able to repay the loans by selling the produce held in storage as collateral, once the emergency has passed. "By expected normal prices we mean the prices that would occur in a free market in a period of high employment and average growing conditions."

The first item of the program speaks of reducing the resources devoted to agriculture, "including both people and land." This suggestion leads to the next recommendation:

"4. Special programs to assist the farmer who cannot make a reasonable living from farming without public subsidy to find a better livelihood in other industries."

This is obviously a desirable measure, entirely aside from any other part of a farm program. It was first emphasized years ago by the Rural Resettlement program. There is a continued drift of farm workers to other occupations; the farm population has been decreasing ever since 1920. Yet there are left many substandard farms which do not produce a decent living—especially in the South, in mountainous regions subject to excessive soil erosion, and in regions without sufficient rainfall or irrigation. (See Table 33/2 on page 397.)

The main question about this part of the program is whether the retirement of these persons from farming—and presumably of their land as well—would much affect the total output of price-supported crops. In general, the low-income farmers grow a very minor part of the crops that come on the market.

Finally, an agency is recommended to supervise the program:
"5. An advisory Agricultural Board, responsible to Congress, to work with the Secretary of Agriculture in applying agricultural policy."

This Board is to safeguard the policy against "crippling exceptions and special privileges," and push the programs "as rapidly as practical toward their stated objectives."

QUESTIONS

1. Would the CED program be effectual in supporting prices of farm products at a level "fair" to the farmers?

The main reliance of the program is on taking land out of production by governmental leasing of agricultural land from its owners, and thus restricting the amount of land and workers devoted to the marketable crops in question.

Ever since 1933, keeping land out of production has been a major element of the farm programs that have been applied. "Acreage allotments," accompanying commitments by the government to support the price of a crop at a predetermined level, have restricted the number of acres any given farmer could plant with that crop. The number of acres so allowed has been calculated with the intention of so limiting the output that the market price would approximate the level desired. Yet, year after year, the actual output has exceeded expectations, and the price could be supported only by the governmentally owned Commodity Credit Corporation, which finances the farmer in holding off the market crops that cannot be sold at the announced support price. The Soil Bank program, recently in effect, though different in several respects from the acreage allotment programs, has also failed sufficiently to reduce output of the crops involved, simply by keeping land out of production. Would a land-leasing program be able to do any better?

The main reason why limitation of land planted has not resulted in maintaining prices at the desired level is the rapidly increasing trend of output per acre. Likewise, the rapidly increasing trend of output per man-hour has made it possible for farmers to produce more and more with a continually declining force of farm workers and manhours. Diminution of the output is less than the reduction of acreage in crops under acreage restriction.

TABLE 33/4

OUTPUT OF MAJOR UNRESTRICTED CROPS, 1953 AND 1957
(in millions)

	1953	1957[1]	Change since 1953	Percent change since 1953
Barley .... acres	9	15	+ 6	+ 67
bushels	247	431	+184	+ 74
Soybean seed ... acres	15	22	+ 7	+ 47
bushels	269	487	+218	+ 81
Sorghum grain .. acres	6	18	+ 12	+200
bushels	116	514	+398	+343

[1] Estimated.

OUTPUT OF MAJOR CROPS UNDER ACREAGE RESTRICTIONS, 1953 AND 1957
(in millions)

	1953	1957[1]	Change since 1953	Percent change since 1953
Corn .... acres	80	72	− 8	− 10
bushels	3,210	3,305	+ 95	+ 3
Wheat .... acres	68	43	− 25	− 37
bushels	1,173	927	−250	− 21
Cotton .... acres	24	14	− 10	− 42
bales	16.4	12.4	− 4	− 25

[1] Estimated.

The argument of the CED Committee is that the Soil Bank has been regarded more as a means of directly increasing farm income by its payments than as a means of sufficiently reducing land in production. It desires this main purpose to be clarified and emphasized in administration. It suggests, wherever possible, governmental leasing of "whole farms."

But the Committee does not favor any compulsion on the farmer to lease his land. Would not the farmers who offered part of their land for rent keep the best part of their farms in production? And would not the farmers who were willing to lease whole farms be only those with the worst land, who could not sell it, at a profit, to other farmers? Farmers abandoned poor land long before there were any governmental price support programs, because they could not compete with more fertile areas.

Anyone who has seen the miles of abandoned farm land in the Northeast can testify to this fact. But that did not stop production from increasing.

2. Is not any program which would prevent farmers from growing crops on land they would use, if the government did not offer to rent it, an interference with the operation of a really "free market"? Is it not a limitation of supply similar to that which is exercised by industrial concerns enjoying monopoly or partial monopoly?

3. If the total land area on which it was possible to grow crops were limited sufficiently to raise prices above the level which would prevail without such limitation, and if entrance into the farming business were thus restricted, would not the larger, more efficient farms tend to combine in order to exert control over the market. Business concerns have done this in many industries to which entry was restricted by private control of natural resources or skills, or by need for large capital investment. Or if farmers did not so combine, might they not be linked into a vertical integration dominated by big concerns engaged in processing and distribution of foods and fibers?

4. Would the recognized disadvantage of competing farmers in a really free market be better alleviated if effectual measures could be taken to prevent monopolistic or other noncompetitive prices of the goods and services farmers buy?

34 / TRADE BALANCE
AND GOLD RESERVE / In 1958 and 1959

some people were worrying about the fact that the United States was losing gold to foreign nations, and that, at the same time, exports were low. Why?

The international account of United States economic transactions with the rest of the world (known as the "United States balance of payments") is so set up that the incoming payments always balance the outgoing payments (with minor errors and omissions).

However, the value of exports—goods and services sold by Americans to foreigners—has usually exceeded the value of imports—goods and services bought by Americans from foreigners. The difference between these two figures is commonly called the "trade balance." The United States trade balance is positive if American exports exceed imports, since in that case more is being paid into the country for sales abroad than is being paid out of the country for American purchases abroad. When imports exceed exports, on the contrary, the United States trade balance is negative.

The other items in the total account of the Balance of Payments compensate for positive or negative trade balances. For example, when Americans lend, invest, or give foreigners more than foreigners lend, invest, or give in the United States, foreigners can buy a value of goods and services in this country larger than the value of goods and services sold here by them.

Monetary gold, though no longer lawfully used as money by individuals, is internationally recognized as a means of payment. A surplus of imports over exports, if not balanced in some other way, will lead to an outflow of gold from the country which has to pay for an import surplus. Likewise, if a country has an export surplus, not compensated by transactions such as loans, investments, and gifts, it will receive payment for that surplus in gold. But transfers of gold across international boundaries do not arise solely from import or export surpluses. Loans, investments, or gifts, for example, may be used to buy gold from the country

404

from which such transfers of capital or other claims on money are received.

The loss of gold by a country may be important for a reason only indirectly connected with foreign trade. Gold serves as the basic reserve of banking systems, even though it no longer can be paid out to individuals for use as money. For example, in the United States, the legal reserves of the twelve federal reserve banks consist of gold certificates, representing gold deposited in the United States Treasury. According to law, nobody can hold monetary gold except the Treasury, yet the gold certificates representing this gold act as the reserves of the central banking system—the federal reserve banks. And, according to law, the reserve banks must have gold-certificate reserves equal at least to 25 percent of their deposit obligations to member banks plus outstanding federal reserve notes, which constitute the bulk of paper money used by the public. (Deposits of the member banks in the federal reserve banks act on the *member banks'* reserves against their own obligations to depositors.)

A loss of gold by the United States may, therefore, if it is large enough, force the federal reserve banks to restrict the circulation of money and credit, unless the existing law is amended. An excess of gold above the 25 percent minimum reserve requirement would permit a corresponding expansion of the money and credit supply, though in this matter the Federal Reserve authorities have legal power to exercise their own discretion.

Ever since 1935, the federal reserve banks have held reserves greatly in excess of the legal requirements—for long periods, approximating 50 percent of their deposit and note obligations, or twice as much as is legally required. Yet in 1958 and 1959 gold was flowing out of the country. Between March, 1958, and March, 1959 (the end of the month in both cases), the gold reserve shrank slightly more than $2 billion, or from $21,804 million to $19,800 million. Partly because of this loss and partly because of credit expansion occurring during the year, the reserve ratio (of gold certificates to deposits and notes) shrank from 47.2 percent to 42.9 percent.[1]

In April, 1959, obviously the reserve was still far larger than that legally required; but if a gold outflow of this magnitude were to be long enough continued, it might in time diminish the United States gold reserve ratio to the minimum 25 percent required by law. This would be especially likely to happen if deposits and federal reserve notes expanded at the same time as the gold hoard was shrinking.

A CRISIS OF CONFIDENCE?

When a nation is in serious danger of marked inflation, people are likely to lose confidence in the soundness of its money. Speculators, and even ordinary bankers, businessmen, and citizens, are likely to exchange

---

[1] *Federal Reserve Bulletin*, April, 1959, page 395.

any of its money that may come into their possession for some other nation's money in which they have more confidence. The reason is obvious. Inflation means rising prices brought about by an expansion of the flow of money and credit more rapid than the increase of goods and services for sale. Rising prices mean diminution of purchasing power of the currency unit in question (say, the dollar).

If people should lose confidence in the dollar, because they expected accelerating price rises in the United States but not similar rises in Britain, Germany, or Switzerland, many who had extra dollars (or claims on dollars) would hasten to sell them for British pounds sterling, German marks, or Swiss francs. This would be especially true of Europeans and others outside the dollar area. Such transactions are handled by banks. Foreign central banks, which are entitled to purchase gold, would hasten to buy gold with their increased dollar holdings which would result from such a dumping of dollars on foreign-exchange markets. In effect, these purchases would mean that the United States would have to pay out large quantities of gold to redeem dollars. This drain on gold reserves would be added to that which might have resulted from ordinary trade or other transactions.

A "crisis of confidence," causing a "flight from the dollar," would create serious difficulties for the American economy and especially for the banking system and government. It would stimulate the very inflation which led to it. Eventually, it might necessitate revaluation of the dollar in relation to gold and foreign exchange. Such crises have beset other countries several times—the most notable recent example being France.

A COMMENT ON THE WORRY ABOUT GOLD

A good summary of the way people were thinking is contained in the following article by Brendan M. Jones in the business section of the *New York Times* of May 10, 1959:

> The fact that exports in the first quarter have continued the downward trend of the past year has been disconcerting for more than the usual reasons. The export weakness has been cited as the key element of a persistent deficit in this country's international transactions.
>
> This deficit, which last year ran to a record of $3,300,000,000, has been marked by a heavy outflow of gold from government reserve holdings. A resumption of this outflow, which hit a record of $101,000,000 for the last two weeks of April, has stimulated general concern.

FISCAL OFFICIALS DISTURBED

> Fiscal officials, though not alarmed, have been disturbed by the trend and its implications that inflation has made serious inroads on the value of the dollar. Together with the downward trend of exports, the gold movement has been taken as a warning of the need to halt the depreciation of the dollar generally.
>
> In all, the export situation and the outflow of gold tends, for the time

being at least, to show a considerable loss in popularity of the dollar abroad. Purchases of gold have constituted a conversion of foreign dollar holdings into the more stable and fluid metal. The lag in export volume is less clear in its significance, although it has bolstered contentions that this country generally is pricing itself out of world markets.

The first-quarter showing of exports has been disappointing in every sense. Volume was some 6 percent less than in the 1958 quarter, a period which itself was one of decline for exports. Expressed on an annual basis, the export showing in the first quarter of this year points to a total of $15,000,000,000 for all of 1959.

This is roughly $2,000,000,000 less than had been generally forecast for the year, and represents a further marked decline in place of the moderate upturn previously expected. This trend, unless reversed, also indicates that the total deficit on United States international transactions will approximate the large figures for last year.

In the above article, the "deficit" in the international transactions of the United States does not refer to an excess of imports over exports. The contrary was still the case, in spite of recent declines in exports, though the margin between exports and imports was somewhat narrowed. The "deficit" refers to a difference between total outgoing, and total incoming, payments, excepting only gold. When gold payments are included, the account was in balance as usual.

TRADE BALANCES AND THE BUSINESS CYCLE

During the last three quarters of 1958 and in 1959 the United States was experiencing recovery from a slump which began in 1957. Is a reduced surplus of exports over imports, such as occurred in this period, characteristic of this phase of the business cycle? A recent statistical study throws light on this question.[2] The author states, "The American trade balance shows inverse conformity [with the American business cycle]; it rose more (or declined less) when American business contracted than when it expanded in twelve of fourteen cycles, 1879 to 1938, and again 1949 to 1956." Since business was recovering in the latter part of 1958 and early 1959, a shrinkage of the positive American trade balance was therefore to be expected in this period, on the basis of historical experience. As far as the effects of the business cycle on foreign trade are concerned, this behavior was perfectly normal.

What *is* contrary to the historical experience as far as the behavior of the trade balance is concerned occurred between 1946 and the recovery which began in March or April, 1958. A footnote in Ilsa Minz's monograph reads: "Since this was written, some very exceptional balance changes occurred in 1957 and 1958: A spectacular rise during the later part of the business expansion and an equally large fall in the 1957–1958

---

[2] Ilsa Minz, *Trade Balances during Business Cycles, U. S. and Britain since 1880.* New York: National Bureau of Economic Research, Inc., 1959.

recession. There is little doubt that special circumstances, connected with the Suez crisis, were in large part responsible for this development. Whether it also indicates some shift in the cyclical behavior of the American trade balance remains to be seen, but all things considered, this seems rather unlikely." The continued shrinkage of the trade balance after recovery began in 1958 tends to confirm this judgment, since it constituted a return to what the study demonstrates is the usual cyclical behavior of the trade balance.

The explanation of the "spectacular rise" of the trade balance in early 1957 offered by Mrs. Minz attributes it to the "Suez crisis." When President Nasser, of Egypt, seized and closed the Suez Canal, the main source of supply of oil for European countries was thereby cut off, and large increases in exports of oil from the United States occurred to replace the supply from Suez. When the Canal was subsequently reopened in 1958, these unusual American exports were correspondingly diminished.

If, then, the trade balance was no longer behaving in an abnormal way after March, 1958, because it would be expected to shrink during recovery—as it did—why is it that this time it is accompanied by persistent loss of gold? Is there anything unusual about this experience?

WHAT ACCOUNTS FOR THE GOLD MOVEMENT?

If we consult the records, we find that from the end of June, 1952, to the end of June, 1956, inclusive, an average of $416 million of gold per year moved out of the United States. This outflow of gold caused no surprise or worry to anyone concerned. Indeed, to some extent, it was planned and thought desirable. The United States had a tremendous gold reserve, but the reserves of Britain, France, and some other European nations were often precariously low. Britain, for example, fighting inflation and a threatened shortage of gold reserves at the same time, kept interest rates in London unusually high, to attract money there. It was the policy of the United States to assist European economic stability for both political and economic reasons.

As far as the United States trade balance was concerned, exports remained large, as they had been ever since the War. The gold did not flow out to pay for a deficit in the export-import balance. It was financed by an outflow of loans, investments, and gifts, including governmental grants. When Britain finally achieved a secure enough position to remove most of her remaining restrictions on foreign exchange, confidence in the pound sterling increased and British gold reserves were strengthened. All this was generally regarded with favor by American bankers, businessmen, and government officials.

During 1956, the United States actually accumulated gold, and this accumulation continued into 1957. During these two years the gold stock of the United States was increased by $1,104 million.

The recent gold outflow began in 1958. In the first nine months of

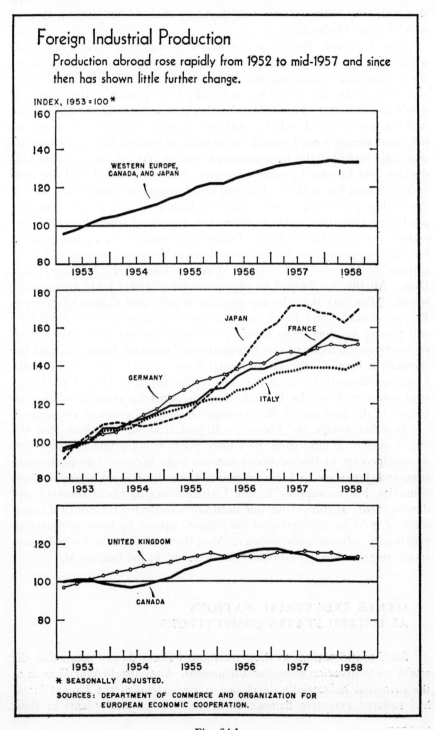

Fig. 34.1.

that year, the United States lost the more than $2,000 million in gold which caused all the flurry.

The *Economic Report of the President* for 1959[3] advances reasons which may account for this unusually large outflow. "The increase in the foreign investments and other payments of the United States in recent years has not been matched by an equally large growth in the exports of goods and services." This obviously left a gap in the balance of payments, which could be filled only by outward shipments of gold. Virtually no informed person would regard an increase in foreign investments as undesirable, provided the investments are sound and help to augment production and income in other countries. Such investment will not only yield a return but will also increase world production and trade. As for the "other payments," these consisted largely of aid to the "primary producing countries"—that is, those less developed countries which sell mainly raw materials to highly industrial countries—" . . . and growing financial support given by the United States through international institutions" such as the International Monetary Fund and the International Bank. All this has helped to strengthen multilateral trade all over the world. "The fact that the net receipts of gold and dollars of Western Europe, Canada, and Japan via multilateral settlements have risen by a still greater amount [than before 1957] in the period since 1956 reflects the increased activity of the International Monetary Fund . . . and the increase in loans by the International Bank. . . . The increase in multilateral settlements, far more than any change in the receipts of the industrial countries from the United States, accounts for the recent large increases in the gold and dollar accumulation of this group of countries."[4]

In other words, the *Economic Report* is saying, in effect, that the recent outflow of gold from the United States is not primarily due either to any increase in United States imports from Western European countries and Japan or to loans or grants from the United States to these countries, but to support by the United States of world recovery and development. If this is true, one need not account for the outward movement of gold by any "crisis of confidence" caused by fears of American inflation or adverse trade balance. Also, if this is true, the United States stands to gain through growth of the economy of the free world.

OTHER INDUSTRIAL NATIONS
AS UNITED STATES COMPETITORS

Such considerations as those mentioned above do not mean that the world trade situation remained unchanged. After World War II most of the principal industrially developed countries except the United States had suffered extensive damage either to their physical plants or their

---

[3] Page 131.
[4] *Economic Report of the President,* 1959, p. 129.

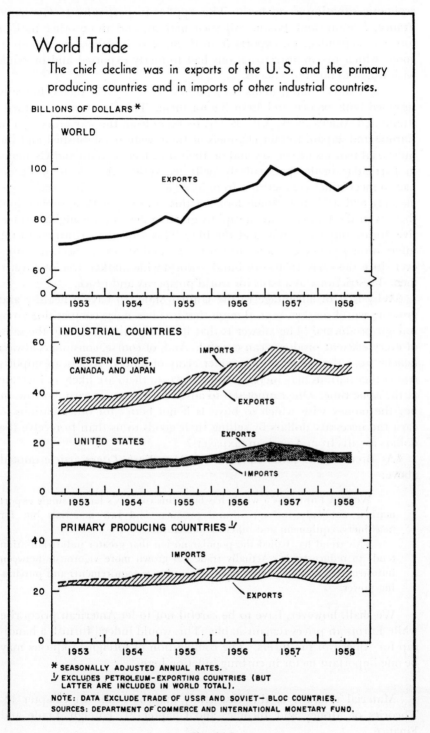

Fig. 34.2

economic situation or to both. This applies in particular to Germany, France, Britain, and Japan. All such nations, and those other nations formerly dependent on exports from them, were in urgent need both of goods which the industrial nations had formerly exported and of funds with which to buy these goods.

The United States, in its own interest as well as in theirs, liberally supplied both exports and financing for them. This situation temporarily stimulated American exports. But as recovery from the war proceeded in Europe and Japan, former channels of trade were re-established and the industrial nations began to stand on their own feet: Britain and Germany in particular made spectacularly swift recoveries. American producers had to meet stiffer competition from foreign producers both in the export markets and at home. Some look on this prospect with apprehension; there is in the United States a rapidly growing demand for higher protective duties, import quotas, and the like. This attitude is contrary to the international policy and aims which the United States has been pursuing ever since the early 1930's—to build a world-wide market, free of governmental restrictions, as a basis for world prosperity and peace.

Why is it of advantage to the United States to have a healthy and growing world market, even though that involves more competition from foreign producers? The answer is that if demand is expanding, the sales of every efficient producer can expand. And, of course, consumers always benefit from the existence of a wider array of sellers. American imports from other nations may increase, but exports to them are likely to increase at the same time. One cannot sell to anyone who cannot earn, borrow, or beg the money with which to buy. Is it not better for other nations to earn the necessary dollars by selling their goods to us than to receive the dollars as gifts from American taxpayers?

As Brendan M. Jones states in the *New York Times* article quoted above:

> Western Europe as a whole has been this country's largest single export market, not only for agricultural products and raw materials but for machinery, equipment and other manufactures.
>
> This trend has belied the popular notion that greater industrialization tends to reduce trade. Actually trade has grown more vigorously between industrialized nations as they have achieved new requirements and purchasing power.

We shall, however, have to be careful not to let American prices rise while European prices remain stable. This would indeed furnish a handicap for American producers. The competition of foreign producers may be one important factor in curbing inflation here.

Material relevant to this case study may be found in Chapter 14, Theories of Money and Income; and Chapter 21, Foreign Trade and Finance.

QUESTIONS

1. Is there any intrinsic advantage to a nation in having a surplus of exports over imports, as the United States has had for the most part ever since the 1870's?

In discussing this question, reflect in what other items of the international balance of payments there can be outgoing flows of payments to match the incoming flow collected by Americans in payment of the export surplus.

2. What advantage, if any, would the United States gain if its holdings of gold should indefinitely increase? Suppose this nation held all the gold in the world, what then?

In considering this question, think of the uses now made of monetary gold, which may be regarded as the "cash" in central bank reserves and in international transactions.

3. The United States Treasury now buys, by law, monetary gold at the rate of $35 an ounce. Suppose the value of the dollar should shrink so low in terms of the goods and services it would buy that nobody would sell gold to the Treasury at this rate, because the dollars he would receive would not buy as much as other currencies he could get for gold. How would this affect the international flow of gold? How would the law have to be modified in order that the United States might retain a sufficient gold reserve?

4. Would people in general still regard American money of any value if the gold reserve were abolished entirely?

In considering this question, ask yourself why people now regard American money as worth anything. What does it depend on, aside from the gold reserve? Can the dollar lose value even though the gold reserve does not change? If so, how?

35 / NEEDS OF AN UNDERDEVELOPED

COUNTRY / In January, 1949, President Truman in his inaugural address announced four principal aims of American foreign policy. The first three were: (1) to give unfaltering support to the United Nations, (2) to continue programs for world recovery from the War, (3) to strengthen freedom-loving nations against possible aggression. Point Four, announced as a "bold new program," was to make available "the benefits of our scientific advances and industrial progress . . . for the improvement and growth of underdeveloped areas. . . . And, in cooperation with other nations, we should foster capital investment in areas needing development. Our aim should be to help the free peoples of the world, through their own efforts, to produce more food, more clothing, more materials for housing, and more mechanical power to lighten their burdens."

Approximately two thirds of the people of the world then lived in underdeveloped areas, with inadequate diets, and often with inadequate sanitation or other protection against prevalent diseases. Among these peoples the average expectation of life at birth did not exceed, on the average, thirty years.

The United Nations adopted a similar program, and Britain, among other nations, attempted to help the spread of the knowledge and means of higher productivity among those nations which needed and wanted an improved level of living for their citizens.

REPORT ON COSTA RICA

Though needs of this sort exist in many parts of the world, it is difficult to know what can be done to satisfy them without an intensive study of specific countries. Situations and possibilities differ, though certain broad generalizations about the problem are possible.

414

Underdevelopment, in the economic sense, may vary in its meaning according to the country, but in general the following situations constitute underdevelopment: inefficiency in the growing of food for the domestic population, lack of sufficient diversification in the number and type of products produced, and a low level of development in manufacture or other modern industries.

Numerous studies of countries and regions have been made. Here let us examine one on Costa Rica, published in 1952 by the Twentieth Century Fund, an American foundation devoted to research in contemporary social and economic problems. The report resulted from a study by five economists, each of whom was familiar with one or more of the fields relevant to the subject—Stacy May, Just Faaland, Albert R. Koch, Howard E. Parsons, and Clarence Senior. The information in the following paragraphs is drawn from their report. The reader should bear in mind that the situation in Costa Rica probably has changed in many respects since the early 1950's. The report is now interesting, not primarily for the sake of acquiring current information about a specific country but rather as an illustration of what considerations may be involved in planning for economic development and of how skilled investigators of such a subject may go about their jobs.

Geography and Population. Costa Rica is one of the smallest of the American republics. It is about the size of Vermont and New Hampshire, 19,700 square miles in area. It is bounded on the south by Panama, on the north by Nicaragua, and on the other two sides by the Pacific Ocean and the Caribbean Sea. The greatest distance between these two salt-water boundaries is about 270 miles. There are three principal seaports on the longer, or Pacific, side, and only one on the Caribbean.

The lower levels on both coasts are tropical, with an average annual temperature of about 86° F. In the center lies a plateau—the Meseta Central—about 30 by 60 miles, with an average temperature of about 68°, and a year-round climate much like that of May and June in the Middle Atlantic States of the United States. Here 70 percent of the population lives. Other parts of the country are mountainous, with climates corresponding to the altitude. There is abundant rainfall, ranging from about 70 inches on the Pacific coast (where there is a dry season from December through March) through 80 inches in the Meseta Central to 100 inches on the Caribbean (where there is no dry season).

The population in 1950 was 794,081 (about the same as that of Vermont and New Hampshire) concentrated on the Meseta Central, partly because of diseases like hookworm and malaria in the more tropical, humid regions; yellow fever also used to be a menace.

Costa Rica, unlike many other Latin-American states, had only a sparse Indian population when the Spaniards arrived, and the European culture "replaced the native culture instead of amalgamating with it." The white population resulting from the Spanish colonization has not been much augmented by subsequent immigration, but has grown mainly by natural increase. The relatively small number of Negroes came from the West Indies, first during the latter part of the nineteenth century to build a railroad and later to work on the banana plantations on the Caribbean coast. Until recently Negroes were forbidden by law to emigrate to other regions.

Costa Rica has been relatively fortunate among Latin-American states, since for about seventy years it has been a democratic republic with regular elections, interrupted by only a few violent overturns. The population is literate; about 13 percent were illiterate in 1949, and the percentage has been steadily falling. The nation is proud of its educational system, having more schoolteachers than soldiers—though, at last reports, not enough. Nor is the number of people pressing hard on the country's natural resources; the population ratio to the possibly cultivable area is still relatively small, and there is no parallel here to the difficulties of a country in which a landed aristocracy holds something like a monopoly of the soil.

The case, then, is neither one of a nation struggling to emerge from a low state of culture or of one beset by famine, pestilence, and widespread misery. In what sense can Costa Rica be said to be "underdeveloped"? This question may be answered best by examining the level of living, the material security of the people, and the economic situation which underlies their difficulties.

The Economy and Its Main Deficiencies. The per capita income of Costa Ricans is one of the highest in Central America, but it is low by standards in the United States and Western Europe. Some exporters and traders live in relative comfort, but there are many citizens with inadequate incomes. The nation as a whole needs a surplus over living expenses (which might, if incomes were higher, be derived from savings or taxation) to provide for needed improvements in health, roads, education, hydroelectric power, and other investment.

A large percentage of family income is spent for food, yet the diet is "not in accord with good nutritional standards." It does not contain a sufficient proportion of proteins, minerals, or vitamins. Yet "agriculture produces more than a third of the national income of Costa Rica; about two thirds of the labor force are engaged in it." In 1949, more than half the value of agricultural products was exported (55.9 percent).

The chief exports of the nation are bananas (efficiently produced by a subsidiary of the United Fruit Company) and coffee of a superior grade, grown by relatively small farmers on the Meseta Central. Cacao (the source of cocoa and chocolate) and abaca (manila hemp) are also exported. With the proceeds of these and a few other exports, Costa Ricans buy manufactured products—durable goods for both construction and consumption, cloth and clothing, and foods not grown in Costa Rica.

More than half the calories in the Costa Rican diet are supplied by corn, beans, rice, wheat flour (which is imported), potatoes, and sugar. Sugars alone "account for almost a fourth of the total caloric value of the

Costa Rican diet. . . . These six food items together account for slightly more than two fifths of the total caloric value of the United States diet, or about 20 percent less than in Costa Rica."

Costa Ricans have available, per person, about one fifth of a pint of fluid milk a day, one pound of butter every three months, "about one-tenth pound of beef" every day, and "less than 2/100 pounds of pork and 1/100 pounds of chicken, and an even smaller amount of fish." There are available about five eggs per month per person. Fruits and green vege-tables are only rarely eaten.

The situation is summarized by the report as follows:

1. Foods grown for domestic production provide neither sufficient nutrition nor variety.

2. Imports of food require the expenditure of a large amount of foreign exchange that might be devoted to development of the country if adequate substitutes for the imported food could be provided cheaply enough at home.

3. Since the purchasing power of the nation for foreign goods depends almost entirely on exports of a few crops, the public welfare would be pro-moted not only if more of these crops could be grown and marketed, but if a wider variety of exports could be developed, so that earnings of foreign exchange would not be so dependent on the vicissitudes of weather, disease and foreign demand for one or two crops.

If a bad growing year occurs for Costa Rican coffee, if a disease at-tacks the banana crop, or if price and market conditions become unfavor-able for either, Costa Rica at once feels the pinch in the supply of foreign exchange required to buy daily necessities, to say nothing of supplies for expansion of productive capacity. This is a handicap of many Latin-American economies, though some of them are more dependent on sales of minerals than on sales of agricultural products.

It is a commonplace of economic experience that the prices of "pri-mary products" such as Latin American countries characteristically ex-port vary much more widely between prosperity and depression than do prices of manufactured goods, which these countries commonly import.

The troubled political situation of the world adds to economic in-security. During the second World War, Costa Rica lost her markets for coffee and cacao in both Britain and Germany, and was unable to recover them for several years afterward, because the European nations, short of gold and dollars, had to restrict purchases in the dollar area of everything but absolute necessities. For a time, also, Costa Rica was unable to buy from these countries the manufactured goods she was ac-customed to importing from them, because their productive resources were devoted almost entirely to war and they had little to sell abroad.

It will be seen that the senses in which a country like Costa Rica is "underdeveloped" are (1) relatively inefficient use of its labor and natural resources in the branches of its agriculture devoted to food for domestic consumption, (2) lack of sufficient diversification in the range of its prod-ucts, (3) deficiency in manufacturing industries which might make more goods for home consumption and so release more earnings from exports for other purposes. It was mainly in these areas that the authors of the study searched for possible remedies.

Suggested Lines of Attack on the Problem.

1. TRANSPORTATION AND POWER. If a nation is to develop its land and other natural resources and is to expand its production and markets, good transportation is essential. Costa Rica already has a railroad which joins the two coasts with San José, its capital on the Meseta Central. A longitudinal traffic artery between the Nicaragua and Panama boundaries—the Inter-American Highway—was under construction when the report was written. Subsidiary roads connecting other parts of the country with these two main routes were, however, scanty or not suited for regular and heavy traffic. Costa Rica also would benefit from improvement of local airfields, often used for transport in countries where the terrain is difficult, and possibly also of its international airport in the center of the country. Port and river improvements were also recommended on the coasts.

Mechanical power is essential also for most types of development. So far as is known, Costa Rica has no deposits of coal or oil, both of which must be imported, so far as they are used. Wood from the abundant forests is universally used as a fuel (as it was in the early days of the industrial revolution in England and the United States). There are, however, numerous possibilities of developing hydroelectric power. A foreign-owned power company already serves the San José region, and a grid of other power stations was planned by the government. The problem was to adjust the relations between these private and public systems and to obtain the necessary capital.

2. AGRICULTURE, FISHERIES, AND FORESTRY. Since the basic problem here was to increase the efficiency of output of agricultural products and provide more and better variety of foods grown domestically, one of the first tasks was to enlarge and improve the agricultural research and education of a sort which has been dramatically effective in aiding output per acre and per man-hour in the United States and other nations. Discovery of varieties of seed and livestock best suited to local conditions; proper use of fertilizer; irrigation where it was needed in the regions subject to a dry season—such projects were properly governmental responsibilities. Also, development of agricultural credit would aid farmers in new ventures.

Specific recommendations were also tentatively made. The extensive United Fruit Company activities in the country were already efficiently conducted in banana culture and other export crops such as cacao. Its new development of palm oil might provide the country with a much-needed source of vegetable fats. The domestic coffeegrowers, however, might improve their practices in several respects. Expansion of production of beef cattle, dairy cattle, hogs, chickens, and eggs could be undertaken in suitable, specified regions. Corn is already grown but not very efficiently, and more of it would be desirable as feed if the output of food animals were increased. Large areas on the Atlantic coast, abandoned by the United Fruit Company as banana land because of a disease attacking the banana trees, would be suitable for two or more crops of corn a year if the second growth were cleared off and artificial drying were provided for the corn in the humid climate. Immigrants from Southern European countries such as Italy might be attracted for corn culture.

There is no region of the country suitable for growing wheat (now imported in large quantities in the form of wheat flour), but a native plant, the yucca, often used as a substitute for wheat, could be grown in large quantities and mixed with wheat flour to economize the use of imported flour. Fruits, nuts, and tubers, now mainly imported, could be grown locally. Rice could be grown more efficiently and extensively by use of modern methods.

Of the nonfood products, the most important might be cotton, grown, at the time of the report, only experimentally. A native supply might encourage the establishment of a cotton-textile industry and so diminish the need for purchasing cloth and clothing abroad. Cotton-textile manufacture is characteristically one of the earliest to be established in a nation turning from an almost exclusively agricultural economy to industrialization.

One of the best sources of protein is fish. Fish are caught in large quantities off the Pacific coast (mainly tuna), and some are brought to Costa Rican ports, canned, and mainly exported. The Costa Rican diet might be improved and the economy might be better diversified by the development of fisheries.

For many years, Costa Rican forests supplied lumber for export, especially of the types which will grow only in tropical regions. Yet no concerted effort has been exerted to make full and efficient use of the possible wide variety of forest products or to cultivate the more valuable trees. Research and development could bring desirable results in this area and might be linked with wood-processing industries of modern design, such as the manufacture of plywood.

3. MANUFACTURE AND MINING. One of the chief needs of a developing country in modern times is cement, used for roads, building, and other construction. Costa Rica imports its cement, though the process of manufacturing it is simple and the necessary materials are available within the country. A modern cement plant was therefore recommended, which might produce all the country's needs and, in addition, a surplus for export, which might be distributed to neighboring countries.

Because of the absence of any known deposits of iron and coal, basic steel or other heavy metal-fabricating industries would not be efficient, even if a large enough market for their products existed. But light industries might well be introduced, such as those already mentioned, like cotton textiles, clothing manufacture, or wood processing. Industries processing food products might also be expanded or introduced. Labor supply for such industries would be released from agriculture as efficiency of agricultural production increased.

There is virtually no mining in Costa Rica, because no deposits of valuable mineral sources have been discovered. Yet there are large areas, especially in the mountainous regions, where neither modern geological surveys nor private prospectors have searched for such deposits. As in most countries except the United States, subsoil deposits are by law the property of the state. The law governing their exploitation has not offered enough incentive to private interests to undertake the risks of discovery and exploitation. The report recommended that this law be suitably amended.

Investment and Savings. If the developments indicated above, or others not mentioned, are to take place, capital for them must be available. Such capital may come from one or more of several sources: (1) domestic saving, invested either in governmental bond issues, in securities of private companies, or expansion of operations by individually owned farms or businesses through reinvestment by the owners and (2) foreign investment, consisting of foreign purchase of government bonds, foreign purchasing of securities of Costa Rican business or utility enterprises, direct investment by foreign concerns in Costa Rican concerns owned by them, and grants or loans by international agencies like the World Bank or foreign governments.

Saving and investment by Costa Ricans have not been sufficient to finance a large program of expansion and must be supplemented by foreign funds if rapid growth is to be expected. Yet it is important not only to increase domestic investment if foreign investments or grants are to be used to the best advantage, but also to change its apportionment among the various uses. In 1949, it is estimated, domestic savings were invested mainly in only two types of property—buildings, land, and mortgages, and imports of durable goods. These together took up more than $20 million of the estimated total of nearly $27 million saved during the year. The next largest item was about $2.7 million paid for insurance, a government monopoly, some funds of which are available for such purposes as low-cost housing. Omitted from the estimates are relatively small purchases of United States government bonds and dollar balances and also investment in domestic business concerns. Moreover, the two largest items to which current savings were devoted, real estate and consumers' durable goods, do not for the most part represent additions to existing productive facilities, since they mainly indicate purchases of land, old buildings, and such consumer goods as automobiles, radios, and furniture.

To stimulate the market for securities, a stock exchange was opened. Sales have been confined almost entirely to government bonds and other obligations with fixed yields. Costa Ricans have not been inclined to invest in common stocks or other equities, but it is hoped that a demand

for such investments will eventually develop. An institution to underwrite and distribute securities is badly needed.

In 1949 it was estimated that, of the long-term foreign investment in
Costa Rica (totaling about $105 million), $92 million was direct investment and $13 million was portfolio (that is, foreign ownership of secu-
rities issued by the Costa Rican government or business concerns). Of the
direct investment, 73.9 percent had come from United States corporations
and some 18 percent from the United Kingdom. Four fifths of the direct
investments were in agriculture, mainly accounted for by the United
Fruit Company with its banana and other exportable crops. The rest
was chiefly in electric light and power, communications, transport, and
petroleum distribution.

The portfolio debt, 69.2 percent of which was held in the United
States and 30.8 percent in the United Kingdom, consisted entirely of
government bonds which, at the time of drafting of the report, had been
completely in default since 1941, but a settlement was about to be
negotiated.

For new international financing, the nation was, for the time being
at least, largely dependent on loans or gifts by governmental or international agencies.

Banking, Credit, and Foreign Exchange. Costa Rica has a banking system composed of a central bank and a series of governmentally
owned commercial banks. The banks are largely engaged in financing
producers and traders of exported crops, primarily coffee. Coffee sellers
in the dollar area sell their dollar exchange to the central bank in exchange for *colones* (the domestic currency). Any boom in exports therefore results almost immediately in an expansion of the domestic money
supply, while a decline in exports has a deflationary effect.

Costa Ricans use currency rather than checks drawn on bank deposits
to a much larger extent than do citizens of the United States.

A considerable part of the nation's savings was kept in the form of
money during World War II. Between 1940 and 1950 the money supply
(currency and bank deposits) rose almost three and one-half times. Expansion of currency was more responsible for this increase than expansion
of deposits; currency quadrupled, and in 1950 it exceeded deposits. During this period the price level rose two and one-half times. This rise,
though a serious inflation, was less than that suffered by many Latin-
American nations. The fact that it was not so great as the increase in the
money supply would indicate that much of the money was being held as
savings; that is, it was not spent and thus did not add to effective demand
for goods and services.

Under these circumstances, central banking policy must be concerned
much more largely with the effect of the balance of trade on the monetary
supply than it needs to be in a nation like the United States. It might
be easier to avoid either inflation or deflation if, consequent to a growth
of domestic production for home consumption, the relative importance of

exports and imports were diminished. (This does not mean that growth in foreign trade is not desirable; it means merely that domestic development is even more desirable.)

If business enterprise in manufacturing and domestic trade grows in Costa Rica, the commercial banks will be obliged to develop new credit avenues to supply its needs for short-term loans.

In any large-scale development program, the danger of inflation would be enhanced by the spending of money for roads, dams, hydroelectric stations, and the like, before additional goods and services became available for the domestic recipients of the money to buy. This danger could be minimized if foreign loans or grants were used almost exclusively for purchases of machinery or other supplies which it was necessary to import, while payment for domestic labor and materials were financed out of current domestic savings and taxation.

Other Needs for Growth. Some of the important needs for stimulation of growth are not material in nature. Among these are:

1. Better statistics so that the essential facts for policy making may be known more fully and promptly.

2. Scientific research and technical advice to improve agricultural practices and efficiency. Agricultural credit backing up the use of such information would be preferable to credit used for price supports.

3. A carefully prepared development program, as a basis for loans from international agencies.

4. An improved capital market which will stimulate domestic savings and their use in expanding needed production.

5. Private foreign investment should be encouraged by such measures as assurances to investors against losses through possible nationalization or scarcity of exchange to pay legitimate capital charges, and revision of laws which discriminate against foreigners in taxes, employment, or use of materials.

Foreign technical aid, such as is contemplated by President Truman's "Point Four," may be of use to Costa Rica in planning and executing a program like that suggested. Properly used, it may help to open the door to any foreign financial aid or investment that may be desirable.

Material relevant to this case study may be found in Chapter 21, Foreign Trade and Finance; Chapter 23, Technology and Production; and Chapter 25, Growth of the United States Economy.

QUESTIONS

1. In the case of a country like Costa Rica, the question of grants or loans from the United States for military purposes (defense against possible foreign aggression) is not at issue. Such help has neither been asked nor offered. In the absence of military necessity or policy, what advan-

tages might accrue to the United States from assistance to economic development?

2. Do nations like Costa Rica prosper more in a peaceful world, where international trade is relatively free and multilateral, or in one where trade is restricted by tariffs, quotas, or other obstructions?

3. The principle of "comparative advantage," roughly summarized, holds that any region or nation will benefit by specializing in those types of production in which the region or nation is more efficient than in other types, even though these other types might be profitable. Has Costa Rica developed in the past in accordance with this principle?

In recommending that the nation should produce more of its own necessities and diversify its economy, are the authors of the report assuming that it would be possible or desirable for Costa Rica to strive to be economically self-sufficient? Are they arguing against the principle of comparative advantage?

36 / DOES INSTALLMENT BUYING
CAUSE UNEMPLOYMENT? / One of the

two main avenues of spending which vary most widely between the top and bottom of the business cycle is consumers' purchase of durable goods. As personal real incomes have increased since World War II, consumer spending for durables has comprised a larger part of the average family budget. The element of instability represented by cyclical variability of this type of expenditure has become more important. The question therefore arises whether it is possible to minimize the swings of consumer durables.

The purchase of consumer durables, like business expenditure, depends to a large degree on credit. The purchaser of an automobile, for example, is likely to borrow on the installment payment plan a substantial part of the price of his new car. Should not the policy of the banking system be directed to dampen down fluctuations of these purchases over the cycle?

EXPERIENCE OF 1954–1955

A survey by the Board of Governors of the Federal Reserve System deals with the effects of a marked liberalization of credit for installment purchase of automobiles in 1954–1955.[1] During the Korean War the Board had received from Congress the power to limit the terms of payment for consumer purchase of cars in order to conserve resources for national security and to minimize inflation. This authority, however, was granted for a limited period and automatically lapsed after 1952. The Board had required that the down payment cover at least one third the price of the car and that the remainder be paid off within a year.

After expiration of the Federal Reserve Board limitations, automo-

---

[1] Board of Governors of the Federal Reserve System, *Consumer Instalment Credit,* Part IV, *"Financing New Car Purchases,"* Washington, D. C., 1957.

424

tive credit concerns began to compete in reducing the down payment and extending the period of installment repayment. Relaxation of installment terms became widespread by 1954. This encouragement of consumer credit occurred—though nobody had planned it that way—at a time when a minor recession was rapidly giving way to the prosperous year 1955. The outcome was spectacular.

In 1955 individuals bought 6,720,000 new cars, the largest number ever sold in a single year. This was an increase of more than one third from the 4,990,000 sold in 1954, already a high figure. The number of cars bought on credit rose, between the two years, by nearly 50 percent, while cash purchases increased by less than 16 percent. "Credit buyers," according to the Federal Reserve report, "in 1955 outnumbered cash buyers 2 to 1 and in middle- and lower-income groups 3 to 1." By the end of 1955 new installment contracts allowed two thirds of the buyers thirty months or more (at least two years and a half) for repayment, while almost half of the contracts permitted down payments of less than 25 percent of the "effective price." The "effective price" is the contract price corrected for overallowances on cars traded in.

Not only did car buyers purchase more cars than before; they bought more expensive ones as well. Car prices rose; in addition, many purchasers bought more expensive models or ordered more optional equipment than they had formerly possessed. Most of the purchasers who had previously bought new cars turned in their cars after a shorter period of use than had been their custom. The median interval for which credit buyers had held the previous car declined from thirty-seven months in 1954 to thirty-two months in 1955.

Another influence which increased the debts assumed for new-car purchases was that "one third of the new car buyers who traded in or sold a car to buy a new one had purchased the trade-in as a used car." And the fraction of buyers on credit who bought new cars before they had finished paying for their old ones rose from one seventh in 1954 to one fifth in 1955.

The net result of these increasing uses of installment credit by automobile buyers was that the total of installment debt increased by $5 billion in 1955, and by the end of the year this debt had reached a record high of $29 billion.

Factors other than easing of credit were at work to boost car sales in 1955, such as rising employment and incomes after the mild slump in 1954 and newly styled models which seemed, temporarily at least, to appeal to the consumers' tastes. Nevertheless, there can be little doubt that the marked easing of credit restrictions on installment sales, which followed expiration of the Federal Reserve System's legal power to enforce such restrictions, played a large role in the great expansion of automobile sales on credit in 1955—a year during which the Federal Reserve authorities began to tighten credit for business uses in order to dampen the inflationary tendency. If the Board of Governors of the Federal Reserve System had retained the power, they might have loosened the previously strict installment credit terms somewhat during the slump of 1954, but they probably would have tightened them again when the booming car market began to coincide with general inflationary tendencies in 1955.

REASONS FOR ADVOCATING SPECIFIC POWER TO RESTRICT INSTALLMENT CREDIT

Why should anyone advocate special controls over the terms of installment contracts? The Federal Reserve System can, and sometimes does, restrict the power of commercial banks to increase loans, by general measures which in varying degree affect credit of all types. Why, then, should these measures not be sufficient to influence the volume of credit extended to finance consumers' borrowing to buy durable goods?

Most consumers, when buying a new car or durable household goods on the installment plan, think mainly of only two requirements—the down payment in cash and the size of the monthly payment. They do not pay much attention to the interest rate they must pay on money they borrow, the total amount borrowed, or the number of monthly payments they must make. A careful business executive, on the contrary, will not wish to borrow more money than he can profitably use or to pay a rate of interest so high that his profit may be substantially reduced or eliminated. A general tightening of credit, therefore, is more likely to restrict business borrowing than consumer installment borrowing.

If the Federal Reserve authorities had retained specific power to regulate installment credit, they probably would have increased the required down payments and shortened the period for installments in 1955.

In 1955 the average monthly payment made by installment buyers of new cars was $72, just about the same as it had been in 1954. The fact that the purchasers were actually paying more for their new cars in 1955 than in 1954 had little or no effect on the family budget for any given month—the additional cost was represented by an extension of the period of payment. Many buyers were attracted, too, by the fact that the required down payments were cut, though of course at the cost of a larger total installment debt, involving a larger interest charge and longer periods of payment.

Indeed, it is probable that most buyers of cars on the installment plan did not even know the rate of interest they were actually paying. A practice of finance companies is to add the interest as a lump sum to the principal of the loan to be paid, charging perhaps 6 percent a year on this amount. For a contract to repay $2,000 by installments extending over three years, the interest charge would be $360, or 18 percent on the amount borrowed. Even this is not the whole story, since the purchaser's monthly payments regularly reduce the principal of the amount he owes. If he were actually paying 6 percent on his outstanding debt, he would owe one twelfth of that percentage on $2,000 for only one month; when the next payment date came around, he would owe one twelfth of 6 percent on $2,000 *minus the first payment on principal of the debt,* and so on. Actually, interest paid often works out at 9 to 13 percent per annum on the real unpaid balance, or 27 to 39 percent in all if the installments run as long as three years.

With interest earnings of this magnitude, running for two to three years on each car purchased, finance companies can afford to pay relatively high interest rates for all they may have to borrow in order to extend increased amounts of credit to consumers. Therefore a general boost in interest rates exerts little pressure in limiting the growth of consumer credit either on car purchasers or on the finance companies which handle the installment contracts. What would be necessary for this purpose would be a special regulation requiring a minimum percentage of the cost of a car which must be met by a cash down payment, and a maximum term (such as a year) during which installments may run.

EFFECT OF EASY INSTALLMENT CREDIT IN SUBSEQUENT YEARS

If easy credit terms helped to stimulate large automobile sales in 1955, why did they not stimulate such sales in subsequent years? On the contrary, sales dropped off in 1956 and 1957, although these were relatively good years for business in general. In 1958, a year of general recession, car sales dropped still further. In retrospect, it looks as if the automobile industry, and the economy in general, would have fared better in the long run if any relaxation of installment credit terms had been withheld in 1954–1955 and somewhat extended about the middle of 1957.

In what specific ways did the installment-buying surge in 1955 militate against continued large sales in the three subsequent years?

1. The buyers of the 6,720,000 new cars sold in 1955 represented an unusually large part of the potential market for new cars. This inference may be drawn from the fact that in no previous year had sales of new cars approximated this figure, and there was no good reason to expect that the long-term trend of growth in automobile ownership could continue upward at a faster pace than before.

Most buyers of new cars cannot be expected to trade them in for a new model within two or three years. (It should be remembered that even in 1955 those who bought new cars on credit had held their previous cars for a median period of thirty-two months, or two years and eight months.) In 1954 the median period for which trade-ins had been held was thirty-seven months, more than three years. The 1955 models were no doubt as durable as their predecessors and were no more likely to be soon outmoded. Therefore the 1955 buyers were not likely to feel the need for new cars before 1958 in any event. And they greatly outnumbered the purchasers of the new models of 1954, 1953, and previous years who might be ready to buy before 1958.

2. Not many purchasers will buy a new model before they have finished paying for their old ones. In 1954 only one seventh of the car

buyers did so; even in 1955 only one fifth did so. Unless the number of months over which payments are due can be sufficiently extended to cover the unpaid balance on the car traded in, this practice must result in higher monthly installments than the purchaser would have had to pay if he owned his trade-in free and clear when he bought his new car.

The fact that the period over which installments were payable was considerably extended in 1954 and 1955 therefore reinforced the probability that purchasers in these years would not soon be back in the market for new cars.

3. The average monthly payments represented a considerable drain on the budgets of many of those who bought new cars in 1955. This average was $72 a month in both 1954 and 1955. The median ratio of the monthly payment to monthly disposable income was 15 percent. Families in the upper-income brackets paid a smaller percentage of their incomes than this on their monthly installments, but the burden was greater in the lower brackets. Incomes below $5,000 were received by spending units comprising about half the population, and this group included a considerable proportion of credit buyers. New-car buyers among them in 1955 allocated 20 percent or more of their disposable incomes to pay installments on the cars they bought; almost two fifths of them paid out one fourth or more of their income for this purpose. For a few months, such payments might be thought a justifiable sacrifice, but no doubt many began to find it too burdensome before the end of the thirty or more months during which they were obligated to pay.

Interviewed in 1956, after they had lived with their new cars between six and thirty months, "about one fourth of the installment buyers expressed dissatisfaction with some aspect of the arrangements, if only that they preferred to buy for cash."

Many of those interviewed expected to buy another car at a later date, but "when asked how they would like to finance the next purchase, these potential buyers expressed a stronger preference for paying cash and for buying on relatively shorter terms than they had demonstrated in their 1954 or 1955 purchases."

About one sixth of the installment car buyers said they had found it necessary to cut back the purchase of other things more than they had expected in order to meet their payments.

This attitude probably had a tendency to restrict subsequent purchases of cars as expensive as those they had bought in 1955 even when the purchasers had completed their payments and were ready to buy new cars. It may also have influenced their friends and acquaintances who might otherwise have bought new cars in 1956 and 1957.

The Federal Reserve Board report sums up the situation as follows:

> The major expansive influences in 1955 were mainly important on a one-time or transitory basis. . . . Such marked changes in buying patterns can hardly be expected to be repeated year after year. . . . The large supplement to spendable funds available to consumers, reflected in rapid expansion of new car installment credit outstanding, could not be maintained for long, if for no other reason than that the rapid rise in credit extension

would be followed, after some lag, by a rise in credit repayments. . . . There is real question whether the increase in credit purchases of the 1955 magnitude can be expected soon.

Material relevant to this chapter will be found in Chapter 15, Business Cycles; and Chapter 22, Consumer Behavior.

QUESTIONS

1. Refer to Chapter 32 on the slump in car sales during 1957–1958.

Assume that installment credit terms had not been relaxed in 1954–1955, and as a result car sales in 1955 had been little or no larger than those in 1954.

Under these conditions, do you think that automobile sales and employment would have been larger than they actually were in 1956, 1957, and 1958? And in that case, would the recession have been more moderate?

Assume, in addition, that installment credit terms had been temporarily relaxed in the fall of 1957, when it was obvious that a general economic contraction was under way. Do you think this action would have boosted sales of cars in that year? Do you, in general, believe that the Federal Reserve Board should have been given permanent power to vary installment credit terms for the purpose of helping to stabilize the national economy?

2. In general, do you approve or disapprove of the general practice of financing the purchase of automobiles by installment credit?

In this connection, consider the case of a person who decides to save up, by regular deposits in a savings bank, the full cost of a car before he buys it, instead of borrowing a large part of the money and paying it off afterward by installments, plus interest and other charges.

A concrete, but oversimplified, example could be outlined as follows:

A new-car buyer assumes an installment debt of $2,200, the contract price of the car over and above the allowance for the trade-in and the cash down payment. This amount, plus interest at 6 percent per year, figured on the full amount borrowed, is to be paid off in twenty-four monthly installments.

Amount of loan	$2,200
Plus interest at 6% for two years, or 12% of $2,200	264
	$2,464
Amount of monthly installment payment ($2,464 divided by 24)	103

(We may assume that incidental charges would be met by the surplus of $8, since 24 × 103 equals $2,472.)

Now suppose that, instead of borrowing the money, the buyer had saved it in advance, depositing $103 every month in a savings bank, which paid interest every six months at an annual rate of 3 percent. How many monthly deposits would he have had to make? What would be his net cash gain?

3. In view of the obvious financial gain accruing to the car buyer who saves the necessary money in advance rather than borrowing it on the installment plan, we may assume that the large number of buyers who borrow either have not sufficient cash savings or do not wish to draw on them for this purpose.

It is difficult, at least psychologically, for many people to save regularly, even though they will pay even larger amounts regularly on installment to prevent their cars or other purchases from being repossessed.

Let us therefore take another example. Suppose, before buying his first car, a prospective car owner formed the habit of depositing $100 every month in a savings bank, which paid 3 percent annual interest compounded semiannually. When he had saved enough to pay the full price of a car, he bought it for cash.

Now assume that at the end of two years after this purchase, the trade-in value of the car, plus $2,200, would buy a new car such as the purchaser wished. If he had kept up his $100 monthly deposits (instead of paying installments), he would have the necessary savings to pay the $2,200, and he would have left $200, plus compound interest, on his two years' savings. Suppose that he kept up this practice for twenty years, buying a new car every two years with a cash payment of $2,200. How large would his remaining savings be at the end of the period?

(Note that he would have sacrificed no more of his current income than the installment buyer who habitually traded in a car every two years for a new car of the same price as those bought by the saver, except for the period when the latter was saving to buy his first car.)

37 / POPULATION AND CITIES / A century

and a half ago the Rev. Thomas Malthus predicted that, if parents did not limit the number of their children, the population of the world would grow faster than the food supply and would, therefore, be curbed by famine, pestilence, or war. So far, in the Western world, his gloomy prediction has not been fulfilled—partly, indeed, by virtue of voluntary family limitation, but to a still greater extent because of unforeseen technological improvements in agriculture.

Nevertheless, rapid population growth can bring serious problems, though in many ways it stimulates business expectations and production. At a recent conference of experts on the subject, a speaker cited a calculation that, if the present birth rate and expectation of life in the United States should continue for another 750 years, there would be only one square foot of land area for each living person. We need not look so far ahead to discover that, in terms of living space—ignoring the question of food supply altogether—population growth can cause headaches. This is now obvious in and around our great cities.

A discussion of these problems, by Colemen Woodbury, Professor of Political Science and Director of Urban Research, University of Wisconsin, may be found in "Economic Implications of Urban Growth," the leading article in *Science*, June 12, 1959. (*Science* is the official organ of the American Association for the Advancement of Science, representing virtually all the major scientific societies of the nation.) This article is the source of most of the material in this chapter.

RECENT POPULATION GROWTH
AND WHERE IT OCCURRED

"According to estimates of the Bureau of the Census," writes Dr. Woodbury, "for the six-year period 1950 to 1956 nearly 85 percent of the very substantial population growth of the United States (14.7 million) was accounted for by the 168 Standard Metropolitan Areas recognized by

431

the census of 1950." Not all of this growth was in the cities themselves—
only about half of it. The rest was in suburbs and neighboring "rural,"
but not primarily farming, areas, often known as "fringe areas."

Within these 168 Metropolitan Regions, startling shifts of population
occurred. During the 1950–1956 period, the central cities accounted for
15.6 percent of the population growth of the nation, the suburbs for 27.2
percent, and the fringe areas for 41.5 percent. The farther away from
the city in a Metropolitan Region, the more rapidly is the land filling up.
To put the situation in another way, in 1956 the increase over 1950 population was only 4.7 percent for the central cities, 17.0 percent for the
suburbs, and 55.8 percent for the fringe areas.

Where did the people come from? Partly, of course, from an excess
of births over deaths, but migration played a large share in the relative
rapidity of growth in the three subdivisions of the metropolitan region.

"The large increases in suburban and fringe area population are, in
important part, made up of outmigration from the central cities." This
migration does not come mainly from the blighted areas, the "slums" of
the city, but from districts inhabited by the moderately well-to-do. The
space vacated by those who move out is filled—indeed, is more than offset
—not so much by people from other cities as by people "from nonmetro-
politan areas and largely composed of Negroes and Puerto Ricans and
other whites well down the income scale." Other central cities are becoming, in this respect, more like New York City, described by the Regional
Plan Association some years ago as the home of the rich, the poor, and
the childless.

THE SUBURBS AND FRINGE AREAS

Suburban areas are largely populated by families with children. But
they are no longer composed mainly of well-to-do people who commute
to their offices in the central city. More and more of those who move to
the suburbs are of middle- and lower-income groups; a recent study indicates that only about two fifths of the suburbs with populations of over
40,000 are "dormitory" towns, where most of the people have jobs in the
metropolis. Suburban towns are becoming urban themselves.

The fringe areas have very mixed populations. They contain many
of the new dwellings not built by speculative builders or general contractors but by their owners, who live in them; such houses comprise
about one fourth of the nonfarm homes built since the postwar building
boom began. They are "the poor man's response to high construction
costs." There are also estates of persons in the upper-income brackets.
Some of the inhabitants are natives; some work in neighboring factories;
some migrated from the city. Not much study has been devoted to these
areas, but apparently they are largely filled with people, rich and poor,
who want more living space than can be found for the same cost either
in cities or in suburbs, where land prices are higher.

WILL THE SPREAD CONTINUE?

There seems to be no good reason to expect present trends in population of metropolitan regions to be much altered, barring a serious depression. There is every prospect of ample food supplies and of adequate transportation to population centers. Automobiles, electric power, modern sanitation, telephones, radio, television, and other devices make household work easier and family living more enjoyable outside crowded cities. There are state and federal grants-in-aid for roads and schools, and federal provisions for facilitating small-house ownership. Nearly one quarter of the revenues of local governments now come from state grants.

Above all, there is evidence of a widespread demand for space (not outer space but space on the earth). "It [space] seems to imply less congestion and tension, more play space and safety for children, more privacy, escape from clamor," and so on. Anybody can extend the list for himself.

This widespread longing for space is coupled with the long-term trend in extension of leisure time. "In my opinion," writes Dr. Woodbury, "this is the most generally underestimated of all the major factors influencing urbanization. . . . More leisure time for more people means more opportunity and more energy for the activities and ways of living common to suburban and fringe areas."

The greatest obstacle to such growth, barring depression, is the high cost of building. The cost of single-family houses more than doubled between 1946 and 1955, while the median dollar income of nonfarm families went up 58 percent. Longer terms for mortgages and smaller down payments have made possible new building, but they cannot long counteract this disparity.

PROBLEMS ASSOCIATED WITH POPULATION SPREAD

The first problem of population expansion arises from the need of cities, towns, and villages for public improvements that cost a great deal of money. As populations grow, this need is intensified. Local government debt increased 92 percent between 1950 and 1956. Schools, hospitals, roads, sanitation systems, water supply, and other public construction are barely adequate now; and the increased family formation soon to be expected when the children born during the years of high birth rate after World War II marry and have families will intensify the need. The difficulty of paying interest on, and amortizing, a large and expanding debt arises from the fact that local governments can levy only a few kinds of taxes, largely on real estate, and the boundaries of the local governments are often too narrow to permit efficient development of public utilities. It is difficult, also, for these local governments to get together either in sharing or in spending their revenues. Their tax rates often vary widely. In addition, the interest rate, in 1957, had about doubled since 1950, and the yield on municipal bonds, which had been below 2 percent, had risen to 3.5 or 4 percent.

Another difficulty is lack of good planning covering large enough areas; "improvements" are made piecemeal when the need becomes pressing enough, often so late as to be more expensive than if the communities had used more foresight. Chances to create parks and open spaces are lost before land prices get too high. It is as if each department of a factory were left to finance its purchase of new machinery and often did not buy a needed machine until work piled up so much as to interfere even with its normal operation.

Some of the difficulties that can be predicted for the future of the fringe and newer suburban areas have already created really serious problems in the central cities and even in the rapidly growing suburbs. The outflow of population with money to spend, combined with traffic congestion, has adversely affected the central shopping districts, especially since the proliferation of supermarkets and shopping centers in the suburbs and outer fringes. But traffic congestion has not ceased; rather it is increased by the concentration within certain districts of tall commercial buildings for numerous types of business offices. The tall buildings are the natural result of the incentive to collect as much rent as possible in the congested districts where rents are highest.

As the expenses of big city governments go up, it becomes more and more difficult to raise the necessary tax revenue: the middle-income people move out; there are too few rich people to supply all the needed money; and the poor people cannot pay the taxes. Buses, subways, and commuter railroads, though often crowded in rush hours, cannot make a profit without raising their rates so much as further to discourage passenger use of these facilities. Main routes into and out of the big cities are so crowded during rush hours that traffic sometimes comes to a standstill. Shoppers and visitors who are now deterred from driving to the city by the parking problem might quickly fill up newly provided parking facilities; and it would not be long before the parking problem became as serious as before, while the traffic congestion would be worse.

"Urban renewal," with the aid of governmental grants, has made headway in removing blighted areas and substituting modern apartments or other buildings with some open space about them; but more areas of housing, deserted by the middle-income classes and overcrowded by the poor, continually become blighted.

Dr. Woodbury is not hopeless of the future of the central city, but he fears things will get worse before they get better. He believes that city planners do not fully appreciate the people's urge for open space and the kind of living that goes with a type of dwelling very different from the big, tall, city apartments. Is the market for these apartments big enough to solve the problem? What is to be done with all the large areas of old city housing about to be blighted? He also believes that suburban and fringe-area governments are not forehanded enough in acquiring "substantial areas for parks, playgrounds, forest preserves, beaches, schools, libraries," and other facilities soon to be demanded.

POPULATION GROWTH AGAIN

These problems might be easier to solve if it were just a matter of shifting population, uncomplicated by rapid over-all population growth. But apparently this is not the case.

"According to the latest projection of the Bureau of the Census," Dr. Woodbury writes, "the population of the United States in 1975 may be between 216 million and 244 million people. For our purposes we may take 220 million as a sound and not improbable figure."

If we do have 220 million in 1975, that would be an increase of about 70 million over 1950.

If metropolitan areas receive 85 percent of the increase, as they probably did 1950–1956, their population would increase by 59.6 million.

In 1950 these areas had 83.8 million. Thus the increase by 1975 would be 71 percent of their total population twenty-five years earlier.

The projected metropolitan area population growth for twenty-five years is roughly equal to the *total* 1950 population of the following metropolitan areas: "New York–Northeastern New Jersey, Chicago, Los Angeles, Philadelphia, Detroit, Boston, San Francisco–Oakland, Pittsburgh, St. Louis, Cleveland, Washington, Baltimore, Minneapolis–St. Paul, and Buffalo, plus 15 million persons more."

As Dr. Woodbury remarks, "This country has a few things to worry about besides the Sputniks."

Material relevant to this chapter may be found in Chapter 16, Government Spending, Lending, and Taxing; Chapter 24, Population and Welfare; and Chapter 25, Growth of the United States Economy.

QUESTIONS

1. Do we need a new form of government for metropolitan regions, combining city, town, village, and county governments? Or can the necessary planning and execution be done by an agency or series of agencies resting on cooperation among present local governments?

2. What is to be done about the present sources of revenue for the local governments? Are the kinds of taxation they are at present allowed to use, combined with federal and state grants, likely to be sufficient?

3. Do you agree with Dr. Woodbury that the longing for open space and the desire for good use of leisure are strong and basic drives of the Americans who are going to found families in the next few years?

4. Do you favor voluntary limitation of families in the interest of curbing population growth? If not, how are the people of the world to find enough space over a long period?

INDEX

437